GW00481987

Noble Merchant

Noble Merchant

WILLIAM BROWNE (c1410-1489)
and Stamford in the Fifteenth Century

Alan Rogers

Published 2012 by Abramis Academic Publishing

www.abramis.co.uk

ISBN 978 1 84549 550 3

Printed and bound in the United Kingdom

Abramis is an imprint of arima publishing.

arima publishing
ASK House, Northgate Avenue
Bury St Edmunds, Suffolk IP32 6BB
t: (+44) 01284 700321

www.abramis.co.uk

CONTENTS

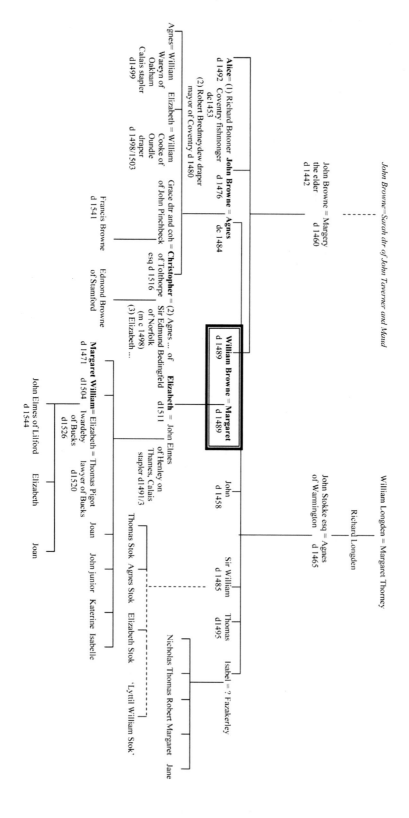

INTRODUCTION

'... these people in this place... [The norms by which we rule our lives] "are often materialised in our socio-cultural context, and in inheriting them as institutions, we inherit a real environment which shapes us but which we also change. We learn this environment in our bodies, as we are taught the conventions". [1]

I first met William Browne early in 1960 when as a University of Nottingham adult education tutor in local history I began working with a group of adult students on the history of the town. But I hardly noticed him at the time, for he was crowded around by many other characters from Stamford's past who clamoured more vociferously for attention – like William Cecil lord Burghley (whom I never quite took to) and William Stukeley (the doctor-antiquarian who was quite mad). But over the years that followed, gradually Browne edged his way into the limelight; wherever I turned in the fifteenth century, WB (as he came to be known) seemed to have left his footprint.

But the responsibility for this book about WB must lie with Henry Summerson who asked me to write the 'official biography' for the Oxford DNB; and that made me draw together the many different pieces of information gathered over such a long time. I am grateful for that invitation, for it forced me to focus – and what I found fascinated me. Here was a man and his wife jointly moving through a troubled society with a focus which I found admirable; a man who had an influence on his days and who left a mark on the local community in which he concentrated his activities. His life throws light on many different aspects of urban life in that most lively of centuries, the fifteenth.

But it has not been easy. Although he was literate and clearly wrote a good deal in the course of his activities, he left no letters unlike the Celys, the Pastons, the Stonors and the Plumptons, nor any business archives except some of his title deeds. The evidence lies buried in many obscure archives and in his artefacts which I have tried to interrogate. And my engagement with WB has been spasmodic; it was interrupted by a lengthy period of absence while I worked abroad, an experience which WB almost certainly knew. It was only resumed after a lengthy gap – and that in itself caused problems

The work then has occupied my attention for many years. And that means that I have incurred many debts, not least in the last few years when I tried (more or

---

[1] Raymond Williams 1965 *The Long Revolution* Harmondsworth: Penguin pp 121-6

less successfully, I hope) to catch up with late medieval studies after my gap years. Among these have been Linda Clarke, Simon Paylin and David Grummitt of the History of Parliament; Professor Caroline Barron and her student Christine Fox, Professor Stephen Rigby of Sheffield University. The University of Nottingham gave me an honorary research fellowship within the School of History for the final stages of the study: I am particularly grateful to Robert Lutton, Gwyllm Dodds and Richard Goddard for their contributions and challenges. The staff of the libraries of the Universities of Nottingham and of East Anglia obtained a wide range of often obscure texts with generous interest; the Institute of Historical Research in London was a constant source of information. Among archive staff, David Crook of the PRO, the staff of Lincolnshire Archives Office, and the staff of many local records offices, among them the Devon Record Office, the City of Coventry Record Office, the Luton Library Services and the Kings Lynn Archives (part of the Norfolk Record Services) have answered queries and provided much help. More locally, the staff of the Town Hall at Stamford have always been supportive, tolerating intolerable abuses of acquaintanceship; the trustees of Browne's Hospital, that mark which WB left on the town for posterity to see, (especially Pam Sharp) have followed the later stages of the search with keen interest and support. I cannot fully express my gratitude to them and to the (now sacrificed) Stamford Museum, to the Stamford Civic Society and its past chairman John Plumb, and especially to all the very patient members of the long-standing Stamford Survey Group (especially Chris Davies). My friend and colleague John S Hartley from a very early period has been engaged on hunting up information for me and sharing thoughts, challenging some of my wilder hypotheses and suggesting new ideas. Andy Hall drew the maps. David Palliser, David Hall, Anne Sutton, Richard Marks, Penny Hegbin-Barnes, Peter O'Donoghue Bluemantle Pursuivant, Eileen and Nigel Bumphrey and many others answered questions willingly and to my great profit. To them all, I am most grateful. But please do not hold them responsible for the reconstruction; for every one writes his or her own story, and this is *my* description of someone I am not sure I would like to have met in person, for he still daunts me at times; it is my experience of an encounter across 500 years.

Two final comments: First, my justification for writing what is at one and the same time a biography and a piece of local history comes from Bourdieu's concept of *habitus*; Bourdieu, like Raymond Williams, stresses that all our beliefs, values, assumptions, prejudices and perceptions (many of them unconscious), which lead to our practices, are created by symbiotic interaction with our context. William Browne's identities were developed through living in his communities of practice – his family, parish, town, the Company of the Staple and his nation – communities which he did not leave unchanged. If we are to try to understand this man and his actions 'in this place', we need to try to deal with both. But this is not a complete picture: there is much more to be done to unravel Stamford in the fifteenth century; and when the archives of Burghley House become available, some further elements in the story will be added. But by looking at the town through one lens, part of the picture has been set.

Secondly, this book has been written for the general public and especially for the residents of Stamford. My concern throughout my career has been to get as many people as possible contributing to the understanding of the history of their own localities. Many years ago at a conference, the local historian was compared with the general practitioner: required to know something about a very wide range of subjects, and incurring the condemnation of the specialist for repeating what is common knowledge and for not knowing the latest developments in every field. Attitudes today towards local historians have changed (although the criticisms still appear), but I am conscious that there is some material here which some professional historians may feel is unnecessary; in particular, the footnotes may appear over-wordy. But my hope is that some people will wish to follow up particular themes for themselves and find such material helpful. I am however aware that both these issues have made the book over-long.

I do not wish to claim William Browne as an archetypal fifteenth-century merchant: he is one case study among many, an example of difference. But like all case studies, he has something to teach us. The theme of the book is set out in the title. William Browne was first and foremost a merchant of his day; unlike his brother-in-law (who became a knight) or his nephew (who became a courtier), William did not aspire to be something he was not; he did not retire to the countryside onto one of his estates. I claim that he regarded being a merchant as a noble calling, and set out to fulfil it to the full; he accepted the designation of his contemporaries of *nobilis mercator Willielmus Browne*. This is a story of some of what he did and what he achieved in the town where he lived all his eighty or so years. But I am conscious that this book will be a more transient memorial than his Hospital.

Alan Rogers
Bury St Edmunds
September 2012

PART I: BEGINNINGS

In this Part, William Browne's context is set out, in terms of the town and the family into which he was born c1410:

- *the history that Stamford carried with it from its beginnings in the ninth century to 1400*
- *the shape of the town in the opening years of the fifteenth century;*
- *the family's origins in Stamford in the middle of the fourteenth century and the inheritance William Browne entered on, 1433*
- *and his early years as a draper in the town before he concentrated on the wool trade and the Calais Staple.*

PART I: CHAPTER 1 STAMFORD'S HISTORY TO 1400

"It is the site and place where every town or city is builded which is the chief cause of the flourishing of the same, or else some special trade or traffic, appropriate to the same, and not the incorporation thereof", A Discourse of Corporations[1]

THE TOWN into which William Browne was born and which he dominated until his death some eighty years later was unincorporated until 1462, but it had already more than 500 years of proud history behind it. How much of this William Browne was conscious of, we cannot know, but the signs of it lay all around him.

But the medieval inhabitants – like their eighteenth and nineteenth century successors – were not above exaggerating and embellishing this rich history. In the 1140s-1150s, Henry archdeacon of Huntingdon wrote in his *History of the English People* that the incoming Saxons fought against the Picts and Scots at Stamford, '40 miles south of Lincoln': "whereas the Picts and Scots fought with javelins and lances, the Saxons were unyielding in fighting back with axes and longswords, so that the Picts were unable to endure their pressure and decided on flight to save themselves. The triumphant Saxons took possession of victory and spoils"[2].

This account is notable for several things. First, it is indicative of a tradition which saw the river Welland as a boundary where north and south met. Crossing the Welland (like crossing the Trent and the Humber further north) would take one into a new province; this may be the significance later of the secession from Oxford University to Stamford on the north bank of the Welland. Here at this boundary, the invading barbaric northerners were halted by the equally invading but heroic Saxons, hints that re-emerged during William Browne's lifetime when 'cruel northerners' were alleged to have 'sacked' towns in the south. Tradition lay at the heart of medieval Stamford as of later centuries.

---

[1] Cited in R H Tawney and E Power (eds) 1924 *Tudor Economic Documents* iii pp 273-4. This chapter is largely based on Alan Rogers 1965 Medieval Stamford, in Rogers 1965 pp 34-57, where detailed references may be found, supplemented by the most authoritative account of the foundation of the town in Christine Mahany and David Roffe, undated, Stamford: The Development of an Anglo-Scandinavian Borough, at http://www.roffe.co.uk/articles/stamfordorigins.htm
[2] Greenway *Huntingdon* pp 78-81

Secondly, Henry of Huntingdon was drawing on oral tradition, for Stamford itself did not exist at the time of the alleged battle – or indeed for some 300 years afterwards. It was the equally invading Danes who chose the crossing of the Welland, half way between the defended Roman sites of Water Newton on the Nene to the south and Casterton on the Guash to the north, for their military camp which developed into Stamford, along with other camps at Lincoln, Nottingham, Derby and Leicester[3].

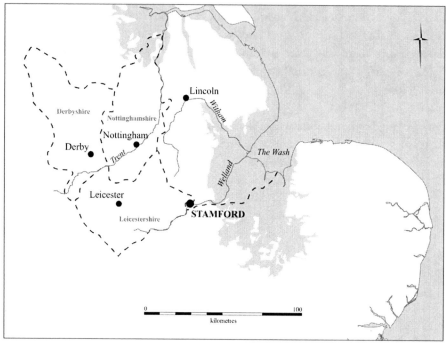

Map 1: Origin of Stamford as one of the Five Burghs

Thus the region later known as the Land of the Five Burghs had a uniquely high concentration of major urban communities in the tenth century. Both military and trading centres, four of these five subsequently became county towns. Leicester was given the land surrounding it for its shire, while Derby, Nottingham and Lincoln were each given the land lying to the north of the fortified borough. Following this pattern, Stamford should have been (and for a time may well have been) given land to the north of the Welland to the Witham as its 'territory'; but this area was given to Lincoln, perhaps in view of threats

---

[3] Phythian-Adams 1977; there may have been an earlier settlement on the site of St Peter's parish to the west of the castle.

from the north, to make that town the possessor of a double (and with the re-colonisation of the wetlands, a triple) county[4].

Stamford thus stood on the edges of three regions, Lincolnshire to the north and east, Northamptonshire to the south and the later Rutland to the west and north; it was very much a 'border' town which benefited economically but suffered politically from its marginality.

But despite this loss of its natural territory, Stamford was still treated as a 'quasi-county town' for at least some 300 years. It held a royal mint; Stamford coins were in circulation for many years. William the Conqueror clearly regarded Stamford as akin to a royal town, ordering a castle to be built there within a year or so of the conquest as in county towns. The Domesday Book of Lincolnshire listed both Lincoln (with its suburb of Torksey) and Stamford as 'towns of the realm', not within any great estate[5]. Recognition of its status was not lacking.

Thereafter, although always with special status[6], it became, first, a royal demesne town with military significance, then seigneurial as the king gave the 'town, castle and manor of Stamford' to royal and loyal favourites. The de Humet family held it from 1156 until 1204, when they were forced to choose between their French and their English possessions – and they chose to remain on the continent. The king gave the de Humet lands to his ally William de Warenne earl of Surrey who made the opposite choice, and his family held Stamford from 1205 until 1347 by successive life grants, with one break in 1240-1263 when it was held first by the king and then by Lord Edward, son of Henry III, and his consort. After 1347 when the Warenne family died out in heiresses, it came to a royal adherent, the Bohun family, and when they too died out, Edward III granted it in 1363 to Edmund earl of Cambridge, one of his sons, from whom it descended to the duke of York of William Browne's day[7].

Stamford then in the high Middle Ages was a hybrid town. It was a seigneurial town but unlike most seigneurial towns. Although part of the estates of the Warennes, Bohuns and Yorks, it was different from its companion town of Grantham which was and always had been a seigneurial town and which developed patterns of local government appropriate to a fully seigneurial town.

---

[4] For Stamfordshire, see Phythian-Adams 1977, and J Glover (ed) 1865 *Le Livere des Reis de Engleterre* Rolls Series 42 p 33; Bolton 1980 p 13

[5] C M Mahany and D Roffe 1986 Stamford and the Norman conquest *Lincolnshire History and Archaeology* 21 pp 5-9

[6] Attreed *King's Towns,* and Shaw *Wells* pp 105-6 distinguish between seigneurial towns and royal towns, but there were shades between like Stamford

[7] For duchy of Lancaster and Stamford, see Somerville *Lancaster* pp 248, 337

But equally Stamford was not a 'king's town', like Exeter, Nottingham, Lincoln, Norwich and York. When the king (during the periods it was in the hands of the king) or the duke of York walked round Grantham, he could claim to be the landlord of every property in the town; when king or duke walked round Stamford, he could only claim to be landlord of a small number of properties; he was overlord of the rest. And that allowed Stamford to develop local government practices which were more appropriate to a county town than to a seigneurial borough like Beverley[8].

Exempt jurisdictions

William Browne's two chief interests in Stamford's past would have been in its governance and its economy. In terms of governance, he would of course have known that the king, and the town's lord who represented the king, would have had ultimate oversight, administering the town from the castle where the royal and seigneurial courts were held and the taxes and rents collected[9]. But as in other towns, there were in Stamford many 'fees', exempt jurisdictions whose tenants owed suit of court to their immediate landlords; in 1274, "the jurors of Stamford identified 11 free courts in Stamford apart from the court of Stamford where the lord of Stamford exercised the king's justice". St Cuthbert's fee based on St Leonard's priory and the abbot of Peterborough's fee, mainly in Stamford Baron, are two of the larger fees. But there were many others, several of which remained in existence (at least nominally) into the fifteenth century. Even the Yorks held a separate fee in the town which had formerly belonged to the Scottish Baliol family. The queens of England seem to have had some entitlement in the town from at least 1209[10].

This last entitlement suggests that, at an early stage, the town's links with Rutland (frequently used as the queen's dower) were close. Hambledon, a key centre in early Rutland, held the church of St Peter's in Stamford as part of its manor. But Stamford and Rutland were joined only occasionally, although the holders of the barony of Oakham often had interests in Stamford[11].

---

[8] Attreed *King's Towns*; Kermode *Merchants*

[9] For steward, see CCR 1254-6/90; 1333-7/735; CFR 1383-91/308; for John Kirkeman receiver in Grantham and in Stamford 1359, PRO, DL 25/735; see CPR 1216-25/157, 189; CCR 1254-6/163, 374; 1259-61/444; 1272-9/63;1369-74/514-5; Selden Soc 46 pp 30, 83-4; *Exch Jews* i pp 170-1; ii p 262. See below p 195

[10] Roffe 1994 p 24. For a dispute over the payment of tolls to the lord of Stamford from the tenants of Peterborough north of the river, see NRS 2 *Pytcheley* p 20; see below p 197. For Baliol/Pembroke fee, CPR 1330-4/124; CCR 1227-31/438. For the queen's interest in Stamford, see e.g. CPL 1198-1304/33

[11] The de Humet family had interests in Rutland as well as Stamford in the late twelfth and early thirteenth centuries; in 1347, Bohun received the barony of Oakham as well as Stamford as part of the endowment for his new title of earl of Northampton. The York family held Oakham

Several noble families and ecclesiastical bodies came to have interests in medieval Stamford and kept their estates separate. King Aldfrith was alleged to have given to St Wilfrid of Durham "the land of ten households in Stamford", and successive lords of the town recognised the exempt jurisdiction of St Leonard's Priory[12]. de Humet, lord of Stamford, exempted the abbot of Peterborough from his courts. As ecclesiastical houses, especially the later friaries, were established in the town or as property came into the hands of monastic foundations which held on all their estates privileges granted by royal or seigneurial charter, so claims of exemption from the existing jurisdictions were made – not just from the seigneurial jurisdiction of the Warennes, Bohuns or Yorks but also from the town's own emerging government. Those claiming free court status in 1274 along with Durham and Peterborough included Thorney, Bourne, Croxden, Sempringham and even the parson of Holy Trinity, as well as a number of laymen[13].

The extent of these exempt jurisdictions in the fourteenth century can be seen in a rental of the gild of St Mary in 1350[14]. Nine properties in Fisher Street, the lane leading to Le Fysshelepes, Bridge Street and the parishes of St Peter, St Mary at the bridge, St George, and elsewhere in Stamford were "held of Robert de Wyke by two 'advents' to his court in Stamford" each year. Four properties were held of the prior of Durham by two suits in the prior's court in Stamford, one was held of the abbot of Croxden by rent only, one of the abbot of Thorney by two suits annually in his court in Stamford; a house in the parish of St Martin and two parcels of land in Stamford fields were held of the abbot of Peterborough by rent and fealty only, and some 27 other properties were held of the lord of Stamford (at that time William de Bohun), most of them by suit of court but some by rent only. Stamford was a patchwork of different jurisdictions.

---

from 1385 until 1402 when it came to William Bourchier and then to his successors, the Stafford family. At the end of the fifteenth century, the barony came to Henry lord Grey of Codnor who again had interests in Stamford, VCH *Rutland* i pp 170-178

[12] Greenway *Huntingdon* pp 684-5; for Durham fee, see CPR 1381-5/10; CCR 1343-6/43; C Ch R iv pp 324-5; HB i fol 25, p 68; CIM ii 1307-49 p 459 (1840). St Leonards had a charter from the earl of Warenne, and it came under royal protection on occasion during the fourteenth century, CPR 1317-21/404; 1327-30/165; VCH *Lincs* ii pp 127-28; Piper 1980; Heale *Priories*, C J Neville 2000 The courts of the prior and the bishop of Durham in the later Middle Ages, *History* 85 pp 216 231; R A Lomas 1978 The priory of Durham and its demesnes *Econ Hist Rev* 2s 31 pp 193-264; reports on excavations in *Med Arch* 12 p 168; *Med Arch* 15 p 139; C Mahany 1977 St Leonards Priory Stamford, *South Lincolnshire Archaeology* i pp 17-22. In the 1520s, St Leonards was said to lie in Ness wapentake, not in Stamford, Sheail ii p 188. The manor "near Stamford" was still identifiable in 1551, WRO, Savernake 9/29/3.

[13] See Hartley and Rogers

[14] *Chron Petrob* pp 44, 47, 100; CPR 1361-4/227-9; Exeter-NRA 95/28 is a terrier of 1362.

From early times, the town secured privileges of self-governance through a council made up of some of its most important residents, balancing out the powers of the castle, and over time increasing their control of trade and the markets. As in some other early settlements, such as Lincoln, Cambridge and Shrewsbury, there had originally been a group of twelve lawmen in Stamford, but if they ever were a 'council', they ceased to be so. By the late thirteenth century, they were property holders who claimed exemption for their properties and probably some form of appellate jurisdiction; vestiges still survived into the fifteenth century[15]. In Domesday Book, the town had wards, five north of the river and the sixth in Stamford Baron south of the river Welland - which seems to imply some measure of local government, if only to collect taxes in these wards. The wards had vanished by the fifteenth century, being replaced by the parishes, although through to the sixteenth century, Stamford Baron were still complaining that they were paying one sixth of the borough's taxes[16].

Under the first lords of the town, the de Humets, the men of Stamford received a charter of some kind in 1202. By this charter (which, they said, de Humet had taken to France with him) the town had been given "borough customs" (almost certainly recognising that it already had some kind of gild of its major merchants), and control of trade and the markets was farmed out to the burgesses, who were probably some 10-15% of the total population of the town[17].

It would seem that over the next century and a half under the Warennes, during the height of the town's prosperity, the burgesses gradually enhanced their control. The gild merchant developed into the town council; craft gilds did not apparently emerge, for the crafts were organised into associations by the town council. Various experimental forms of local government were tried. While in the king's hands, the town was for a relatively short time (1240-54) farmed to a group of merchants under the leadership of Walter de Tickencote; and in 1257

---

[15] Roffe 1994 p 58. F M Stenton (ed) 1930 NRS 4 *Early Charters from Northamptonshire* p 129; NRS 5 *Assize* pp 116, 712. They seem to have paid a fee for their exemption: "9s rent from 9 tenements of the lord in Stamford held of the lawmen's fee each at 12d p.a. as appears in new rental made by Thomas Willoughby former auditor at Michaelmas 21 Henry VI on information of John Kirkeby, Robert Loryng and other tenants of the lord", PRO, SC6/1115/7. See Miller and Hatcher pp 32-33. For 'Lawmensforthe' in Stamford in 1402, see CAD ii p 346 (B2903).

[16] See below p110. Stamford Baron had its own hereditary reeve, NRS 2 *Pytcheley* p 88. William de Burghle was reeve in 1120s, *Chron Petrob* p 167. This may be the so-called 'sheriff of Stamford', CCR 1272/-963; 1296-1302/11,76; see VCH *Northants* ii pp 523-4

[17] *Rot Parl* i p 462; LRS 22 *Assize* p 5. In the 1220s, the town was fined on several occasions by the king for various misdemeanours, and that implied some mechanism by which the major residents could speak and act on behalf of the community; e.g. *Pipe Roll Society* 47 p 11; 48 pp 160-1.

when the town was in the hands of Lord Edward, a 'commune' was set up for the town under an agreement granting to Stamford the privileges that Oxford held, including the use of the title of 'mayor' for the chief officer of the borough, exemption from the tolls of the lord of the town (although the 'commune' could impose and collect their own tolls on their own traders and on 'foreigners' who traded in the great fair and markets), and freedom from arrest to the lord's court (i.e. the burgesses could plead in the town court rather than the lord's court)[18].

This arrangement did not last long, for the town was granted back to the Warenne family. John de Warenne earl of Surrey became for the town something of a traditional hero; he is attributed with having founded the bull-running, and he gave his coat of arms to the borough council for their seal. In 1275, a stronger agreement was made between Warenne and the major town residents. They were granted powers to elect annually a chief officer, now once again called Alderman instead of mayor; he would occupy the position of 'governor and justiciar' in the town, offices which presumably had been held by one of the lord's officials[19].

This 1275 grant was consolidated in 1313 by Warenne in another charter which the king confirmed. By this, he gave

> *to the burgesses of Stamford, his resident tenants and tenants in chief, that they may freely buy and sell in their town as their ancestors used to do, and that they shall elect one of their number as Alderman to rule them, who on election shall be sworn before the earl or in his absence before the steward of the town.*

The status of Stamford was recognised by invitations to the town between 1298 and 1322 to elect and send members to the king's parliament[20].

Such charters often recognised what was already in practice, and if they did not, then practice tended to continue unhindered despite the charter. Thus during the fourteenth century, it would seem that Stamford borough was to a large extent relatively independent from the county (Kesteven) in which most of it stood. Under its lord, it was seemingly governed by a group of thirteen men who each

---

[18] C Ch R i p 472; *Calendar of Plea Roll of Jews* iii p 104; see Selden Soc 46 p 316

[19] Peck ix 3

[20] CPR 1330-34/23; original charter in French, Spalding, 7 July 6 Edward II [1313]. See CCR 1302-7/215, 316; F Palgrave 1827 *Parliamentary Writs* (Rec Comm) vol i cclx; Roffe 1994 pp 23-32. Warenne had a dispute with the king over the return of writs from Stamford in the 1290s – and lost: M T Clanchy 1967 Franchise of return of writs, *TRHS* 5th series 17 pp 59-82; CCW vol i 1244-1326 pp 2, 577; F R Fairbank 1907 The last Earl of Warenne and Surrey and the distribution of his possessions *Yorkshire Archaeological Journal* 19 pp 193-264

year chose one of their number as Alderman. These practices may well have existed from earlier times. In all of this, the status of Stamford Baron, the suburb to the south of the river Welland, was ambiguous.

Stamford's peak period

Through these changes, Stamford continued to grow in terms of populace, power and prestige. It was something of a military centre. Stamford was part of a larger scene; the area from Oxford bridge to Stamford bridge (a link with Oxford which may account for Stamford coveting that town's privileges), with its chief centre at Rockingham, was designated as an area for tournaments, acknowledged by the English medieval nobility as a playground for hunters and athletes. Grants of rights in the forest were a feature of royal patronage, mainly to those close to the royal family. Thus the town with its main road, bridge and wide meadows, became the venue for national and international tournaments, great festivals creating a colourful and noisy spectacle.

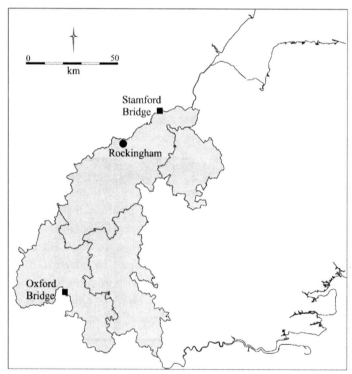

Map 2: The forest area between the bridges of Stamford and Oxford was designated as the hunting and tournament grounds for the nobility, used as an excuse for plotting against the king

With defences built in the twelfth century, Stamford castle played a significant part in the civil wars between Stephen and Matilda, withstanding at least one siege in 1153 before surrendering to prince Henry after King Stephen (then besieging Ipswich castle) refused to come to its relief. During the 'troubles' which afflicted the country in the reign of Henry III, the castle was held against the king in 1264. This combination of playground and castle led to a number of musters of retinues in the town; meetings were held and plots were hatched. It was under cover of a tournament that the greater barons of the realm met in Stamford at Easter 1215 prior to meeting king John at Runnymede and forcing him to sign yet another agreement, later called the Magna Carta; and similarly Richard earl of Cornwall mustered his troops in Stamford against his brother Henry III in 1227[21].

And Stamford had political influence, in part because of its proximity to the king's family and in part because of its location on the main road to and from the north. This road system is immensely important in Stamford's history - but not just the north-south route. The town also lay on the main road from west to east, from Coventry and Leicester to the ports of Boston and Lynn. It is significant for Stamford's early history that all the north-south streets are very narrow (except Ironmonger's Street which housed a market area), while all the east-west streets are wide, indeed often very wide, indicating that the original orientation of the town was east-west along the river terraces, not north-south. But the north-south route came to take precedence.

The king often included Stamford in his itineraries round his kingdom and conducted business while in the town. Royal councils were held in Stamford on many occasions. Parliament met there in 1309, and the 'Statute of Stamford' relating to alien trading in wine, cloth and other merchandise was passed. In his first year (1327), Edward III set up the chancery in Stamford for a month, and in 1337, the administration was again established in the town while the Great Council which rejected Philip of France's annexation of Gascony and thus started the Hundred Years War was held between May and June. In June 1392, another Great Council was held, "almost a parliament" as contemporaries said, which made a truce with France. The king seems to have stayed in one of the town's friaries rather than the castle: in 1309, during the parliament, Edward II held a private meeting with Piers Gaveston "in his chamber in the Black Friars".

---

[21] Greenway *Huntingdon* pp 768-9; CPR 1258-66/318; NRS 5 *Assize* p xv; the constable of Stamford castle and others were accused of the abduction of a cleric in 1216-18, *Diplomatic Documents* i 1101-1272 (1964) p 34; *Rotuli Selecti* 1834 ed J Hunter p 190; see CCR 1272-9/63.

Many nobles passed through: for example, John of Gaunt the controversial duke of Lancaster was in Stamford in 1374 and again with Richard II in 1392[22].

We cannot over-estimate the importance of such meetings and visits to the (c3000) residents of a town like Stamford. We can take 1337 as an example. In that year, the king, accompanied by the king of Scotland, stayed for some time, and the town and its residents benefited. The castle was repaired so that the sessions could be held there, and presentments were made before the king himself. The nuns of St Michael, at the request of the king of Scotland, obtained licence to acquire land; the canons of Newstead by Stamford obtained a confirmation of their possessions; the monks at St Leonard's received a licence to acquire more land; and the White Friars, who were expanding their house by acquiring various domestic dwellings, received licence to take over three more houses. Henry de Tiddeswell, the town's leading wool merchant, was licensed to grant a messuage to St George's church in mortmain for a light in the church. William de la Pole (who may well have met Tiddeswell for the first time in this year and started to plot with him the creation of a company of English wool merchants to challenge the alien merchants and make loans to the king) laid the foundation for his family's holdings in the town by acquiring property.

But there were also dangers in such visits. Alleged criminals from some distance around the town were brought into the royal household court (the Court of Verges) which superseded the local courts, and the royal clerk of the market's jurisdiction took precedence over the town's own courts. It was during this visit that the Bohuns were granted a succession right to the town of Stamford after the death of Warenne, and that the government became aware of the wool smuggling in which merchants like Tiddeswell engaged[23]. Extensive exposure to royal attention might not always be a good thing.

Religion and education

The presence of three large and prestigious friaries (and a smaller one) supported by royal and noble families not only helped to make Stamford a suitable focus

---

[22] CCR 1354-60/582; 1360-64/100; *Rot Parl* i pp 444-6; *Chron Petrob* p 24; J R Lumby (ed) 1886 *Polychronicon Ranulphi Higden*, Rolls Series p 265; *Knighton*, p 318; V H Galbraith (ed) 1970 *Anonimalle Chronicle 1330-1381* Manchester University Press p 158; F C Hingeston (ed) 1858 *Capgrave Chronicle* Rolls Series p 256. Great councils were held at Stamford in 1301, 1307, 1309, 1326, 1337, 1377, 1392. For the king in the castle, see Selden Soc 46 p 30. See also CCR 1307-13/225; 1337-9/75; E C Lodge and R Somerville (eds) 1937 *John of Gaunt's Register 1379-1383* Camden Society 3rd series vols 56-57 i p 89; CPR 1396-99/561; NRS 12 *Peterborough Local Administration* p xviii

[23] CPR 1334-38/417, 460, 509, 534; CCR 1337-9/75, 131-143; E B Fryde 1988 *William de la Pole, merchant and king's banker (d 1366)* London: Hambleton; Attreed *King's Towns* p 75

for royal visits but also revealed it as a religious centre. Stamford was not a place of pilgrimage but one of debate and study, particularly among the Carmelites. The Grey Friary was for a time the *studium specialem* of the Franciscan custody of Oxford, the Austin friary for the Lincoln 'limit'. All of them hosted provincial chapters during the fourteenth century, and religious councils were held in Stamford on many occasions. In May-June 1392, a major council under archbishop Courtenay was held at the Carmelites (White Friars) in Stamford which condemned some of the doctrines of Wycliffe[24].

This can perhaps help to account for the number of schools known to have been in Stamford. St Leonard's certainly had students. From time to time, the main training centres for some of the religious orders, especially the friars, were located at Stamford. The Whitefriars had a 'house of study' in St George's Square. Master Robert Luterell founded a cell of the Gilbertines in Stamford in 1302 which later had students. An inscription in a book reads, "written by the master who taught in the school at Stamford" (1309). The Austin friars had a school from at least 1343 to at least 1392. A number of medieval scholars are known to have studied or taught at Stamford[25].

All of which gives credence to the story of the secession in the 1330s of northern masters and students from Oxford, first to Northampton and then to Stamford north of the river Welland, a secession which the archbishop of Canterbury and the bishop of Lincoln used their influence with the king and queen to extinguish firmly and quickly. Although later accounts of this are unquestionably exaggerated, with the result that some historians have continued to decry it, a

---

[24] Peck xii 25-28; M Aston 1967 *Thomas Arundel* Oxford University Press pp 326-7; W J Courtenay 1987 *Schools and Scholars in fourteenth century England* Princeton University Press pp 66-7, 74; Hartley and Rogers; OHS 20 p 85; Workman *Wycliff* ii p 293. The church council was primarily a defence of the friars. The bishop of Bangor, Thomas Ashburne, John Langton who is said to have written down the charges against the Lollards, Ralph Spaldyng, John Beverley, John Kenningham, Bertram Fitzalan were all Carmelites. In 1373, the clergy of the archdeaconry of Lincoln met in St Mary's church to elect proctors to parliament, LRS 86 p 54 (157).

[25] A F Leach 1896 (reprint 1968) *English Schools at Reformation* p 192; Harrod i p 24; J A H Moran Cruz 1985 *The growth of English schooling, 1340-1548: learning, literacy, and laicization in pre-Reformation York Diocese* Princeton University Press pp 451-471; Ker *Libraries* p 182, and supplement 1987 p 64; Owen 1971 p 80; Orme 2006 pp 178, 269, 326, 366; D Knowles and R N Hadcock 1971 *Medieval Religious Houses* Longman pp 199, 244. Some writers are still doubtful, see B Golding 1995 *Gilbert of Sempringham and the Gilbertine Order c1130-c1300* Oxford: Clarendon, but the number of scholars known to have studied and taught at Stamford in the late thirteenth and fourteenth centuries is steadily increasing – John (de) Berewick, John de Twislington, William Ludlington or Lyddington, William Wheatley (master of the grammar school in Stamford in 1309), John Burley, Robert Graystanes of St Leonard's, Robert Wodehous, John Rodington, Walter Heston, Uthred Boldon of St Leonards; see PRO E328/16; E326/4541; ODNB sub nomina; G C Brodrick (ed) 1885 OHS 4 *Memorials of Merton College* p 197; A G Little and F Pelster (eds) 1934 OHS 96 *Oxford Theology and Theologians c1282-1302* p 74; OHS 52 ii p 15.

more balanced account indicates that it happened, and that it took place in a context where already a good deal of education and training was going on, where many churches, religious bodies, gilds and associations already existed, and where there was a tradition of subversion, so that the threat of a permanent home was real and had to be addressed with resolution. But teaching in some form continued in the town after the suppression of the university schism; in 1335, 38 persons (half of them Masters) were accused of continuing to teach in Stamford after the banning order, including the parsons of the churches of St Peter, St Andrew, All Saints beyond the bridge, and St George; "Philip le Manciple atte Brasenose" held school in Stamford. There were later secessions in 1334 and in 1349, and as late as 1362-4, there are mentions of students at Stamford. Clearly William Browne would have known about this event, for its tradition continued for a long time; Spenser mentions it in the Faerie Queen[26].

Brasenose Gate, Stamford, from illustration in Stamford School (with permission)

And it is emerging that Stamford was something of a cultural centre. Towns of course had a wider range of literacy practices than the surrounding countryside[27], but Stamford seems to have developed a significantly greater number of cultural activities. It is possible that the Luttrell Psalter was illustrated in part in Stamford in the 1320s. An alliterative poem of about 1400 related to the cult of St Katherine which we know was followed in the town can now be traced to Stamford. We know that there was a workshop of highly regarded medieval glass in the town. Scientific experiments were probably carried out in St Leonard's priory. Books have been recorded in significant numbers: Hebrew

---

[26] PRO, C145/127/23; BL Royal 8A IV (inscription relating to the Stamford secession); VCH *Lincs* ii pp 468-474; VCH *Oxfordshire* iii; Workman *Wycliff* i p 82; OHS 32 p 11; Orme 2006 p 80

[27] e.g. Thrupp pp 155-163

books belonging to the Jews were auctioned at Stamford in 1290 and some were bought by the prior of Ramsey. The nuns of St Michael, several of the friaries and Newstead and St Leonard's priories are all known to have had books. Wills refer to books of meditations and of statutes; primers and psalters were held by local residents, and the wool town's links with the continent gave it an opportunity to access books which were being produced there. The town had its own cycle of eleven Corpus Christi *pagentes*, town waits and organ-player – and at the end of the fifteenth century, Deeping close by produced in Robert Fairfax one of the outstanding musicians of the age[28].

Henry Elyngton's tomb 1400 in St Paul's church includes the words: *Katerine et Margarete preiez pour li* (photo: Rob Foulkes)

A trading centre

All of these achievements were of course based on what Browne would have been most interested in, a strong basis of trade and industry. That Stamford was prosperous is clear: its 'fee farm', to be collected annually from the major citizens and paid at first to the king and then to the town's lord as king's representative, was substantial, £50 per annum, similar to other major towns in the country[29].

---

[28] M P Brown 2006 *The Luttrell Psalter*, London: British Library, introduction; Kennedy 2003; R Greenhill *Incised Slabs* 2 vols 1976 pp 455-482 (Lincs Slabs). For glass, see below pp 237-8. For music, see NRS 9 *Peterborough Local Administration* p 77; ODNB Robert Fairfax; F L Harrison 1963 *Music in Medieval Britain* Routledge and Kegan Paul; Clive Burgess and A Watley, Mapping the soundscape: church music in English towns 1450-1550 in *Early Music History* 19 (2000) pp 1-46. Stamford features in the works of Henry Daniel, an eminent horticulturalist and Dominican friar of the late fourteenth century, J H Harvey 1987 Henry Daniel: a scientific gardener of the fourteenth century *Garden History* 15 pp 81-93; J H Harvey 1990 *Medieval Gardens* pp 118-9, 189-192. For plays, see below pp 192-3

[29] Roffe 1994 p 28. For the fee farm, see T Madox 1726 *Firma Burgi* London; Bridbury 1992 p 11. Ipswich fee farm was £60, *Tooley* p 9

"The destiny of towns is inextricably bound up with the fate of the economies in which they lie"[30]. Stamford was set very fortunately. To the east lay the wetlands: the town was tied to the country around the Wash through trade and drainage commissions. This region was transformed during the early Middle Ages into "delightful meadows and arable land", rich, fertile, with a flexible seasonal economy of fish, fowl and reeds etc in winter, and salt and grazing in summer, supporting the ports of Lynn and Boston which were known internationally for the import of lead, wine, furs and dyes. Commissions of sewers were established to ensure that adequate drainage of the fens and passage along the waterways were maintained; these took Stamford as their western focal point, and Stamford residents were called upon to play their part in enforcing the regulations for that region[31].

To the north lay the woodlands of Kesteven with barley uplands – the limestone landscape was said to be particularly valuable for sheep and for fulling. To the immediate west lay mixed and prosperous arable and livestock farming. To the south-west lay the forest of Rockingham and to the southeast the area of Peterborough which was called occasionally 'the forest of Stamford'. Around the town were the quarries famous all over the country and abroad (Barnack, Clipsham, Ketton, Collyweston etc).

With such a rich and varied hinterland, held together by road and water systems centred on Stamford, the town was always likely to flourish. But the region was not all good news, for this picture is perhaps rather too optimistic. The area to the east was characterised by floods and by many disputes, often violent, over conflicting rights of drainage or pasturage. Roads became impassable with inundations, navigable rivers with droughts, floods or blockages; the frequency of the commissions of sewers show that they were not always kept clear. The forest areas around were one of England's most notorious centres of Robin Hood-type gangs where "the men of Lincs, Northants and Rutland have formed groups against those whom they think to be rich, to extort ransoms and such sums of money as they assess from them by threats .., have imprisoned those who refuse to pay such ransoms and have killed some .. so that merchants and others cannot pass by the highways without very great peril of death" (1341). In 1335, the king ordered the bailiffs and good men of Stamford to look after the king's messenger on his way from London to York because the area was so

---

[30] Alan Dyer 2000 p 282

[31] Carus-Wilson, Wash pp 183-4, 201; for the wetlands around the Wash, see C Woolgar 1995 Diet and consumption in gentry and noble households: a case study from around the Wash, in Archer and Walker 1995 pp 17-32; J A Galloway 2009 Storm flooding, coastal defence and land use around the Thames estuary and tidal river c1250-1450 *JMH* 35 2 pp 171-188

dangerous; and a Genoese merchant taking jewels from York to queen Philippa in London was murdered between Grantham and Stamford: "many robberies and murders are committed by day and by night by felons lurking in the highways and woods within the county of Lincolnshire and especially in the neighbourhood of Stamford"[32].

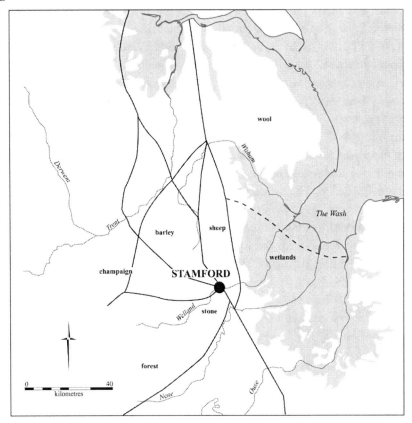

Map 3: The location of medieval Stamford

But despite this, its natural advantages meant that Stamford grew not only into a major trading centre but also into an industrial centre. Its early pottery largely died out by the thirteenth century, but in its heyday 'Stamford ware' found its way through much of the country and abroad. Iron-working flourished for a time before the manufacture of woollen cloth took its place; and although medieval *stanfortes* cloth may not have owed their name to the town (it may mean *stamen forte*, strong web), the cloth known as habergets and other kinds of cloth were undoubtedly made in the town and neighbourhood and sold widely. While Lincoln and Leicester were probably more renowned for their cloth, the cloth of

---

[32] CPR 1334-38/163, 174 210-1; 1338-40/79; 1345-8/176; 1350-4/90, 449 etc; NRS 5 *Assize* pp 114 (696, 698), 116 (712)

Stamford held up well against other towns such as Coventry and Norwich[33]. Browne as a draper would have been fully aware of this past.

But it was as a trading centre that Stamford was best known. At the junction of a major road and river system from north to south and from east to west, many merchants and other traders passed through the town. Wool of a high quality was traded in large quantities from all over the midlands through the east coast ports; in 1305, wool "of a better quality" was obtained by the Frescobaldi merchants from the area. The wool from the lands of Vaudey and Fineshade abbeys, for example, went via Stamford. Stamford wool merchants were well known: Gilbert de Casterton was one of the richest wool merchants in the country engaged in the royal trade, and Henry de Tiddeswell formed a partnership with de la Pole to promote the English wool trade[34]. Stamford was one of the places named as a staple town for the sale of English wool, as Edward III sought for a convenient location to control and tax the trade, before the staple was finally located at Calais.

The great international fair was held in mid-Lent in every open space in the town and (when not flooded) on the Meadows. One of the great fairs of England in the thirteenth century alongside St Ives, Boston and Winchester, it was the range of goods and the credit facilities available which attracted merchants from all over Europe. Woad and other dyes, fish, wine, corn, cloth and horses were all available at Stamford fair. This fair was a major source of income for both the residents of Stamford and for the town's lord, and the 'keepers' of the fair were seen as great men – in 1248, Henry III, while holding the town, appointed a royal servant as 'warden' of Stamford fair to collect his tolls and regulate disputes. Much illegal trade was identified in and through Stamford. The fair was the occasion for the settling of international debts, and Stamford fair courts were known and used by merchants of London and other towns. Tolls on goods going to Stamford markets and fairs were collected over a wide distance around the town. Until the early years of the fourteenth century, the Stamford mid-Lent fair was fitted into the annual calendar of merchants throughout the realm and across the continent of Europe[35].

---

[33] K Kilmurray 1980 *The Pottery Industry of Stamford, Lincolnshire AD850-1250* Oxford; H R Loyn Anglo-Saxon Stamford, in Rogers 1965 pp 25-26; Roffe 1994 p 6; CLBL Book E 1314-1337 pp 54, 65; Carus Wilson, Haberget; Bridbury *Clothmaking* p 36; P Nightingale 1995 *A Medieval Mercantile Community* New Haven: Yale University Press p 39; N B Harte and K G Ponting 1983 *Cloth and Clothing in Medieval Europe* Heinemann pp 107, 161-3.

[34] PRO, E210/7015; SC1/38/159; CFR 1347-56/6, 270. For John Longe wool merchant, see CPR 1388-92/454; 1391-6/629; CCR 1377-81/236-7. Carus-Wilson, Wash p 185; CPR 1292-1301/335; CCR 1339-41/45-6 etc; 1341-3/219; 1343-6/144, 479. See L V D Owen 1928 Lincolnshire and the wool trade in the middle ages *AASR* 39 pp 259-263.

[35] Bridbury *Clothmaking* pp 33-34

The thirteenth century then was the great period of Stamford's prosperity. Although the history of Stamford at its peak still has to be written, the documents which have survived and much of the surviving architecture (ecclesiastical and domestic) show something of the nature of the town at this time. Here Jews with their synagogue (despite a massacre in 1189), Lombards and Germans (like Terricus of Cologne[36]), merchants like Eustace Malherbe of Amiens and the extensive Fleming family, traded and owned property, sharing with English merchants a common interest in the prosperity of the town. Artisans and traders lived cheek by jowl. The parish churches flourished, and the new friaries, although outside the walls, increased pressure on town space. It was probably the expulsion in 1290 of the extensive colony of Jews which began the town's decline; their place was taken first by continental merchants and then by English merchants who found resources to lend to a cash-strapped king[37].

Well before the Black Death hit the town severely in 1349-50, Stamford was in decline[38]: one parish (Cornstall) had gone by 1309, another (Clement) became a chantry by about the 1360s *per pestilenciam*. By the 1330s, when most of the alien merchants had left, Stamford's pre-eminence was beginning to pass: in the taxes of that period, the town was assessed at between £31 and £36 with Stamford Baron at a further £8-£10, but Lincoln was assessed at £100 and Boston (taxed at a lower rate of tax, a fifteenth rather than a tenth) was assessed at £73. It was still ahead of neighbours such as Grantham (£19), Grimsby (£9), Peterborough (£25), Northampton (£27), Oakham (£12) and Leicester (£16) - though Spalding at £42 came close to Stamford in assessment[39]. In the 1340s, when towns were called upon to provide the king with men, Stamford was assessed at being able to pay for six men, while Lincoln could afford 20 men, Coventry 15 men, and Bury St Edmunds 30 men[40].

---

[36] J P Huffman 1998 *Family, Commerce and Religion in London and Cologne* Cambridge pp 180-89

[37] Bridges *Northants* ii p 593; PRO, SC11/426; NRS 5 *Assize* pp 114 (698), 116 (712)

[38] See B M S Campbell and K Bartley 2006 *England on the Eve of the Black Death* Manchester University Press p 344: in 1349 a property in the town was described as *vasta et ruinosa et nihil valet in aliquibus exitibus propter debilitatem eiusdem*, PRO, C143/290/9. For the decline in value of the Stamford estate, see below p 111

[39] PRO, E179/135/15; figures from R E Glasscock 1975 *The Lay Subsidy of 1334* British Academy and Oxford University Press, except Leicester, taken from J Thompson 1849 *History of Leicester* pp 451-5; see also A R Maddison (ed) 1888 *Lincoln Wills* i, *AASR* 19 p 20. In 1335, Stamford paid £10, the same as Grantham; Leicester paid £26, Northampton £33, CPR 1334-8/133. Many of these figures are of course notional, but they reflect local perceptions of relative wealth, so that Stamford was judged by contemporaries as poorer or wealthier than these other places. Some of the large rural parishes in the wetlands such as Spalding, Gosberton and Pinchbeck at times exceeded Stamford.

[40] CFR 1337-47/497, 501: Leicester was called on to provide 12 men, Northampton 8 men, Boston six men, and Grantham and Spalding three men each. But these figures were individually negotiated according to perceived prosperity at the time: in 1336, Stamford was called to

Before that, it had been at the centre of an international trade web - which helps to explain the many linkages Stamford had with other towns. The ports of Lincoln, Boston, Lynn, Ipswich (not so much Norwich) all feature in the surviving records; Huntingdon and Cambridge and places towards London (which obviously had a predominant influence on the town) are recorded. Westwards lay Leicester which had a special relationship with Stamford ("those shops there which the merchants of Leicester are accustomed to keep"), but that relationship was weaker by the late thirteenth century[41]. Beyond Leicester stood Coventry where again (as we shall see) Stamford had strong links. The merchants of Northampton to the southwest had privileges in Stamford fairs and markets in the thirteenth century. There was regular correspondence between Stamford and neighbouring towns such as Nottingham, Leicester and Northampton.

And it was trade which largely encouraged many religious houses to acquire property in the town which would give them income, trading rights and access to the markets and fairs - Beauvale, Vaudey, Sempringham, Laund, Croxden, Croxton, Garendon, Thorney, Belvoir, Bourne, Brooke (Rutland), Crowland, Fineshade, Huntingdon, Ouston, Pipewell, Southwick, Swineshead, apart from the major holders Peterborough and Durham. This was not of course unusual in late medieval English towns[42] but the ecclesiastical interest in the town was substantial. Some neighbouring manors held property within the town, such as Little Weldon in Northants, Wingfield in Suffolk and Wakerley manor in Rutland; Grantham manor also had property in Stamford. Many nobles had residences or other interests within or close to the town. The Beaumonts held property in Stamford as of Bulby manor (Lincs); the Despenser family (related to the dukes of York) had a residence in the town and members were buried in the Black Friars[43].

The biggest and most influential of these by the end of the fourteenth century (after the Yorks) was the de la Pole family. Originally of merchant origin from Hull, this family became courtiers and soldiers and very wealthy – "Edward III's

---

provide 10 men, Grantham 10 men but Lincoln 80 men, LRS 78 *Inquest* p xii; in 1350, Stamford paid for 3 armed men, Lincoln 4, Grantham 2, Boston 4, *Foedera* iii i p 193

[41] e.g. Bateson *Leicester* i p 82: the sheds "which the burgesses of Leicester were wont to hold there", 1258; NRS 18 *Peterborough Local Administration* pp 5-6; the men of Stamford and Leicester had reduced tolls in Peterborough.

[42] R Goddard 2007 Church lords and English urban investment in the later middle ages, in Dyer et al *Hilton* pp 148-165

[43] Hartley and Rogers. Thorney's liberty was particularly important, CUL Add Mss 3021 fold 261v-262v; H A Cronne and R H C Davis (eds) 1968 *Regesta Regum Anglo-Normannorum 1135-1154* Clarendon vol iii p 242 (1665); ii pp 322 (879); Gibbons *Wills* p 98; *AASR* Wills p 74; see below pp 70-71; CCR 1279-88/384; 1413-19/145; CIPM 23 1427-32 p 102; CCR 1447-54/216. See D Roffe 1977 Rural manors and Stamford, *South Lincolnshire Archaeology* 1 pp 12-13.

principal financier"[44]. The family was in Stamford and Burghley[45] by 1338, and William de la Pole bought up a good deal of the property of Henry de Tiddeswell, his fellow wool merchant, but this caused him to get entangled with the law, for Tiddeswell owed the king a great deal of money for "uncustomed wool exports", as it was put (perhaps smuggling, perhaps a genuine dispute over unpaid taxes) and his property became forfeited to the crown, though de la Pole recovered a good deal of it[46].

Writing Stamford's medieval history

Stamford then by the beginning of the fifteenth century had been and remained a town of national significance by many standards: almost a county town, a great international fair town and industrial centre, a birthplace of the struggle for Magna Carta (although in the fifteenth century Magna Carta did not hold the place in the national consciousness that it came to hold later), one end of the forest that lay "between the bridges of Stamford and Oxford", the origin of the Statute of Stamford that regulated fairs, the home (for a time) of scholars, and the starting point of the Hundred Years War. Why then has it been neglected by medieval historians, especially urban historians?

There are several reasons for this. One is that Stamford has not been well served by its earlier historians in at least two ways. From Lambarde in 1584 (who provided notes on the 'hystorie of Stanforde' to William Cecil lord Burghley) to the historians of the nineteenth centuries, Stamford attracted many antiquarians, largely because of its surviving buildings. But they were over-zealous, making unfounded claims to greatness which could not be supported (e.g. that Queen Boadicea chased the Roman legions over the ford at Stamford, a legend which despite the pleas of eminent archaeologists still survives![47]). Stukeley and his colleagues in the eighteenth century often made weird statements about the town. So that a reaction against such exaggerations is not unnatural. Secondly, these historians plundered the town's records. Thus Francis Peck had in his

---

[44] CPR 1354-58/158-9; Loans p 52; Horrox 1983

[45] This village on the edge of Stamford is given in medieval sources as 'Burley' but I have used the later version of Burghley to distinguish it from Burley in Rutland.

[46] CPR 1338-40/79, 528; 1354-58/158; CCR 1360-64/180; PRO C143/224/23; 242/2. Tiddeswell was collector of the taxes in Lincolnshire and farmer of the king's wools, accused of many extortions and abuses, see e.g. LRS 78 *Inquest* passim; his property may have been seized because of his abuses as well as for uncustomed exports of wool. For Pole in Stamford, see CPR 1381-85/60, 450; 1385-89/67; in Burghley, VCH *Northants* ii pp 523-4; CCR 1377-81/236-7; Pole also had a manor called Westwode, CAD v p 60 (A10892). CIM v 1387-93 pp 66-7 (93), 91 (115); BL Harl Ch 54 C7, C9-10; 50 I15; PRO, C1/24/90; Peck xiv 17; see pp 282-3.

[47] BL Lansdowne 43 21; W F Grimes 1965 The Archaeology of the Stamford regions, in Rogers 1965 pp 11-12.

possession, for a time at least, medieval documents, including a roll of Aldermen of the town. The town clerk Richard Butcher in the middle of the seventeenth century accused the town councillors of taking the borough's archives (and he probably also did the same). There are today virtually no records before 1465 when the first Hall Book starts, and very few afterwards until the middle of the sixteenth century[48].

Other records are also missing - for example, wills; in Stamford, most wills were proved in the court of the dean of Stamford, and if a probate register were ever written, it has not survived[49]. To build the history of Stamford thus requires a wide search for evidence over a long period. One major source has been a collection of medieval deeds drawn from many sources relating to property in the town[50]. But the rich resources of Burghley House are not yet available, and other sources are scattered; many are in unexpected locations. Chasing material concerning William Browne and his town around the country has been an arduous task.

But there is the physical evidence. The archaeology of the town is fruitful until the thirteenth century; thereafter, it is surviving buildings which provide much material. Archaeology and architecture suggest that by the time William Browne was born, Stamford's greatness lay to a large extent in the past. The prosperity of the thirteenth century was followed by a period of decline, due as much to changes in trade and industry as to the plagues. By the mid-fourteenth century, the military value of Stamford was gone, its castle in ruins and its town walls breached. Its industries – the mint, potteries, iron-working and the making and finishing of cloth - were either gone or in decline; the greatest days of its international fair lay in the past, it was more of a centre for local marketing. But yet surprisingly it did not feel like that in the town; the two Great Councils of 1392 and Richard II's chapel to his mother are witness to that. There was still enough greatness around to keep the flame alight, even if it depended on a few persons like William Browne and his brother John.

---

[48] See Butcher 1717 p 18: the Town Clerk inveighs against "the Generation of Vipers .. Men [in this Town] who have been begotten into prime Offices by the Votes and Suffrages of others ... purloyning from her her ancient Records, Charters, and Miniments ..."; in his revised edition, 1727, p 26, he speaks of "records being ill-kept ... many of the antient records lost or imbezzeled".

[49] See below p 228

[50] This collection of title deeds, in Alan Rogers 2012 *People and Property in medieval Stamford: a catalogue of title deeds from the twelfth century to 1547*, (abramis) contains few other documents such as wills, bonds or recognizances; they are private collections, not the products of courts – few show signs of enrolment.

How much did William Browne know of his town's history? I suspect he knew a lot. He would have known that the borough used the charter and bore the arms of the Warenne family for at least 120 years. The castle would have reminded him of the story of the lordship of the town, just as the dynastic struggles of his own time constantly referred back to the fourteenth century. And one activity in particular would have given him a sense of passing time – his purchase of property. As we shall see, like others of his day, he collected large numbers of property deeds; one of his manors brought no less than 113 deeds reaching back to the early 13th century when the handwriting and language used would have made reading such documents difficult for the fifteenth century owner. And in rebuilding his parish church, he would again have been reminded that earlier generations were different from his own. William Browne like his contemporaries would have absorbed a sense of the history of his own town and of the country in which he lived, even if not formally taught.

PART I: CHAPTER 2 THE SHAPE OF THE TOWN IN 1400

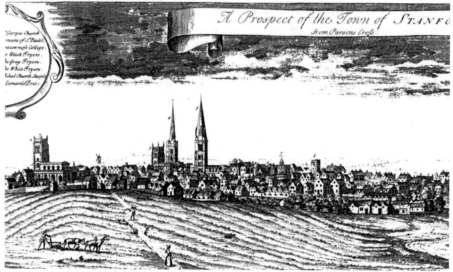

View of Stamford (from Peck 1727): Browne's Hospital is marked by '7' on the skyline

"a medieval town did not lose itself in extensive suburbs of factories and villas; girded by its walls, it stood forth as a compact whole, bristling with innumerable turrets. However tall or threatening the houses of noblemen or merchants might be, in the aspect of the town the lofty mass of the churches always remained dominant"[51]

It is important to remember that Stamford, like all towns, was not so much a physical space as a location where people lived, where activities took place, and where changes occurred. It was above all a culture or set of cultures. Living in a town meant that William Browne and his family absorbed certain values and practices, and were constantly adapting to the changing nature of Stamford and the region around, while at the same time contributing to those changes.

Nevertheless, the space was important and specific. Stamford is sometimes regarded as one of those towns which have retained its medieval layout more faithfully than most. The line of the town walls and the suburbs beyond them, the medieval churches and street pattern appear to have continued with relatively little change. But this is illusory: for what has gone from medieval Stamford is more, and more important, than what is left. The survival in Stamford of a remarkable number of medieval fragments must not mislead us into ignoring the

---

[51] Huizinga p 10

fact that most of what was built before 1500 has now gone, mainly during the Reformation and the rebuilding activities of the eighteenth and nineteenth centuries, but some more recently. For example, only one third of the medieval parish churches remain; eight have vanished, five and part of one other remain. But more significantly, three other major changes have completely altered both the skyline and the whole feeling of the town.

The first is the removal of the castle. This stood on a terrace above the river (where the bus station is now located) on a natural and artificial mound which was higher than at present; much of the hill was removed in the 1930s. Below the mound, on the river side stood a large courtyard with the great hall in which most of the business of the lord was done; and a wall and gate stood between it and the Meadows. The area to the south between the castle and the Meadows was an area where the town and the town's lord contested the possession of the Pinfold. To the east was Castle Dyke, a street which ran alongside the stream which bounded the castle on that side.

This view of Stamford c1900 shows how – even as late as this – the castle dominated the town; its removal c1935 changed the face of the town (photo: Stamford Survey Group collection)

Under the shelter of the castle to the north nestled St Peter's church, as in a number of other medieval towns[52]. To the west lay the king's fee, what appears to be a planned part of the town with regular streets and fairly uniform sized burgage plots, with the 'king's mill'. The castle towered over the town and could

---

[52] The association of medieval urban churches dedicated to St Peter with Norman castles is striking. e.g. Nottingham; A. Rogers 1972 *Parish boundaries and urban history: two case studies* *JBAA* 3rd series 35 pp 46-64.

have been seen from most points in medieval Stamford and, although by the middle of the fourteenth century it was in ruins, it would have been a constant reminder that the town had a lord, even if absent; courts were certainly held in the castle and prisoners detained there[53]. But the castle has now gone, built over by modern developers.

The castle was supported in its military purpose by town walls and large gates. St Clements Gate with its 'Turret' at the north entrance to the town, the East Gate at the end of St Paul's Street, St George's Gate, the Westgate, and the gate at the bridge were the main gates; other lesser gates such as Water Gate and Saltby Gate allowed local traffic. Although by the fifteenth century military functions had all but disappeared from both castle and town walls, the physical presence of the walls and gates remained, symbols of the town's status and prestige[54]. But they too have gone. Some sections of the walls and bastions remain, but all the town gates have been removed. These were important features, restricting traffic and enabling the collection of tolls, controlling trade, giving a feeling of enclosure, even perhaps claustrophobia, to both residents and visitors, as much as a sense of security.

Seven towers along the wall were manned by freeholders allotted to watch and ward in time of need. Murages (a tax on residents to maintain the walls) were granted regularly from the mid-thirteenth century to at least 1352, but by the fifteenth century, this charge seems to have been replaced by the responsibility of adjacent landholders for the maintenance of their section of wall, supplemented with ad hoc levies as required[55].

But the third removal has been even more important than the removal of castle and town gates. Outside the town walls to the east lay a complex of buildings, all now gone, alas, except for part of a priory and one friary gateway. Here was the town's main religious focus, with three very large friaries and a not unsubstantial

---

[53] In 1340, it was stated that the site of the castle consisted of two acres "and is called 'the manor'" which consisted of 15 cottages; "the castle is old and the walls decayed; within are an old tower, a great hall, a chamber with solar, a chapel, a turret, a house used for a prison", CIM ii 1307-49 pp 418-9 (1703); PRO, C145/139/20; CCR 1337-9/75; 1339-41/140; for Kings Mill, see Pipe Roll Soc new series 33 pp 138-9.

[54] Attreed *King's Towns* pp 184-7 suggests town walls were symbols of civic pride, of a communal image, of loyalty to maintain the king's peace, etc; but they also had practical uses.

[55] For walls, see below p 91; *Placitorum Abbreviatio* 1811 p 264; CPR 1247-58/103; 1258-66/155, 469; 1266-72/121; 1292-1301/512; 1307-13/493; 1327-30/361; 1330-3/523-4; 1350-54/237; RCHME *Stamford* pp xli, 4; HB i fol 7, p 19; fol 18d, p 50; fol 38d, pp 113-4; Hilary L Turner 1970 *Town Defences in England and Wales: an architectural and documentary study, AD 900-1500* London: John Baker; O Creighton and R Higham 2005 *Medieval town walls: an archaeology and social history of urban defences* Gloucester: Tempus pp 68, 88

monastery, St Leonard's, together with a smaller house of Austin canons, Newstead, further east at the bridge between Stamford and Uffington. It would have been a populous and no doubt somewhat unruly area with students and novices, friars and monks, visitors visiting and tenants calling to argue about leases and rents. There was a friary outside the walls on the west side of the town, the Austin Friars, but that was a smaller building and did not have the magnetic attraction of the eastern suburb[56].

We have little idea what those friaries looked like. Two of them, the Grey Friars (where the hospital now stands) and Black Friars (south of Wharf Road) occupied large sites; White Friars (between St Paul's Street and St Leonards Street) was more cramped and took over at least eleven dwellings in the thirteenth century[57]. Their churches were large and housed the tombs of a number of noble families. They were patronised by the great and the good: the Despenser family built a chapel in the Black Friars, and Sir Anketil Mallore, Alice lady Bassett and Elizabeth widow of lord Grey of Codnor of Castle Bytham all sought burial there. Blanche daughter of the earl of Lancaster (grandson of Henry III) and wife of lord Wake was buried in the Grey Friars under an "image of copper and gilt and bed laid on marble". The White Friars was regarded as a royal foundation, which gave the king rights to reside there if he wished; but it was the larger Grey Friars which was used more frequently for the royal household. The entrance gate survives, bearing the arms of Edward III; and beside the church stood the chapel which Joan, the mother of Richard II, "the most beautiful lady in England and by far the most amorous", built for her first husband Thomas Holland earl of Kent and where she herself was buried in 1386 in the presence of the king under a monument built for her by her royal son.[58].

These large and busy convents may have looked similar to some of the Oxford colleges - solid stone buildings round courtyards with entrances on the streets which both excluded and yet gave tantalising glimpses of life within. The towers of their churches with their bells would have been conspicuous to local residents, and the eminent visitors to them would have been visible.

---

[56] VCH *Lincs* ii pp 225-230; CCR 1374-77/390; CIM iii 1349-77 p 386 (994); PRO, C143/379/12; CPR 1330-4/456; 1334-8/325; 1348-50/512

[57] CPR 1317-21/54

[58] *Froissart* ed K de Lettenhove 1870 edn ii p 243

Noble support for the friaries: Memorial to Blanche daughter of Henry earl of Lancaster and wife of Thomas lord Wake; she died in 1380. The stone, now repaired and in St George's church, was found in a house in High Street in the 1960s (photo: Alan Rogers)

To the south lay two nunneries, St Michael's beside Stamford and the smaller house of St Mary's Wothorpe. Because St Michael's was so poor, in 1354 the bishop of Lincoln merged Wothorpe, which was in even worse straits, with it, to try to keep it going[59]. Both have now gone and hardly any remains survive, but in its day, the combined nunnery was a significant player on the Stamford stage. And scattered throughout the town were a number of hospitals. The most important and the largest was the combined Hospital of St Thomas the Martyr and St John the Baptist at the southern end of the town bridge: an old and well-established institution mainly for pilgrims, it was a substantial landholder in and around the town. At the southern end of the town stood St Giles leper hospital which, like "the house of St Sepulchre"[60], became something of an annexe to St Thomas' Hospital. Not all the hospitals lay on the verges of the town or in the suburbs. A parish *domus dei* stood on the south side of Eastgate (St Paul's Street), and the Callis which stood close to St Peter's church may have been a parish almshouse[61].

And gildhalls. We are not certain where all the gildhalls stood. That of the main fraternity, the rich combined gild of St Mary and Corpus Christi, stood on the south side of St Mary's Place; what is probably part of its undercroft survives[62].

---

[59] CPR 1354-8/27; see CPR 1350-54/320; 1348-50/2; 1343-45/145; 1334-8/460; LAO Register Gynewell VIII

[60] C Ch R iv p 275; Exeter-NRA 53/3, St Giles 'at the town's end'. The free chapel of St John the Baptist was described as "upon the Hill in Stamford", which suggests it stood at the south end of St Martin's parish, L and P Henry VIII 16 1540-1 pp 573-4.

[61] It is not clear what this was – perhaps a small almshouse or a parish hall; as it was not lawful to eat and drink in church, a parish hall or gild hall was required; Salter 2006 p 13.

[62] Exeter-NRA 89/3; Peck xiv 6; WRO, Savernake 9/29/75.

Some of the parish gilds did not have their own hall: St Katherine's gild did not have one until William Browne refounded it in 1480; and All Saints gild had no hall until Browne built his Hospital and shared its use with the gild. Most met in one of the parish churches.

Browne would have seen all of this and felt it. As we shall see, his own inclinations seem to have been rather hostile to friars and monks, but undoubtedly business would have taken him regularly out into the eastern suburbs, or to see the steward in the castle hall in the courtyard under the high keep. However, his main field of activity in Stamford would have been in the area between these two focal points.

Here lay the town's marketing and industrial activities. Areas where specific trades and crafts were concentrated can be identified: the shoe-booths in Red Lion Square area, the street of the bakers, Fishmonger Street and Butchers Row (le Bocherye) as well as le Drapery[63]. The earlier potteries to the south of what is now Wharf Road had largely ceased to function by 1400, and the iron smelting which succeeded the potteries (mainly in the St Leonards Street area) also were less productive. For by the fifteenth century, apart from weaving, Stamford was very largely a trading town. To the north of the castle and up to the church of All Saints in the Market lay the market, heavily overbuilt from an early period, with very narrow lanes and crowded buildings. Even the present space of Red Lion Square was covered with buildings and lanes. Jumbles of streets and buildings also lay between St Mary's Street and the river. Further east were more spaces. Broad Street was open although it ended at the eastern end in a very narrow lane: Star Lane was less than half its present width. High Street too was wide and used for market stalls, as was Ironmonger Street with its market cross. Around some of the churches were more open spaces: St George's Square and St Mary's Place were both used as regular markets, as was the wide area of the corn market (Cornstall, now St Leonard's Street) just inside the eastern walls. The Tolboth, the collecting office for the markets, is mentioned on several occasions[64].

Scattered throughout this area were the thirteen parish churches. The burial grounds formed open spaces which assumed considerable importance in a busy town, being used for many functions[65].

---

[63] CPR 1361-4/229; HB i fol 34d, p100; PRO, SC6/1115/7, 13; SC11/414-427

[64] CIM v 1387-93 pp 66-7 (93); CCR 1454-61/35; PRO, SC6/913/25; SC6/1115/6-13; C1/26/443.

[65] *Feudal Aids* vi 364-5. J Barrow 1992 Urban cemetery location in the high Middle Ages, in Bassett 1992 pp 78-100

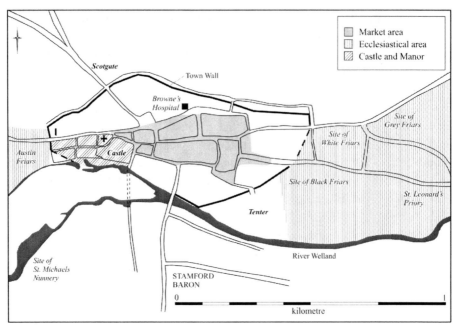

Map 4: Map showing the three main areas of medieval Stamford; the religious quarter to the east, the royal castle and manor to the west and the commercial and industrial area in the centre

The contrast between this central trading area of medieval Stamford and the two other areas was large. Apart from the parish churches, three kinds of buildings would have been seen, remnants of two of which still survive.

First, there were small but substantial stone houses which can best be visualised by looking at the north side of St Paul's Street. By the time of William Browne, these were already some 150 to 200 years old. They represented the wealth of the town during the thirteenth century but were only partly rebuilt during the later Middle Ages. Today regarded as small houses or shops, at the time, they were home and workshop to some of the more substantial tradesmen of the town.

But by the fifteenth century, the wealthier residents would be living in more modern and larger buildings of stone, or more recently substantially of timber, often jettied. Many of these would combine residential and working activities, with elaborate undercrofts, smaller halls and more private rooms, but some larger commercial buildings like wool halls existed. Fragments of these substantial buildings can still be seen around the town – in St Mary's Street, for example, or inside Walkers Bookshop in High Street[66] (for a fuller discussion, see below pages 121-7).

---

[66] see RCHME *Stamford;* Alan Rogers 1970 *Medieval Buildings of Stamford* University of Nottingham

North side of St Paul's Street – largely laid out in the thirteenth century but with fifteenth century and later adaptations (photo: Stamford Survey Group collection)

And thirdly squeezed in all over the town, occupying any spare space, would have been the homes of the poorer elements of Stamford's society. These ranged widely from single or two roomed dwellings of relatively substantial build to hovels made up of insubstantial materials. Mud and stone and brick and timber and no doubt cloth would all be pressed into use for building materials – they would have used corrugated iron if they had had it. None of these remains, and like most of the friaries no signs of them can now be found – but they would have formed the majority of the built-up element in the town; the documents constantly speak of 'cottages' in Stamford. The surviving buildings are not typical of the domestic and commercial buildings of Stamford in the Middle Ages – only the more substantial ones have survived.

None of these domestic and commercial buildings would have stood very high – the highest can be seen in the hall over the Central Café and the adjoining shop on the south side of Red Lion Square, built just before William Browne was born. Many of the roofs would have been of thatch or wooden tiles, liable to catch fire, a perpetual hazard of medieval towns like Stamford. The only buildings which would have caught William Browne's eye above the roofs would have been the castle and the church towers and steeples. So that I do not believe it is too fanciful to think that the Hospital that he built on the highest point in the town, the hill of Claymont overlooking Broad Street market, was put there to form another focal point in the town. It could be seen from long distances outside the town (see View of Stamford at head of this chapter). It was a statement of what a merchant rather than a prince or a churchman could do, an

31

assertion of the importance of trade and finance alongside religion and government to the town's welfare.

To the south of the walled town flowed the river, a vital element in at least two ways. First, as the name reveals, Stamford was grew up at a ford, later converted into a bridge, across the Welland. It was the 'stony ford' in the surrounding wetlands: Henry of Huntingdon speaks of "the marshes at Stamford"[67], so that a crossing with a firm underfoot would be worth protecting.

But secondly the river Welland was itself a major artery of communication, although not as important as the Nene-Ouse complex which was the main route for persons and goods through the wetlands. These rivers tied the town both to the east, the ports of the Wash, and to the west, reaching back far into the midlands. Although these routes were showing signs of silting up[68], they were still busy. Stamford stood at the head of the navigable Welland, the very edge of the wetlands, an inland port; and the wharves on both sides of the river would have been areas of bustle and hubbub, of special concern to the Browne family firm because from here wool and cloth would go out to Lynn and Boston. No doubt even in their short journeys to Deeping Gate where they had friends, and further afield to Boston, the Brownes (like the Coventry merchants on their way to and from the Wash) would use water as much as, if not more than, road. And it would also serve for fishing and for mills along its course, especially Hudds Mill to the east, Kings Mill to the west, Bradcroft mills further west and Wothorpe mills on the south side. The town council had diverted the course of the Welland for a mill and paid St Leonard's priory regularly for this privilege[69].

The bridge was now the main feature of the town rather than the ford. The town gildhall was built over its northern end and the hospital of St Thomas at the southern end[70]. To the west of the bridge stood the Meadows, a wide flood plain, often under water despite the cuts which were intended to drain the land and provide the mills with powerful streams. At other times, this was an open space used for markets and fairs, for grazing cattle before slaughter, for leisure and exercise, for military training and wooing - the lungs of the town[71].

---

[67] Greenway *Huntingdon* pp 354-5

[68] See Carus-Wilson, Wash pp 185, 195; Blair 2007; Wren *Ports*, Rigby *Grimsby* p 13

[69] R Holt 1988 *Mills of Medieval England* Blackwell; Langdon *Mills*; M Yates 2000 Watermills in the local economy of a late medieval manor in Berkshire, in Thornton 2000 pp 184-201

[70] For bridges, see D F Harrison 2004 *Bridges of Medieval England: transport and society 400-1800* Oxford

[71] For the importance of meadows and marshland, see Salter 2006 p 57

And finally there were the suburbs. Stamford Baron south of the river was much more substantial than the other suburbs of Scotgate straggling either side of the road from the north with its Eleanor Cross, or Bradcroft (actually in Rutland) with its ovens and grazing lands to the west[72], or Eastgate beyond the walls until the friaries largely depopulated it. Probably built on the site of the fortress created by king Edward the Elder to conquer the Danish burh north of the river, Stamford Baron (St Martin's parish) lay in Northamptonshire, marking the edge of the jurisdiction of the abbot of Peterborough with two large standing stones. Here stood the nunnery of St Michael and the hamlets of Wothorpe (with its gildhouse and mills) and Burghley, both of them closely linked with Stamford[73].

To the north, beyond the town walls, lay the agricultural area, well over 1000 acres in three fields, East, Middle and West. Most of the open fields lay in the parish of All Saints in the Market, probably the oldest of all the churches, but St George's church had substantial areas of land in the open fields; the other parishes were confined to small areas of the town itself[74]. Very little of these fields had been enclosed – few closes can be identified even in close proximity to the town. It was crossed by roads to Tinwell and Leicester, to Empingham, Oakham and Melton Mowbray, to Casterton and the north, to Ryhall and Bourne, and to the Deepings, Spalding and Crowland. Undulating land, stony with patches of heavy clay, the underlying limestone only a short distance below the surface, the fields were dry, good for barley and some short grazing. To the south, Stamford Baron had its richer fields, as did Wothorpe and Burghley.

Agriculture was then a dominant concern in fifteenth century Stamford. Farmhouses were inside the walls scattered throughout the town, barns and granges in the suburbs, with all that that implied for livestock in the streets. Most

---

[72] Bradcroft has been neglected – it does not appear in VCH *Rutland.* See F M Stenton 1920 *Documents illustrative of the social and economic history of the Danelaw* London: British Academy p 329; F M Stenton *Danelaw Charters I* pp 325,327, 329-30, For courts there, CPR 1301-7/186; CCR 1318-23/482-3; CIM ii 1307-49 pp 297 (1210), 418-9 (1703); CIPM 18 1399-1405 pp 206-7 (629, 634); it paid tax at one tenth with Stamford, PRO, E179/135/20, 24; *Feudal Aids* iv 208; BL Harl 52 A22; Add Mss 20242 etc

[73] PRO, E210/644; see *Deserted Villages Northants.* Stamford Baron was assessed for tax as a rural area at one fifteenth, not at one tenth as an urban area; its returns were at times made in the Lincolnshire wapentake of Ness, not in Stamford, nor Northamptonshire. HB i fol 11, p 30; PRO, E179/136/296; for two 'stupendiston' (large stones), one "outside Stamford" and the other "beyond the house of the nuns", see NRS 9 *Peterborough Local Administration* p xiv; by Peck's time, only one seems to have been standing, Peck viii 10-11. The language used for Stamford Baron is interesting: it is always referred to as 'beyond the bridge'; while Stamford in Lincolnshire is 'near side', Stamford Baron is 'far side'. The view point is always from the north looking south. See e.g. LRS 78 *Inquest* pp 810-811.

[74] See Hartley and Rogers; Miller and Hatcher p 26. Mahany and Roffe suggest that the missing church of St Peter was the original church in this part of the town and that the rural areas of All Saints parish came from amalgamation with St Peter's church.

parishes kept a pig house, and crops were stored inside the urban areas. Acreages or grazing rights in the common fields were attached to most properties[75]. The Meadows were not just an amenity area but a tool of agriculture. The town council regulated crops and ploughing, fallow periods, and the grazing of cattle, pigs and sheep. The town council had arable and pasture lands which it let out[76].

And beyond the walls and fields of the town, as we have seen, lay the hinterland, the villages and surrounding areas of forest and fen which contributed to and relied on Stamford, land in which William Browne came to take a keen interest as he built up a portfolio of property in Lincolnshire, Rutland and Northamptonshire.

The town was plentifully provided with good water; indeed, at times there was too much water - on several occasions during the fifteenth century, floods broke the mills and did much damage. A number of springs arose from the underlying limestone; wells could be dug. There was a stream which ran down from Scotgate to castle dyke and thence into the Welland. Conduits in Eastgate and High Street are known from early periods.

Indeed, the town was noted at the time for its healthy situation – at least when compared with the wetlands to the east. In 1535, Walter Graver schoolmaster wrote to Thomas Cromwell from Crowland asking Cromwell to find him a new situation for his health. After suggesting Kirton and Boston, he added, "there is one at Stamford without a master which he should prefer to all others for its healthy situation and for not being very far from Cambridge"[77]. Was this perhaps one reason for the longevity of so many in the town in the fifteenth century? Or was this due to less crowding in the town?

Population

For by the fifteenth century, the town seems to have been housing fewer people than in the thirteenth century. We have little evidence of the population of Browne's Stamford. The taxation returns of the 1320s-30s (c215 taxpayers), of the 1370s-80s (1218 poll tax payers), and of the 1520s (242 taxpayers), together

---

[75] The estate of Peterborough in Stamford had 42 houses with land and only 17 without land, *Chron Petrob* pp 165-6.

[76] See S Reynolds, 1977 *Introduction to the History of English Medieval Towns* Clarendon pp 176-8; PRO, REQ 2/4/77; most Stamford title deeds relating to urban property carry with them land in the fields, see Rogers, *Deeds*, HB i fol 6, p 15; fol 13d, p 36; fol 22d, p 59; fol 42, p 125; PRO, SC6/913/25; 1115/6-13; SC6/913/26; 914/1-4; 1260/1-25; SC2/188/2-3, and Durham Cathedral Archives. There was a 'swinesherd's place' in Cornstall and parish piggeries, PRO, SC6/913/25, see below p 112. Miller and Hatcher p 26; Kermode *Merchants* p 62

[77] L and P Henry VIII ix 1535 p 380 (1107)

with a return in 1450 (30 taxpayers in Stamford in Lincolnshire, and 29 in Stamford Baron), which are often used to try to guess population figures, only tell us of the numbers of taxpayers recorded by officials, and these figures can be adjusted to meet different taxation targets. Such figures do not tell us how many were not taxed in these records (for example, the clergy, of whom there were a large number in Stamford) or who were taxed in other places of residence, or how many managed to evade being recorded; and if at least one fifth of the urban male population were too poor to pay to the lay taxes, as has been suggested[78] (a fraction which seems too small to me), then the margin for error is very wide indeed.

It is now recognised that in all medieval towns, there were large numbers of persons "living near subsistence level", and these "urban poor remain virtually hidden from sight". Thus when we learn that in the poll taxes of Richard II, a total of 1218 lay men and women above the age of 14 were registered in Stamford for the tax, it would be risky to deduce from this a permanently resident population of the town of some 2500-3000. And since "we have no agreed figures for England's population in 1377 or 1524, for the extent of decline after 1377 or for any revival before 1524", we cannot use national population trends to help plot Stamford's changes during the fifteenth century[79].

---

[78] Phythian-Adams *Desolation* p 134. Rigby points out that in 1327 and 1332, when the tax was doubled, Stamford doubled the number of tax payers to keep the tax levels much the same, while in Grimsby, each tax payer was asked to pay double; between the poll taxes of 1377 and 1381, the number of taxpayers fell by 32%, which may have been deliberate to save the very poor from paying the tax, Bridbury 1981 p 11; in the 1524 tax, only 70% of those listed in the musters of 1522 are recorded, Rigby *Grimsby* pp 25, 36, 127; see PRO, E179/135/15, 76; E179/136/315; E179/276/44. (1450, omitting the three gilds which paid tax). The correlation between taxpayers and total population is too hazardous to make. See S H Rigby 1979 Urban decline in the later middle ages: some problems in interpreting statistical data *Urban History Yearbook 1979* pp 46-59; S H Rigby 1984 Urban decline in the later middle ages: the reliability of non-statistical data *Urban History Yearbook 1984* pp 45-60; P J P Goldberg 1991 Urban identity and the poll tax of 1377, 1379 and 1381 *Econ Hist Rev* 2s 43 pp 194-216

[79] Historians' estimates vary greatly: the tax exempt could amount to 2.5% or 25%; Rigby 2010 pp 397, 399; Rigby *BJRL* pp 69, 73; Phythian-Adams *Desolation* p 134. Cornwall *Wealth* p 222 suggests that in some towns such as Norwich, some 21-22% were living in poverty: "few could have reached the tax threshold in 1524-5". National population could be 2 or 3 million in 1377; it could be 1.8 or even 2.75 million in 1524; and decline could be 6% or 33%! See Hatcher *Plague*. Various multipliers have been suggested for various tax returns – e.g. 6 or 6.5 for the 1524-5 returns; 1.9 for the poll tax is often used, which would give us some 2400 for Stamford – but the figure is full of doubt, and the non-taxed population is unknown. Hatcher, Slump p 245; J Laughton and C Dyer 1999 Small towns in the east and west Midlands in the later middle ages: a comparison *Midland History* 24 p 46 suggest Stamford lost two thirds of its population between 1300 and 1524/5; J C Russell 1948 *British Medieval Population* Albuquerque: New Mexico Press pp 303-5 says the town was losing population badly; but there is no evidence for this.

Such figures may however be useful more to compare with figures for other towns than to give an indication of whether the town were growing or declining; they may reveal how brightly our star is shining compared with neighbouring stars.

Numbers of taxpayers [80]: Towns arranged in hierarchy: Stamford slides slightly by 1524

1370s	1524
Lincoln 3412	Lincoln 798
Boston 2871	Northampton 474
Leicester 2101F/2380	Leicester 401
Northampton 1518F/1477L	Nottingham 295
Nottingham 1447	Boston 294
Stamford 1218F/1400L	Spalding 250
Spalding 893+	Stamford 242
Peterborough 850	Peterborough 212
Grimsby 562	Grantham 183
	Grimsby 118

But even this is hazardous, for the light comes to us through centuries of dust which obscures it. Comparing sums paid in taxes or grants rather than numbers of taxpayers is equally unsatisfactory, for population does not always equate with wealth. All we can say is that the town of Stamford was always behind neighbours like Lincoln, and probably falling behind other local towns; Northampton and Leicester seem to have been pulling ahead.

Current guesses suggest a resident population in the late fourteenth century of about 2000-2500; and it is likely that Stamford in the fifteenth century was typical of the country as a whole where population seems to have fallen. But even a statement like that means so little. By 1400, it was not a very crowded town. The dense packing in of houses and people only came later as the population grew but the town area did not expand, restricted as it was by the lands of the later Earls and Marquesses of Exeter: disputes between landholders over the ownership of the waste land which surrounded the town walls meant that land was unavailable for building until the Parliamentary Enclosure Act as late as 1875[81].

---

[80] figures L are from Laughton et al 2001 pp 340-342; F is Fenwick
[81] See J M Lee 1965 Modern Stamford in Rogers 1965 pp 91-115

Open spaces and gardens

But in William Browne's town, there were still many open spaces. The gardens of late medieval Stamford are of interest for the balanced economy and social implications they reveal. Gardens can be traced in almost all parts of the town. They were clearly valued and cherished, carefully sub-divided and leased or sold, and dimensions were noted with precision. Most were looked after by women.

The eastern end of the town within the walls (the parishes of St Paul and St George) seems to have had the most, often in small allotments. About 1406-7, John Longe acquired part of a garden in Cornstall measuring 15½ yards "by the king's standard" by 8 yards, surrounded on all sides by his own garden and the garden and 'orchat' of his father. In 1419, Margery Makesey 'in her free widowhood' sold to Emma Salteby the southernmost part of her garden amounting to 7 yards by 9 yards lying between John Longe's garden east and Emma's own garden west and south – again a consolidation. Sometime about 1424-5, the Browne family acquired a garden in the same area at the extreme east end of the walled town, bounded by the town walls on the south and east and by St Paul's Street on the north. Most of these plots seem to have been small but some gardens were larger, running from St Paul's Street through to Cornstall. Other gardens in the Cornstall area both north and south of what is now St Leonard's Street are known. Further south in the same parish by Watergate Lane, a house with four separate gardens was sold in 1542 to Richard Cecil[82].

Most other parishes had gardens. William Browne acquired a messuage in Estgate (now St Paul's Street) on the corner with Star Lane with adjacent garden. St Peter's parish had several gardens - off Gledgate and the road which leads to 'le Waterzate' beside St Peter's church, and four gardens in that part of the parish which had come from St Mary Bynwerk where again garden met garden. Even in the heart of the town, the parish of St Michael the Greater, there were gardens – one off Cheyne Lane, and another in "the street called Racon-rowe". In St Mary's parish, the town council in 1472 leased a garden on St Mary's Street bounded on the south by another garden called "Lytyll Paradys"[83].

---

[82] Peck xiii 7-8; xiv 1-2, 14, 45, 47; Stamford parish records, now in LAO, PG 2/1, PG 3/6, MCO 11

[83] MCO 23, 7, 9; LAO, Stamford parish records, PG1/6; 1/7; 1/8. There are references to two Watergates, one in St Peter's parish which would seem to relate to some gate below the castle near King's Mill, and one in St George's parish, PRO, E210/4200; Peck iii 33; DCD Reg III fol 223r-d; Reg IV fol 135; Peck xiv 21, 22; MCO 27; PRO, E315/44/34; Town Hall Stamford records (TH) 13/1/6

Travellers and visitors

The town then had space; although there were cottages squeezed into small plots such as those off Cornstall, there were still openness and green spaces. But in assessing the size of the town's population, urban historians today try to take into account not only the permanently resident but also the transient population, the people it catered for, those who turned up for one or a few days to attend the weekly markets or the fairs or events such as the bull running. Further, there were (in a town like Stamford) always a large number of visitors simply passing through, often staying the night – and they all had to be accommodated and catered for. The evidence we have suggests that it was not uncommon for a merchant to settle in Stamford for a few years and then move on. The scale of migration into and out of Stamford, as with other towns like Ipswich or Colchester, is not known. Later in the fifteenth century, we can see that some came from Wales or Cheshire like Sir David Phillips, David Cecil or the Malpas and Williams families or David ap Howell[84].

Migration might not indicate population growth. Indeed, it is possible that there was some depopulation in Stamford, but it is not clear when that took place. In 1428, there were less than ten taxable persons in the suburban parish of Holy Trinity, but that may have occurred earlier as the friaries expanded. There may have been some recovery; for in the 1530s, there were some 400 "houslings" (parish communicants) in Stamford Baron, so that a population of about 2000-2500 suggested for 1377 could have been recovered by the 1540s[85].

Urban development

We should not imagine that Browne's Stamford was a static town, fixed throughout his long life. As we shall see, there was much building in progress. Medieval houses needed far more regular maintenance than modern houses, and there was always some work going on, reroofing, extending, creating the new fangled chimneys. There was some encroachment on open spaces and examples of empty sites in late medieval Stamford, some of which were sold or leased for development. There were in the late fourteenth and early fifteenth century

---

[84] L and P Henry VIII 1 ii 1513-14 p 1366 (3226(12)); see *Tooley* p 3; Esser 2007; for outward migration from Stamford, we know of some who went to Colchester, W Gurney Benham (ed) 1907 *Oath Book or Red Book of Colchester* pp 96, 126, 137. See Johnson *York* pp 228-9, 234.

[85] Hartley and Rogers pp 27-28, 31; PRO, E179/136/315; *Feudal Aids* iii 338; vi 364-5. Miller and Hatcher p 244 suggest that by the 1360s, Stamford ranked with smaller places like Melton Mowbray and Market Harborough; that is unlikely. For numbers of parishioners in 1548, see *AASR* Chantry; VCH *Northants* ii pp 522-9

properties which had been allowed to fall down and from which no rent could be had[86].

In a number of other towns, the thirteenth century investment in the parish churches was replaced in the later Middle Ages by investment in the friaries. There are however few signs of this in Stamford; what investment in friaries took place was by outsiders. Here, most of the parish churches in the fifteenth century were undergoing extensive 'restoration', especially the erection of new towers. Browne himself was responsible for part of this activity, as we shall see, but he was not the only one: merchants and outside patrons contributed, and the nuns of St Michael, poor as they were, rebuilt their chapter house and dormitory.

All of which helps to explain the concern which the town council showed in requiring that all streets should be surfaced and kept unobstructed: "in no wise shall [the streets] be obstructed with timber, stone or [other obstacles] … on pain for each [offence] etc 40d"[87]. The parish refuse tips were to be re-located outside the town walls. While some of this concern for litter and pollution may have been for health and amenity reasons, some of it undoubtedly related to the encouragement of trade. For the traders, the open spaces would have been as important as the buildings. While some streets would have been paved, most would simply have been beaten by the feet of thousands of animals and human beings over centuries into solid concrete with a mixture of clay, dung and straw. The broad wheels of the wagons and carts would have consolidated them rather than broken them up as the narrower wheels of the eighteenth century transport were to do later. The runnels in the centre or at the sides would have been choked with plant and animal waste, fortunately (without plastic) most of it being biodegradable, but with consequent health hazards and amenity disadvantages.

For it was in the streets that the stalls for the markets and the fairs were laid out. Stamford fairs were still operating, although it would seem not on the scale of the twelfth and thirteenth centuries with their international clientele. By this time, the weekly markets were just as important as fairs. Stamford fairs and markets seem to have concentrated on food, livestock and cloth; it is noticeable that to purchase iron goods, the nuns of Stamford went to Grantham[88]. Horses

---

[86] PRO, SC6/1115/9; E326/4777; E210/4927; for fuller discussion, see pp 116-9

[87] HB i fol 4d, pp 11-2; fol 7, p 18; fol 30, pp 86-7; etc

[88] PRO, SC6/1260/4; but nails were bought at Stamford in 1450-1, NRS 16 *Morton* p 39. The Sunday market of Stamford had been changed to Monday in 1202, LRS 22 *Assize* p 119 (no. 676). For markets, see Britnell *Commercialisation*. C Dyer 1996 Market towns and the countryside in late medieval England, *Canadian Journal of History* 31 p 23 suggests the hinterland was up to some 8 to 12½ kilometres; see J A Galloway 2003 Urban hinterlands in later medieval England, in Giles K and Dyer C (eds) 2003 *Town and Country in the Middle Ages: contrasts, contacts and*

were purchased and a white horse was stolen from Stamford fair. "Fat winter-fed oxen" were bought for the army, and fish for a funeral at Rippinghale in south Lincolnshire. The duke of Norfolk was among those whose households made purchases at Stamford fair. The impact of the fair was not confined to Stamford but spread out to the surrounding area, as far as Wansford in the south. And not just in trade: the abbot of Peterborough in 1446 was reported to have gone to the mid-Lent fair at Stamford to enjoy some shooting "like a layman"[89].

It was not just the trading streets of Stamford which were of concern. The roads through the town were of great importance, both for carriage and for the sake of visitors. The obstructions were most noticeable and most objectionable in the narrow main route through Stamford from the north to the south and midlands. The bridge was subject to continual maintenance: the gild of St Mary in the church of St Mary by the bridge was founded to maintain the bridge, merchants left bequests to the repair of the roads and the bridge, and the council also contributed to such repairs[90].

Royal visits continued. Although Henry VI showed a "disinclination to travel", keeping within a narrow area around London, William Browne would have seen him in the town in 1448 and 1452. Edward IV came through more often (1462, 1464, 1466, 1470 and 1473), in connection with his interests in Fotheringhay or the conflicts which marked his reign; in 1473, the king was residing at the Grey Friars. Browne would have had the opportunity to lobby both Richard III and Henry VII on behalf of his Hospital when they passed through in 1484, 1485, 1486 and 1487. Such visits would inevitably involve the Alderman and council members, and cost the town, a great deal.

Many were the travellers through the town: the bishop of Lincoln was in Stamford almost every year during the century, so far as we can see, for it lay on his main route from Lincoln to his residences at Lyddington and Buckden. Nicholas von Poppelau on his journey through England in 1484 passed through Stamford[91]. The town was a convenient place for meetings, a conference centre,

interconnections 1100-1500 Leeds: Maney pp 111-130; D Perring 2002 *Town and Country in England: frameworks for archaeological research*, CBA Research Report 134

[89] NRS 33 *Obedientiaries* p 121 etc; F Devon 1836 *Issues of the Exchequer* London p 291; L and P Henry VIII 1 i 1509-13 pp 1118-9 (2544); *Stonor Letters* i p 40. CY *Visit* iii pp 296-7; A Crawford (ed) 1992 *Household Books of John Howard duke of Norfolk 1462-71 and 1481-83* Sutton i p 268; LRS 18 *Gilbertine* pp xiv, 3; C Ch R vi pp 253-4; Carus-Wilson, Wash pp 192-3, 195, 201; the later fairs and markets would be to the profit of the town, not the York estate.

[90] HB i fol 54; Westlake *Gilds*; AASR Wills p 74

[91] C A J Armstrong 1969 *Usurpation of Richard III* Clarendon p 137; Wolffe *Henry VI* pp 367, 370; Griffiths *Henry VI* pp 562-3; CCR 1468-76/318-20 (1164); CY *Visit* i pp i, ii, xxii, xxiv, xxxii, xxxviii, xl etc

a location where the councils of the realm could be held; and for this, large buildings were available in the friaries, and a rich hinterland to provide provisions.

Apart from the accommodation provided by the friaries and monasteries, a number of substantial 'inns' could be found in the town. The George inn south of the bridge is noted early, the Bull, the Swan and the Greyhound later in the century. Inns and their staff occupied the attention of the town council on several occasions; for (as travel centres) they were most open to, and yet resistant to, new cultural influences from outside, and were often the focus of disorder in towns; and through their carriers, they disseminated news and propaganda to the region around. Brewing was a major industry, and although all the named buildings do not necessarily imply hostelries, the number of such buildings in the town, such as the Garland, le Hart, the Antelope, the Moon and Stars, the Belle, the Aungel, the Chequers, the Eagle and Child, the Bluebell, the (Black) Bull, and the Tabard (by the churchyard wall of St Michael the Greater), is striking[92].

During Browne's later years, both the king and the king's enemies continued to muster their troops at Stamford, and councils were held in the town. Just as "towns attempted to make use of casual visitors", especially royal household members[93], so too a wealthy and well connected merchant prominent in the community would have many opportunities to enlarge the circle of his contacts in such a town.

---

[92] For inns, see Salter 2006 pp 60, 78; Alan Everitt 1973 The English urban inn, in A Everitt (ed) 1973 *Perspectives in English Urban History* Macmillan pp 91-137; for house names, see Huizinga p 229. For the Antelope: HB i fol 16d, p 45; Moon and Stars: HB i fol 31, p 87; LAO, Stamford parish records, PG deeds; Angel: PRO, C1/26/443; Blew Bell: Exeter-NRA 87/7; Bull: HB i fol 45, p 134; PRO, C1/629/3, 6; SC2/188/2,6; Surtees Society vol 76 p 338; Garland: PRO, SC2/188/2/1-3; George: HB i fol 15d, p 42; Tabard: PRO, C1/26/236, CY *Visit* i p 109; *AASR* Chantry; HMC de l'Isle i pp 216, 218; le Hart HB i fol 14, p 38; the Swan: NRO FitzWilliam 433 fol 30; PRO, C1/24/90; C1/629/3, 6; SC2/188/2/2, 6; tavern in behind-ye-bak: CPR 1388-92/340; the New Tavern: PRO, SP46/123/57.

[93] Horrox, Patronage pp 148, 160

PART I: CHAPTER 3 THE BROWNE FAMILY AND STAMFORD c1350-1433

Ubi sunt qui ante nos fuerunt[94]

Even if he did not know much about the past of the town he lived in (and I suspect he knew a good deal), one thing William Browne would have been aware of was the history of the Browne family in Stamford. It was a distinguished one, stretching back nearly one hundred years.

In Stamford, as in other towns, few merchant dynasties can be identified during the fourteenth and fifteenth centuries: "the risks of long-distance trade, combined with high mortality among urban populations, meant that enduring concentrations of power within urban dynasties were rare"; "relatively few sons followed their fathers into office because relatively few officials had sons who survived long enough to hold office". Perhaps, as elsewhere, Stamford merchants sent their sons to other towns for apprenticeships[95]. The names which predominate in the fourteenth century, such as Tickencote, Apethorpe, Stainby[96], have all but vanished by the fifteenth century; and (apart from Browne) the names of those who occupy official positions most frequently in the fifteenth century cannot be found in the fourteenth. In part, this may have been the result of continued outbreaks of the plague, especially in the late fourteenth century. But it may also have been the changing nature of the economy of the town which saw a localisation of trading and a down-sizing of industry (especially cloth). Those families whose names did survive appear to have lost status: to give but one example, the Apethorpe family was very prominent in the fourteenth century - Alderman, JP, commissioner, making loans - but after the reign of Henry IV, they appear only incidentally[97]. Of the thirteen leading townsmen listed in 1388, only two families, the Brownes and the Coks, feature

---

[94] "Where are those who lived before us?" Medieval poem, B Stone (ed) 1964 *Medieval English Verse* Penguin p 67

[95] Fleming, *Oligarchy* p 178; Kermode *Merchants* p 41; Esser 2007; for urban dynasties, see Phythian-Adams *Desolation* pp 221-237; for apprentices, see Shaw *Wells* p 175

[96] With various spellings from Stenby to Styandeby

[97] LRS 78 *Inquest* p 377; CFR 1347-56/6; PRO, KB27/347; CPR 1350-4/90; CCR 1377-81/42; 1389-92/390; CIM ii 1307-1349 p 459 (1840); *Feudal Aids* iii 252; Peck xii 28, 41; PRO, C143/361/6; NRS 33 *Obedientiaries* p 45; Gibbons *Wills* p189. They do not appear in the Hall Book at all; PRO, SC6/1115/6; Peck xiv 21-22; PRO, CP25/1/145/161/8; CP25/1/293/72/361, 364

among the eminent citizens of the second half of the fifteenth century[98]. None of the families known to have served as Alderman between 1350 and 1450 appears as Alderman after 1450 apart from the Brownes. And even when some merchant families did pass their businesses on to their sons, later generations did not follow into public office. The Leche/Leke family (which had interests in Grantham as well) held offices in Stamford from at least the 1360s; in the fifteenth century, one (a goldsmith) was churchwarden of St Mary at the bridge in the 1430s, another was a household servant of the dukes of York, one daughter became prioress at the nunnery, and another daughter became the town's anchoress; but they did not serve in any office or on any commission in Stamford. The family may have moved out of the town into the surrounding area, for none of the family appears among the freemen of the town[99]. Similarly, the Longe family of wool merchants were very active in Stamford in the 1370s and early 1400s, Alderman in 1381, 1387, 1393, 1400 and 1431, and collectors of taxes – but although an occasional reference to them can be found as late as 1504, they vanish from the official record[100].

Few of the freemen appear to have been born in the town. Enrolments of freemen are only recorded from 1465, and of the 314 freemen listed up to 1492, only 21 (6%) were listed as exempt from the entry fine because born in the town[101]. And most of those who were exempt came from minor families, few from the politically active residents. Only one of these 21 (Browne) came from the first tier councillors, six from the second tier councillors. Almost all of the

---

[98] *Rot Parl* iii p 444. For Cok, see CFR 1383-91/72; Exeter-NRA 203/8; CIPM 21 1418-22 p 62 (216); CPR 1452-61/318; PRO, C1/26/443. Henry Cok yeoman of the kitchen of duke of York 1446; bailiff for the duke of York in Deeping and Stamford, Johnson *York* p 230; PRO, SC6/1115/7, 9; bailiff for the nuns, SC6/914/1; SC6/1260/18; see C237/43/188; Alderman 1478 and commissioner of gaol delivery; Alderman and died in office 1488.

[99] CIPM 21 1418-22 p 62 (216); John Leke mercer 1485 *AASR* Wills pp 68-9, 198; CY *Visit* ii pp 347-356. One John Leke became escheator in Northamptonshire in 1450; household officer for duke of York, see Hampshire Record Office 23M58/57b; PRO, SC6/1260/20; *Feudal Aids* iii 335; Peck xiv 4; BL, Vesp A24 fol 3d; CFR 1422-30/221; PRO, E179/136/198; 276/44; C1/56/258; C1/74/62; E210/8224; see below p 213; ROLLR Conant DG 11/113; PRO, E329/66; L C Lloyd and D M Stenton (eds) 1950 *Sir Christopher Hatton's Book of Seals* NRS 15 pp 4-5; BL, Egerton 8787; *AASR* Wills p 67

[100] Their name is not recorded in the Hall Book. Peck xiv 9; CCR 1377-81/236-7; CFR 1383-91/17; CPR 1388-92/454; *Rot Parl* iii p 403; CPR 1391-96/114, 629; CFR 1391-99/74, 99; PRO, C143/422/12; C255/20/1 (Alderman 1388); PROB 11/18 fol 85; C47/67/14/573 (now C88/41/8); C258/41/8; SC11/419; CFR 1415-22/152; CPR 1408-13/134; 1416-22/333; CIPM 18 1399-1405 p 296 (862). They may have moved to Lincoln: PRO, C1/273/15.

[101] This does not necessarily mean that they came from outside the town; they could have been born in Stamford but to fathers who were not at that time freemen; for in some towns, such as Ipswich, it was birth to a freeman rather than birth in the town which exempted sons from paying an entry fine; see Amor *Ipswich* p 45. So there could be more family continuity than the freemen lists suggest.

main families of Stamford seem to have been one- or at the most two-generation families. Only occasionally do we find among the minor families some extended mentions.

So that the Browne family was unusual; they did not share "the short lifespan of most urban families"[102]. The Brownes can be traced among the leading citizens of the town from the 1360s, if not earlier, and they were still taking leading positions in the town in the late sixteenth century. They were the dominant family in the town from at least the 1380s until the Cecils arrived.

The first Browne who can be traced in the area[103] is John Broune who from the 1330s acted as attorney in a variety of locations, especially in London. As king's merchant of London, he was commissioned by the king in 1341 to sell the king's wool, and in 1352 was loading wool in Lincolnshire for a French port; as deputy to a royal serjeant at arms, he was alleged to have connived at illegal trading in wool during a witch-hunt against smugglers associated with the beginnings of the staple system of wool exports[104]. By 1348, he was described as merchant of Lincolnshire (Easton in North Stoke by Grantham) when sued in Rutland; in 1352, he was exporting through Boston; in 1366, he was a witness in Stamford. By 1368, he was called 'of Stamford'. This John Broune held commissions in Northants (Geddington) along with the Zouche family who had residence in Stamford[105].

A London wool merchant with royal household connections, then, moved into Lincolnshire in the 1350s and settled in Stamford by the 1360s. John Broune's entry into Stamford was facilitated by marriage to Maud the daughter of Sarah

---

[102] Rorig 1967 p 123

[103] Despite some possible links, the Stamford family does not seem to have come from the Oxfordshire Brounes who were royal servants, or from the Buckinghamshire family of Leighton Buzzard. For John Broune king's servant, king's yeoman, serjeant at arms with an annuity at the exchequer, who served the Black Prince in Wallingford castle, see CPR 1330-34/27; 1338-40/58; 1348-50/595; 1350-54/154, 455; 1354-58/66; 1358-61/584; 1361-4/ 287; 1364-7/68, 109; 1367-70/66; of Oxfordshire: CPR 1330-34/580; 1334-8/199, 383, 511; 1343-5/415, 423, 576; 1348-50/62; 1361-4/501; see CPR 1340-43/166, 173. For Leicestershire Brounes, see CPR 1327-30/277; 1334-8/216, 364, 369; 1343-45/72, 184, 420. There was a John Broune of Burton, Leicestershire, CPR 1345-8/556, 561, and another of Burbage, Leics, CPR 1348-50/454

[104] CPR 1327-30/102, 199; 1330-34/192; 1334-38/461; 1340-43/160, 164, 296; CCR 1341-3/34, 227, 296; CPR 1348-50/217; 1350-54/338

[105] CPR 1348-50/101; CCR 1364-7/63; CFR 1368-77/165, 279; CCR 1374-77/472; PRO, E315/34/138. It is possible, though somewhat unlikely, that he was the John Broune who in 1349 with William his son was accused in Northamptonshire by William de Bohun earl of Northampton of slander; for Bohun at this time had just become lord of Stamford, CPR 1348-50/172-3, 529.

wife of John Taverner of Stamford, a local official and tax collector. Taverner and Sarah in 1358 obtained property in Stamford from Richard Ardern, a merchant with whom John Broune of Stamford later had connections, and in 1394, Sarah left property in Stamford and Spalding to John Broune husband of her daughter Maud[106].

Thus by 1366 (and probably several years earlier), one John Broune[107] was established in Stamford. He or his son headed the family from the 1360s to the early 1390s. As John Broune of Lincolnshire, he was witness in London in 1364. He may have been trading on a substantial scale, for in 1368, John Broune of Stamford sued his 'receiver' Robert Stybbyng of 'Sauneby' (presumably Saundby in Nottinghamshire near Gainsborough, a port in this period) for his account. As draper, he witnessed property transactions in Stamford in 1366 and 1371, and in 1370, John Broune burgess of Stamford and the rector of St Mary Bynwerk obtained from Durham Priory a plot of land outside the east wall of the town, almost certainly in some official (perhaps gild or town council) capacity. In 1371, at the request of Humphrey de Bohun earl of Hereford (the lord of Stamford), John Broune of Stamford was pardoned for killing John de Helpeston of Stamford, a soldier who had fought in France and had been accused of robberies and other felonies in a wide swathe of the country[108].

The family was thus established in Stamford, freemen and traders in cloth and wool. In 1376-7, John Broune merchant of Lincolnshire, with Henry Bukeden of Stamford and other merchants of the region, was engaged in a dispute with Florentine merchants over wool. In the poll tax of 1378-9, John Browne "menuwe merchant" was assessed in the parish of St Paul, Stamford, with two

---

[106] CPR 1358-61/63; this property can be traced back to a grant by John de Warenne earl of Surrey to Thomas de la Saucerie, a household official, see CPR 1350-54/525; 1348-50/265; 1330-34/538; PRO, E40/14365; C143/228/13. CPR 1391-96/496; CFR 1391-99/152; Peck xii 22, 29 (that this relates to our family is shown by the fact that the will, now lost, was among the Browne's Hospital records); PRO, C136/85/11; Wright *Domus Dei* pp 3-4 gives the wrong date, 1384. Peck transcribes her name as Tanner but other records show clearly it was Taverner; the reference in Peck to John Broune of Stamford taverner in 1394 (Peck xii 30) is probably an error; there is no other reference to a John Broune taverner but there are references to John Taverner; and it is noteworthy that this reference occurs in 1394, the year John Broune inherited from Sarah Taverner. For John Taverner and Sarah, see PRO, CP25/1/141/128/3; Peck xii 2.

[107] There is no consistency in the spelling of the name but a general tendency to use the form Broune in the earlier period and Browne in the later period. I have followed that inconsistency!

[108] CCR 1364-68/63; CPR 1367-70/116; LAO, Stamford parish records, PG1/5; Durham DCD Reg. 2 fol. 275; CPR 1370-74/158; 1358-61/520 (1361). In 1369, soon after receiving the grant of Stamford and Grantham, Edmund Langley was commissioned to hear and conclude (*oyer and terminer*) law suits in Yorkshire, Grantham and Stamford (his own estates); a series of pardons were obtained from the king which seem to be related to this commission, CPR 1367-70/187, 457; 1370-74/78, 122, 127, 489; 1374-77/154.

servants[109]. Although a 'small-scale' trader, he was one of the wealthier members of the town, but others were more highly taxed, among them Geoffrey Casterton esquire in St Paul's parish and John de la Panetrie esquire in St Andrew's parish. Sometime before 1375, John Broune was serving as Alderman of the borough and acquiring property in St Mary's parish, property which came down to William Browne[110].

We must not of course imagine that all this took place in a vacuum; it is only too easy to detach family history from its context. The Browne family lived in a town in which (as we have seen) royal visits and councils occurred at regular intervals; and that town stood in a region and a country, so that regional and national events impacted on the locality. As the yield from the king's own estates (the royal demesne) increasingly failed to meet the cost of government, especially the wars with France, various devices were invented to raise money from his subjects; and the customs on exports and imports and the lay and clerical taxes which parliament and convocation granted from time to time had to be assessed and collected. Thus, in the last year of Edward III's reign (1376-7), John Broune was appointed as one of the collectors of the king's taxes in Kesteven (someone from Stamford regularly sat on that commission, and it was presumably his turn); and in 1377, he was collector of the subsidy in Stamford with Stenby, Taverner and Ardern. The government of the new king Richard II appointed him, as Alderman (for at least a second time), to assess a new tax to build ships for the king's navy; the borough of Leicester shared that task with Stamford[111].

A more immediate and continuous way in which Stamford (and with Stamford, the Browne family) was involved in the politics of the wider world was through the nobles and greater gentry, as well as monasteries, who (as we have seen) held

---

[109] CCR 1374-77/472-3; CFR 1368-77/389; PRO, E179/135/76; Fenwick p 28: 'menue' means 'small' (as in 'menue peuple' – lesser people) or 'fine' as in 'fine lace', Carus-Wilson, Haberget p 149; the term was often used in the context of trade and money. The tax returns for Stamford are not complete.

[110] Peck xii 2. For deeds witnessed (as Alderman of Stamford) in 1375-6, PRO, E315/31/198; Wright *Domus Dei* p 3; MCO 33; Peck xi 66; xii 2. Peck is wrong in suggesting that John Broune served as Alderman in 1375 and again in 1377; these dates are those of the deeds, not the date of service as Alderman; see Rogers, Aldermen. A deed involving the family of Burton of Tolthorpe in Rutland, close by Stamford, misled an antiquarian to suggest that the Browne family purchased the manor of Tolthorpe before 1376. It seems clear however that John Broune was called upon to act in connection with a property deal; James Wright 1684 (reprint 1973) *History and Antiquities of Rutland* London pp 128-130; T Cox 1720-31 *Magna Britannia et Hibernia* vol. iv *Rutlandshire* London pp 566-7; for Burton, see J S Roskell, L Clark and C Rawcliffe (eds) 1993 *History of Parliament: the House of Commons 1386-1421* Sutton ii pp 441-43; VCH *Rutland* ii pp 238-9.

[111] CFR 1369-77/389; 1377-83/55; CPR 1377-81/203, 324; Bateson *Leicester* ii pp 161, 186; POPC iv 320

property in the town. The doings of the town's lord (Warenne, Bohun, and Cambridge, the king's son) at court or on the battlefield would thus be of concern in the town. Edmund of Langley, Richard II's uncle, has been described by one recent historian as someone who was "not a strong character, had very little ambition, and .. [was] unpopular". As duke of York, he remained loyal during the troubles of his nephew in 1386-89, which may be why the king held the important council of 1392 in York's town of Stamford[112].

Relations between their lord and the town's political elite were not always easy. The main controversy seems to have been over the respective jurisdictions, with the town council trying to assert their right to hold a court for all offences committed in the town, presumably under the charter of 1313 from Warenne. Only occasionally does this friction come into the open, but it must have been running continuously - and Browne was caught up in it, like other merchants in the town. Indeed, the family seems from an early stage to have taken the lead in the borough. In 1379, the earl of Cambridge complained that John Broune of Stamford and others (unnamed) were preventing his officials from holding his courts and collecting his dues in the town (some inhabitants of Grantham were similarly accused). It would seem that the earl's officials entered into possession of Stamford (and Grantham) expecting to find one form of seigneurial jurisdiction but they found another; and John Broune led the Stamford citizens' resistance to the new lord's claims. Some agreement was clearly reached, almost certainly in favour of the town, for nothing further was heard of these petitions. In 1388, when oaths were taken throughout the country to keep the peace and defend the five Lords Appellants' agreement with Richard II, a list of thirteen names from Stamford were recorded, headed by John Longe the Alderman, followed by John Broune[113] and eleven other names; almost certainly these were the twelve members of the town council with the Alderman. A member of the Broune family was among the leading citizens of and one of spokesmen for the town from at least the 1360s.

The actions in 1379 which offended the town's lord clearly did not harm John Broune locally, for in 1384, he was elected as Alderman again. The government appointed him to a commission of array (1385), to summon and inspect the fighting men of the town and region around. In 1388, John Broune served again on the Kesteven tax-collecting commission. The family's connections with the nobility continued; he was witness to the establishment in Ely of a chantry by Hugh la Zouche knight in 1387 and 1391 (the Browne connections with the

---

[112] Ian Mortimer 2008 *The Fears of Henry IV: the life of England's self-made king* Vintage p 75.

[113] given in the printed version as John 'Brom'; *Rot Parl* iii pp 400-3; CCR 1385-89/405; PRO, C255/20/15; CPR 1377-81/357-8

Zouche family remained strong for many years)[114]. For, as we have seen, there were others than the Plantagenet dukes of York in and near the town, and such interests were important.

The most important in Stamford, after the dukes of York, was the de la Pole family. Successive de la Poles and successive dukes of York became bitter enemies. Michael de la Pole stood high in the favour of Richard II and, having been made Lord Chancellor 1383, to the disgust of many of the greater peers of the realm, he was created in 1385 earl of Suffolk (at the same time as Edmund earl of Cambridge became duke of York). But Suffolk was impeached in 1386 for having undue influence with the king, and his estates (including the Stamford property) were forfeited. The property was substantial: a great inn called 'Kyngesin' on the west side of Bridge Street (now St Mary's Hill) with great gates opening into the street[115], a garden, dovecote ("a place called Duffecotegarthe"), a forge and a wine-tavern. The whole had been leased out "with furniture" for £20 p.a.. In addition, there were three messuages, two shops in Colgate (High Street), another tavern, a cottage, an "empty place near the Friars Minor", 64 acres of arable and 4 acres of meadow. The estate carried a number of annuities to servants of Suffolk's household. His local interests were strengthened by acquiring offices and property rights in Rockingham forest and in Burghley nearby[116]. This was a major interest in the town,

Richard II restored Suffolk in 1387, only to cause an outbreak of violence from a group of nobles (the Lords Appellant, Gloucester, Arundel and Warwick), and at the king's command, he was exiled to France where he died in 1389. The Browne family was somehow involved: for on several occasions, John Broune acted as a witness to property transactions by the de la Pole family, and in 1390, John Broune was appointed to investigate whether two of Suffolk's servants should continue to enjoy their annuities from the earl's Stamford property, a dispute which rumbled on for several years[117]. While this should not be taken as implying that Broune was a Suffolk adherent, it is probable that the government felt he would be sympathetic.

---

[114] PRO, E326/4775; Peck xii 10; CPR 1381-5/589; 1388-92/340, 347; CCR 1385-89/458; CFR 1383-91/216

[115] CFR 1383-91/248, 308. Its name suggests that this large house had originally belonged to the castle which stood immediately behind it but it had become detached as the castle had declined.

[116] CPR 1388-92/291, 513; 1391-96/210; CIM iv 1377-88 pp 225-6 (412); v 1387-93 pp 66-7 (93), 91 (115); CPR 1388-92/291-2, 340-1; CCR 1389-92/300; 1392-96/399

[117] e.g. MCO 33, 199; CCR 1377-81/236-7; Stamford town hall records, TH13/1/1; CCR 1389-92/389; CPR 1388-92/340-1, 347.

Apart from his trade and the town's government, he was also involved in handling property for the town's gilds, especially the gild of St Mary and Corpus Christi in the parish church of St Mary at the bridge. He continued to be involved in property transactions, primarily as a witness, both in the town and outside. In 1395, we find John Broune holding a messuage and garden in Cornstall, property which remained with the family until William Browne settled it on his Hospital[118].

In 1399, Henry of Bolingbroke deposed Richard II and he immediately confirmed the forfeiture of the Suffolk property which Richard II had persuaded parliament to annul in 1398; but Henry quickly restored the heir Michael de la Pole in 1399 as earl of Suffolk in an attempt to buy his loyalty which seems to have been successful. Edmund duke of York died in 1402 leaving two sons, Edward duke of York and Richard earl of Cambridge. The town and the Brownes would have watched with interest as the new political complex worked itself out.

John Broune the father

The John Broune we see from 1409 was the father of William Browne. By that date, he was established as a draper in the town and outside. He may have been the John Broune commissioned to make arrest in the port of Lynn in a case which involved Hanseatic merchants in 1406, but we first see him clearly in 1409 when as John Broune draper he bought two adjacent shops in the parish of All Saints in the Market, Stamford, next door to the wool hall of John Longe[119], and converted them into one warehouse. He would no longer be a *menuwe* merchant. The extent of his trade may be seen from his suit against an Italian merchant for a debt of £91 7s and from the wide range and high quality of the cloth provided[120]. John Broune draper was witness in 1411 and again in 1414, and served as Alderman of the town in 1414. As John Broune of Lincolnshire, he acted as surety with a merchant of Kent in the grant of a wardship in Cambridgeshire. John Broune draper was a witness in 1416 for the nuns of St Michael, and witness in St George's parish in 1419[121].

---

[118] PRO, C143/422/12; CPR 1391-94/114; BL, Add Ch 6092; CCR 1396-99/80; LAO, BHS 7/2/6.

[119] He appears to have bought up some of the interests of John Longe, see Peck xi 35 38, 64 65; xii 2, 13, 21, 33; xiii 7-8; xiv 1, 12, 21-22. He had another property in Woolrow.

[120] Wright *Domus Dei* p 4; *Calendar of Plea and Memoranda Rolls of the City of London* 1437-1457 p 40; John Botoner was one of the valuers, and John Browne's daughter Alice was married to a Botoner of Coventry.

[121] CPR 1405-8/232, 416; PRO, E326/4777; MCO 23; Peck xiii 9; PRO, E315/35/19; CFR 1413-22/125; LAO, Stamford parish records PG2/1

The Browne family also acquired property in the countryside around Stamford. In earlier periods, members of the family had acted as witnesses for transactions in neighbouring villages, including Carlby, Lincs, and Barnack in Northants. By 1408-9, John Broune of Staunford was holding Peterborough abbey land in Pilsgate; and at the same time, John Broune of Warmington, Northants, was a tenant of the nuns of St Michael, Stamford, and collected some of their debts. This John Browne married one Margery, and (as John Broune of Marholm with his wife) in 1418 and 1426, they held property in both Stamford and Marholm, Northants[122].

But the main focus of the family remained Stamford. John Browne draper became Alderman of the town again in 1422-3. In the same year, the business expanded significantly; he acquired another two shops immediately adjacent to his existing two shops, and joined the four together, making a substantial storage capacity. Located in what is now the cleared area of Red Lion Square[123], it was surrounded by narrow streets, bounded on the east by the king's highway (Scobothes) and on the west by the narrow lane of 'Behinde-ye-Bak'; it stood between other properties north and south. It cannot have been easy to work with large wool bales in such a confined area. One can see what such a property would have been like by looking at Dragon Hall, which another draper and mercer, Robert Toppes, formed out of four adjacent properties in Norwich at about the same time. Browne acquired further property in the town; this may be a sign of the boom which some towns experienced in the early fifteenth century[124].

The reign of Henry V, with its vigorous defence of the dynasty against rebellion and campaigns in France, touched Stamford: for in 1415, Richard earl of Cambridge, the younger brother of Edward duke of York, together with lord Scrope, was accused of treason against the king, tried and beheaded just as the king was departing for France. This became of immediate significance to Stamford, since Edward duke of York was killed at Agincourt, and the son of the executed earl of Cambridge, another Richard, became the town's lord at the age of four years. What made these events more significant was that the main

---

[122] LAO, BHS 7/3/3; 7/2/6; NRS 43 *Pilsgate* pp 168, 392; there may have been an earlier John Broune in Pilsgate, see ibid. p 164. NRO Fitzwilliam (Milton) Charters 1213, 1219; PRO, SC6/1260/17; NRS 33 *Obedientiaries* p 119. Thomas Broune husbandman appears in Pilsgate in 1397, Richard in Warmington in 1397-8, PRO, SC6/1260/11,12.

[123] Wright *Domus Dei* pp 4-5; Peck xiv 1. For Woolrow in Stamford, see PRO, SC6/913/25. It has been suggested that the hall above 6-7 Red Lion Square is William Browne's Wool Hall. It is not. That stands in St John's parish, not All Saints; it dates from the end of the fourteenth century, not from the 1420s; and it is the wrong shape. It is not even certain that it was a wool hall.

[124] Toppes p 212

accuser of Richard earl of Cambridge in 1415 was Michael de la Pole earl of Suffolk; but both Michael and his eldest son (another Michael) died in France, and his second son William (aged 19) succeeded to the title and estates (though, like the duke of York's estates, somewhat impoverished by dowagers).

Henry V, like York and Suffolk, died in France; he left a nine-months-old child as heir to the kingdom. Surprisingly, in view of the rebellions faced by Henry IV the usurper and by Henry V, the minority passed off relatively peacefully in England. There was of course continual fighting in France, but Henry VI assumed personal control in 1437 at the age of about fifteen. John Broune played his part in the war effort: he served as a member of both the lay and clerical tax commissions for Kesteven in 1428 and the Kesteven lay subsidy commission in 1433-4, taxes needed to fund the war being waged by John duke of Bedford, the young king's uncle[125].

But war did not prevent Broune from expanding his interests. In 1424-5, he acquired a garden in Cornstall, and was Alderman for a third time in 1427. He acquired a further messuage in Woolrow in 1431, and acted as witness twice for one Robert Browne (perhaps a relation) in 1432. As John Broune draper of Stamford, he witnessed other property transactions in the town and in Rutland between 1425 and 1436[126]. With Alexander Mercer and John Smyth, he was feoffee (trustee) for Jane the wife of Robert Torold with instructions to pass her property in Stamford, Ryhall and Belmesthorp to her executors to find a chaplain to sing masses for her soul; after her death, her husband and executors sued Browne and Mercer (Smyth was by then dead), since they were alleged to have refused to pass over the estate to the executors. His increasing status may be seen when he became one of the feoffees with Ralph lord Cromwell for Sir William Mallore in lands in south Lincolnshire[127]. His interests thus spread into Lincolnshire, Rutland and Northamptonshire. John Broune of Stamford with John Godale and John Page of Stamford (a former Alderman) was alleged to have assaulted John Brampton of Stamford mercer (probably a servant of the earl of Suffolk) on the high road to Thornhaugh in Northants[128].

---

[125] *Feudal Aids* iii 338-9; vi 364-5; CFR 1422-30/221; 1430-37/144, 359

[126] Peck xiv 2-3, 4; CFR 1422-30/221; 1430-35/194; BL, Add Ch 66631; for John Browe esq of Stamford, Wodehed, Rutland, and of Pilsgate Northants gent, CPR 1461-67/90; Exeter-NRA /6/59; Peck xiv 5, 9; MCO 23, 27, 46, 7, 9, 25, 12.

[127] PRO, C1/7/202. Some of these suits are fictitious, intended to record property transactions for greater security. LAO, Holywell 71/15B

[128] PRO, C1/6/155, beating Brampton senseless and leaving him for dead and later threatening to kill him, so that the alleged victim claimed that he dared not live in his own house in Stamford; this is undated. In the 1390s, John Brampton was feoffee for the earl in settling lands on his new *domus dei* in Hull, CPR 1391-96/210; and a John Brampton clerk is recorded in Papley

In 1432-3, John Broune handed his business over to William his son, and in December 1433, made his will. John died nine years later in 1442; Margery his wife did not die until 1460. The making of the will and the retirement of John Broune senior in 1432-3 suggests that he was ill at this time, although he was named once again as the Stamford representative on the Kesteven tax commission in 1437[129]. John asked to be buried in the chapel of St Thomas the martyr in the parish church of All Saints in the Market, Stamford; the family had moved its base from St Paul's parish in the east of the town into All Saints parish in the centre. He left enough household goods to his wife to ensure her necessities were met, and a belt and gold seal to his son John. His executors were Margery his wife, William Lewes of Oakham (a merchant), … Browne of Stamford 'my son' (clearly William but the will is torn at this point), and Robert Ballard rector of Helpston. William bought for his father and mother a brass depicting male and female figures but without an inscription; he waited until his mother's death to order the inscription to go with that brass[130].

Brass erected by William Browne in 1460 to his father (died 1442) claiming him as Calais Stapler and using the Browne merchant mark (photo: John Hartley)

What of other members of the family? A Robert Browne husbandman appears in 1431-2 when he acquired property in Stamford, John Browne draper acting as one of the witnesses for him; in 1441-2, Robert Browne glover was Alderman of the town. He was dead by 1452 when a deed refers to Joan the widow of Robert Browne glover and to a former wife Elena (now dead) in an transaction

(Warmington, Northants) in 1457, Simcoe 1038 M/T/13/122. Many of these pleas exaggerate the harm done to ensure the attention of the royal council.

[129] Peck xiv 12, 15. This deed is undated; Peck puts it under 1440 but there is no evidence for this. It would seem to be part of the settlement of 1432-3. CFR 1430-37/359, 394

[130] Emmerson, Brasses

(unfortunately not dated) for which William and John Browne acted as witnesses[131]. He may have been a relation.

Thus it would seem that at least three generations of drapers (also dealing in wool), property dealers, tax collectors, town councillors and office holders in Stamford, with interests in the surrounding countryside, lay behind William Browne and John his brother. Foundations had been laid, in terms of business, property and participation in local government, on which William and his brother could build[132].

---

[131] MCO 5, 27, 46; Peck xiv 15; Butcher 1727 p 26; Stamford Borough records, TH13/1/4; MCO 18: PRO, E210/4927; MCO 25, 31, 42, 57. He may be the Robert son and heir of Maud Broun later the wife of one William Stokes; this Robert was born about 1405, CIPM 22 1422-27 p 648; he married Joan de Brynnesley, see CIPM 21 1418-22 p 262 (770); CIPM 22 1422-27 p 649 (745). Another Robert Browne was a juror in 1480, MCO 44. Peck xiii 7 records a Raphe Browne as Alderman of Stamford in 1409 but this is almost certainly a misreading for Ralphe Bonde who is known to have been Alderman in 1410-11, Rogers, Aldermen. It is important to note that the references to Robert Browne in Wright, *Domus Dei* pp 3-5 are misreadings.

[132] There is an intriguing issue: in 1413, a group of wool merchants were pardoned taxes on their wool exports from Ipswich: they included William Lewes, William Lessyngham, Robert Wodecombe, John Pykwell, John Fildyng, William Prodhomme, John Sapcote, John Clerk, William Browne, Hugh Martyn and Nicholas Squyer merchants; CPR 1413-16/127; their wool in Ipswich port had been burnt, PRO, E404/29/183. One William Lewes was executor for John Browne the father, and our William Browne became executor for William Lewes of Lynn and Oakham; the Sapcote family joined in several wool sales. But this William Browne cannot be our William Browne since he would have been too young. And it is unlikely that a member of the Stamford family called William was operating without there being other evidence of him at the time.

PART I: CHAPTER 4   WILLIAM BROWNE'S EARLY YEARS c1433-1449

And some chose trade · they fared the better,
As it seemeth to our sight · that such men thrive[133]

The lyf so short, the craft so long to lerne[134]

We do not know when William Browne was born; we can only assume from the start of his public career, 1432/3, a date of birth of about 1410. But it could be a few years before that. Named William, we can assume that he was not the first-born, who would have been named John but did not survive, so a younger brother was named John to make good the loss.

Nor do we know how he and his brother were educated. Educated they certainly were. Both were literate: William wrote his will ("In wittenes wherof I have put my seale to the same and subscribid with myn owne hand the day and yere above wretyn"), and his brother-in-law Thomas Stokes spoke of "my brothers own hand in his rede bok". He presumably was fairly fluent in various forms of French for trading purposes; he almost certainly had some knowledge of Latin. As we have seen, there was plenty of choice for his education in or near Stamford. Although the schools of national and indeed international significance in the town seem to have declined (see p13 above), schooling in fifteenth century Stamford remained substantial and, it would seem, attractive. A schoolmaster in Stamford is mentioned in 1404, and John the teenage son of lady de la Pole dowager countess of Suffolk spent several months in Stamford during 1416-7. St Leonard's priory maintained a school, and both Henry Helay in 1422 and Richard Barton in the 1430s, new priors of St Leonard's, brought books with them from Durham[135]. All the friaries had centres for training novices, and some of these are likely to have been open to paying pupils. Dr Nicholas Kenton, head of the Carmelites at Stamford, and John Milverton who studied at the White Friars Stamford in the early 1430s, confirm this tradition. John Shepey of New College, Oxford, left books to the Franciscan friary, Stamford, in 1412, and John Kynton studied with the Franciscans in the 1450s. Elizabeth lady Grey

---

[133] D Pearsall (ed) 2008 *Piers Plowman: a new annotated edition of the C-Text* University of Exeter Press, Prologue lines 31-32

[134] W W Skeat (ed) 1924 *Complete Works of Chaucer* Oxford University Press: Chaucer, *Parlement of Fowles* 1

[135] CY *Visit* ii pp 152, 156; iii pp 346-7; CY 73 *Fleming* p 136; BL, Add 41063 fol 75; Heale *Priories* p 126

of Codnor who asked to be buried in the Black Friars of Stamford in 1444, left ten marks to "friar Thomas Gray [perhaps a relative] and to the school". Religious houses like Sempringham and Vaudey who owned property in the town seem to have offered some schooling, as several of the parochial clergy would have done. And there were places outside of the town: we know of one boy from Stamford who attended 'the song school' at Burton Lazars. "... schools may have been declining in importance in the fifteenth century, as emergent inns of chancery and of court in London attracted their potential clients, but they had certainly not disappeared"[136].

We have some details of the school in Stamford run by the nuns of St Michael in Stamford Baron. The convent took in boarders who were placed under the supervision of the prioress, but their numbers fell off in the latter part of the century, perhaps as the reputation of the nunnery declined, from 8 in 1440-5 to three in 1470, to two (both boys) in 1472 and only one in 1481 but three in 1482. There must have been day pupils, for there are references in the nunnery accounts to 'le skolemaystre' whose income almost certainly came from the fees the pupils paid[137].

William and John Browne may have attended the nuns' school. But it is also possible that there were chaplain-schoolmasters attached to some of the gilds of the town. We have evidence for such a position in the Corpus Christi gild in the early sixteenth century, and it is likely that some chaplains provided by this or other gilds were teaching local children before that time. In view of the connections between the gild and the town council and the fact that the Brownes had been town councillors for several generations, a gild 'school' (however informal) would have been the obvious place for John Browne the father to send his two sons[138].

---

[136] PRO, REQ 11/199; see *AASR* Wills p 108. Griffiths, Bureaucracies p 119; N Orme 1973 *English Schools in the Middle Ages* Methuen p 237; Orme 2006 p 269; A F Leach 1915 (1968) *Schools of Medieval England* Methuen (Blom) p 192; VCH Lincs ii p 230; NRS 33 *Obedientiaries* p 131; BL, Egerton Rolls 8776 (although dated 4-5 Henry IV by BL, it should be 4-5 Henry V); Peck viii 45; x 14; Owen 1971 p 86; BL, Stowe 141 fol 37; R E Archer 2003 Jane with the Blemyssh: a skeleton in the de la Pole cupboard, *Ricardian* xiii p 13. OHS 32 p 11; OHS 52 ii p 15; Heale *Priories* p 126; ODNB sub nom.; Peck xi 25-27; Gibbons *Wills* p 168; *Cal Papal Reg* 1455-1464 p 634. Nigel Ramsay has listed book collections in medieval Stamford in N Ramsay and J M W Willoughby (eds) 2009 *Hospitals, Towns and the Professions* British Library and British Academy pp 403-411

[137] CY *Visit* iii p 349; E Power 1922 (1964 edn) *Medieval English Nunneries c1275-1535* Hafner; the daughter of Robert Crane (Alderman 1498) was in the school in 1482. The schoolmaster assisted the convent at time of harvest with cartage and other services, for which the nuns paid him, PRO, SC6/914/4; SC6/1260/13,16, 17

[138] *AASR* Chantry p 101; CPR 1549-51/271, le Scolehouse in St George's parish, see VCH *Lincs* ii p 230; C P McMahon 1947 *Education in fifteenth century England* Baltimore: John Hopkins p 158.

After the basic schooling, there were three possible routes for professional development – the inns of court or chancery, the universities, or apprenticeships. Margaret Spencer left money for one of her sons "towards his fynding and exhibicion to the courte [one of the inns of court] there to lerne diligently the lawes of the kings grace of this his Realm of Englonde". Thomas Stokes left £100 (a very large sum) "into the keping of Sir Henry Wykes and maister Thomas Hykam for the exhibicion of ij prests" including "maistre John Taylour scolar of Oxford ..., the said maistre Taylour to have his stipend to Oxford by cause of his Lernyng there viij marcs by yere" [139]. William Browne would most likely have proceeded along the third route, apprenticeship, perhaps under his father; he learnt the skills of the trade on the job[140].

Taking over: 1432-1437

William's business career took off at the same time (1433) that the duke of York (about the same age as William Browne) was entering into control of his inheritance, including Stamford, and just before the young Henry VI took charge of the government for the first time (1436-7[141]). Browne's first known activity (1432) is as witness to the deed by which his father was feoffee for Robert Browne. In 1432-3, John Browne of Stamford draper granted to William his son "all his entire shop, lately four shops together" in Woolrow in the parish of All Saints in the Market; John Halyday vicar of All Saints was charged to put William in possession of the property. A few months later, in December 1433, John Browne named William as one of his executors. This was a settlement of the business on the son, with the father passing into some form of retirement[142]. At about the same time, certainly before 1437, William Browne purchased from John Smyth chaplain (a fellow feoffee with William Browne's father) a substantial property in the parish of All Saints (now 1 All Saints Place), and soon afterwards he acquired and passed on to his father the property next door (now 17 Barn Hill), with the vicarage of All Saints on one side and his own tenement on the other side, with grounds stretching back to the town walls, a house in which his father and mother lived until the father died in 1442 (his mother probably stayed on there until she died eighteen years later) [143].

These arrangements may have been caused by William's changed family circumstances, for it was during these years (1433-37) that William Browne

---

[139] PRO, PROB 11/16 fol 118; PROB 11/10 fol 29.

[140] For apprenticeships, see Withington 2005

[141] J L Watts 1994 When did Henry VI's minority end?, in Clayton et al 1994 p 117

[142] Peck xiv 12. For John Browne's will, see above p 52. In 1427, a York merchant gave all his property to his son in return for a life pension, Kermode *Merchants* p 41.

[143] Peck xiv 13, 14, 15; for Smyth, see above p51

married. His bride was Margaret daughter of John Stokes, a royal household esquire of Warmington, a village of Northamptonshire where William Browne's father already held property. At about the same time or somewhat later, his brother John married Margaret's sister Agnes. A daughter Elizabeth was the only child to survive, but it is likely there were earlier children who died at a young age. Elizabeth, stated to have been aged about 48 in 1489[144], was apparently born a year or two on either side of 1441.

And the same time (1432-3), William Browne draper was feoffee for a prominent Stamford merchant, William Storeton baker, in a property transaction in the parish of St Paul where the Browne family had recently lived. John Browne draper, the father, was a witness to this deed[145].

This transaction provides an example of the kind of property dealings which feature throughout William Browne's life. In 1412-13, Elizabeth Mercer of Stamford widow, the daughter of Henry Kyrkeby of Stamford, owned a largish property on the south side of Estgate (now St Paul's Street) between the property called 'Goddeshowse' belonging to the parish of St Paul and the property of Holy Trinity Gild, and running through to Cornstall. Elizabeth set up feoffees to hold this property for her use, and got the then Alderman and other burgesses including John Broun draper (the father), a neighbour in Estgate, to witness this transaction. In 1424-5, those trustees who were still alive passed the holding of this property to new trustees including one Alexander Mercer who may have been her son; many of the same witnesses including John Browne draper were used for this transaction. In 1436, the one surviving trustee passed the property back to Elizabeth and her new husband William Storeton baker of Stamford and to their new trustees, including the young William Broune draper (again John Broune draper was a witness); and Alexander Mercer released to the new feoffees any rights he may have had in the property. Storeton (a councillor and Alderman of the borough) was a friend of William Browne; he acted as feoffee for him in some of his more important property transactions, and like Browne, he was not above a spot of sharp property dealings (see pp 282-4 below). The two families kept in touch: Elizabeth outlived her new husband and must have become very old, for as late as 1470, William Browne released to Elizabeth, widow of William Storeton, any rights that he may still have had in this property[146].

---

[144] CIPM Henry VII i pp 202 (476), 219 (525), 523 (1179). The ages in these inquisitions were often widely out, sometimes by ten years; Elizabeth Elmes was said to be aged about 48 in October 1489 but about 50 in 1496. For Stokes, see Rogers, Stokes

[145] MCO 12, 16.

[146] MCO 23, 7, 2. Alexander Mercer was a feoffee with John Browne draper of Stamford (the father) in another property dealing, PRO, C1/7/202; MCO 12, 16, 53. For Storeton, see PRO,

William Browne then, as a young man, began to take over some of his father's responsibilities in relation to neighbours and friends in their property dealings, at the same time as he took over his father's business, his networks and his place on the town council.

The transfer of the business, taking the form of a 'sale' of the wool hall from father to son, tells us several things about these two men. The first is a concern for exactitude, an attention to detail. These four shops were purchased by John Browne senior in two separate transactions, each of two shops: but the previous deeds were carefully kept and recorded each time there was a new transaction. As we have seen, William Browne was very preoccupied with documentary evidences[147]. Secondly, the appointment of the vicar of All Saints as attorney for this transaction is an example of the tendency for the family to use secular clergy, especially the incumbent of their own parish church, extensively in their business dealings.

But the question arises why such a formal transfer should have been necessary. The answer may lie in the fact that William was the eldest surviving son of John Browne senior. The pedigrees of earlier writers have been contradictory on this matter, several saying that William Browne was the older son, some the younger (no one has suggested the two boys were twins; they could have been but it is unlikely). William's appointment as executor to his father and his taking over of the business indicates his seniority; and John his brother, alive in 1433, does not appear actively until 1448, sixteen years after the first references to William Browne.

Why then the deed of transfer of the business? This must be because much of the property was held by the custom of borough English (that is, inheritance by the youngest son, not the oldest son). A feature of all Five Boroughs except Lincoln, borough English was known as "the custom of Stamford" in the fourteenth century, and it survived into the sixteenth century[148], as the will of John Elmes, his great grandson (1540) shows:

C1/26/236; Harvard Deed 343; Peck xiv 66; PRO, E179/276/44; KB9/65A/36; the family may be related to the Stourton who acted as feoffee for Margaret duchess of Somerset in Maxey, Exeter-NRA 203/9

[147] Rogers, Archives; see above p 23

[148] CFR 1319-27/418; CCR 1381-85/64; PRO, E321/15/7; C Roberts (ed) 1865 *Calendarium Genealogicum* ii 643; Peck i 21-22; xiv 21; Roffe 1994 p 22; see Hill *Medieval Lincoln* p 293

Item I wyll that all suche stuff as I caused to be fetchyd from my house in Stamforde be layed there agayne and there to remayne to thuse of the heyre that borough Englyssh make heyre theyr[149].

So William as the elder son could not inherit without some special provision such as this. William Browne took over the business, and although his brother John Browne was a partner, he was always a junior partner, his name rarely occurring on its own in the records, and when jointly with William Browne, coming after William Browne on almost every occasion; his trading was usually on a smaller scale than that of his brother.

This assumption of the drapery business in 1433 was followed by property dealings and civic duties. William Browne can be seen as early as 1433-4 purchasing a tenement in Stamford Baron (Hyegate, now High Street, St Martins). In the following year, he was elected for the first time as Alderman of the town for the year September 1435 to 1436[150]. I think this reflects on the status of the family in Stamford as well as William Browne's burgeoning reputation, for at this time, service in the town's chief post would normally have been reached after several years on the town council (see p 184 below); it must have been unusual for a person as young as William Browne in 1435 (say 25 years of age) to have jumped straight into that position, even if his father had served as Alderman on three occasions. Here was a young man going places and fast.

The first decade of trading – William Browne draper, 1439-1449

From an early date, William determined to control his own career. In September 1439, William Browne of Stamford secured from the king a comprehensive exemption for life from being put on royal commissions such as assize or inquisitions, from being made mayor, bailiff or constable in any town, and from being appointed to any royal offices such as sheriff, escheator, coroner, assessor or collector of taxes etc, against his will[151]. This does not betray an unwillingness to serve in any of these offices; it might even be in his interest to do so on occasion – and in fact he did so serve. Rather, it was a statement that William

---

[149] PRO, PROB 11/30 fol 21; a garden in St Peter's parish and a garden in Gleydgate came to Thomas youngest son of William Elmes, William Browne's grandson and heir, by borough English, PRO, C1/629/3

[150] Peck xiv 11, 14: the title deed dated 29 March 18 Henry VI (1440) refers to 1433-4 when Richard Lee wright who was witness was Alderman; a title deed, MCO 12, dated 20 July 1436 (i.e. during William Browne's Aldermanship) which mentions John Page Alderman as a witness must relate to 1432-33 when Page was Alderman. For a full discussion, see Rogers, Aldermen

[151] CPR 1436-41/341; such exemptions were (in theory) later annulled, *Rot Parl* v p 225; Attreed *King's Towns* pp 55-59

intended to serve on his own conditions and at times of his choosing; he would decide for himself what duties he would undertake and when. And he saw himself as someone with a national remit as well as a Stamford focus. Such an exemption probably cost him or his family a good deal.

The main records we have of William Browne for the first few years are in connection with property transactions, in 1437-8, in Scotgate outside the town walls to the north, and in 1441, as feoffee in Star Lane, a trusteeship which lasted until 1481[152]; this property eventually came into William Browne's hands. Family matters also occupied his attention during his first ten years of business, including the death of his father (1442).

Despite the exemption, in 1442 William Browne like his father served his turn as the Stamford representative on the commission to collect the lay subsidy in Kesteven. The position may have given the young William Browne an opportunity to look around the Kesteven countryside to see which estates may have been available and desirable for investment; for he seems to have started purchasing outside of Stamford about this time. In 1446-7, he acquired property in Bradcroft (Rutland). And he may have been working on a wider scale, for soon after the truce of Tours in 1444 which led to the marriage of Henry VI to Margaret of Anjou, the surrender of much of the territory in France which Henry V had won, and the (in the end abandoned) "viage for pees" which Henry VI planned to make to cement the truce, one William Browne was appointed to a commission to the duke of Burgundy concerning the grievances of merchants of Holland, Zealand and Flanders; this is probably William Browne of Stamford[153].

Both brothers must have been elected to the town council (the First Twelve) from a very early date, for in 1444-5, William Browne served for a second time as Alderman of Stamford. Four years later, his brother John became Alderman, and in the following year 1449-50, William Browne became Alderman for a third time, during which time, he acted with his brother John as witness to a marriage settlement in Stamford[154].

During these years, the only designation given to him was 'draper of Stamford'. As William Browne draper, he was witness in 1443 to a deed of the nuns of St

---

[152] Peck xiv 13; LAO, Stamford parish records PG1/6-9

[153] CFR 1437-35/223; PRO, E28/76/18 - his name heads the list of the commission; Peck xiv 21:
Richard Lee Alderman in 1446-7 was witness; Pugh , York p 119; J Ferguson 1972 *English Diplomacy 1422-61* Clarendon p 188

[154] Peck xiv 18, 22; MCO 38

Michael concerning the lease of a mill in Stamford; in 1445 he was witness along with John Page the Alderman, William Storeton and Richard Lee, all town councillors[155].

But things changed sometime before 1448-9. William was called 'draper' until at least 1443, but election to the Calais Staple must have occurred in the middle of the 1440s, for from this time, both William and John Browne invariably used the title 'merchant of Stamford', even in their many pardons when it was incumbent to give all possible titles under which they might have operated. The first known reference is in 1448-9 when as 'merchant of Staunford', they both acted as feoffee for Robert Browe of Rutland (steward of Stamford for the duke of York); and in October 1449, as Calais Staplers, with William Lewes of Oakham, they received a licence to export wool from Ipswich in repayment of their share of the Staple loan to the king. And this is important, for "It should be understood that by this time the word 'merchant' was used to describe only relatively wealthy members of the urban elite who engaged in overseas trade". The Browne brothers were no longer Stamford traders or manufacturers; they were overseas traders based in Stamford[156].

The economy of Stamford in the 1430s-40s

But the time was inauspicious. The 1430s was a time of terrible weather, especially the years 1437 to 1440 - the coldest period between the eleventh century and the twentieth century. Some historians have described the "agrarian crises of the 1430s" as leading to 'the Great Slump' – a period of rising rents and rural wages, and the lowest harvest yields for over 100 years, despite which agricultural prices, especially of grain, were often so low as to be not worth taking it to market; livestock experienced epidemics. "Dearth and disease", and a sense of gloom pervaded the country[157]. But other historians see this as a period of opportunity, with a lively land market, long term leases and the conversion of arable to pasture for sheep, in part because of a shortage of tenants and land workers; with some industries such as leather working and especially brewing growing more specialised and on a larger scale; with therefore more opportunities for apprenticeships and training, with shops becoming

---

[155] MCO 12, 16, 53: in two deeds dated 20 July 1436, he is simply William Browne of Stamford; in a third deed dated 21 July 1436, he is William Browne draper of Stamford. Peck uses the term 'William Browne merchant' in one of his notes, Peck xiv 13, but this is so out of keeping with all the other entries that it is likely to have been Peck's insertion; the original is now lost.

[156] PRO, E326/5553; CPR 1446-52/314-5; ROLLR Gretton DE1431/274. See Britnell Elites. Butcher 1727 noted the change and suggested there were two William Brownes, the draper who served as Alderman in 1435 and 1444, and the merchant who was Alderman in 1449, 1460, 1466, and 1470, but this is not possible.

[157] Hatcher, Slump pp 243-246; Griffiths *Henry VI* p 598; Langdon *Mills*, Dyer, Capitalists

separated from workshops and an increase in carriers to move goods around, increasing mobility of workers and the expansion of domestic service[158].

The picture then is mixed. Agriculture was clearly changing, with greater production for the market (especially sheep) and long–term leases. It still underpinned the economy of a trading centre like Stamford (see above p 33). Margaret Browne in her will speaks of her cattle and sheep, and other wills contain references to sheep and crops. The nuns' accounts and those from St Leonard's Priory are full of concerns about sowing and harvesting; Robert Browne was both husbandman and glover. So that the weather impacted on Stamford more then than it would today. William Browne would have been concerned with agriculture, not just in terms of the product of flocks of sheep but also arable and meadow land also, with more leasing than direct exploitation of land[159].

But Stamford relied more on trade and manufacture than agriculture – and these too were changing. Reliance on the twin pillars of the international fair and cloth making which had characterised the town during the thirteenth and early fourteenth centuries was declining; the markets were taking over. Stamford's mid-Lent fair was still important on a regional basis but its great days were clearly past; in Stamford, as elsewhere, the international fair was being replaced by "more ... permanent urban trading networks". The request for two more fairs made in the 1481 charter was probably not so much a reaction to an increase in trade but, like other such grants at that time, "an attempt by local grantees to defend a dwindling share of aggregate trade"[160].

Add to this the fact that the wool trade was shrinking, especially in 1436 to 1439, and (as we shall see) the Calais trade was in chaos. The war in France was beginning to go badly, and this impacted on the general climate of the day. John duke of Bedford, the king's uncle, who had been relatively successful in France, died in 1435, and England's ally, the duke of Burgundy, changed to side with the French king against the English. French ships patrolled the coasts of England, acting as pirates, and Calais was soon under siege (1436). The Flemish towns

---

[158] e.g. McIntosh 1986; Mate 2006; Kermode *Enterprise* p 12; Hatcher, Slump pp 247-9; Bridbury 1992

[159] See PRO, C1/26/236; C1/48/332-40; REQ 2/4/77; PROB 11/16 fol 118; SC6/913/26; 914/1-4; 1260/1-25; SC2/188/2-3, and Durham Cathedral Archives, St Leonard's account rolls; see also PRO, E315/42/226; Kermode *Merchants* p 62

[160] S R Epstein 1944 Regional fairs, institutional innovation and economic growth in late medieval Europe *Econ Hist Rev* 2s 47 pp 459-60; see J Masschaele 1997 *Peasants, Merchants and Markets* Macmillan

with which much of Stamford's cloth trade was conducted rose against their Burgundian masters, and the city of Bruges was closed in 1436-8[161].

Markets had always been important for Stamford, catering week by week for the neighbourhood. Held on different days of the week, they occupied their own corners of the town. The importance of local markets can be seen from the request for a new Monday market in the charter of 1481. The cloth-making industry in Stamford seems to have been declining, and few new industries appear to have been taking the place of clothmaking – except perhaps some building[162] (including glass) and some leatherwork.

Craft groupings

In 1465, the town council listed twenty-two crafts into 12 groupings for the purposes of admissions of freemen, several trades sharing the same entry fines. The occupations listed are fairly comprehensive – drapers and mercers, tailors and hosiers, shoemakers, glovers and tinkers (whitesmiths), bakers, brewers and innkeepers (although bakers appear again on their own), fishmongers, butchers; all other handicrafts, husbandmen, labourers, and flax chapmen were grouped together for their admissions and entry fees. But a different set of eleven groupings called 'pagentes' and 'wardenryes' (and a wider range of 42 occupations) were listed for the presentation of the eleven Corpus Christi pageants[163], and it was these groupings which elected wardens to search and oversee the trades and crafts:

> *Theys be the names of all manner crafts sett together in pagents whiche shall within them selfs chuys them wardeyns for to serche and overse all manner poynts longyng to the same crafts that they be chosen of for the welfare and worshipe of this sayd towne and boroughe; and yff any wardeyn so chosen fynd any manner of defalt within his craft or in the master or servant of the same that wyll not be amendid by hym, he shall then complayn to the Alderman that he and his bredern and counseyll may therin take a dewe correccyon and reformacyon[164].*

This time, drapers, hosiers and tailors are grouped together, while the mercers went with the grocers and haberdashers. While there was an attempt to ensure that crafts were usually compatible, some groupings may have been made to

---

[161] Childs 1991 pp 70-72; Griffiths *Henry VI* pp 195-208. For the rebellion in Bruges, see J Dumolyn 2007 The 'terrible Wednesday of Pentecost': confronting urban and princely discourses in the Bruges rebellion of 1436-8, *History* 92 pp 3-20.

[162] for building see pp 116-128, 237-8

[163] See below pp 192-3

[164] HB i fol 2d, 3, pp 6-9; fol 5d, pp 13-14. For craft gilds, see Giles pp 56-57

ensure a balance of numbers – for the arms trades of bowyers, fletchers and stringers were linked with the turners and dyers. One significant sector was made up of scriveners, glasiers, painters, stainers, plus barbers and chandlers; the bakers (who were important enough to ensure they were kept distinct in the earlier regulations) were joined with the brewers, vintners and millers. Weavers joined the walkers and shermen; shoemakers, cobblers and corriers made a group separate from other leather workers, barkers, glovers, skinners and whitawers. The builders included carpenters, masons and slaters, and the victuallers were made up of butchers, fishmongers, hostellers and cooks. The decline of the metal workers can be seen in that the ironmongers and smiths were combined with the saddlers and bottlemakers and all other crafts.

The only evidence we have of the economy of the town on anything like a systematic basis is a list of pardons in 1452, when 118 persons were named, most with their occupations. Of these, the cloth industry and trade amounted to a quarter - six 'merchants', seven mercers and six drapers with only four weavers but ten tailors. Victuallers were some 15% and leather workers 14% – tanners, saddlers, shoemakers and skinners. About 16% gave a social title rather than occupations (gent, esquire, yeoman)[165].

A less useful indication of the main economic activities of the town is the list of admissions to the freedom, recorded only from 1465. In Stamford, entry fees were graded according to the occupation, whereas in some other towns, they had become standardised. But fees became difficult to collect, and the council took steps to try to enforce payment, changing the dates of payments, splitting the entry fines into instalments, and reiterating the order for payments several times; but arrears mounted until in 1476, they reached £3 2s 11½d for the past three years[166].

Enrolment of freemen in Stamford may have been political: for example, William Browne admitted only four men in his two years of recorded Aldermanry, 1466-7 (4) and 1470-1 (0), while Robert Hans fishmonger admitted 60 in his three recorded years, 1465-6 (8), 1472-3 (26) and 1481-2 (26). The graph indicates, I think, the rate of enrolments registered in the Hall Book rather than any general economic trend; registration as a freeman as a requirement for trading was not strongly enforced in late medieval Stamford.

---

[165] PRO, C67/40; see below pp 83-4; for cordwainers in Stamford, see CCR 1377-81/369

[166] HB i fol 9d, p25; fol 10d, p 28; fol 23, p 60. For urban freemen, see Withington 2005; Shaw Wells pp 143-153. Ipswich freemen paid 40s, Amor Ipswich p 16; see also R Britnell 2006 Town Life, in Horrox and Ormrod 2006 pp 134-178.

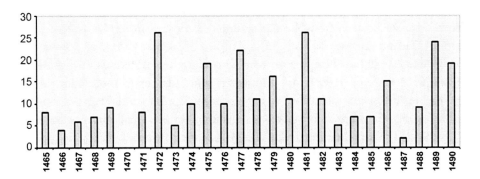

Occupations are not always given. Of the 253 (80%) whose occupations are known, the major trades were as follows:

clothworkers 58

labourers 39

leather workers 32 (12 in one year, 1490)

victuallers 28

building 28

metal workers 18

mercers 15

agriculture 15

other crafts 15

Only one grocer is recorded.

Although borough regulations required apprenticeships to be registered at the end of the first year, very few apprenticeships are recorded in the Hall Book, none by the Browne brothers. Most of the enrolments were made at the end or in the middle of the term of service (five to ten years); only two were enrolled within one year of starting. Either there were very few apprentices in the town or enrolment of apprentices in the borough court was not enforced. Of the nine enrolments, six were for mercers (four for the same merchant), two for drapers and one glover. Freemen admitted without entry fine on the grounds they had been apprentices were a baker and two mercers[167].

But such lists omit many of those who worked in the town, especially in occupations such as domestic service. Some of these can be seen in the Hall Books but always in a negative sense, since they only appear when summoned for some alleged offence or other. But they constituted a large part of the working population of the town.

---

[167] HB i fol 3d, p 9; fol 27, p 74; fol 30d, pp 85-6; fol 33d, p 96; fol 39d, p 115. One of the mercer apprentices changed masters before finally graduating.

Wool merchants are not included in any of these lists. But the importance of the merchants can be seen from the occupations of those who served as Aldermen during William Browne's long life. From 1430 to 1500, we know the occupations of all but four persons who were elected as Alderman. Of these 66 elections, 19 were of 'merchants', 12 mercers and 7 drapers - more than half[168]. Of the rest, 7 went to bakers, five to glovers, four to wrights and four to fishmongers. The impression given is of a town with a small group of traders who engaged in a range of activities to enhance their personal wealth and status; it was personal wealth built up by multiple economic activities and personal initiative which accounted for their power base, not the craft or trade to which they were apparently officially attached.

How many other wool merchants there were in Stamford when William Browne took over the business, we don't know. The Spycer and Longe families had been trading in wool at the end of the fourteenth century but do not appear to have been very active by the 1430s. There were several drapers – John Page (Alderman three times) and Thomas Kesteven (Alderman and MP) seem to have been the leading figures. John Basse draper exported cloth through Lynn[169]. Of the mercers, the Gregory family were prominent, and George Chapman mercer and merchant was Alderman three times. Other merchants, Staplers and mercers there were like William Colom who did not serve as Alderman (see below p 184).

The significant thing about William Browne at this period was that he changed his designation from William Browne of Stamford draper to William Browne merchant of Stamford or merchant of the Calais Staple, and he stuck with these designations. He was no longer a draper and never appeared as a mercer; he was a merchant. At some time prior to 1449, he experienced a turning point in his career – presumably by purchase of membership of the Staple, along with his brother John. He even made his father posthumously a member of the company of Calais Staplers; the brass which William erected for his father twenty years after his death describes him[170] as 'merchant of the Calais Staple', although John Browne used no other title than 'draper'.

---

[168] See Rogers, Aldermen. On occasion, the same individual was elected but with a different designation. George Chapman was both mercer and merchant, Thomas Kesteven was draper and merchant (Calais stapler), Thomas Phelip was draper and mercer.

[169] CPR 1391-96/629. See Hanham *Celys*; Rogers, Calais; Rogers, Parl; PRO, E122/96/37; E122/97/8

[170] It seems that this ascription of membership of the Calais Staple was a posthumous ascription to John Browne the father, as there was (for example) of the Garter to Sir Hugh Elsing of Elsing, Norfolk; see Norris, Brasses p188

PART II: BROWNE, STAMFORD AND THE WARS OF THE ROSES[1]

In every shire .. misrule doth rise and maketh neighbours war

- - - - - - - - - - - - - - - - -

For in your realm is no just peace[2]

William Browne's recorded working life covered the years 1432 to 1489, the period of what later became called 'the Wars of the Roses'. In this chapter, we look at how the town of Stamford and its leading citizen reacted to the conflicts of this period, especially in

- *1450-52 when the town was accused of rising in support of the Yorkists;*
- *1461 when it was allegedly 'sacked' by the Lancastrians as punishment for its Yorkist support;*
- *and 1470 when the Lincolnshire Rising led to a battle on its doorstep.*

Through it all, Stamford, and Browne, kept their heads down and avoided serious involvement, unlike Browne's brother-in-law – until towards the end of his life a party emerged in Stamford committed to one side of the conflict.

---

[1] This chapter is based on the detailed account given in Rogers, *Wars of the Roses*. Fuller references are given there

[2] Ballad cited in H Cole 1973 *The Wars of Roses* St Albans: Hart-Davis MacGibbon p 24

PART II: CHAPTER 1   THE CRISIS OF 1450-52

'These matters be Kings' games, as it were stage plays, and for the most part played upon scaffolds'[3]

The context

Stamford could not but be involved in the dynastic struggles of the mid-fifteenth century, not just because its overlord was the duke of York whose son Edward earl of March deposed Henry VI and became Edward IV. More important was its location on the main route between north and south.   Further, the concentration of substantial noble residences in and around the town seems to have increased during the century. Three miles to the south lay Collyweston, where Ralph lord Cromwell lived; on his death in 1455, the house he built there came to his successor Humphrey Bourghchier lord Cromwell, and then to Margaret Beaufort, mother to Henry Tudor; she expanded it into a great palace where she held court[4]. Further south but within easy distance of Stamford stood the castle and church of Fotheringhay, the York family home: Leland, talking of Edward IV, spoke of "the love that he bare to Foderingay". Margaret Beaufort spent part of her childhood at Maxey Castle to the east, one of the homes of the Beaufort dukes of Somerset, where her mother, Margaret Beauchamp, had a residence which her successive husbands used as their base[5].

To the north lay Castle Bytham, home to the family of lord Grey of Codnor. The royal castle of Oakham to the west housed the sheriff of Rutland. Rockingham castle to the south-west was in royal patronage – possession of an interest in it was a sign of royal favour. Richard II's widow queen Anne and Henry IV's widow queen Joan had interests in Rockingham by way of dower, and both the Holland family (earls of Huntingdon) and the de la Pole family (earls and dukes of Suffolk) held offices in the castle and honor of Rockingham. Humphrey duke of Gloucester and then Richard duke of York were granted interests in this estate, and in 1465 it came to Edward IV's new queen Elizabeth Wydeville.

---

[3] Sir Thomas More, *Life of Richard III* (ed P Kendall 1965, Folio Society)
[4] VCH *Northants* ii pp 551-3; RCHME *Northants* pp 30-32; M K Jones 1987 Collyweston, an early Tudor palace, in D Williams D (ed) 1987 *England in the Fifteenth Century* Boydell pp 129-141; see M W Thompson 1981 The architectural significance of the building works of Ralph lord Cromwell 1394-1456, in A Detsicas (ed) 1981 *Collectanea Historica: essays in memory of Stuart Rigold* Maidstone: Kent Archaeological Society pp 155-162; HKW iv ii pp 67-68
[5] VCH *Northants* ii pp 502, 550, 569-76; *Leland* i pp 4, 22; HKW ii pp 563, 649-50; iv i pp 248-251

William Browne's brother-in-law Sir William Stokes was appointed parker there[6]. It was a significant landmark in the landscape around Stamford.

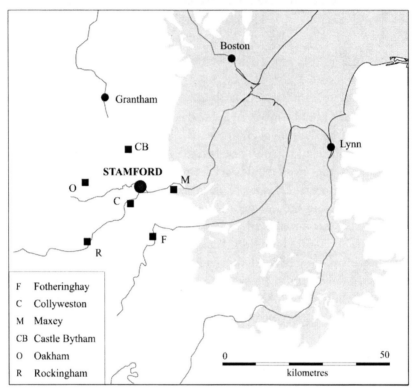

Map 5: Major residences round Stamford in fifteenth century

These were the major residences; but other nobles had estates in the town or vicinity, and they and their key servants would visit these from time to time. The family of lord Grey of Codnor and Castle Bytham was prominent and members were buried in the town. John lord Beaumont held property, as did lord Scrope, lord Zouche and lord Roos. Sir Anketil Mallore, various branches of the Knyvett, the de la Warre, Despenser and Holland families, all had estates in and near the town[7]. The earl of Warwick held Essendine, Barrowden, Greetham and

6 CFR 1377-83/109; CPR 1377-81/407; CCR 1389-92/257; CPR 1391-96/119, 387, 450; 1413-15/398, 402; 1429-36/262; 1436-41/77, 438, 479; 1441-46/198; 1446-52/217, 413; 1461-67/13, 430, 481 etc; HKW ii pp 815-18; S A Mileson 2009 *Parks in Medieval England* Oxford University Press; R Liddiard (ed) 2007 *The Medieval Park: new perspectives* Windgather. For Anne, see J Hunter, J Caley (eds) 1810 *Valor Ecclesiasticus* (Rec Comm) p 142.
7 PRO, E40/15839; E326/4687; Peck xii 6; CIM vii 1399-1422 pp 248-9 (457). For Lord Grey and Stamford, see CCR 1441-47/314-7; HB i fol 43d, p 130; PRO, C139/116/35; C139/144/34; Elizabeth daughter of lord Grey of Codnor married John lord Zouche of Stamford, Rogers, Fairfax; CCR 1381-5/64; Gibbons *Wills* p168; PRO, CP25/1/293/70/283; lady Grey appears to have been a member of the gild of St Katherine, Stamford, GCC 266/670 fol 34; Rogers,

Luffenham in Rutland, all within eight miles of Stamford, as well as Easton on the Hill, Northants, almost a suburb of Stamford; Sir John Tiptoft, later earl of Worcester, was in Ryhall, like Easton less than three miles away[8]. Stamford was surrounded by great lords whose households would have used the town not only for acquiring goods and services but also for recruiting servants and borrowing cash in an age notably short of liquid currency. It has been pointed out that, while magnates could act as "special friends" for the borough, "the presence of too many of them, with their estates in close proximity to one another, was likely to promote rivalries, disorder and violence"[9].

Urban disturbances and Stamford

In September 1448, John Browne was chosen as Alderman of the borough of Stamford for the first time, and in the following September, William Browne was chosen for that office for the third time[10]. William was probably about 40 years of age and John some years younger. William's year ended as Stamford's first crisis of the Wars of the Roses was just beginning. The government alleged that the town was the site of rebellious assemblies in favour of Richard duke of York, first in November 1450 and again in February 1452. In the widespread disorder between 1449 and 1452, Stamford and Grantham, York's towns, so it was alleged, were full of the sound and fury of armed treason[11].

Since the subsequent inquiry found evidence of violent disorder in both towns, it is necessary to distinguish these two incidents from the more normal disturbances which characterised every medieval town. Fifteenth century towns with their ordered ceremonies of mayor-making and gild feasts have at times been seen as islands of peace, stability and security in a countryside characterised by gangs led by war lords like William Tailboys of Kyme castle, "a common murderer, mansleer, riottour and contynuell breker of the peas" who terrorised large areas of Lincolnshire; the woods around Stamford remained hazardous for travellers[12]. But towns too had their violent side; and places like Stamford with

---

Gild Book p 91; *Feudal Aids* iii 261, 267-70, 273, 283, 289, 296; CIPM 23 1427-32 p 52 (102); PRO, REQ 10/92

[8] Exeter-NRA 76/87; 45/25, 44; CPR 1452-61/578; VCH *Northants* ii p 565; VCH *Rutland* ii pp 270 1

[9] Kermode *Merchants* pp 32-3; Griffiths *Henry VI* p 563

[10] Peck xiv 22

[11] Hardly the "meaningless anarchy" which some historians have alleged: Richmond 1998 p 66; see Watts 1995

[12] *Rot Parl* v p 200; R Virgoe 1972-3 William Tailboys and lord Cromwell: crime and politics in Lancastrian England *BJRL* 55 2 pp 459-482; CIPM 25 1437-42 p 518 (614): king's tax collector robbed of his tax money "in the wood by Stamford", June 1420.

large gatherings at markets and fairs were particularly prone to violence, for fairs were occasions when debts were settled, and not just in currency[13].

We must be careful not to exaggerate, for the term 'riot' was often used to draw the king's attention to some local fracas. Disorder in urban communities in the fifteenth century was a wide-embracing term: it covered, for example, breaches of the regulations for the production and sale of bread and ale, and misdemeanours such as Sunday trading. And the evidence we have consists mainly of allegations, some of which were false and malicious; while guilty verdicts were sometimes made more for political or personal reasons than in pure justice[14]. But there was real violence in urban communities, so that much of the disorder which the inquiry found in Stamford was of the 'normal' sort: thefts, robberies, breaking and entering, murder and 'rape' (which often meant abduction) - local people against local people, or involving 'strangers' such as the Newcastle merchant murdered in the town. We see the town bailiffs arresting both residents and visitors[15]. Bye-laws in 1478 show that violence was of concern:

> ... that every man comyn to this toune and market kepe the kynges pees, pyke no quarells, gyve non occasion [on] payn of corporall punysshment, And that no man deynysyn [denizen], nor other nor none artificer ne journeyman bere no gleve [spear], pollax, longe staffe, clubbed staffe, swerde, wodeknyfe, baslard [dagger], ne hanger [short sword] except a gentilman to have a wepyn born after him, payn of forfatour of all such wepyns born to the contrary. [16]

The Hall Book records some warrants against individuals, sureties or recognisances to keep the peace, arrests and fines. Details of the offences are occasionally given: in 1467, William Browne as Alderman accepted nine sureties to "behave peaceably", ranging from street brawls to domestic violence. The Hall Book does not record all such events, but what we have suggests that 1468-9 and 1476-81 were troubled periods; after 1481, recognisances average only one or two each year. But, however we interpret the figures, violence was a continual issue with the council.

---

[13] Dimmock 2001; Dyer 1992; Carrel 2000; Mackman 2008; Griffiths *Henry VI* pp 566-7

[14] Attreed *King's Towns* pp 249, 283. A coiner of Stamford was accused of forgery, but inquiry exonerated him and he continued to work in the town, CIM vii 1399-1422 pp 21-22 (28). McIntosh 1998 shows how 'violence' in this period covered a very wide range of events; see B S Tuten and T L Billado (eds) 2010 *Feud, Violence and Practice* Ashgate; S A Throop and P R Hyams (eds) 2011 *Vengeance in the Middle Ages: emotion, religion and feud* Ashgate

[15] PRO, C244/79/11; C258/7/12 (formerly C47/67/8/308); C260/123/37; C88/96/37; C88/41/8; CIPM 19 1405-13 p 176 (470); PRO, C1/3/46; C1/6/155; Carus-Wilson, Haberget p 151; NRS 5 *Assize* pp 696, 698

[16] HB i fol 25, p 69

But fifteenth century Stamford was probably no more violent than in the thirteenth and fourteenth centuries so far as we know[17]. Not all incidents were recorded: in 1450, a servant murdered his master, or so the wife alleged - but this is recorded in an unusual source, otherwise we would know nothing about it[18]. The divided jurisdictions of the town gave criminals the opportunity to seek sanctuary in one or other of the 'free fees' or to cross the river into Stamford Baron to elude the justices. Some of those accused left the town: in 1408, the property of an alleged murderer was seized since he had fled abroad. Religious houses like St Leonards provided refuge to alleged criminals, which may in part account for the alleged attacks on church property. Especially the friars: in 1414, John Hempstede, the dean of Stamford, was accused of having by night violently broken the close of the Austin Friars and unlawfully pulled down their walls (since the dean was parson of the church of St Mary Bynwerk which adjoined the Austin Friars' site, there may be an explanation, for the Austin Friars were expanding their site at this time); two weavers were accused of having, on Sunday 29 March 1416 (the day may have been significant), assaulted two Black Friars, "beat, wounded and ill-treated them, so that their lives were despaired of [a common form accusation], and committed other enormities"; and John Longe gave security to keep the peace with the Black Friars, 1420-2[19].

Sometimes gangs and mobs were involved, and accusations of treason were voiced. In 1404, the Franciscan friars of Stamford were accused of supporting the deposed Richard II, and the head of a friar was displayed in the town. In 1417-8, there was apparently a riot in the town. The charge *"en maner de gerre arraiez"* was levelled against a group in a property dispute in 1433. But this was not new. In 1346, a group of men tried to eject the rector of St Peter's church from his living, particularly dangerous in this case since he had been presented by the king. In 1360, Robert de Wyke (a prominent citizen) was accused of 'rebellion' for organising a demonstration while the captured King of France was hurried through the town "as secretly as possible"; and in 1371, one of the town's constables was killed in a riot. The annual bull running may have provided an occasion for disorder, and there were other incidents, though

---

[17] See LRS 30 (1937) *Sessions of the Peace 1360-75* pp 162-3; LRS 49 (1955) *Sessions of the Peace 1381-96* p 5; NRS 5 *Assize* pp 114, 116, 157; CPR 1232-47/426; CCW 1244-1326 p 139; CPR 1364-67/148-9; 1367-70/121, 187, 457; 1370-74/78; 1381-85/60, 556; CCR 1288-96/166, 173; 1296-1302/331; 1302 7/411; 1307 13/279; 1327-30/438; 1343-46/43; 1385-89/83; CPR 1416-22/439; LRS 65 (1971) *Sessions of the Peace in Lincoln (1351-4) and Stamford (1351)*; LRS 78 *Inquest* passim; CIM ii 1307-49 p 459 (1844); Platts *Medieval Lincolnshire* pp 241-4, 258

[18] BL, Harl 773 fol 36, item 131; this is a common-place or precedent book of Nicholas Bowet, sheriff of Lincolnshire in 1441, 1448 and 1452; for details, see below p 282

[19] PRO, C258/41/8; CCR 1402-5/166-7; CIM vii 1399-1422 p 303 (535); CCR 1405-9/411. Hempstede was still being summoned for this in 1418 but refused to attend the hearings, CPR 1416-22/99

perhaps fewer than in some other towns[20]. There are, for example, no signs of quarrels over the election of the Alderman, little violence against the duke of York's officials, and few signs of disputes between the burgesses and the non-burgesses, as seen elsewhere.

Just passing through

One factor would have made violence in Stamford potentially common and visible. The main road through the town means that it experienced large retinues and groups of royal servants passing through fairly regularly with their horses, weapons and measured tread[21]. *Through* here means winding through narrow streets: for unlike Grantham, there was no wide and straight road through Stamford. The town, with its east-west orientation, straddled and blocked the route. Goods trains and military bands from the north came down Scotgate, through St Clements gate and into the market place by the church of All Saints; there they entered the narrow streets with their sharp turns (Red Lion Square was built up in those days). At the end of St John's Street, travellers would either turn right down into Castle Dyke, then left along the stream to the river, across the causeway over the Meadows, over the further watercourse into the back road to the south; or they would turn left into St Mary's Street, sharp right down Bridge Street (St Mary's Hill), to clatter over the bridge and ride furiously up the steep hill to the south. Everything had to come this way: to go into East Anglia, you branched left after Stamford; to go to Northampton, Oxford and the south west, you branched right after Stamford; for London, you went straight ahead. The town of Stamford stood in your way whichever route you followed. So the town knew all about armies and noble retinues and caravans of goods and the trouble they caused in their passage. And, despite the decline in the castle, Stamford still had a military element in the fourteenth and fifteenth centuries; the number of soldiers from Stamford serving in some of the major retinues of the day was considerable[22].

But assemblies for rebellion were different, and the charge of this would have brought to mind earlier days when seditious tournaments had been held at Stamford. We can be sure that this history was remembered; so that large scale 'armed gatherings' at Stamford in 1450 and 1452 would have been regarded as

---

[20] CCR 1402-5/389; BL, Harl 773 fols 74d-76; PRO, C1/12/157; CPR 1343-45/374, 579, 584-5; CCR 1360-64/111; CPR 1370-74/127; Toulmin Smith p 192; Kermode *Merchants* pp 53, 57; *Medieval Norwich* chapter 8

[21] L and P Henry VIII 1 i 1509-13 p 815 (1798); L and P Henry VIII 1 Addenda p 160 (478); L and P Henry VIII 4 i 1524-26 p 309 (694)

[22] e.g. CPR 1358-61/30, 504, 520; Deputy Keeper's Reports 48 *French Rolls Henry VI* pp 282, 308, 322, 342, soldiers recruited from Stamford into the retinues of the duke of York, the earl of Salisbury, Sir Thomas Beaumont and Sir Thomas Rempston.

particularly significant. The king and his government saw this as rebellion in favour of Richard duke of York by one of York's estate towns.

The assemblies of 1450 and 1452

But closer examination reveals a different story. That something happened in the town between 1450 and 1452, with the duke of York at the heart of it, is clear[23]. Richard duke of York had entered into his inheritance, including Stamford, in 1433. But his servants ran the town: local bailiffs managed the day to day administration of the estate, and a steward came to Stamford and Grantham on a regular basis to preside over the lord's court in the great hall, collect rents and administer justice. So far as we can tell, York like his predecessors showed little personal interest in Stamford, despite the fact that one of his main residences was close by. The main concern of the York family in the fifteenth century was in building up Fotheringhay, the focus of their estates in eastern England, and Ludlow, their favourite residence and centre of their western estates in England and Wales[24]. Theirs was a hands-off administration[25], like Warenne before them - until 1450, that is, when Richard fell out with Henry VI's government. For in the fifteenth century, estates were also valuable as a source of retinues – and great lords had to travel with a suitable attendance to demonstrate how important they were; the duke of Gloucester was said to have damaged his standing in 1447 because his retinue at parliament was only 80 attendants.

And standing was what concerned Richard of York. He claimed to be the king's nearest kin and, as long as Henry had no child, his presumptive heir. He felt that he was not being given the position in government he ought to have had. True, between 1436 and 1445, he had served as the king's lieutenant in France and apparently did the job well. However, gradually the difficulties mounted, first with the Beaufort duke of Somerset, and after his death (perhaps by his own hand) in 1444, with William de la Pole earl of Suffolk, created marquess of Suffolk in 1444, who made himself indispensable to the king and excluded York. Richard never forgot that Suffolk's father was one of those who had tried his father, and no doubt Pole's wool merchant origins were remembered[26].

---

[23] For this period, see Watts 1995

[24] In 1415, on the death of the duke of York, Stamford (apart from the dower due to the duke's widow) was included for a time among the estates settled on trustees to create at Fotheringhay a castle and collegiate church worthy of a great dynastic family, CPR 1413-16/349-50; BL., Campbell x 5

[25] The Alderman and council complained to the duke when local officials overstepped the mark, e.g. Exeter-NRA 53/1

[26] The hostility of York to Suffolk was personal and yet pragmatic; while Suffolk was negotiating with the king of France for a truce and a bride for Henry VI, York asked him to find a bride from the French royal family for one of his young sons, and in 1458 York married his second

It is not clear whether York and the experienced and able soldiers around him could have halted the French advances, but it was certainly believed in England that he could have done so. But soon after York returned to England, although the war in France went disastrously in his absence, York was sent in the opposite direction – to Ireland. The appointment may not have been entirely displeasing, for the duke had interests there, and the position enabled him to keep an army in the field. But the French war went from bad to worse, and attempts by the king to obtain peace with France were very unpopular. Local disorder, which had been growing for some years, broke out all over the realm.

The crisis came in 1450. Early in that year, two bishops, royal servants, were murdered; Normandy was finally lost to the French, and disbanded soldiers returning from France increased local discontent and disturbances. Suffolk was impeached by the parliament and murdered while on his way into exile in France, and Jack Cade led the Kentish men onto the streets of London, reminiscent of the Peasants' Revolt of 1381. Throughout the country, there were riots and treasonable discussion[27]. It was fortunate for York that he was not in England, for such events tended to increase the popularity of the absent duke, and demand for the return of York to remedy government abuses and restore England's greatness abroad rose[28]. York had two main demands, a place for himself on the royal council and the removal of those (especially the new duke of Somerset who replaced Suffolk as "chief adviser" to the king) who had overseen the disastrous collapse in France and allowed the country to become almost ungovernable. Local conflicts were increasingly violent, as those involved turned not to the king or to law but to the greater lords to settle their disputes. York returned unannounced from Ireland in September 1450 and marched from north Wales on London to take his place in parliament[29].

This is where Stamford (and Grantham) became involved. Wishing to make an impact on the parliament, York and his ally the duke of Norfolk mobilised large

---

daughter Elizabeth to the young John de la Pole the new duke of Suffolk at considerable cost to his estate; Pugh 2001 p 77.

[27] Griffiths *Henry VI* p 564; Virgoe 1450 p 128; see J N Hare 1982 The Wiltshire Risings of 1450: political and economic discontent in mid-fifteenth century England *Southern History* 4 pp 13-31; I M W Harvey 1991 *Jack Cade's Rebellion of 1450* Clarendon; M Mate 1992 The economic and social roots of medieval popular rebellion: Sussex in 1450-51, *Econ Hist Rev* 45 pp 661-676.

[28] Griffiths, Intentions p 192; John Harries at Stony Stratford spoke of the duke of York as a 'flail' come to winnow the realm of traitors like Somerset.

[29] For York's financial embarrassment at this time, see Smith 2000; Pugh 2001; C D Ross 1966-7 The estates and finances of Richard duke of York *Welsh Historical Review* iii pp 299-302. Somerset was better at getting the government to pay his dues than York was. York himself was not above local violence: on at least one occasion (1448), "a large force, headed by an usher of his chamber and composed of his Essex tenants", was used in a local dispute, Johnson *York* p 72. Griffiths *Henry VI* p 591.

retinues to attend them. York sent out letters to various towns, asking them to support his claims to amend the government, and we can presume that Stamford and Grantham received such messages[30]. There are no signs that any from Grantham or Stamford went to London to join the duke, and they may not have been needed; the intention may simply have been for an assembly to be held locally as a demonstration of the support York enjoyed throughout the country.

But parliament "faded away" in the violence of the time, and during the next few months, the king and his justices pursued Cade's rebels in Kent in what one chronicler called a "harvest of heads". Nothing seems to have been done about Grantham and Stamford except that the council sent one of the quarters of an executed rebel ("a poor wine drawer from Kent") to Stamford for display, probably on the town gate at the bridge, as a warning. The period which followed was one of great tenseness. York went on tour through East Anglia, visiting Bury St Edmunds where the duke of Gloucester had died during parliament only four years earlier (the popular belief was that the duke of Suffolk had hastened the death of 'Good duke Humphrey'), before going to Fotheringhay close to Stamford, and then to Ludlow by November 1451[31].

From there, York decided to back his appeal up with a display of force; and once again he mobilised his tenants and supporters, sending letters to towns such as Shrewsbury to justify his actions. We can again assume that Stamford received letters. In February 1452, York and his followers set out from Ludlow to London[32]. But refused entry to London, he circled round the city and took up a position on Dartford Heath. The king and York met but in the confrontation, Henry VI came off best. York was conducted into London surrounded by royal troops and swore an oath in St Paul's church never to rebel again.

Thus the duke of York called upon his tenantry and local supporters on two occasions – in November 1450 and in February 1452. By 1452, the government and the king himself were clear that those tenants and supporters who had turned out must be punished. And this time Stamford could not be overlooked.

---

[30] Griffiths *Henry VI* p 581 says that York appealed to Stamford and Grantham but since lord Cromwell refused to support the duke, the towns did not raise troops; but there are no signs of this. Bristol received such letters and Beverley in Yorkshire copied them into its town council minute book, Griffiths, Intentions p 204

[31] Wolffe *Henry VI* p 231; R Virgoe 1965 The death of William de la Pole, duke of Suffolk *BJRL* 47 pp 489-502. The other quarters were sent to Coventry, Newbury and Winchester. CPR 1446-52/320, commission to try John Frammesley of London vintner, March 1450; POPC vi 107-9, execution before 28 June 1451; "another traytour callyng him silfe John Rammesey wyne drawer", C L Kingsford 1914 Historical collection of fifteenth century *EHR 29* p 514; see E N Simons 1963 *Lord of London* London: Muller; Pugh, York p 127

[32] H Ellis 1825 *Original Letters* i pp 11-13; ODNB 46 p 754 [Richard duke of York] says he was "thinly supported".

In July 1452, a commission was appointed to suppress sedition in Lincolnshire, and in September 1452, another commission was appointed to investigate the risings in Stamford and other places[33]. Inquiries were held in Grantham and in Stamford, perhaps in York's castle at Stamford.

The evidence of the trials

We only have the charge sheets, not the pleadings, and sentences exist in only two cases; these reveal that in November 1450 and in February 1452, 'assemblies' were held in these two towns. But when we look in more detail, these 'risings' fade away into insignificance.

This cannot be attributed to the weakness of the commissioners, for Henry VI himself intended to supervise the work as he had done in Kent. On 19-25 October when most cases were heard, the king was at Peterborough and Newark, and he arrived in Stamford on 26 October 1452[34]. He probably stayed in one of the friaries where other kings had stayed, and during his visit he exhibited his majesty and benevolence by granting pardons to all and sundry - at a price. Such a royal visit would no doubt have struck fear into the heart of Thomas Gregory mercer, the Alderman for that year, who was himself accused of participating in the 'rising' of November 1450 and who subsequently took advantage of the royal pardon in November 1452; for the king was known to be "harsh and vacillating", unpredictable, wayward in his decisions, inclined to display extremes of compassion and harshness[35]. With the king's presence close at hand, the justices were meant to make an example of those who stood accused. Which makes it all the more striking that so little emerged from the trials for either incident.

Local disorder

The commissioners held sessions in Stamford on 19, 20 and 24 October and in Grantham on 19 and 23 October 1452; other sessions were held in Boston and in Kirton in Holland. Cases from all over Lincolnshire which did not relate to the treasonable activities of 1450 and 1452 were included, for parts of Lincolnshire, especially Kirton and the region around Spalding, were in turmoil. The Grantham area experienced considerable disorder. But only two of these other cases came from Stamford itself: William Kave (or Kane) of Sandwich

---

[33] CPR 1446-52/579, 585; 1452-61/54.
[34] The king had been in Stamford in September and October 1448, Wolffe *Henry VI* p 367; Laurence Milton was Alderman for the first visit, and John Broune was Alderman for the second.
[35] ODNB sub nom Henry VI. Griffiths calls Henry VI and his regime "discredited, .. ineffective and partial, .. an inexperienced and short-sighted monarch". Wolffe suggests he was partisan, vicious, unpredictable and showed lack of character.

yeoman was accused of having stolen a white horse belonging to Richard Joseph in August 1452 at Stamford; while on 13 March 1452, nearly three weeks after the end of York's second uprising, a small group from Stamford, *vi et armis*,[36] attacked Robert Babthorp (a royal servant) against the peace of the king.

One accusation was clearly political[37]. John Lylleford, Dominican friar of Stamford, *alias* John Depyng of Stamford, was accused of preaching sedition in various churches in August 1451, exciting lieges of the king to wage war against the king and to help the duke of York – by which (it was charged) several people [on 23 February *deleted*[38]] waged war against the king. But the accusation with its confusion over dates is clearly bungled, and the man cannot now be traced. His name is not even certain, for one "*Robert* Lilleford black friar of Staunford alias Robert Depynge frere prechour" was pardoned in 1452[39]. It is very doubtful if this were a serious accusation: friars preaching in churches or elsewhere were always open to accusations of treason or heresy, for while popular with some, they were unpopular with others.

The assemblies

So much for the other crimes investigated by the justices. What of the two assemblies at Stamford in November 1450 and February 1452? These cannot be separated from the Grantham assemblies.

Forty-five named persons from Grantham with seven from surrounding villages were alleged to have assembled in Grantham on 11 November 1450 in support of the duke of York; they were mostly substantial persons - gentlemen, yeomen, merchants, mercers, drapers, and other tradesmen; there was one servant and one labourer among them. It does not appear that they marched on to the Stamford assembly which took place the next day, 12 November.

---

[36] Thomas Taillour tailor, Robert Hille tailor, David Sawyer sawyer, Geoffrey Lewes tailor and John Taverner sawyer. For the exaggeration behind the use of the terms *vi et armis*, see Attreed *King's Towns* pp 283-306. For the polarisation of Lincolnshire in 1448-9 between Cromwell (with Willoughby and Welles) and Suffolk (with Tailboys and Beaumont), see R L Storey 1979 Lincolnshire and the Wars of the Roses, *Nottingham Medieval Studies* 14 pp 64-83; and revision by Bohna 2008.

[37] We may notice that (apparently in 1451-?) Nicholas Bowet sheriff of Lincolnshire arrested one John N of Bourne yeoman for treason, BL Harl 773 fol 63d.

[38] The deletion is interesting, for preaching in August 1451 could scarcely have urged men to join the duke of York six months later in February 1452.

[39] PRO, KB9/65A; C67/40 m6; there are many John Depynges around at the time; the abbot of Peterborough up to 1439; the bishop of Lincoln's chancellor; a canon of Newstead, CY *Visit* i pp lii-vii ff ; PRO, SC11/419; it is interesting that an earlier John Depyng was to be arrested in Stamford 1389, CPR 1388-92/56. Owen 1971 p 89 gives the name as William Lilford.

Four lists of the Stamford 'assembly' exist. The first two have some 28 names, of whom more than half are known to have served or were soon to serve as Alderman or councillors of the town. A third list has thirteen names with on the whole humbler occupations (furbour, barber, sowter, cutler, brewer, stainer, tailor, mason and slater), and a fourth list, headed by John Bullok of Stamford yeoman, has 21 names, a mixture of substantial and less substantial men of the town. Many of these persons were future town leaders; at least three became Alderman.

A total of 62 persons were thus reported to have assembled in Stamford on 12 November 1450 in support of Richard duke of York. No further action was taken against any of them. And the nature of the lists does not suggest an armed rising. The first list in particular, with 16 names headed by 'John Browne of Staunford merchant' who precedes even the Alderman William Storeton baker, reads like a list of the Alderman and town council with a few extra persons. This view is strengthened by the fact that the second list includes 'John Kyrekby toun clerk', the only time we have a name for that office. This was no riotous assembly but a meeting of the town's elite to debate what they should do about the crisis and the appeal of their overlord Richard duke of York for their understanding and support and to see how they might avoid trouble.

The 'assembly' in February 1452 has larger charges but even less substance. It seems clear that York or at least his servants did attempt to mobilise the tenants this time; early in February, Edward Mulso, a York household servant, was alleged to have been encouraging people to assemble at Fotheringhay[40]. And first at Grantham and later at Stamford, some did assemble. One record accuses three Grantham men of having met at Stamford and elsewhere with 40 (unnamed) men and more, and later with 1200 men; and almost all the charge sheets contained the phrase "and many more" when naming individuals.

But those named are fewer than in 1450, and most of these came from outside. Twenty men from Yorkshire, led by Sir William Skipwith of Hatfield, Yorks (a servant of the duke of York), assembled at Grantham on 23 February 1452, allegedly to help the duke of York. Only three local people are said to have joined these men, Simon Welby of Harlaxton near Grantham, John Sapcote merchant of Grantham and John Sherman of Stamford skryvener.

Some Grantham men did go to Stamford where an assembly had been taking place on the same day, 23 February.

---

[40] Johnson York p 235

"John Trompe of Staunford sadiler and many other false traitors with the assent, will and connivance of many other traitors rebels etc unknown on 23 February 30 Henry VI at Staunford and elsewhere in Lincolnshire imagined and compassed the death and destruction of the king and in diverse illicit conventicles congregated ... to deprive the king of the realm and rule and power; they assembled vi et armis in support of the duke of York at Dartford field".

The Grantham contingent arrived the following day: John Wynawey yeoman, William Walcote yeoman and Roger Gaddesby cook, all of Grantham "and many others" met with three Stamford men, John Bullok, John Veske and John Trumpe in Stamford on 24 February 1452.

But the men from Yorkshire remained in Grantham, doing some local damage: on 2 March, "William Torton of Wakefield yoman, alias William Torton of Wakefield knave, Nicholas Torton, Thomas Torton, John Torton and Richard Torton all of Wakefield yomen"[41] (all of whom had been at Grantham on 23 February) assaulted John Wodehous, one of valets of the crown and *nuncius* of king, at Houghton, just south of Grantham.

Although the numbers alleged to have met in Stamford in February 1452 are said to have been large, only four men from Grantham and four from Stamford are named; the others are said to be 'unknown'. It may be that the commissioners intended to make an example of a few individuals *pour decourager les autres*.

Only two convictions were secured: not even Trompe was punished, although the jurors found the accusation was 'a true bill'. John Wynawey of Grantham and John Bullok of Stamford were said to have 'confessed' to high treason and were condemned to be hung, drawn and quartered. But these two were the bailiffs of the duke of York in Grantham and Stamford respectively; and both were pardoned, not just on the pardon rolls but with the stronger safeguards of confirmation by letters patent[42]. The duke's officials may have been specially targeted, either by the government or by the residents of Grantham and Stamford: William Estington yeoman, a former bailiff of the duke, was also

---

[41] PRO, KB9/65A; the date ("Thursday after the feast of St Mathew 29 Henry VI") would seem to be confused; as given, it would be 24 September 1450 in which case it had nothing to do with the alleged assembly. But since exactly the same people are alleged to have been at Grantham in February 1452, the saint's day could have been St Mathias, not St Matthew, and the year 30 Henry VI, in which case we get 2 March 1452, which would fit their stay in Grantham. As R L Storey 1999 edn *The End of the House of Lancaster* Sutton, has shown, many dates in these records are inaccurate, perhaps deliberately so.

[42] PRO, C67/40. John Wynawey of Nuneaton, yeoman, bailiff of Grantham, PRO, C81/1371/31; C237/43; CPR 1452-61/23-4; John Bullok yeoman, bailiff of Stamford, CPR 1452-61/26; PRO, C81/1371/32; C260/199/10 (formerly C47/67/9/373);

accused not only of involvement in assembly but also of extorting tolls. The duke of York was at Fotheringhay during part of the summer of 1452[43], and it may have been his presence locally which assured his officials sufficiently for them to provide the commissioners with a 'confession', knowing they would not suffer the fate of traitors. The king and his government got what they wanted – evidence of treason; but all those accused went free.

Not quite free – for the king extorted from Stamford (and from Grantham and other towns like Hitchin) a heavy toll in terms of payment for pardons; a large number of persons from Stamford took out pardons during 1452. But listing on the pardon rolls does not imply involvement in treason; taking out a pardon simply meant that these citizens wished to shield their backs against false charges and minor misdemeanours.

The follow up reveals how little substance there was to the allegations. During the inquiry itself, a Stamford jury of twelve men, seven of whom had been accused of treasonable assembly, made a presentment of a separate breach of the peace which took place in Stamford subsequent to the alleged assembly. Life was resumed: Stamford elected as its Alderman for the year 1451-2 Richard Blogwyn, a merchant accused of assembly in 1450, and in September 1452, Thomas Gregory (another accused of assembly) was elected Alderman to receive the king on his visit to Stamford.

What can we make of all this? Fifty-three persons from Grantham and area were alleged to have met at Grantham on 11 November 1450, and 59 persons at Stamford on 12 November in support of Richard duke of York. There is good evidence that the men arraigned for assembling on this occasion were the town council and major citizens who met to discuss what to do; they all continued to serve in office and carry on their businesses unimpaired by the accusations. There are no signs that anyone went to join the duke's forces in London. In February 1452, three men from the Grantham area and one from Stamford 'assembled' in Grantham with twenty persons from Yorkshire on 23-24 February. In Stamford, 40 (unnamed) persons were alleged to have arrayed there, and some 1200 assembled in arms, but only six men were named. One was accused of having raised the Yorkist cause in Stamford on 23 February, and on the following day, three men from Grantham and three from Stamford met; two of these men were the duke of York's bailiffs in Grantham and Stamford, the others from Stamford were a saddler and an innkeeper.

---

[43] Johnson *York* p 125 says the duke visited Stamford in July 1452, that is, before the trials commenced, but the reference he provides does not support that statement, and I have been unable to find the source for this visit. The duke was certainly in Stamford in June 1453 according to PRO, E368/267; see Pugh 2001 p 76.

We must also remember the two towns were closely connected. For example, Robert Hikeham baker of Grantham was related to William Hikeham baker of Stamford; both were accused of participating in these assemblies. Henry Cok had interests in both towns, and several other families like Haryngton and Curteys held property in Stamford and Grantham. There were members of the Leche family in both towns, and Grantham manor held property in Stamford.[44]. So that the fact that, at a time of crisis, the officials in both towns saw it necessary to meet should not surprise us.

Five men were accused of having taken part in both the 1450 and 1452 assemblies. Three were clearly troublemakers, Simon Welby of Harlaxton and John Veske and John Trumpe of Stamford (all three were accused separately of acts of violence during 1451); the others were officials or their attendants. The rest of those listed as involved in 1450 seem to have kept away from the trouble of 1452.

In neither incident can we speak of a 'rising' or even an 'assembly' in favour of the duke of York. In 1450, Stamford town council called a meeting to discuss the situation; in 1452, a smaller meeting of the duke's officials was held in Stamford. True, there were some hotheads like Welby, Trumpe and Veske and a family gang from Yorkshire who visited Grantham but soon turned back. No serious attempt was made to discover the 40 men or the 1200 men alleged to have assembled in support of the duke of York.

Further light is shed on these two incidents by the pardons taken out in 1452[45]. The king issued his general pardon on Good Friday, 7 April 1452; on that day several pardons were enrolled. Between May and June, three more Stamford residents took out pardons, and in July, John Veske got his pardon enrolled. There were then no more until the commission finished its work. Early November saw eight more pardons including lord Zouche[46] of Stamford. Then came 27 November 1452 when the king re-issued the general pardon, and 116 names from Stamford were listed in two separate lists. In all, no less than 118 persons from Stamford took out a pardon during the year, some more than one[47]. Almost all those named in the charge sheets in both Grantham and Stamford received a pardon, even the band who came from Yorkshire to

---

[44] CPR 1381-85/556 etc; *Feudal Aids* vi 481-2; PRO, CP25/1/145/156/30; CPR 1452-61/577
[45] For pardons, see H Lacey 2008 *The Royal Pardon: access to mercy in fourteenth century England* York Medieval Press; H Lacey 2008 'Grace for the rebels': the role of the royal pardon in the Peasants' Revolt of 1381, *JMH* 34 i pp 36-63
[46] Zouche was not named in any charge sheet during the investigations at Stamford
[47] Johnson *York* p 118 says 139; this is the total number of pardons granted

Grantham. Simon Welby of Harlaxton, against whom six violent crimes were alleged, also received pardons – several of them.

One immediate (and no doubt short term) consequence of these events was that the administration of the York estates seems to have suffered some dislocation. An account of the York estates covering the period Michaelmas 1451-2 appears among the Ministers Accounts in the National Archives[48], in which, uniquely, the Alderman of the town (Richard Blogwyn) rendered accounts for the fee farm of the town, a function normally undertaken by the duke's bailiff. It is possible that no new bailiff had yet been appointed after the trial of Bullok, and thus the Alderman accounted directly for the fee farm, the rents of the mills and other items.

The Browne family and the crisis of 1450-52

What of the Browne family during these events? William Browne's term as Alderman came to an end just as York was returning from Ireland. York's first appeal (if there were one) came in November 1450 when William Storeton was Alderman. Despite the fact that William and John Browne and their firm were known to have been lending money to the king, John Browne was one of those charged in 1450, but nothing further is heard of this and he resumed his career quickly; he was not named in 1452. William Browne was not involved in either incident. In October 1450, he was in mid-Lincolnshire, for he attended the county court in Lincoln for the election of the shire MPs. Whatever happened to others, the Browne family came through unscathed; nevertheless, although no charges were laid against him, William covered himself with no less than three pardons during the year 1452, one taken out on the first day the pardon was made available. He may even have profited from the troubles, for in 1451-2, William Browne accounted for the property of one John Kyngespere, a felon[49].

So life continued for the Brownes. John Browne was Alderman of the town again in September 1453, and in 1454 the firm obtained further licences to

---

[48] PRO, SC6/1115/6

[49] PRO, C219/16/1; see A Rogers 1966 Lincolnshire county court in the fifteenth century, *Lincolnshire History and Archaeology* 1 pp 64-78; PRO, SC6/1115/6; C67/40. On 14 November 1452, Thomas Flete gent, Thomas Folkyngham gent, Ralph Tallon gent, Thomas Dygby yeoman, Thomas Lacy gent and John Murdok gent, all of London, stood surety for William and John Browne in separate bonds, PRO, C237/43; C244/79/11. Flete, a duchy of Lancaster official, JP in Kesteven and collector of customs in Boston 1436-1446, also stood surety for several of the more prominent men of Grantham including Simon Welby of Harlaxton; he may be related to William Flete, rector of St Peter's church Stamford until he resigned in 1422 to go to Gainsborough, CY 73 *Fleming* pp 83, 138, 408; for Thomas Flete, see Somerville *Lancaster* p 574. Thomas Lacy, like Flete, seems to have been someone regularly used by London citizens and others as a trustee, CPR passim. For Murdok and Lacy links later with Stamford MPs, see Rogers, Parl

export wool to reimburse their loans. It is possible that William was appointed by the Yorkist administration to a commission to investigate piracy in 1456. There may have been some grumbling in the town about the trials, for in July 1453, the government ordered the sheriff of Lincolnshire and the Alderman of the borough to inquire into all treasonable acts and speeches in the town since the king had last been there in October 1452[50]. But local justices could now deal with local troubles, and nothing further is heard of this.

How then can we summarise the involvement of Stamford in the troubles of 1450-2? One possible explanation is in terms of the king's personal intervention. In the years 1450 to 1452, Henry VI showed unusual energy when faced with Cade's revolt (did he imagine he was another Richard II facing the peasants down?), York's unsanctioned return to England from Ireland, and his challenge at Dartford. But Henry could swing rapidly from one extreme to another. Insecure in himself, he was always attention seeking, but in his attempts he lost respect.

This seems to be the explanation for much in the 1450-2 affair. The king launched a savage attack, exaggerating the accusations of treason and the numbers involved; and then when the trials showed there was little substance to these accusations, he granted large numbers of pardons which many people took up as an insurance in case the accusations should be revived later. Later historians have unjustifiably taken the accusations and the pardons as firm evidence of insurrection at Stamford. But it is not true that "a town like Stamford, which was part of the duchy of York, was inevitably 'Yorkist' in the 1450s"[51]. There was no rising at Stamford in either 1450 or 1452. In both years, there were discussions about what the town should do, and this involved the duke's officials as well as the town councils at both Stamford and Grantham. And in the end, they did nothing. The attitude of the Browne brothers is seen in their multiple pardons taken out immediately they became available. Their concerns were to ensure respect both for their office of merchant of the Calais staple (especially their loans) and for their persons, and to keep the town from too close involvement in the politics of the day.

---

[50] CPR 1446-52/579; PRO, CP25/1/293/72/361; among the other merchants were Lewes and Sapcote who had been accused of involvement in the Grantham assembly, CCR 1454-61/35; Peck xiv 43; LAO, BHS 7/1/3. The William Browne commissioned with others to conduct an inquiry into the seizure by English pirates of a Portuguese ship in June 1456 and its detention in Portsmouth may not be the Stamford merchant since the other commissioners came from Sussex, CPR 1452-61/306-7

[51] Horrox, Patronage pp 148, 160

PART II: CHAPTER 2   THE 'SACK' OF THE TOWN AND THE CHARTER, 1461-2

All the lords of the north they wrought by one assent
For to destroy the south country they did all their intent
Had not the Rose of Rouen been, all England had been shent"
(Ballad of the Rose of Rouen in praise of Edward IV) [52]

Soon after the inquiries in Stamford, in August 1453, Henry VI became ill; the royal household tried to conceal this, but by early 1454, it became impossible, and Richard duke of York was appointed Protector. But Stamford does not seem to have benefited from the first York ascendancy, 1453-4, so that for the next few years, the town's inhabitants probably watched to see how things would unfold.

York's Protectorate did not last long; early in 1455, Henry resumed his authority and restored his favourites. So York had his last fling as a loyal subject: he withdrew from the court and raised troops. This time, there are few signs that he expected his loyal but undisciplined and often ill-armed tenantry to turn out on his behalf; he relied more on his "competent fellowship", a smaller, more loyal and trained band of professional soldiers, especially those drawn from his days in France and Ireland. He and his allies intercepted the king on his way from London to a Great Council in Leicester, and at a short sharp encounter at St Albans (May 1455), they engaged in a series of "political assassinations"; among those killed was Somerset. Henry VI was 'captured' by the Yorkist group and soon after was declared to be ill again, so that York assumed control of the government[53]. A parliament was called, one which, at least in theory, should have affected many people in Stamford, for the pardons purchased in 1452 were affirmed not to be effective and a new general pardon was issued, reinforced this time with parliamentary authority. But significantly, not one of the residents of Stamford who secured a pardon in 1452 renewed it in 1455[54]. The danger was felt to have gone.

In October 1455, York's administration agreed with the Staplers for the payment of the wages of the Calais garrison, a matter which William Browne would have

---

[52] Rossell Hope Robbins (ed) 1959 *Historical Poems of the XIVth and XVth Centuries* New York: Columbia University Press pp 215-8

[53] Wolffe *Henry VI* pp 321, 312; C A J Armstrong 1960 Politics and the battle of St Albans 1455, *BIHR* 33 pp 1-72

[54] PRO, C67/41

watched with care, for in October 1454, with the support of the Yorkist parliament, he and other Stapler merchants received licences to export wool[55]. But again York's Protectorate did not last long. Early in 1456, Henry VI resumed personal control backed by his Council, but he proceeded more cautiously than before. York remained principal councillor, and his ally the earl of Warwick obtained control of Calais.

But Queen Margaret of Anjou came to the defence, if not of her husband, at least of her son. She retired with the king to her stronghold of Kenilworth and the nearby town of Coventry – "this best ruled of cities", as Henry himself described it, which she seemed to see as a new capital for the country. Thus commenced the "fugitive royal household" for the last years of the reign, a period when Henry VI "held the government of the realm in name only", as the abbot of Crowland put it[56]. Henry exhorted the city fathers to "allow no riots and conventicles and take no liveries from lords, knights or esquires". Both of the Browne brothers were at this time visiting Coventry regularly, so they would have been well informed. York seems to have sworn to turn his back on violence, "the wey of fayt", as a means of settling political differences. Henry arranged a Love Day in March 1458 in St Paul's church in London; York and the Queen are said to have walked in procession hand in hand (no doubt both hating every minute of it).

But Henry's hopes, as so often, were doomed to failure; both sides went deeper and deeper into opposition. In May-June 1459, affairs came to a head. Henry retired to Coventry, York issued another condemnation of the favourites around the king. A Great Council was summoned to Coventry but the earl of Salisbury (a York supporter) met troops of the Queen at Blore Heath (September 1459) and defeated them. Warwick came over from Calais and joined York and Salisbury, and the three found themselves facing a large royal army outside Ludlow (October 1459). But when some of the Calais troops (who seemingly had not been warned that they might have to fight against the king) went over to the royalist side, the Yorkist leaders fled, York to Ireland, Warwick, Salisbury and the young Edward earl of March, York's second son, to Calais, while asserting they were still loyal to king Henry. But the king was no longer loyal to them. A parliamentary assembly was summoned and on 20 November, the Yorkist lords were attainted, their offices forfeited and their lands seized.

---

[55] CPR 1452-61/210-2, 226; CCR 1454-61/6, 13-16, 35; for fuller discussion, see Harriss, *Struggle*
[56] Laynesmith 2003; D Dunn 1995 Margaret of Anjou queen consort of Henry VI: a reassessment of her role 1445-53, in Archer 1995 pp 107-143; Helen Maurer 2003 *Margaret of Anjou: Queenship and Power in Late Medieval England* Boydell

Stamford citizens must have been full of apprehension, for immediately the carve up of York's estates commenced. The royal administration appointed new officers in the York estates, and parts were granted away. On the same day, 20 November 1459, Henry Percy earl of Northumberland was given Warwick's manor of Easton by Stamford. In December, Viscount Beaumont was appointed for life steward of Stamford and Grantham "and all other lands late of the duke in Lincolnshire ... for his labours against the rebels and traitors Richard duke of York, Richard earl of Warwick and Richard earl of Salisbury and their accomplices". Thomas Haldenby of the royal chamber, for his good service against the rebels, was granted the office of bailiff of [the duke's estates in] Stamford, also for life in January 1460. Reginald Grey esquire, formerly a servant of York and now a royal household servant, had his annuity of 20 marks from Stamford confirmed by the king (his desertion of York at Ludlow helped to cause his erstwhile master to flee, for his writ explains, "he had this rent from the duke by letters patent which with other stuff and goods to the value of £40 he lost at Ludlow with his withdrawal from the duke"); and the king's serjeant Thomas Tresham esquire was granted £20 p.a. from Stamford (and £40 p.a. from Grantham) "for his losses in the king's service and for service in parliament"[57].

But all had not yet been played. What followed was a period of some eighteen months of a seesaw. The government issued commissions of array[58], and the Yorkists issued propaganda. In June 1460, Warwick came from Calais and met the royal forces at Northampton (July 1460). Lord Grey of Ruthyn now deserted the Lancastrians, and the troops of Warwick held the field. Again a number of Lancastrian leaders (including Beaumont) were killed and the king was taken captive.

In this period of uncertainty, Stamford turned once more to its chief citizen to steer it through what lay ahead. The pretensions of the Yorkist family to become king of England cannot have been unknown to the town. Having watched Beaumont take over as steward of York's estates and then be killed at Northampton, with the town in the king's hands (officially) but the Yorkists in control of Henry VI, the borough elders in September 1460 elected William Browne as Alderman for the fourth time; and it was on his watch that the town

[57] CPR 1452-1461/533, 553, 573, 577. A prominent Northamptonshire landowner whom William Browne would have known well, Tresham had been MP several times and was Speaker in the 1459 parliament which had condemned York and his adherents. See Johnson *York* pp 128, 189, 206, 209, 232 for Grey; CCR 1454-61/407; for Tresham, see Wedgwood *Biographies;* J S Roskell 1965 *The Commons and their Speakers in English Parliaments 1377-1485* Manchester University Press pp 368-9

[58] CPR 1452-61/559-61; Scofield i p 68

weathered the changes of fortune caused by the Yorkist usurpation. And yet the choice, if it were influenced at all by current political issues, could have been dangerous; for Margaret Browne's brother, William Stokes, with whom William Browne and his family were very close, was a member of Henry VI's household; his loyalty was both assured and rewarded by a valuable marriage and his appointment in February 1460 as receiver in Yorkshire of a number of Yorkist estates; sometime after that date he was knighted for his services to Henry VI, presumably on the field[59]. And the Browne brothers were coping at this time with the death of their mother (1460).

Henry (under the control of Warwick) called a parliament in Westminster, October 1460, to revoke all the acts of the Coventry parliament. When York came from Ireland, however, he claimed the throne for himself, but most of the lords stood against him. A compromise was found by which Henry would reign for the remainder of his life but he would be succeeded by Richard of York, a similar arrangement to that which had been made in Henry VI's name with the king of France. The Queen and her son were thus to be dispossessed and needed to be dealt with in the name of the king. So Richard of York marched north in December 1460 to face Margaret's army, but at Sandal (Wakefield) on the last days of December, he was defeated and killed together with his eldest son Richard earl of Rutland, leaving Edward earl of March as Richard's heir to Henry's succession.

The 'sack' of Stamford 1461

The Lancastrian forces, joined by the Scots and strong in the aftermath of their success at Sandal, marched south to face Warwick and enter London. And here we encounter one of Stamford's historical myths, that in January-February 1461, the army of Margaret of Anjou sacked every town, Grantham, Stamford, Royston etc on their way south – and "Stamford suffered badly". The 'sack' of Stamford has featured in every history book of Stamford since it happened. It has been given as the cause of the reduction of the parish churches of medieval Stamford from fourteen to six, and the reason why there are no medieval records from the town – they were (it is alleged) burnt. It is the explanation of the rebuilding of much of the town fabric in the late fifteenth century. Everything that can be explained by a sack has been laid at its doors[60].

---

[59] Rogers, Stokes

[60] Griffiths *Henry VI* p 872; J Simmons 1974 *Leicester Past and Present* Eyre Methuen p 54, draws on VCH *Lincs* ii p 268 to suggest that "Stamford never really recovered from this disastrous raid". I too accepted it in my first publication on Stamford in 1965; Rogers 1965 p 39. One or two historians have doubted the 'sack', see Platts *Medieval Lincolnshire* p 226. For a full treatment, see Rogers, Wars of Roses pp 88-94

But, if it happened at all, it has been greatly exaggerated. For one thing, none of the other towns listed (Grantham, Peterborough, Huntingdon, Royston and Melbourne) made such a great thing of this event in their histories as Stamford did. Further, architectural and archaeological evidence for a 'sack' does not exist. Three of the vanished churches had gone before 1461, while all the other churches survived until the middle of the sixteenth century, when an Act of Parliament of 1546 united them for reasons of population decline[61]; no church was destroyed by the 'sack'. What is more, the churches do not seem to have been damaged greatly. Glass from before 1461 survived in considerable quantities in all the churches, especially St George and St John the Baptist; and the rebuilding of the churches started well before 1461. Some archival material (though probably not in substantial amounts) did survive into the seventeenth century, and the lack of borough records continues *after* 1461 as much as before: maintaining Stamford's borough records was never a strong point of the town's administration.

Stamford had been warned of the possible attack: on 17 January 1461, Warwick's government from London had issued a commission to William Browne Alderman and the "burgesses or jurats" (a phrase which suggests that this was drawn up by staff who were not very experienced) of Stamford to arm and to keep watch, to arrest traitors, to muster and to proclaim that none assist the guilty. Whether such a commission was sent to any other town on the Lancastrian route, we do not know; but Warwick may have hoped to stop the Lancastrians at the Welland crossing. The queen was still at York on 20 January and arrived at Dunstable by 16 February, so the passage through Stamford probably took place in the first few days of February; Warwick's warning should have been received in time. One incident suggests the authorities of Stamford acted on this commission: John Belyngham husbandman of Wisbech came to Stamford purposing to ride into Nottinghamshire, but was arrested and searched by the bailiff on the grounds that he might be carrying letters "to the north" (presumably to the queen's army) [62].

---

[61] St Michael's church in Cornstall had gone well before the 'sack', and in Stamford Baron, the church of All Saints by the Water had been annexed to St Martin's by 1434. St Mary Bynwerk was amalgamated to St Peter's church by 1454. St Peter's was still in use in 1543; St Andrew was joined with St Michael the Greater in 1546, St Clement with St John the Baptist in 1548, Holy Trinity (by then called St Stephens) to St Michael the Greater in 1556, St Paul to St George some time in the sixteenth century. Detailed information on all these churches is in Hartley and Rogers. There was no parish church of St Thomas despite later legends. Hamilton Thompson in his edition of *Alnwick's Visitation 1440* ii p 348 asserts that St Andrews church disappeared at the sack of 1461 but it was still in existence in the first half of the sixteenth century.

[62] CPR 1452-61/657; Scofield i pp 134-6; PRO, C1/28/435; he was searched, but "noo maner of letter nor other suspesious thynge was founde"; therefore he asked licence to ride on to Nottingham, offering sufficient sureties within Stamford in the very large sum of £100 "for his trouth and liegance", but the bailiff "wold not in noe wise delyver hym" without a bribe of 40s "and so kepith your said oratour in strayte prison and duras ayens all trouth and conscience".

But there is evidence that the alleged 'sack' was a minor event. From 1472, only a few years after the so-called 'sack' and soon after the battle at Empingham near Stamford (1470), the town council gave permission to several citizens to make gates in the town walls. Such permissions may have been granted earlier, but the first recorded is in November 1472:

> *This day William Hykeham begged licence of Robert Hans Alderman and of the whole community to have one 'le postern yate' under the boundary wall of the aforesaid town in a certain garden of his next to his inn called le Anteloppe which he [Hykeham] had in exchange from the fraternity of the Gild of Corpus Christi; and it was granted by the said Alderman and the whole community of the town or borough aforesaid to the aforesaid William Hykeham to make le postern yate[63].*

Grants to Robert Hans, the serving Alderman (1472), Robert Nevour furbisher in 1474, and to Thomas Stokes at the vicarage of All Saints and his brother-in-law William Browne (for his new Hospital) in 1475 followed:

> *On this day was granted to Master Thomas Stoke vicar of All Saints a postern gate to be made by him in the boundary wall at the north end of his garden, viz between the gardens of William Browne and John Browne; and the aforesaid Master Thomas and his successors shall fully and sufficiently repair, sustain and maintain the aforesaid boundary wall there in everything on pain of forfeiture of this postern.*

Later came William Browne (for one of his tenanted properties, 1479), Richard Forster, one of the town MPs (1479), Thomas Hikeham rector of St Peter's church (1486); and in 1489,

> *… was granted to John Fissher a postern in the north part of his free tenement in the parish of St Paul to be made by him in the boundary wall. And the said John shall have and execute this grant, and shall well and sufficiently repair the said wall in all things as he used to repair it anciently and sustain and maintain it on pain of forfeiture of the said doorway and postern.[64]*

This is the last recorded licence, but in the early 1500s, Lady Margaret Beaufort arranged for a door to be opened in the town wall behind the anchorage of St Paul's church[65]. The walls were apparently seen more as a nuisance than a useful

---

[63] HB i fol 16d, p 45

[64] HB i fol 49, p 146; the walls were maintained by adjacent landowners; collections for the walls were taken in 1479 and 1486, and repairs to the walls, gates or ditches are mentioned occasionally, HB i fol 7, p 19; fol 31, p 88; but the town dunghills were located in the town ditches from at least 1465 until they were forbidden in 1486.

[65] see below p 221

defence. However interpreted, this shows a surprising lack of concern for the integrity of the town defences after such a traumatic event – if Stamford suffered severely in 1461.

St George's gate: all the medieval town gates have been removed.

This bastion is almost the only part of the town's defences to have survived; the postern gates were mainly in the eastern section of the north walls (photo: Alan Rogers)

How then did the story of the 'sack' arise? It came mainly from the Crowland abbey chronicle, a strongly Yorkist partisan record. Crowland panicked; they hid their treasures and muniments, as much perhaps from the refugees who flooded into the monastery for protection as from the Lancastrian army. So they exaggerated to justify their reaction, and their account spread.

For this was an age when rumour abounded. In the 1450-1452 crisis, "The countryside was humming with rumours" from government as well as from hostile elements: "moche straunge langage ...", "tittle tattle of slender foundation ... an undergrowth of rumours and hearsay", "grett grutchyng and romore that is unniversaly in this your reame" were everywhere. York and others proved adept at creating propaganda and getting it into widespread circulation. During the 1470 crisis, the government expressed concern about the *fabula* and *rumores* which were spreading[66].

---

[66] *Foedera* xi 657; see Holland 1988 p 868. Griffiths, Intentions pp 189-193, 199; BL Add Mss 43,488 fol 7, printed in Griffiths, Intentions p 204; Steel *Exchequer* p 234; Ramsay ii p 151; Loans p 54. See A Allan 1979 Yorkist propaganda: pedigree, prophecy and the 'British History' in the reign of Edward IV, in C Ross (ed) 1979 *Patronage, Pedigree and Power in later medieval England* Sutton pp 171-192; I M W Harvey 1995 Was there popular politics in 15th Century England? in R H Britnell and A J Pollard (eds) 1995 *The McFarlane Legacy: studies in late medieval politics and society* Sutton pp 155-174; C A J Armstrong 1948 Some examples of the distribution and speed of news in England at the time of the Wars of the Roses, in R W Hunt, W A Pantin and R W Southern (eds) 1948 *Studies in Medieval History* Oxford pp 428-454; J A Doig 1995 Propaganda, public opinion and the siege of Calais in 1436, in Archer 1995 pp 79-106; Richmond 1998; C D Ross 1981 Rumour, propaganda and popular opinion during the Wars of the Roses, in Griffiths

And the story was given 'spin' in three ways. First, the conflict was represented as one between north and south: "The men of the north, treacherous men, men quick to rape". The government of Warwick in London emphasised this in their statements, and the Paston letters repeat it: "the people in the north rob and steal and been appointed to pill[age] all this country and give away men's goods and livelihoods in all the south country"[67]. Secondly, religious houses like Crowland and St Albans denigrated the Lancastrians as worse than heathens or infidels; thus they wrote that the objects of their wrath were religious centres: churches, abbeys and houses of religion (so it was alleged) were ransacked; they carried off books, vestments, chalices and church ornaments; they broke open pixes and threw away the Holy Sacrament, and if priests or the faithful resisted them, they were murdered in their churches or churchyards; they acted "as they had been Paynims or Saracens and no Christian men". This was taken up by later writers[68].

And thirdly, a political element led to exaggeration: if Queen Margaret could not control her troops from looting, how could she be trusted to run the government? Among those most fearful were the Londoners, and a panic broke out about the Queen's adherents and their looting – a panic which in the end denied Queen Margaret her victory, for the Londoners refused to allow her to enter the city. The London chronicles (especially Stow), reflecting this, influenced later historians and led Leland in the mid-sixteenth century to assert that the vacant plots he saw in Stamford were caused by the sack of the town 80 years earlier, a myth which has persisted to this day[69].

Almost certainly the army of Queen Margaret did do some damage in Stamford as they passed through; this was after all normal, for armies of the day were "ill-disciplined", forced as they were to live off the land[70]. We may have one piece of evidence of such damage. In 1463, William Colom, a Calais Stapler, merchant of Stamford and colleague of William Browne, sued five men from the north for having, *vi et armis,* broken and entered his closes and houses at Stamford and taken away his goods to the value of £40. The defendants were outlawed, and Colom appealed for justice several times. The presence in Stamford of five

---

Patronage pp 15-32; J L Watts 2004 The pressure of the public on later medieval politics, in L Clark and C Carpenter (eds) 2004 *Political culture in late medieval Britain: Fifteenth Century* vol IV Boydell pp 159-180

[67] Gairdner *Paston Letters* i p 540 (367)

[68] H T Riley (ed) 1872 3 *Whethamstede,* Rolls Series i 388-9, 394, 400: "Gens Boreae, gens perfidiae, gens prompta rapinae"; Gairdner *Paston Letters* iii pp 249-250; Pronay and Cox pp 421-3; *Engl Chron* p 109; J Gairdner (ed) 1880 *Three 15th Century Chronicles,* Camden 2nd series vol 28 pp 76, 155, 172; C L Kingsford (ed) 1905 *London Chronicle* Oxford: Clarendon p 172

[69] M R McLaren 1994 The aims and interests of the London chroniclers of the fifteenth century, in Clayton et al 1994 pp 158-176 ; Leland v p 5

[70] "The march of armies was inevitably associated with some looting and rapine", V H H Green 1955 *The Later Plantagenats* Arnold p 356.

armed men from Cumberland and Northumberland can most easily be explained during the passage of the northern army of Queen Margaret through the town in February 1461. But if so, the offence was relatively minor, hardly consistent with a 'sack'[71].

It is also possible that some borough archives were destroyed; Grantham complained in 1463 that "the king's great rebels coming out of the north country had taken all the earlier charters of the town", and they asked for a confirmation of them (instead they got a new charter). It was again normal for documents to be burned during war in the late Middle Ages; and it was January-February, when soldiers would be looking for fuel to keep themselves warm. But as we have seen, some archives survived into the seventeenth century[72].

There was then no wholesale 'sack' of Stamford; Stamford suffered no more (but equally no less) severely than any other town on the route of a fifteenth century army. The exaggeration which later historians have given to the event is typical of much of Stamford's historiography – to copy and expand on what earlier writers have written. The claim to have suffered severely out of loyalty to the Yorkist cause (especially after the apparent failure to support the duke in 1450-1452) could be useful, in that it gave increased credibility to the request for a charter of incorporation made soon after the incursion.

The accession of Edward IV

Margaret marched on to face the troops of Warwick at the second battle of St Alban's on 17 February 1461 – and won. She took possession of king Henry, and Warwick fled again to join up with Edward earl of March who had not yet arrived from the Welsh marches. But the Yorkist lords now claimed that Henry had broken his oath, and so March (who had defeated a small Lancastrian force at Mortimer's Cross in February 1461 on his way to join Warwick) with characteristic decisiveness entered London while Margaret dithered – for having the king, the Lancastrian army could only do what he decided and he decided nothing. Edward now determined not to wait for Henry to die before acceding to the crown; he claimed the throne on his arrival in London, and a group of lords supported him when he declared himself king with popular support.

---

[71] Watts 1995 p 37. LAO, BHS 7/ 9/115; PRO, C88/157/11; the northerners were listed as William Martyndale of Neweton in Alderdale Cumberland knight, Richard Kyrkebride of Wydon in Alderdale armiger, Bartholomew Laucher of Wygdon in Alderdale yoman, John Nele of Newecastell wever, Richard Mofford of Irynham in Cumberland yoman
[72] Scofield i p 136; PRO, C81/1492/20; G H Martin (ed) 1963 *The Royal Charters of Grantham 1463-1688* Leicester University Press pp 13-14; Butcher 1717 p 18

The Yorkist army immediately set out to follow Margaret as she retreated northwards, perhaps avoiding Stamford. At Towton, the armies met on 29 March 1461 and the Lancastrians were decisively defeated. Henry, the queen and their son fled to Scotland, and Stamford could draw breath again – the duke of York's son, their lord, was king. The first six months of William Browne's Aldermanry had been hectic; the second six months would be a time of greater calm.

And of some reward - Edward IV granted to Stamford a borough charter. We do not possess any preceding petitions, unlike Grantham; nor was it stated (as with Norwich) that the charter was given "in consideration of the good conduct and great costs and expenses of the citizens of the said city and moreover of the free services many time borne by them for us against our adversaries and rebels". Given the time required to compile a charter of incorporation, the initial approaches were almost certainly made by William Browne as Alderman rather than his successor from September 1461, George Chapman mercer. By 12 February 1462, the new charter had been drafted and promulgated[73].

But Margaret Browne's brother, William Stokes, suffered his fate for being on the losing side. He was condemned as a traitor and his goods confiscated by an act of attainder passed in parliament in 1464. He continued to fight against the Yorkist regime until he surrendered at Harlech in 1468; imprisoned in the Tower of London, he was however pardoned in 1469 and restored in 1472. And William Browne's son-in-law John Elmes of Henley on Thames, was also accused of being a rebel during a lengthy suit about illegal wool trading, from which he did not escape until well into the reign of Edward IV (see p 136 below). Political disaster came close at that time to the Browne family, but they and Stamford emerged unscathed. William Browne's leadership had proved effective.

---

[73] Attreed *King's Towns* p 36; C Ch R vi pp 164-67; original letters patent in Town Hall, Stamford; Newbury supported York actively in the crisis of 1458-60, Yates 2007 pp 227-8. Ipswich supplied funds to Edward to "resist Margaret queen of England" as early as 11 February, *Bacon's Annals of Ipswich of 1654* (edited 1884) p 118; they had their charters confirmed in 1464.

PART II: CHAPTER 3 THE FINAL BATTLES: LOOSECOAT FIELD AND BOSWORTH FIELD, 1461 to 1489

"I see daily kings, pryncys and other estates from the highest to the lowest ... , now high, now low, now rich, now poor, now alive, now dead"; letter of Thomas Kesteven of Stamford, 1482[74]

The year 1461 thus saw a change in Stamford's status; their lord became king. Within a few weeks of returning to London (1 June 1461), Edward IV granted Stamford and Grantham lordships to his widowed mother, Cecily dowager duchess of York[75]. This did not mean that Edward ran the estate for her, although we know that at times she asked his advice on the appointment of officials. Equally we find the king writing to his mother asking her to consider the appointment of a favourite to a post on one of her estates. In 1469, she surrendered Fotheringhay to Edward IV and spent most of her time at Berkhampstead. She outlived even William Browne; and in 1492, Stamford and Grantham were granted by Henry VII to Elizabeth his queen after Cecily's expected death which occurred in 1495. Cecily left the profitability of the estate to her officials; she continued the traditional 'hands off' attitude of the Yorks towards the town. Her steward was left to run affairs; for she was heavily involved in the politics of her son's reign[76].

Edward IV's first reign (1461-70)

The period 1461 to 1465 was spent tidying up after the Lancastrian defeat. But "rejoicing at the succession of Edward IV and at the Yorkist solutions for the maladministration and financial debacle of Henry VI's government" soon faded, and there was in any case a core of resistance to the new regime. A period of unrest, calling for the deployment of local militias and some royal forces, ended in 1465 when Henry VI was captured. Stamford must have become used to bands of troops passing through the town. Musters were ordered and

---

[74] PRO, SC1/53/175 ; see Rogers, Calais

[75] CPR 1461-7/131; BL Add Mss 6693 fol 57; Add Mss 16564; Egerton 8782; she may have held Stamford during Henry VI's last years despite the attainder of her husband, since the wives of Yorkists attainted were apparently exempted in 1459, *Rot Parl* v p 350; see R E Archer 1984 Rich Old Ladies: the problem of late medieval dowagers, in Pollard 1984 p 22. Cecily's political involvement may have been exaggerated, as also her interest in religion; see ODNB Cecily duchess of York; Pugh 2001 p 73; Pugh, York p 112; VCH *Northants* ii pp 569-76; see also Hughes 1988 p 102. She was buried at Fotheringhay. See below pp 277-8

[76] CPR 1485/369-370

commissions of array issued several times: "the common people are so tired of war that they are more or less desperate"[77].

Edward IV was in Stamford in March 1461, mustering troops to attack the army of Margaret of Anjou who had now retreated towards Scotland. The king spent more than a week in the town in March 1462, shortly after the town charter had been sealed in Westminster. After more musters of troops in April 1464, the king held a council in the town in August, and he was there again in 1466. It may be no coincidence that in April 1464, both William Browne and his brother (who served again as Alderman in 1462-3 and was appointed to a commission of arrest in Lincolnshire and Rutland) obtained (no doubt at a cost) another general pardon[78].

Once the Lancastrian threat had been more or less neutralised, this king paid attention to government finances, collecting 'aids' and 'benevolences' from his subjects and securing several Acts of Resumption. He set out to improve the management of the royal estates, but it is unclear if the revised practices affected the duchess's estates including Stamford. For in Stamford, life continued much as before; the charter made little difference. In 1466, William Browne was Alderman again, and two months later (November), he was appointed sheriff of Rutland for the first time. During his Aldermanry, he collected from the First and Second Twelves a 'gift' to Humphrey Bourghchier lord Cromwell (who had acquired the interests in Stamford of Ralph lord Cromwell) and a collection for work done on the West Gates of the town; the council banned dicing and cards, at the same time as parliament (with two royal servants as the first recorded MPs for Stamford) was trying to ban the same games by statute[79].

Between 1466 and 1470, Edward IV and his main supporter the earl of Warwick were at odds, both pursuing a different foreign policy. Warwick sought peace with the new king of France; Edward married his sister to the new duke of Burgundy, a marriage which was soon to stand Edward in good stead. Many in Stamford would have been interested, as they traded with the Low Countries as well as with Calais.

Warwick found an ally in Edward's younger brother, the duke of Clarence. Wayward, indecisive, easily influenced, Clarence was a tool for others to use[80]; in

---

[77] F W Brie (ed) 1908 *The Brut or Chronicles of England* EETS vol 136 ii p 503

[78] CPR 1461-67/532; *Rot Parl* v pp 512, 601; *Vale* p 137; CPR 1461-7/313, 351

[79] CFR 1461-71/191; HB i fol 7, pp 19-20; fol 26, p71. The entry in HB i fol 8d, p 23 is undated.

[80] M A Hicks 1992 *False, fleeting perjur'd Clarence: George duke of Clarence 1449-1478* Bangor: Headstart History; C Carpenter 1986 The duke of Clarence and the Midlands: a study in the interplay of local and national politics *Midland History* 11 pp 23-48

1469, Warwick and Clarence slipped off to Calais and there contracted a marriage which the king had expressly forbidden; they returned to England demanding the kind of reform which Richard duke of York had called for, to remove those who were influencing the king against them. Fighting broke out again in England. 1469-70 was Edward IV's *annus horribilis*, as 1450 had been to Henry VI. Risings took place in the north and a pitched battle was fought at Edgecote Moor which led to Edward himself being detained for a time by Warwick but soon released – it was not possible for Warwick to keep two kings of England in prison at the same time.

For the first time, we can catch a glimpse of Stamford being involved. In 1469, on his way to face Warwick, Edward IV passed through Stamford (July), staying long enough to send letters to various towns calling for troops to assemble; so it is not surprising that during the summer of 1469, the town council sent troops with the king to Nottingham and again rather later "to the north". And then the fighting came close to Stamford – which may have led one citizen to conceal his wealth in a pot in St George's churchyard, not to be recovered until 1866[81].

The Lincolnshire Rising 1470[82]

Early in 1470, a local dispute escalated into a violent conflict – the so-called Lincolnshire Rising. Sir Thomas Burgh of Gainsborough, a royal supporter, was attacked by a band of men of Richard lord Welles, including Sir Thomas Dymock and Sir Thomas de la Launde[83]. Edward IV summoned Welles and Dymock to him and held them hostage. Lord Welles' son Sir Robert Welles raised a force and marched towards Coventry to meet with Warwick and Clarence. Edward moved from London to Fotheringhay, summoning his army to assemble at Stamford. When he stopped at Stamford to "get his bait", Edward heard that Robert Welles had changed his route and was marching towards Stamford, to try to rescue his father or to come between the king and London. Edward promptly had lord Welles executed in front of his army under Eleanor's

---

[81] Scofield i pp 491-2; Ross *Edward IV* pp 129, 304-5. For the Stamford hoard, see below p 154

[82] See Holland 1988 pp 849-869; while some historians have argued that Warwick and Clarence provoked the rising or used it against the king, Holland argues that Edward IV took advantage of the rising to attack Warwick and Clarence. Two recent analyses have suggested that the king himself was indirectly responsible for the outbreak, since he encouraged a royal party in the county: see Bohna 2000 and Mackman 2008. The Crowland chronicler is the major source for this; Pronay and Cox; J G Nichols (ed) 1847 The Chronicle of the Rebellion in Lincolnshire 1470, *Camden Miscellany* Camden Society 1 series vol 39; J R Lander 1965 *Wars of the Roses* Secker and Warburg pp 163-9.

[83] It is odd that on 3 March 1470, Richard lord Welles and Willoughby and Robert Welles knight his son both took out pardons, PRO, C67/47 m8. Lord Welles may not have been a member of the gang which attacked Gainsborough but his men were.

Cross just outside the walls of the town[84], and on 14 March, he marched out of Stamford to meet Sir Robert. At Empingham in a field called Hornefeld (near a copse which later was called Bloody Oaks), a brief encounter took place; but Welles' band fled so fast that the battle was called Loosecoat Field. Edward returned to Stamford where he stayed for two days and issued a proclamation concerning the suppression of the rising, before continuing north, executing Dymock, members of the de la Launde family and the "grete capteigne of Linccolnshire", Sir Robert Welles[85].

For the next few months, events moved swiftly. In April 1470, Edward summoned Warwick and Clarence to come to him, but they fled to France. There Warwick made peace with his greatest enemy, Margaret of Anjou, and plotted to restore Henry VI. In September, Warwick and Clarence invaded England and their forces nearly captured Edward in Yorkshire. He in turn fled through Lincolnshire to Lynn where he took boat to Holland and appealed to his sister, the wife of the duke of Burgundy, for help.

Given these "troublesome tymes", it is not surprising that Stamford in September 1470 turned once again to its senior citizen William Browne to take on him the role of Alderman, as he had done in the crisis year of 1460-61. And he agreed — unlike the situation in York in that same year where they could not find anyone to serve as mayor, or in London where the mayor took to his bed with "fegned sicknesse". It is perhaps not surprising that in August 1470, William and John Browne took out yet another general pardon[86]. Things did not look good for the country as a whole; the now absent Edward IV was felt to have failed in his enterprise and accused of having hurt trade badly.

In October 1470, Warwick took Henry VI out of the Tower of London, dusted him down and put him back on the throne for a few miserable months. New sheriffs were appointed by his administration and a parliament was called: it is not clear if Stamford chose any MPs for that parliament which never met. For in March 1471, Edward was back. At the urging of Cecily his mother, Clarence deserted Warwick and went over to Edward; a family reconciliation was held in Baynards Castle, London, presided over by the duchess. Two quick and decisive victories won by Edward, at Barnet in April (at which Warwick and others,

[84] "The lorde Willoughby beheded beside Stannford the xij day of marche in the yere ml cccc lxix": *Vale* p 179.
[85] CCR 1468-76/134 (528); J Fenn (ed) *Paston Letters* Dent vol ii p 84 (295). Paston called it 'Lincolne Feld', presumably because the rebels came from Lincolnshire, Gairdner *Paston Letters* ii p 413 (655). For Welles' 'confession', see S Bentley (ed) 1831 *Excerpta Historica* London p 283; *Rot Parl* vi pp 144-5; the de la Launde family later contributed to the endowment of Browne's Hospital
[86] Ramsay ii pp 363, 366; CPR 1467-76/315-6; granted by Edward IV's administration

including Humphrey Bourghchier lord Cromwell, were killed) and Tewkesbury in May, followed by the death of Henry VI, ended the threat from the revived Lancastrians.

Stamford played a bit part in these contests. With armies assembling in the town in 1469 and again in 1471, the town could not avoid involvement. But William Browne, during his term as Alderman (1470-71), faced both ways, giving "good contenans and interteynement to both parties". He ordered troops to join "the king [i.e. Henry VI] with Warwick", perhaps in March 1471, no doubt under some duress since the earl of Oxford was in Stamford[87]; but he also sent two bands of soldiers to Edward IV – 40 men on 22 April (a week after the battle of Barnet had been fought and won) and a smaller band (perhaps ten men) at an unspecified date. The town had to raise the not inconsiderable sum of £59 11s 6d to pay for its part in these acts of the Wars of the Roses.

The rebellion of the Welles family concerned Browne, for he acquired two manors from the family and had to obtain the exemption of these manors from the act of attainder and the act of restoration of the family in 1472 and 1475. There was always the threat of legal action for alleged trespasses in his trading through the Staple and for his office of sheriff: hence yet another pardon taken out in January 1472 for offences and arrears of fines and other payments [88].

The later years 1471-89

The period 1471 to 1483 was perhaps the longest period of calm and stability which the country had known since the 1440s. The main element of disorder was the ongoing but constantly changing quarrel between the king's brothers, the dukes of Clarence and Gloucester, over a number of different issues. The uncertain behaviour of Clarence made him an unreliable ally, as Warwick had found; his death in 1478 removed this rogue element.

Three issues faced by the king in these years would have concerned Stamford and William Browne. First, out of gratitude to the ships which brought him back to England in 1471, Edward resolved a dispute between the Hanseatic merchants and the English merchants in favour of the Hanse (Treaty of Utrecht 1474), and trade resumed. Secondly, Edward – during what contemporaries described as the biggest invasion of France the country had seen – deserted Burgundy and made peace with France, gaining an annual pension but losing popularity. When the duke of Burgundy died, France annexed Burgundy but the Low Countries, Stamford's trading partners, came to the duke's heir, Maximilian of Austria; a

---

[87] Attreed *King's Towns* p 299; M E Christie 1922 *Henry VI* Constable p 361; HB i fol 14d, p40
[88] *Rot Parl* vi pp 145, 287; CPR 1467-77/315-6, 508-9; LAO, BHS 7/12/21

trade agreement was made which involved an attempted settlement of various disputes over rates of exchange, a matter on which William Browne would have had strong opinions. Thirdly, the pension altered Edward's financial situation. He continued to borrow, especially from the Staple, but these loans were repaid and a royal surplus was built up, particularly through benevolences, some of which were drawn from the towns (there are no signs that Stamford paid such benevolences, but it is almost certain that they did).

William Browne used these years for two main concerns – his trade and his foundation of Browne's Hospital. The latter probably started to occupy his mind from about 1471, and the first stage was completed by 1475, but he continued to work on it until his death. Trade through the Staple was a continuing preoccupation; in 1472, William secured another general pardon with a group of other Calais staplers[89]. Parliament in 1473 renewed the agreement with the Staple over the customs and the payment of the Calais garrison.

Edward visited Stamford in 1471 and again in July 1473, a visit which seems to have caused consternation. In January 1473, William Hussey (king's attorney and Cecily's steward) sat with the town council for one of the sessions of the peace; he may have been in town in preparation for the Great Council which Edward IV was planning for Stamford for the summer of that year. On 8 July, during the "grete hote somere", the Alderman called a session of the town council to make "ordinances for the coming of our lord king Edward the fourth to hold his council in Staunfford and other things to do"[90]. The Hall Book does not record what was discussed and decided. But for once, a glimpse is given of how the court operated when in Stamford. On 27 July 1473, a group of royal officials (including Hussey) collected the great seal from the lord chancellor, who was ill in London, and delivered it in a sealed bag into the king's own hands in "the refectory of the Friars Minor of Stamford" in the presence of the bishops of Winchester, Ely, Coventry and Lichfield, Exeter, and Lincoln (keeper of the privy seal) and of the earls of Essex and Kent and a group of lords of the king's council and others.

And after a short interval the said king in their presence delivered his seal to Laurence bishop of Durham whom he appointed Chancellor; and committed the seal to him; and the said Laurence on the same day at 2 p.m. in the hospice within the priory of St Cuthbert's, Staunford [St Leonard's] had the bag opened and sealed several writs and letters patent with the great seal[91].

---

[89] CPR 1467-77/316
[90] HB i fol 17, p 47; *Rot Parl* vi p 82; Morgan 1973 p 17
[91] CCR 1468-76/318-32 (1164); CPR 1467-77/318-320

The responsibilities which fell on the Alderman (Robert Hans fishmonger) must have been considerable. But a royal visit was also an opportunity; with the king being accompanied by many nobility and influential officials, it could be a time for making contacts and seeking favours, as well as a time of trading. But equally there would be heavy charges for hospitality and display.

Three years later, Stamford witnessed another display from the royal court when the body of Richard duke of York passed through the town on its way from Pontefract for reburial in Fotheringhay. On Saturday 27 July 1476, the procession arrived, "received by the lords of the neighbourhood and the citizens of the said town, all dressed in black [led no doubt by John Gybbes mercer, the Alderman] and by all the archers of the crown". The hearse was accommodated in the Grey Friars; "and there it was during the Saturday and the Sunday and everything belonging to and decorating" the hearse was given away as alms "and large gifts were given there especially to the churches and to all who came, great and small". On the Monday, it moved on to Fotheringhay. The cortege was accompanied by Richard duke of Gloucester, the earl of Northumberland, lords Stanley, Welles and others, various bishops, at least twelve heralds, men at arms, and sixty "poor men who each held a burning torch"; the display in Stamford for these few days must have been impressive[92].

This event may have been a sign of a change in the geo-political scene in which Stamford was placed. From the 1470s, royal officials such as William Hussey became more active in Stamford, presumably in the name of Cecily duchess of York. Edward IV seems to have been planning an East Midlands appanage for his second son Richard duke of York based on Fotheringhay, to include Stamford and Grantham, the duchy of York estates in Lincolnshire, Rutland and Northamptonshire, and the extensive duchy of Lancaster estates in the east, especially Bolingbroke. The reburial of Edward's father at Fotheringhay in 1476 may have been part of this plan. Nothing came of it (Richard was only a child, so the plan must have had more to do with Edward's sense of local administration than with any political ambitions for a royal second son) but it formed a precedent for Henry VII[93].

---

[92] A F Sutton and L Visser-Fuchs with P W Hammond 1996 *The reburial of Richard duke of York 21-30 July 1476*, Richard III Society pp 16-18, 21, 25

[93] HB i fol 17, p 46, William Hussey lawyer is recorded for the first time as sitting with the town council as justices. For appanage, see Ross *Edward IV* p 335; Morgan 1973 p 18: "the creation of an apanage [sic] for the king's second son Richard…. By 1475, the plan was to endow him with a collection of lands in the east midlands – Fotheringhay, Stamford, Grantham and the other Duchy of York lands in Northants, Rutland and Lincolnshire; the Duchy of Lancaster honours of Bolingbroke and Higham Ferrers .. and the former Welles-Willoughby estates in Lincolnshire".

Through these years, William Browne remained busy. Involved in litigation over property and debts, acting as feoffee for his sister Alice in Coventry, and continuing his trade, he found time to act as sheriff for Rutland for a second time (November 1474-5). During 1477, despite his age (he was in his late sixties), William would have had much travelling to do as sheriff of Lincolnshire, the only time he served in his own county; he supervised the election of the county MPs in Lincoln in January 1478. Yet he was also serving about this time as mayor of the Calais staple. In 1480, perhaps on surrender of that office, Browne received a pardon as merchant of the staple [94]. In 1481, he was suing a merchant of Boston for debt, and served as Alderman of the gild of Corpus Christi in Boston; he received a pardon again as a Calais stapler, and was trading through London.

But he still found time to engage intensively within the town – as feoffee for local merchants and as surety for new freemen and building his Hospital. In 1476, John, William's brother, died; as Christopher, John's son, was not in Stamford until 1481, William took responsibility for Agnes, John's widow. In 1480, William was Alderman of the gild of Holy Trinity, and in November, he refounded the gild of St Katherine. He sorted out his widowed sister's affairs in Coventry and brought her back to live in Stamford. He helped his wife Margaret with her duties as executrix for Thomas Philip of Stamford. In the following year, he acted as feoffee again. His pace of activity would leave a younger man breathless - apart from the very hard winter, late spring and bad harvest which contemporaries commented on. In 1482, William Browne of Stamford was appointed sheriff of Rutland for a third time [95].

In 1481, the town received a second charter. It is hard to determine the context within which this arrived. It may be related to the political changes in the town from the late 1470s associated with Christopher Browne (discussed below pp 204-6), for negotiations must presumably have been started by at least 1480, and some elements in Stamford seem to have become more closely involved in national politics than in earlier years [96].

The death of Edward IV in April 1483 threw out William Browne's plans for a finalisation of his Hospital. William was confirmed as sheriff of Rutland, first by Edward V's government, and then by Richard III when he ascended the throne

---

[94] CFR 1471-85/38, 84; BL Harl 4795 fol 47; Pishey Thompson 1856 *History and antiquities of Boston* Boston p 120; PRO, C219/17/1; Rogers, Elections; CPR 1476-85/118-9, 243.

[95] Durham DCD Reg 4 fol 191d, 216r; GCC Mss 266/670, Rogers *Gild Book* p 4; CPR 1476-85/266; BL Harl 4795 fol 48d; Cobb 1990 pp 110 (450), 114 (456), 166 (602); *Cely Letters* i p 134; Butcher 1727 p 27

[96] C Ch R vi pp 253-4

in June; and it may have been at this time that Browne received a reward for his costs as sheriff of that county. He must have been seen as a safe pair of hands, as he was now made a JP and a collector of lay subsidy in Rutland. He received a pardon from Richard III in 1484 - the new government needed men like William Browne. It would seem that the Browne family of Stamford was much in the mind of the government: a list of men required to take knighthood at the coronation of Richard III included one 'John Browne of Stamford'. But John Browne of Stamford had been dead since 1476; and the John Browne referred to was John Browne formerly of Oakham and now of London, a later mayor of the city[97]. The slip of a chancery clerk reveals the prominence with which the Browne family of Stamford was regarded at the time. But if the government needed Browne, Browne also needed the government; he was at the stage in his foundation when he required government approval to incorporate it and to endow it.

The revolt of the duke of Buckingham, which embroiled several Yorkist towns like Newbury, seems to have passed Stamford by without much impact, although, as we shall see, the town administration appears to have been disjointed during the years 1483-5. In 1484, William was Alderman of the gild of Corpus Christi, and he acted as feoffee in Lincolnshire. Richard III passed through the town twice in 1484; and it may have been through personal contact on one of these visits that William obtained the licence to endow his Hospital (January 1485)[98].

There are no signs in the Hall Book of the town's reactions to the continual state of alert and the various summonses to muster troops which Richard III's government issued throughout 1485 leading up to the battle of Bosworth - except that Richard III personally ordered the town council that one Thomas Turton should be pardoned for breaches of the peace[99]. And I am not at all certain what William Browne's reaction must have been to the invasion of Henry Tudor in 1485, accompanied (so Christopher's son Francis claimed later) by Christopher Browne, or to the nearby battle of Bosworth in which no doubt some Stamford partisans participated on one side or the other, or to the first parliament of Henry VII to which Christopher Browne was chosen as one of the

---

[97] CFR 1471-85/245, 257, 268; see p 182 below; CPR 1476-85/148, 396, 570; Wedgwood *Biographies* p 119; Thrupp p 327. See A F Sutton and P W Hammond (eds) 1983 *The Coronation of Richard III : the extant documents* Sutton p 318; A N Kincaird (ed) 1982 *Sir George Buck's History of King Richard III* Sutton p 47; Horrox and Hammond iii pp 11-12.

[98] PRO, SC6/1115/13; LAO, Stamford parish records PG/1/43; Horrox and Hammond i p 254; ii p 118; CPR 1476-85/505

[99] HB i fol 37d, p 109: the name Turton may be significant; it is the same as the Yorkshire men who rebelled against Henry VI in the 1450s. For the period, see L Boatwright 2008 The Buckinghamshire Six at Bosworth, *The Ricardian* vol 13 pp 54-66

town's representatives. But William does not seem to have suffered from his apparent closeness to Richard III's government. The new king stayed in Stamford for at least three days in March 1486, and in November of that year, the ageing William was appointed sheriff of Rutland for a fourth time and JP for the county for the rest of his life (he must have been in his mid or late seventies by now)[100].

Stamford's hinterland changed radically under Henry VII. Not only did the new king adopt a more hands-on approach to the towns[101]; more importantly for Stamford, Fotheringhay was no longer the centre of power in the region. Instead, Collyweston, only three miles from Stamford, where Ralph lord Cromwell had built a favourite residence, now became the home of Henry VII's mother Margaret, countess of Richmond and Derby. Here she established a court; here her council was recognised by the royal council as one suitable to administer justice over a wide area of the east Midlands[102]. The appanage which Edward IV had planned now seems to have been established at least in embryonic form; Margaret Beaufort rather than the elderly Cecily of York needed to be built into all considerations. Her officials like Sir Reginald Bray and Sir David Philipps were active in Stamford, and she herself visited the town on several occasions; her court became for many the court of first instance. Christopher Browne was a member of her council[103]. 'The times they were a-changing'.

And William Browne was slowing down, giving attention to the refounding of his Hospital and to the settlement of his estates. He did not apparently get his licence to endow the Hospital renewed by Henry VII, although his executors did in 1494. His last known public activity was in 1488 when he was named as one of the collectors of the lay subsidy in Rutland. He finalised arrangements for the endowment of his Hospital late in 1488 and made his will in February 1489. He

---

[100] CFR 1485-1509/54, 150; CPR 1485-94/ 83, 85, 192; the king again passed through the town in August 1487

[101] Lee 2009

[102] Jones and Underwood p 87 88; PRO, REQ 2/4/216; Rogers, Fermour; M K Jones 1986 Lady Margaret Beaufort, the royal council and an early Fenland drainage scheme, *Lincolnshire History and Archaeology* 21 pp 11-18. The abbot of Peterborough visited Lady Margaret at Collyweston on several occasions in 1504-5, NRS 13 *Peterborough Local Administration* ii p xvi

[103] *Test Vet* pp 516-524; David Cecil was steward of Collyweston in 1523 and later, see Rogers, Parl for biography. For Bray, see D J Guth 1998 Climbing the civil service pole during civil war: Sir Reynold Bray (c1440-1503), in S D Michalove and A Compton Reeves (eds) 1998 *Estrangement, Enterprise and Education in fifteenth century England* Sutton pp 47-62.

died in April 1489, in his late seventies or even older, after a richly rewarding life. Margaret his companion for at least fifty years died some six months later[104].

When William Browne died in 1489, it would have been by no means clear that the 'Wars of the Roses' were over – that Henry Tudor would survive longer than some of his predecessors. There were still claimants to the throne, although the direct Yorkist and Lancastrian lines had been more or less eliminated. The land still felt insecure – as it had done throughout almost the whole of William's life, certainly since the 1440s when William Browne was burying his father and when the country buried Humphrey duke of Gloucester. In May 1489, the town was ordered by the king to supply goods for the royal army[105]. Trading, buying property, making and spending a substantial fortune in this climate, while avoiding too close involvement in the major conflicts of the day, must have been an achievement matched by a relatively small number of other merchants. William Browne succeeded with the help of Margaret his wife; and their trustees, led first by Thomas Stokes canon of York, Margaret's brother, and then by William Elmes, William Browne's favourite grandson whom he had educated in the inns of court, ensured, despite some opposition from Christopher Browne, that the symbol of his achievements, his Hospital in Stamford, stands today high above the town.

---

[104] CPR 1485-94/243; Rogers, Wills; CFR 1485-1509/88, 116, 118; PRO, E150/670/9; REQ 2/5/93; CIPM Henry VII i 1485-96 p 230 (551); CIPM Henry VII iii 1504-9 pp 508-9 (992), p 606
[105] HB i fol 46, p136.

PART III: EARNING A FORTUNE

In this section, we look at how William Browne made his fortune

- *in the context of a town of which the economic basis was changing and of a country undergoing a major slump -*

- *through trading;*

- *through money-lending;*

- *and by building up a portfolio of estates in Stamford and the surrounding countryside.*

PART III: CHAPTER 1 WINNERS AND LOSERS: ECONOMIC CHANGES IN FIFTEENTH CENTURY STAMFORD

"ye be not of such richesse as ye have been in tyme past"[1]

William Browne became the wealthiest man in Stamford in the later fifteenth century. In 1450, he paid 9s in taxes; the next nearest was 6s. In 1466, a subvention for improvements to the Westgate was collected: William contributed 40s, his brother John paid 20s; no-one else paid more than 10s. At the same time, William paid 3s 4d towards a gift to Humphrey lord Cromwell; the next nearest was 2s, and the rest were well below this. Clearly everyone was aware of William Browne's relative wealth[2].

We need to see the context for that wealth. It has been assumed that fifteenth century Stamford, like many other towns, experienced economic decline; at best it "stagnated"[3]. There is some evidence for this. Holy Trinity and St Clement's parishes in the suburbs were depopulated. It was reported (1440) that some of the parish churches "are come to such slenderness of means" that pensions to monastic houses were not being paid[4], and some parishes were amalgamated: St Mary Bynwerk joined St Peter's and All Saints beyond the bridge joined St Martin's by the 1450s (see above p 209). The town experienced a period of dearth during the middle of the century: the 'slump' of the mid-century, the bad harvests of the 1480s and the general recession of the final decades of the century, especially the "unyversall dethe" in the years around 1471, must have impacted on the town. During the century, flooding did long-lasting damage[5].

But if we judge by the building work in the town, there are few signs of an overall 'decline' in Stamford; indeed, the town may have been experiencing something of a boom. Debating "the probably irresolvable" issue of the growth or decline of late medieval English towns may hide from us the fact that general trends conceal local variations. This was not an age of general decline or growth

---

[1] Edward IV to city of York 1482, Attreed *King's Towns* p 195
[2] PRO, E179/276/44; HB i fol 7 7d, pp 19 20
[3] Rigby *Grimsby* p 141; Palliser 2000 pp 627, 632; see Bolton 1980 p 201; G L Harriss 2005 *Shaping the Nation 1360-1461* Clarendon p 275; Kermode *Merchants* p 7; C Dyer 2002 *Making a Living in the Middle Ages* Yale p 301
[4] The non-payment of pensions may not of course have been caused by poverty
[5] LRS 14 p 348; RCHME *Stamford* p xlii; for dearth and distress in the 1460s-70s, see PRO, C1/45/306; SC6/1115/9. C Dyer 2005 *An Age of Transition? Economy and society in England in the later Middle Ages* Oxford University Press

but one of change. Our concern is to try to see what was happening in Stamford, and who benefited and who suffered from these changes[6].

The wealth of Stamford

It is hard to make any judgment about the wealth of Stamford. That the farm of the town of £50 had fallen to £40 by 1452 does not indicate poverty. Tax records for Stamford provide little guidance to the relative prosperity of the town. In 1436, the town made a 'gift' to the king of £40, well behind Boston (£166.66), on a par with Grimsby (£40) and ahead of Grantham (£20). In the 1520s, Stamford with Stamford Baron was assessed at £90, similar to Northampton (£91) but behind Leicester (£103), whereas Nottingham was assessed at £56, Peterborough at £44 and Grimsby at only £14[7].

But the levels at which taxation, aids and benevolences were assessed depended more on power than on a realistic assessment of wealth. For example, when in 1433, parliament provided a remission from tax for poor towns, Lincoln received significant reductions, Stamford only a small remission. Indeed, Lincoln became exempt on the grounds of its alleged poverty, the result almost certainly of its friendship with Ralph lord Cromwell of Tattershall, Lord Treasurer of England 1433-1443; yet between 1442 and 1452, the city of Lincoln made large loans to the government. Stamford had few such friends in high places. The York family showed no signs of being interested in the town from which it drew some of its wealth; the de la Pole family had other concerns. Few of the sheriffs of Lincolnshire and Northamptonshire and none of the MPs came from the region around Stamford, and until 1467, Stamford sent no members to parliament who could argue for its interests[8].

---

[6] C Phythian-Adams 1978 Urban decay in late medieval England, in P Abrams and E A Wrigley (eds) 1978 *Towns in Societies* Cambridge pp 159-185; *Medieval Norwich* p 387; see Bridbury 1975; Dobson 1977; Dyer *Standards* p 195; Rigby *Grimsby* pp 114-5, 138. Both the RCHME *Stamford* and D M Loades 2009 *The Cecils: privilege and power behind the throne* National Archives p 12, say that the town was prosperous at this time; Palliser 2000 pp 3-15: there is no "consensus on the direction or extent of change in the urban share of the population", Palliser 1988 pp 1-21. The literature on late medieval English towns is too extensive to list here. But see Britnell 1998; R H Britnell 2009 *Markets, Trade and Economic Development in England and Europe 1050-1350* Ashgate; Dyer A 2000; R H Britnell 2003 England: towns, trade and industry, in S H Rigby (ed) 2003 *Companion to Britain in the later Middle Ages* Oxford: Blackwell

[7] POPC iv p 320; Sheail ii pp 188-9; J Dillon (ed) 2002 *Performance and Spectacle in Hall's Chronicle*, Society for Theatre Research p 165. Stamford Baron was assessed at £15 10s, almost exactly one sixth of the total sum of £90 3s 4d. It would seem that a larger percentage of the population of Stamford Baron paid to the tax but they paid less than those taxed in the town: Stamford Baron paid an average of 5s 5d, while Stamford town paid an average of 7s 10d. See above pp 19-20. Hadwin 1983 p 200 argues that there is serious under-valuation in these tax records.

[8] PRO, E179/136/224, 296; in 1469, Stamford's tax bill of £35 17s 8d was reduced by 4 marks (£2 13s 4d), Stamford Baron's £10 was reduced by 16s 8d, HB i fol 11, p 30; for Lincoln and lord Cromwell, see PRO, SC8/121/6024; Hill *Medieval Lincoln* p 280; Steel *Exchequer* p 265; Gray

Winners and Losers

Stamford in the fifteenth century was changing – and in the process, some people gained and some lost. The clearest evidence for those who lost most comes from surviving estate records, especially those of the York estate[9]. The value of Stamford to its lord declined in the fourteenth century[10], so that the town was not a major source of income for the Yorks; in 1412, Stamford and the York lands in Rutland and Northants were assessed at £20 p.a., Grantham with the Lincolnshire lands at £71 p.a.. In 1415, on the death of the duke of York, it was reported that Stamford was worth only £20 because of life annuities amounting to £26 6s 8d – a total yield of at least £46 p.a.. But a rental of Joan dowager duchess in 1403 indicates at least £80 p.a. coming from two watermills, houses and shops, wastes, tolls of markets and fairs, forfeits, escheats and the profits of the courts[11].

The documents are difficult to interpret, for much of what is recorded was the 'charge' for which the official needed to account, "his own personal liability"[12], rather than 'real' receipts, so that many of the entries are formal and hide more than they reveal. A "new rental" was drawn up in 1441-2, soon after the duke of York entered into his inheritance, and this was revised in 1459, probably when the estates came (temporarily) into the hands of Henry VI on the attainder of York. Nevertheless, some items stand out. During the fifteenth century, York's rents were falling in Stamford. Farms for one part of the property fell from £14 9s 6d p.a. in 1400 to £7 in 1459 and to £5.3s 4d in 1485. The tolls and 'window tax' (from street-side shops) taken from the bakers, brewers and butchers fell

---

1436 p 607; Hadwin 1983 p 214; Horrox, *Patronage* p 153. Ralph lord Cromwell, who had interests in Stamford, may have received gifts, as did his successor Humphrey Bourchier lord Cromwell in 1466, HB i fol 7d, p 20.

[9] PRO, SC6/ 910/4; 913/23-25, 31; 1094/11; 1108/22; 1115/6-13. A fragment of a household account for 1450-1 is in Hampshire Record Office 23M58/57b. For the estates and finances of Richard duke of York, see J T Rosenthal 1965 Estates and finances of Richard duke of York 1411-60, *Studies in Medieval and Renaissance History* ii pp 117-204; J T Rosenthal 1964 Fifteenth century baronial incomes and Richard duke of York *BIHR* 37 pp 233-9; Pugh, *York*; Johnson *York*; Smith 2000.

[10] In 1317, Stamford yielded £124 p.a., Grantham and the Lincolnshire estates yielded £158 p.a.; by 1340, Stamford had fallen to £94, a figure it continued to account for at the start of the fifteenth century, whereas Grantham yielded over £130, CIM ii 1307-49 pp 87 (347), 419 (1703); CCR 1346-9/313.

[11] CIPM 20 1413-1418 p 120; annuities to Roger Flore of Oakham and William Wolverton, CIPM 18 1399-1405 p 296 (862); PRO, C145/80/8; SC6/1115/6; *Feudal Aids* vi 478. In 1415, the estates were forfeited for a time, and the low valuation may be an estimate of the clear value after all outgoings and annuities are taken off. The duke's estates may be compared with those of the earl of Suffolk in Stamford (£20 p.a. in 1388; £10 in 1412) and John Haryngton of Grantham whose property amounted to £30 p.a. in Grantham and Stamford, CPR 1385-88/513; *Feudal Aids* vi 481-2.

[12] Davies 1968 p 213

from nearly £10 p.a. in 1400-1 to just under £6 by 1485-6; and the profits of the courts fell drastically from over £37 in 1400-1 to £6 5s 4d in 1485-6. The profits of the 'Pembroke lands' in Stamford fell from £3 6s 8d to £2 2s 8d. Rents for the mills on the estate fell from £18 in 1459-60 to £14 13s 4d in 1485-6[13].

Even clearer are the 'decays' recorded. In 1459-60, a total of £6 13 4d in rents was written off in all parts of the town: in St Paul's parish, Butcher Street (3 shops 'destroyed'), the Fishmarket, le Shobothes, St Peter's parish and Colgate. Pigsties in St George's and St John's parishes and 8 shops in St Mary at the bridge were listed as "all vacant", two shops as taken into the lord's hand because the tenants had died and they could not be let, and several acres of land, meadow and pasture as 'destroyed'. That this year was not exceptional can be seen from the account roll for 1466-7 which recorded a flood which destroyed the mills on the river and damaged several other properties. 8 acres of meadow could not be let this year - "no-one wished to take them". There was nothing from the tollbooth; 22 stalls were empty at a loss of 26s. One shop containing two stalls, two shops needing repair, three shops in Butcher Street 'destroyed', pigsties in the parishes of St Michael and of All Saints in the Market, a shop in le Shobothes (formerly let at 8s 6d but on offer for 7s 6d but still "no-one wants it") and a shop taken into the lord's hand because the tenant did not repair it – all these yielded no rents. The list of such decays is much longer than the lists for the early years of the century.

Also suffering were ecclesiastical landlords. The account rolls for St Leonard's priory show a decline in the yield from St Mary's church from £3 6s 8d in 1407 to £2 in 1456-7 and in some years much lower. The pixide oblations at St Leonard's fell drastically from £3 6s 7¾d in 1389 (a figure which had fallen from over £5 in 1364-5) to only 1s 8d in 1497-8: the biggest and permanent fall came between 1390 and 1407. Rents from all sources fell from about £50 to some £34, and the profits from tenements fell from £1 9s 8d in 1420-1 to 16s in 1507-8. In 1424-6, this priory was in "dire financial straits" and the monks were recalled to Durham: in 1440, "the priors of this place are so removed and have not the will to abide therein" because of the poverty of the cell. The account rolls of the nunnery of St Michael similarly show their rents in Stamford falling from £4 8s 8d in 1399-1400 to £3 0s 9d in the 1450s. A new rental made under pressure from the bishops of Lincoln took these up to £8 8s 1d in 1481-2 but they fell again. Total receipts fell from £91 (1398-9) to £46 11s 4½d in 1473-4;

---

[13] PRO, SC6/1115/7, 9: tolls of markets: £9 17s 2d in 1400-1 down to £5 18s 8d in 1485-6; court profits: £37 17s 5½d in 1400-1, £11 2s 6d in 1466-7, £6 5s 4d in 1485-6. For declining urban rents, see Carus-Wilson and Coleman 1963; Kermode *Merchants* p 291; Butcher, Rent; Mate 2006 pp 24-25; for refusal to pay rents, see C Dyer 1968 Redistribution of incomes in fifteenth century England, *Past and Present* 39 pp 11-33.

they rose to £64 18s 5d in 1481-2, only to fall again to £42 7s 4d in 1490-1. There was much concern at the poverty of this monastery (see p 28 above)[14].

But there is evidence that other rents were holding their own. The crown held some property in Stamford which had come to Edward III from Galvin Southorp, a soldier who had been captured in Brittany in 1347 and ransomed with help from the king. The property was substantial, and was leased to "speculative farmers", sometimes duchy or royal servants, sometimes local merchants, on an auction basis – if someone made a higher offer of rent for it, the earlier agreement was cancelled. Leases are complete for the century; and although the rents charged varied only slightly, a property yielding 24s 8d in the first years of the century was valued at 25s in the 1480s – there was here no decay of rent[15]. Which suggests that, although traditional landlords with customary rents and long-term leases suffered, individual merchants and household servants wealthy enough to take short-term tenancies and free to charge new rents did not suffer and may even have profited from the changes.

Who gained? the evidence from building

The building work which Stamford saw at this time, much of it of a high quality, presents a different picture of the town. My impression is that major building work was going on somewhere or other in the town for most of the century. It

---

[14] CY *Visit* iii p 347. This is based on an analysis of a run of surviving account rolls of St Leonard's Priory at Durham, and the rolls in the PRO, SC2/188/1-3. See Piper 1980; Heale *Priories,* especially pp 137, 223, 250; PRO, SC6/910/26; 914/1-4; 1260/1-24.

[15] Originally one messuage, two shops, 63 acres of land, 10 acres of meadow and 4 acres of pasture in Stamford and Bradcroft, all for a debt of £128 6s 8d owed to the government; a few years later, it had become two messuages, one shop, 64 acres of land and 17 acres of meadow and 10d p.a. rents; by the fifteenth century, the property had been reduced to a garden, a shop, 30 acres of land, 3 acres of meadow and 4 acres of pasture, CPR 1327-30/492; 1345-48/45-6, 148, 360-1; 1354-8/137. There was competition for it, but equally a limit to the rent it could raise:

1434 John Chevercourt 10 years 24s 4d
1440 Thomas Burton esq 10 years 24s 4d +12d
[1445 John Broune king's clerk rent of 31s from Burton and reversion when it falls in]
1453 John Chevercourt 24s 4d + 8d
1456 Thomas Luyt and John Murdok 25s + 4d
1464 John Chevercourt 5 years 25s 4d +4d
1464 William Huse and John Murdok 10 years 25s 8d + 20d
1465 John Trunke yeoman of chamber and Richard Forster yeoman of buttery 5 years 25s 4d + increment
1476 Richard Forster 25s no increment
CFR 1430-37/199; 1437-45/171-2; 1452-61/28, 164; 1461-71/124, 135, 150-1; 1471-85/134; CPR 1441-46/372.

A second property which the king retained in Stamford was from Henry de Tiddeswell, (see above p 12) forfeited to the crown in the 1340s, CCR 1346-9/375, 391, but we do not have enough tenancy agreements to see trends in rents from this property.

was substantial and costly and covered all sectors, ecclesiastical, civic and domestic.

The evidence for this comes from both documents and architecture. As we have seen, few wills survive to provide evidence for ecclesiastical building, but a large number of property deeds for domestic and commercial properties exist, either in original or secondary form. Unlike some other towns, Stamford had a strong property market in the fifteenth century[16].

The evidence of title deeds:

The deeds suggest a pattern of building work in the town during the period. During the first third of the century, leases give a sense of dilapidation. References to 'empty places' occur, for example in Behinde-ye-Bak (1402) on which there were "formerly situated two shops with solars above". In 1411, a vacant place (adjacent to another vacant site) used to have two shops and solars above them; the same two sites were still empty 36 years later (1447-8). One lessee (1418) was enjoined that he "shall build new houses" on a tenement leased from the nuns. In 1421, the executors of a deceased owner, "seeing that the lands and tenements were going to great ruin and dilapidation, with the consent of the parishioners and neighbours, went to [the previous owner's widow] to incite and implore her to put the same in a fitting state of repair, and thus fulfill the last will and declaration of" her husband. A plot in St John's parish (the most densely occupied area of the town) "was ruinous and not built", so that "for many years past they [the nuns] have received nothing" (1422). In 1426, William Morwode and John Sibily took a fifty-year lease in St Martin's parish with an agreement that they "will build anew a house on the aforesaid empty plot"; and in 1430, John Englyssh of Staunford lockyer agreed, when he took an eighty-year lease from the nuns of a vacant plot on the north side of St Mary's Street, that he would "build a shop and solar over on the plot at his own expense within the first two years" – although four years later when he renewed this lease for 100 years, the shop had not been built and the same condition was included in the new indenture. Sometimes the building material and form were specified: the prior of Durham (1438) leased "a tenement now waste, in Stamford, in the lane called Cornewelsty or Chynelane", requiring that William Syngalday "within two years build and subsequently maintain a stone house on the waste with a door onto the high road by which the lord may effect entry and distraint as necessary"[17].

---

[16] Kowaleski 1995 p 90; Butcher, Rent. See Rogers *Deeds*
[17] e.g. PRO, E315/41/267; E315/35/19; E329/66; E326/4778; SC6/913/25; SC11/1115/7; CAD iii p 687; PRO, E326/2903; E326/4777; Peck xiv 21-2; PRO, E210/4190; NRO FitzWilliam

There are few signs of such vacant sites during the middle third of the century, but in the final third, leases reveal building on a larger scale. William Ledys tailor leased from the prior of Durham two adjacent cottages in the street called "Brigstrette super Westrawe" (St Mary's parish) on the understanding that "William will, within twelve years, rebuild and maintain at his own expense the two cottages, viz, on the one … a hall and a chamber with a solar, and on the other a parlour and a kitchen". In 1461, a lease of nunnery property included a clause recovering arrears of rents from two cottages which had been allowed to decay. In 1470, property in High Street Stamford Baron was being repaired; in 1478, "a messuage lately built, formerly divided into two houses in the parish of St. Mary Staunford" was settled on trustees. In the same year, "a place standing in the parish of the Holy Trinity … where it is faulty and ruinous", was to be rebuilt. In 1484, two plots were being used for a new hall, shop and solar, and in 1486, both Hudds Mill and 'le Cressaunt' in the parish of St Mary at the bridge were the subject of repairs. In 1497, "a small, empty plot, now built upon" in Est-by-the-Water in Stamford Baron was leased[18].

We need to remind ourselves of three things in relation to this evidence. First, provisions in deeds for the repair of buildings does not mean that these buildings were always in a poor state of repair; a repossession clause such as "if at any time during the aforesaid term the said shop with solar is not competently repaired"[19] means no more than it says, that if the tenant does not maintain it, the landlord retains the right of re-entry. Secondly, title deeds, which tend to survive in bundles relating to the same property, may exaggerate the evidence by repeating information concerning the same property. And thirdly, such leases may indicate a relatively healthy market rather than the reverse. While empty and ruinous sites suggest a decline, the fact that deeds relating to vacant properties exist indicates that there was some demand for such properties and wealth enough for people to acquire these sites and at a convenient time redevelop them. Equally, while the building activities of the final years of the century imply that there were properties which had fallen into some measure of dilapidation which required attention if they were not to deteriorate further, turning two smaller properties into one larger property can be seen as a sign of prosperity.

498; PRO, E210/4927; E326/4779; E315/31/8; E315/41/38; Durham DCD Register III fol 223

[18] Durham DCD Register III, fol 310; Register IV, fol 127; Peck xiv 21-22; PRO, E326/4781; MCO 2, 11; PRO, E210/2676; Exeter-NRA 53/4; Stamford Borough records, TH 13/7; MCO 37, 39; PRO, E210/799

[19] PRO, E326/4778

The architectural evidence

The architectural evidence makes the picture clearer. Judging by the buildings, "there is little direct evidence of decline" before the 16th century; and in particular "the churches which have survived ... show that Stamford remained a relatively rich town". "If buildings alone provided evidence for the changing fortunes of the inhabitants of fifteenth century towns, we would have to conclude that they were passing through a period of unparalleled prosperity"[20]. Or perhaps *some* of the inhabitants.

Religious buildings: Most of the religious buildings of Stamford had extensive work undertaken on them during William Browne's lifetime. The Austin friars in the west of the town was being enlarged. It has been suggested[21] that Richard III gave the White Friars materials from the decayed castle for building work (the castle was one of the buildings in the town not apparently repaired at this time, perhaps because Richard duke of York and later his son Edward IV concentrated their funds and attention on Fotheringhay nearby, page 69). The building of chapels in the friaries in the 1380s may have continued into the fifteenth century. We have no evidence of building at poverty-stricken St Leonard's, but work was undertaken at the nunnery of St Michael, despite its poverty: in 1445, John Fox of Wisbeche contracted with William Boydall alias Wryght of Great Casterton to take down all the timber of the "chapetre hous atte ye nonnes of Staunford and to make a lowe flore and a new rofe"; the work was to be completed in eight months. Boydall was also to make a new roof for the dorter; this work was not to take more than twenty months. Other work included the cloisters[22].

The building work on the six parish churches which remain today is remarkable. Although we have no evidence of what was done at the seven 'lost' churches[23] or

[20] RCHME *Stamford* p xlii; Dyer *Standards* p 204; see Dobson 1977; Dyer A 1995; P Hughes 1992 Property and prosperity: the relationship of buildings and fortunes of Worcester,1500-1660, *Midland History* 17 pp 39-58; Bridbury 1981; P Borsay 1982 Culture, status and the English urban landscape *History* 67 pp 1-12; Dyer C 1989; S H Rigby 1985 'Sore decay' and 'fair dwellings': Boston and urban decline in the later Middle Ages, *Midland History* 10 pp 47-61; K D Lilley 2000 Decline or decay? urban landscapes in late medieval England, in Slater 2000 pp 233-265; Palliser 1988 (reprint in D M Palliser 2006 *Towns and Local Communities in medieval and early modern England* Ashgate).

[21] Butcher 1717 p 45; Harrod i p 23; C Nevinson 1879 History of Stamford *Journal of British Archaeological Association* 35 pp 159-168; G L Dunning 1936 Alstoe Mount, Burley, Rutland *Antiquaries Journal* xvi pp 410-1; PRO, C47/67/11/441; see CCR 1374-77/390; CPR 1370-74/235; CIM iii 1349-77 p 386; CPL 1342-62/69; CPR 1446-52/79; PRO, C143/379/12

[22] PRO, E101/504/19, printed in Salzman 1967 pp 519-520; PRO, SC6/1260/12.

[23] St Michael in Cornstall, St Mary Bynwerk, St Peter, St Andrew, St Clement, Holy Trinity/St Stephens and All Saints by the Water in Stamford Baron have all gone. Part of St Paul's church remains; new glass was inserted here in c1397, CIPM 21 1418-22 p 62

at the church of St Michael the Greater which fell down in the nineteenth century, a great deal of work was undertaken at the other churches: indeed, it may have been because of this work that these churches are the ones which have survived.

"During the second half of the fifteenth century, the character of [St Mary's] church was transformed": the nave, aisles, clerestory, chancel arch, south porch and windows all underwent reconstruction. The nave roof is late fifteenth century. The north aisle chapel (the Corpus Christi chapel) was rebuilt and decorated about 1480. Some surviving glass is of the same period[24].

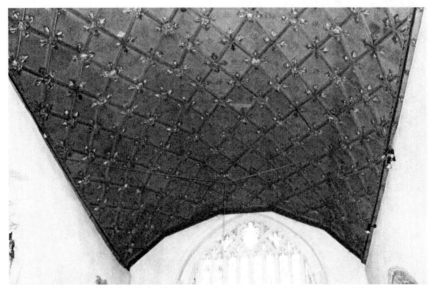

Chapel of Corpus Christi gild, St Mary's church, the roof of which was remodelled by William Hykeham baker and his wife in the 1480s (photo: John Hartley)

At St George's church, Sir William Bruges, first Garter King of Arms (1450) paid for much of the rebuilding and the extensive and expensive glass provided[25].

And All Saints church was extensively reconstructed (see below pp 239-41). Apart from the towers, most of which seem to have been erected first, these churches were being rebuilt all in one campaign, although over a long period.

---

[24] RCHME *Stamford* pp 23-27
[25] For Bruges, see below p 212

The new towers built at St John the Baptist and St Martin display an uncanny "uniformity of design", and the same model was used for the tower of the church at Easton on the Hill, some three miles from Stamford (photo: Alan Rogers; drawing by Nattes from Stamford Survey Group collections). See RCHME *Stamford* pp xlvi-vii; there are similarities with the tower of Great Ponton south of Grantham built by the Ellys family, Calais staplers.

118

The whole of St John's church with its angel roof was rebuilt, mainly by merchants as shown by their brasses and the glass; the work was probably completed by 1451 when elaborate glass was inserted. Here, masonry, timber and glass were all of a very high quality (photo: Alan Rogers)

St Martin's church was completely rebuilt during the century, tower first and then the nave and aisles. The newer style of large windows and wide, light and more flexible processional and devotional spaces within the church with its large numbers of images were major features of the work (photo: John Hartley)

This is a substantial record for a town the size of Stamford – and no doubt there was more now lost. The merger of some parishes may have given impetus to parish-funded rebuilding, but much of the building seems to have been funded by patronage, the costs borne by local merchants and others. The families of Fox (possibly John Fox alias John Kirkeby town clerk in 1452 and perhaps related to Fox of Wisbeach, builder at the nunnery) and Richard Sapcote and his wife were recorded in the glass of St George's church; Nicholas Byllysdon dyer and William Gregory mercer left brasses, and John Marchaunt and at least five other patrons provided glass, in St John's church, which would have implied some contribution to the building work. William Hykeham baker and Alderman and Alice his wife rebuilt the Corpus Christi chapel in St Mary's church in an elaborate style, highly gilded. But there were outsiders like Sir William Bruges at St George's and Sir David Phillips at St Mary's church. The patrons of St Martin's church, the nuns of St Michael, must have watched the reconstruction there with mixed feelings, for they cannot have contributed much to the cost, as their house was very poor; but the coats of arms of successive bishops of Lincoln from at least Fleming (1421-31) to Rotherham (bishop of Lincoln 1472-80 and archbishop of York 1480-1500) may give a hint of some of the patronage behind the rebuilding of this church. The work was still in progress in 1509, as can be seen from the will of Margaret Spenser: "I will that my executours cause to make and perfourme the Rodelofte and both the Iles accordinge to that which is nowe made in the body of the churche"[26].

Secular buildings too were rebuilt. The town hall over the bridge underwent substantial work in the 1480s, the council meeting in the Corpus Christi gildhall in St Mary's Place; that too was rebuilt in the fifteenth century, as the surviving fragment of the undercroft shows. To this we must add William Browne's gild hall cum hospital in Broad Street (Claymont); Browne also supervised the building of St Katherine's gildhall in the 1480s. There was much building of commercial premises – particularly the mills along the Welland damaged by floods: in 1486, William Bewshire of Stamford had a lease from the borough council on condition that he "shall build anew … one house with two water mills and all other necessary appurtenances belonging to the mill" at St Leonard's Ford (this may be the origin of the present Hudd's Mill). Kings Mill was rebuilt, and Wothorpe mills on the south side of the Welland were in need of major repairs in 1416, 1443 and 1497[27]. John Browne's wool hall of the 1420s has now disappeared.

---

[26] Peck xiv 24, 35-36; PRO, PROB 11/16 fol 118-9
[27] HB i fols 38d, p 112; fol 41, p 121; Rogers, *Gild Book;* Peck 1727 speaks of the Corpus Christi gildhall as "yet standing in Monday mercat street", Peck xiv 6; Exeter-NRA 89/3; Stamford borough records, TH 8A/1/7; PRO, E315/35/19; E315/42/148; E326/5673, 6374

Domestic buildings: The quality of the surviving domestic buildings from this period reminds us that what we possess today are only the very best of these buildings; the poorer ones will have disappeared.

Much building from the fifteenth century survives, often hidden behind later (frequently Georgian) fronts. Some 25 surviving properties wholly or largely built in these years have been identified. Courtyard houses, the sign of substantial prosperity, are rare but are known in High Street, St Martin, in St Mary's Hill, and in Barn Hill; David Cecil's house in St George's Square was a large courtyard house containing a hall, a great parlour, and that most modern development of the period, a gallery[28]. But the majority of fifteenth century houses in Stamford consisted of hall and cross wing.

Examples of the many hall and cross-wing buildings of the fifteenth century: St Paul's Street and the Vaults in St Mary's Street (photos: Alan Rogers and John Hartley

---

[28] Will of David Cecil, PRO, PROB 11/29; fol 2d-3; also "the gesse [guest] Chambre bye the strete", "the clossett wher she [my wyff] lyeth", a nursery, and a bed "at the stayr hed". For Cecil's biography, see Rogers, Parl. The Hermitage, now part of the George Hotel, was a courtyard house. The 'great gates' of the 'Kyngesinn' held by the earl of Suffolk suggest a courtyard. In 1444, the nuns leased "a tavern with two shops situated in the street called Brigstrete [next door to] the great gates of the tenement lately Richard Wykys of Stannford", PRO, E210/8897; the Wykes' property was the inn which Joan Veske later leased which consisted of a main building set back from Bridge Street (now St Mary's Hill) with two shops outside the gates, one on the north side and the other on the south side of the entrance, PRO, C1/26/236; see below pp 282-4

The newly developed properties are scattered throughout the town – from Barn Hill to High Street St Martins, from St Paul's Street (Estgate) to St Peter's Street. Most of them were in the core: in what is now Red Lion Square, in the parishes of All Saints, St John the Baptist, St Mary at the bridge, and St Paul, and in Cheyne Lane in the centre of town. Fewer of these properties were in the suburbs; very few are in Scotgate, but several were in Stamford Baron, in High Street, East-by-the-Water, Webstergate and Wothorpe. There was still enough space within the walls for the rich to build larger and more comfortable homes and working places, sometimes buying up adjacent properties and converting them into one larger property.

Although one or two of the newly erected buildings like All Saints Vicarage and the house in Cheyne Lane were in stone, the majority of these buildings were timber-framed, not (I believe) out of economy or lack of available building material, but for reason of fashion.

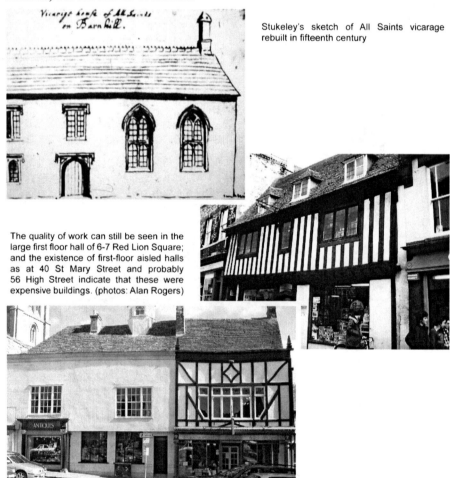

Stukeley's sketch of All Saints vicarage rebuilt in fifteenth century

The quality of work can still be seen in the large first floor hall of 6-7 Red Lion Square; and the existence of first-floor aisled halls as at 40 St Mary Street and probably 56 High Street indicate that these were expensive buildings. (photos: Alan Rogers)

To these we can add buildings which have now disappeared but which Stukeley and others recorded; these are even more revealing of the size and quality of the domestic building of this period.

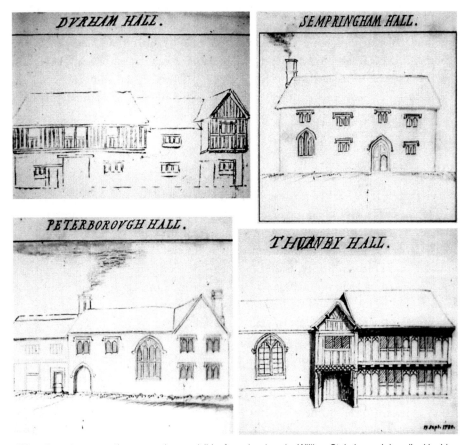

Fifteenth century properties now no longer visible, from drawings by William Stukeley and described by him as Black Hall; Durham Hall; Peterborough Hall; Sempringham Hall; and Thorney-Vaudey Hall (Stukeley Collection, Stamford Historical Society)

Most of these newer buildings occupied the full length of the street frontage. This helps to explain the grants of gates through the town walls into the rear gardens and yards of properties on the north side of the town - to gain access not so much to locations outside the walls as into these yards and gardens. In some houses, side passages allowed entry to the rear of the property, but in other cases, the continuous occupation of the street frontage meant that the only way to make the yards of these properties useful for commercial activity without going through the house itself was through a rear entry. The full use of the burgage plots and separation of private accommodation from commercial usages were growing apace during this century[29].

Much of this work was of course normal development and maintenance; some may have been repairing the decay of the fourteenth century. Some was upgrading of existing properties: chimney stacks were inserted - which helps to account for the small plots of land which changed hands[30]. Certainly, building on this scale did not start in the fifteenth century and it did not stop with the coming of the sixteenth century, which again witnessed substantial building, despite increasing urban poverty, as can be seen in St Mary's Hill and at the north end of Cheyne Lane.

Winners and losers

When therefore we ask who was benefiting and who was suffering from the economic and social changes in Stamford, the picture becomes clearer. The changes of this period involved considerable redistribution. Those with formal long-established interests in the town such as the dukes of York, the nuns of St Michael, and Durham priory, found the yields of their estates declining. All over the country from 1350 onwards, there was a "sharp contraction in the number of markets and in the amount of trade which was carried on in them", so that the collectors of the tolls and rents of stalls suffered.

Quite why traditional landlords found their rents falling is not clear. It may be that they did not maintain their properties as assiduously as the newer 'buy-to-let' landlords and thus their rents fell. Maintenance clauses were often included in the long leases (often 80 or even 100 years) now issued, but since these usually involved a largish initial payment (to assist immediate cash flow) and a lower annual rent, it is clear that income would decline. But no new income lines were now available. In addition, such landlords often found themselves unable to reduce their outgoings in line with their reduced income. The priory of Deeping St James illustrates this. Given by Guy Wake property in Behinde-ye-Bak (All Saints parish) which initially yielded £3 12s but by the early fourteenth century was providing £3 p.a. (with an additional 6d to be paid to the chief lord of the town for some steps to an upper chamber), the priory complained in 1331 that it was saddled with a stipend of £3 6s 8d for a chaplain to pray for the Wake family, so that this income line was in deficit from very early. By the fifteenth century, income from these properties had fallen to £2 p.a., and in a new rental

---

[29] Kowalweski and Goldberg 2008; see du Boulay 1970; Dyer *Standards* p 204.
[30] e.g. LAO parish records, Stamford PG 2/1

drawn up in 1473, Thomas Kesteven the tenant became liable for less than half the sum (£1 6s 8d) these houses had yielded 250 years earlier[31].

But Kesteven (draper and Calais Stapler) was one of those who found new opportunities to prosper. The wealthiest seem to have been merchants and mercers, like the Gregory brothers and John Marchaunt, but others were also wealthy, like William Hykeham baker and Nicholas Billesdon dyer[32]. William Spenser notary was clearly very rich, as his widow's will shows. What surplus there was in Stamford seems to have been used in the town; it was not until the end of the century that the wealth generated in Stamford began to be taken out into the countryside, although as late as 1532, William Radclyffe used his wealth to found a grammar school in the town.

How far wealth came to be concentrated in fewer hands while more and more of the town's population declined into poverty is uncertain. The 1524 tax returns do not of course show us the poorest of the poor but they do reveal that the bulk of the town's low tax payers were congregated in the parishes of St Mary at the bridge and All Saints in the Market. The richest parishes of the town north of the river by far were those of St Michael the Greater and St John the Baptist. But even the poorest taxpayers were not very poor; just under 30% of all those assessed at £3 or less were assessed at £1; nearly 20% paid £3, while 52% were in the middle category of £2. Of course, as we have seen, there were the many invisible residents; only some 240 persons were caught in that year, probably less than a half of all the households in the town[33].

And there were some very wealthy taxpayers. Fourteen were assessed at £40 or above. The richest was in St Martin's parish (Stamford Baron): Thomas Wylliams was assessed at £120[34]. He was followed by John Thomas of St Peter's parish at £100. Four more (including William Radclyffe) were assessed at £80, each in a separate parish. It may be significant that they were incomers who married well and made fortunes.

---

[31] BL Harl 3658 fols 19v, 49-56v, 69; W E Lunt 1934 *Papal Revenues in the Middle Ages* New York: Columbia ii p 191

[32] Peck xiv 67 and plate; RCHME *Stamford* p 26. Pugh suggests that the duke of York's income from other sources was increasing, and other historians have urged that total income might rise when rents fell, see Hatcher, Slump p 247; Pugh, York; Smith 2000: Britnell 1993; C D Liddy and B Dodds (eds) 2011 *Commercial Activity, Markets and Entrepreneurs in the Middle Ages: Essays in Honour of Richard Britnell* Boydell

[33] Sheail ii pp 188-89; I have omitted the churches and gilds from my list of taxpayers.

[34] St Martin's needs to be treated as a separate entity, because the taxable population seems to have the profile of a separate town, with a significant number of wealthy merchants and a large number of very small taxpayers; there are several detailed surveys of this area between the early fifteenth century and 1595 in NRO

It is not until the 1540s that claims of poverty begin to be made publicly in Stamford. Leland spoke of vacant sites. The amalgamation of the parishes in 1548 was on the grounds of poverty. That is not to say that there was no decline earlier – such trends are often long term and may be hidden from view for many years. But during William Browne's life, not only he but others in the town found themselves able to create enough wealth to enhance their own community substantially and leave a heritage which survived for many years. Stamford was the richer architecturally and culturally because of men like the Browne brothers and their contemporaries. They earned much and spent much.

There was then considerable wealth - but it was in the hands of relatively few merchants, of whom the Brownes were the outstanding examples. Much of the building was undertaken by a handful of richer inhabitants. Compared with the thirteenth century urban expansion in Stamford, where wealth seems to have been spread throughout the community, and building, though on a smaller scale, was more widely based[35], in the fifteenth century wealth seems to have been in fewer hands, the gap between rich and poor was very wide, and the building work was on a narrower but grander scale. It may be suggested that the spending on building in Stamford in the thirteenth century was for investment; the spending of the fifteenth century was for consumption.

The fifteenth century saw in Stamford a town that was shrinking – "smaller, more provincial and with fewer men of great substance". Its population was certainly smaller than it had been in the thirteenth and early fourteenth century. The town's hinterland too was probably shrinking; here, as elsewhere, those who attended its fairs were fewer and were local rather than international[36]. But this does not necessarily mean the town was poorer: "vacant premises and abandoned town churches might by themselves denote merely declining population rather than diminishing per capita prosperity"[37].

---

[35] See Rogers *Medieval Buildings*; in 1333, the average tax paid was 2s 11d, but 58% of the taxpayers paid 2s or less, 31% paid between 2s and 6s, and 11% paid more than 6s, PRO, E179/135/15. In 1524, 240 lay taxpayers paid an average of 7s 6d; 65% of taxpayers were assessed at less than £5, 22% at between £5 and £19 and 13% at £20 or more, PRO, E179/136/315

[36] Shaw *Wells* p 103; see J Laughton 2008 *Life in a late medieval city: Chester 1275-1520* Windgather Press. J Laughton and C Dyer 2002 Seasonal patterns of trade in the later middle ages: buying and selling at Melton Mowbray, Leicestershire, 1400-1520, *Nottingham Medieval Studies* 46 p 181, suggest that there was an upsurge in local fairs such as Melton's; this would have affected Stamford's fairs.

[37] Hatcher, Slump p 269. For hinterland, see Miller *Medieval England* p 10; Platts *Medieval Lincolnshire* p 226; Galloway 2003. The Stonors bought fish at Stamford in the 1420s, *Stonor Letters* i p 40. NRS 33 *Obedientiaries* pp 119, 121, 171 etc show purchases at Stamford, especially horses; and Lady Margaret Beaufort's household accounts in St John's College Cambridge again reveal many purchases there, especially cloth and food. The army of Henry VIII obtained some

PART III: CHAPTER 2   MAKING MONEY: FROM WOOL

Wool: "noble lady, goddess of the merchants"[38]

William Browne accumulated large sums of money – but not through war, royal service or the law. He drew his income from a number of activities, but he was first and foremost a merchant – that is how he described himself and how he acquired his initial wealth[39].

William Browne and the cloth trade

He was at first a 'draper of Stamford'. In this, he was in a long tradition; for, as we have seen, Stamford had for centuries been known throughout the kingdom and abroad for its cloth. The manufacture and trade of cloth in the town continued into the fifteenth century. But cloth manufacture had changed; the introduction of horizontal treadle (rather than upright) looms and later broad looms which needed more space than small town workshops could provide, and the concentration of fulling, had resulted in some of the better quality cloth manufacture relocating to other places, leaving Stamford with more standard varieties of cloth, especially the cheaper heavily fulled woollens such as black kersey. But cloth manufacture in the town remained relatively strong throughout the century. Between 1465 and 1492, thirteen weavers were admitted to the freedom, and weavers, dyers and fullers formed one of the largest craft groups. Nicholas Billesdon dyer became Alderman and left a brass in St John's church. But signs of capitalist organisation in spinning, dyeing, weaving or fulling in Stamford at this time are missing, unlike earlier years[40].

Cloth was exported as well as manufactured, mainly through the ports of Lynn, Boston and Ipswich. William Browne was thus joining a flourishing community of drapers in Stamford. At least 13 drapers were active in the town at this period;

---

of its provisions from Stamford fair, L and P Henry VIII 1 i 1509-13 p 1118 (2544). See J Thirsk 1965 Stamford in the sixteenth and seventeenth centuries, in Rogers 1965 pp 58-76

[38] G C Macauley (ed) 1899 *Complete Works of John Gower* i pp 280-1

[39] Payling 1992; Rigby *Grimsby* p 71. There is a large literature on fifteenth century provincial merchants; see e g Kermode 1982; Kermode *Merchants*; Kermode *Enterprise*; Horrox 1983; Hanham *Celys*; Power *Medieval People* (Betson); Tooley; Richmond *Hopton*

[40] PRO, E101/340/16; see Carus-Wilson, *Wash* p 187; Bridbury 1982; J H Munro 2003 Medieval Woollens: textiles, textile technology and industrial organisation, in D Jenkins (ed) 2003 *Cambridge History of Western Textiles* Cambridge University Press i pp 181-227. Peck xiv 67; Butcher 1727 p 27; the dyers had workshops in the dyke beneath the castle, PRO, SC6/1115/9. Kermode *Enterprise* p 19; Ralph Stokes of Stamford was an early entrepreneur engaged in 'putting out' in the 1270s, Miller and Hatcher p 116

four were admitted to the freedom in the years 1465-92, and four served as Alderman on a total of 10 occasions during the century. There was a town Drapery. When we add the mercers (some of whom, like Thomas Kesteven and Thomas Philippe, also called themselves drapers), we have a powerful group of cloth traders in the town: eight mercers were admitted between 1465 and 1492, and seven mercers served as Alderman on 13 occasions[41].

But by mid-century, the international cloth trade had diminished; it has been estimated that between 1438 when William Browne was just starting and 1482, a few years before his death, the English overseas cloth trade fell by one third, though it rose again in the last years of the century. The fastest period of decline seems to have been 1448-1450 - which may provide one reason why William Browne came to concentrate on wool trading in these years. And, since that meant trading through Calais, some time before 1449, he and his brother John were admitted to the company of the Calais Staple, "the most remarkable body of traders in England". They gave up the title of 'draper' and took to themselves 'merchant of Stamford' or 'merchant of the Calais Staple'. It is unlikely that they served the apprenticeship which some undertook; more likely they purchased their membership[42]. But from then on, 'merchant' or 'Stapler' are the only titles by which they were known.

The wool trade

English wool was still the great product of England, recognised both in the country and on the continent as the backbone of the country's economy: the Treatise concerning the Staple spoke of

> *The speciall gift of the fynes [fineness] and goodness of the staple wolle, which Godd by his first day of everlastyng light by vertu of his holy spirit gaff into the erth for the common welth of Englande.*

Wool was stated to come to the value of half the land. The demand from the continent for English wool from at least the twelfth century was very great. Since the middle of the fourteenth century, the bulk of the wool for the continent was supposed to go via Calais. There were exceptions of course; wool for some Mediterranean cities, exported usually by alien (mainly Italian) merchants, went

---

[41] CPR 1361-64/229; PRO, E122/96/37; E122/97/8; SC6/1115/7; HB i passim; Rogers, Aldermen

[42] Power *Medieval People* p 124; see Tooley p 21; Munro 1972; Carus-Wilson, Wash pp 196-7; Bridbury 1982 *Clothmaking*, Britnell *Closing* pp 241-251. John Barton of Holme Calais Stapler requested in his will that his son "should make John Tamworth a free man of the Calais Staple", presumably by purchase, Power *Medieval People* p 201. Rich *Ordinance Book* p 6; Sutton, Staple p 137

via the south coast ports, though some went by Calais and overland. Wool for the Scandinavian ports went largely from north-east ports. But most wool went to Calais; from Calais, much of it went to Flanders and Brabant or the newly emerging Dutch towns to be made into cloth to be sold back to England[43]. The trade was politically important, for the customs on wool financed much of the government's special needs such as war or a royal marriage, and through loans from wool merchants (often an advance of customs payments), they increasingly played a part in the more normal expenditure which the government incurred.

The trade was changing. From about 1350, wool exports declined, so that when William Browne joined the Staplers, exports had fallen to just over 5000 sacks a year from a height of some 34,000 sacks in 1350. As with the cloth trade, after what seems to have been something of a boom in the first few years of the century, the middle years of the fifteenth century witnessed "an enduring and wide-ranging slump of precipitous proportions"[44]. English wool exports are said to have declined by one sixth between 1438 and 1471, and other commodities, after a rise which in part compensated for the decline of wool exports, also fell. The sharp fall between 1452 and 1462 may be related to:

> the contynuall debate contention and warre that hath bine in many yeares past, which hath stayed not onely the emperors subjectis and Frenchmen to come to Caleis to buy the said staple-merchandises but also hath stayed the said staplers to adventure their goodes into their handes[45].

Wool prices fluctuated greatly during the century, but overall they fell, reaching in the 1450s their lowest point of which parliament complained bitterly in 1453; there were years when not all the wool could be sold[46]. Interruptions were caused by wars and diplomacy. There was something of a rally in overseas trade

---

[43] Power *Wool Trade* pp 21, 28, 73; Carus Wilson, Wash p 189; see O Coleman 1963 Trade and prosperity in the fifteenth century: some aspects of the trade of Southampton *Econ Hist Rev* 16 p 14; Power and Postan pp 39-90; Lloyd *Wool Trade*. A Venetian merchant of c1500 said that "the riches of England are greater than those of any other country in Europe because of their extraordinary abundance of wool", *Italian Relation;* see also G Warner (ed) 1926 *The Libelle of English Policy* Clarendon pp 5-7. A good short account of the Calais staple in the fifteenth century is in S Rose 2008 *Calais, an English Town in France 1347 to 1558*, Boydell. pp 95-111; see also G A C Sandeman, 1908 *Calais Under English Rule* Oxford: Blackwell

[44] *Medieval Norwich* p 387. The nuns' accounts show that sheep on the lands of the nuns of Stamford increased in the late fifteenth century, from about 100 in 1472-3 to over 200 in 1515. Wool exports are summarised in Nightingale 1990 p 561; Hatcher, Slump pp 241-5; H L Gray 1933 English foreign trade 1446-1482, in Power and Postan pp 12-16.

[45] Rich *Ordinance Book* p 8; Kermode *Merchants* pp 165-200; Hanham, Wool; Britnell 1998.

[46] "the Wolles growyyn withynne this Reaume heretobefore hav been the great comodite, enriching and welfare of this land, and ... now late the price of the said Wolles ys so gretly decayed and amenused in the hondes of the growers", *Rot Parl.* v p 274; see Childs 1991 p 82; T H Lloyd 1973 *Movement of wool prices in medieval England* Economic History Review Supplement.

from the 1470s, brought to an end in 1477 when the king of France invaded the Low Countries on the death of the duke of Burgundy[47]. Add to this the more 'normal' risks of shipping – fire, wrecks, storms at sea, and William Browne's task of making a fortune from wool was harder than some of his predecessors' had been. Almost the only feature favourable for the Brownes was that the hold of London on the trade was somewhat weaker; although the London merchants still dominated the regulation of the trade, their trading seems to have diminished, so that it is doubtful if the Calais Staple were "coming to be more and more a London merchants' colony" [48]. There was room for William Browne of Stamford.

Corbel in All Saints church showing sheep's head (photo: Rob Foulkes)

And for many Staplers, the trade was becoming less important. The decline in exports and the fact that a growing number of persons had a hand in it meant that it became more difficult to make a good living from wool alone. Many of those who engaged in the wool trade as Calais Staplers had other means of income. Some MPs were "intimately involved in the wool trade". Edward IV himself is said to have traded much wool, and he gave licences to members of

---

[47] Sutton *Tates* p 71. It has been estimated that in the second half of the fifteenth century, wool was worth 25% less than in the first half of the century, and it was 40% less than it had been worth in 1300-1350. Sutton *Tates* p 65 speaks of a rally in the reign of Edward IV. Hatcher, Slump p 270; wool prices were high 1465-75 and again 1480-89 but low at other times, Britnell *Closing* pp 231, 270-1; a stone of wool 1400 cost 4.2s; in the 1440s, 3.1s; in 1447-8, 2s; in the 1450s, 2s – 2.3s. A sack of wool in 1453 cost £3 6s 8d, and this was said to be low. Fleeces declined in weight starting in the 1370s; by the 1450s, they were on average only half of 1350s. They fell in value from the early 15thC (4d or 4½d) to the mid-15thC (2½d and sometimes as low as 1½d).

[48] Lloyd *Wool Trade* pp 252-3; Power 1926 p 28; Steel *Exchequer* p 264; Kowaleski 2000. See PRO, E404/29/183 for wool ship burnt in the port of Ipswich.

the royal family, including his mother Cecily duchess of York, and others[49]. For many Staplers, overseas trading in wool was a part-time occupation.

There was of course always the home market which was growing; English cloth manufacturers were demanding that more wool should remain in the country: "The cloth industry of England was making considerable inroads on the amount of wool being exported". But to this market came overseas merchants, especially Flemings and Lombards, to buy up wool at source. The presence of these alien merchants, who held about one fifth of all the English wool trade and had access to wider networks of finance, was of great significance. The government sought to woo them, for economic and political reasons related to the various conflicts of the day - with Charles of France, the duke of Burgundy, and the Italian and Hanseatic merchants. But these alien merchants were very unpopular in the country, especially after the loss of Normandy in 1449-50. They were often treated as scapegoats for local troubles: Lynn and Grimsby saw disturbances in the late 1450s. Although the taxes on alien merchants were increased substantially (their poll tax rose from 16d to 40s, and their wool subsidy from 53s 4d to 100s), there were riots against alien merchants in 1456- 8, especially in London, which was given as one reason why Queen Margaret took the royal court out of London to Coventry[50].

But not so far as we know in Stamford. Through the practice of hosting, Browne would of course had had dealings with many alien merchants in the ports and in towns like Coventry as well as abroad; but long-term resident alien merchants are not recorded in Stamford during the fifteenth century, unlike towns such as Lynn and Ipswich.

The Calais Staple

The field then in Stamford was held by local merchants. In joining the Staple company, William Browne and his brother joined a well-established group of

---

[49] CPR 1476-85/441. Griffiths *Henry VI* p 555; Sutton *Tates* p 65; Power 1933 p 70; Carus-Wilson *Merchant Adventurers*, A F Sutton 2002 Merchant Adventurers of England: their origins and the mercers' company of London *History Research* 75 pp 25-46; Power 1926 pp 21-2; Scofield ii p 84; it is possible that the use of the king's name was granted by licence to men who called themselves 'king's factors' to escape customs in return for benefits to the government. Cecily had her licence to export wool renewed by Henry VII

[50] *Rot Parl* iv p 387; see Power and Postan p 12; Kermode *Enterprise* p xi; Rigby *Grimsby* p 145; Griffiths *Henry VI* p 171; M S Giuseppi 1895 Alien merchants in England in the fifteenth century *TRHS* 9 pp 75-98; Childs 1991 pp 70-72; Griffiths *Henry VI* pp 171, 551, 554-6, 560, 564, 790-5; Kermode *Merchants* p 26; J L Bolton 1998 *Alien communities of London in the fifteenth century: subsidy rolls of 1440 and 1483-4* Stamford: Watkins; Attreed *King's Towns* pp 152, 231-2; A A Ruddock 1951 *Italian Merchants and Shipping in Southampton 1270-1600* pp 162-179; Helen Bradley and Matthew Davies 2005 *The alien commodity trade, 1440-45*, ESRC Report

about 250-300 merchants. Some would export only an occasional few sacks or bales, while others would export substantially and regularly. What held these merchants together was the Calais market: they all had to use the Staple. Joining the Company was a *sine qua non* for the trade of wool to the continent. The Staple was a centre where wool, fells and hides were sold under supervision, primarily so that the customs on such sales could be the more easily collected, prices negotiated and the quality of the wool controlled[51]. Calais was regarded by contemporaries as part of England, and as such came under increasing attack from the French king. Defended by a ring of fortresses and a permanent garrison, it was a key factor in the government's policy-making and in the financial burdens on the royal revenues. So the king and his government turned to the wool merchants – through their company of the Calais Staple – to help finance the wars in return for various trading privileges, and the Staplers gradually became more and more embroiled in the royal finances, at first through loans and then payments for special purposes; thus the Company found itself funding expeditions to France for the war or for diplomatic purposes. The loan repayments to be taken from exemptions from the customs or other sources of revenue were however threatened by successive Acts of Resumption which tried to restrain the king from granting away revenues to his favourites and creditors, and arranged for the taking back of many grants which had already been made. So that from 1451, a different approach was adopted. The Company of the Staple was from time to time required to raise troops to go to Calais and pay for them, and from 1466 the Staple Company took over the farm of the customs and the revenues of Calais with obligations to pay the garrison and other charges in Calais as well as to recoup their debts[52]. The Staplers thus became responsible for paying for the garrison in Calais directly, perhaps seen as a way to control the unruly garrison which from time to time caused trouble.

By 1454, Henry VI's government was felt to be working against the Staple. The law that all wool for sale abroad must be sold at Calais led to smuggling and attempts at evasion, especially through export licences[53] issued to Staplers and other traders to send the wool to some other market. Licences were granted to Staplers to export wool to Calais with reduced customs payments. Both were issued to obtain repayment of loans or for other favours to king or government. By 1458 when everything was beginning to come apart, many licences to export wool went to people known as 'king's factors', sometimes aliens, which led to more wool being exported without going through Calais.

---

[51] Sutton, Staple pp 135-6; approximately 272 members in PRO SC1/57/111 (1472).

[52] Steel *Exchequer* p 210 ; Sutton, Staple p 137. Between 1451 and 1455, the Staplers (including Browne) paid no less than £43,500 for the expeditions of the duke of Somerset and the earl of Warwick

[53] For smuggling, see Power 1926 p 19; Postan 1973 pp 356-360; Kermode *Merchants* p 195.

So that, as with the cloth trade, it was a bad time for William and his brother to join the Calais Staplers. At home, trouble was brewing up since the death of Humphrey duke of Gloucester in 1447, the tipping point of the century. Overseas, relations with the duke of Burgundy who controlled Flanders deteriorated, undermining the commercial treaty which had been made in 1439. Calais was closed for a time, as it had been in 1421 and was to be again later (1468)[54]. The war with France was going badly; for many years, the English had been holding their own, despite the new life put into the French armies by Joan of Arc (burned in the English-held town of Rouen in 1431) and despite the (rather half-hearted) reconciliation of the duke of Burgundy with his French overlord in 1435, but from 1447, the situation deteriorated. The conflict encouraged and at times legitimated piracy, and ships laden with English wool were being captured or lost at sea. The demands for the 'saf kepyng of the see' became loud, as Chaucer had noticed earlier. The duke of Burgundy imposed a ban on the sale of English cloth in his territories from 1447 until 1452. And in 1449, just as the French king was winning the war in Normandy and threatening Calais, increasing hostility, especially in the east coast ports such as Lynn, between English merchants and those from the Baltic who had formed their association of the Hanse, resulted in outright war which lasted until 1473 and closed the northern markets to English traders from time to time[55].

The English government, hard pressed to fund the war, was demanding that the Staplers provide more and more cash. It is true that this gave the company leverage[56]; and parliament at Leicester in 1449 responded by making some provision for the Staplers. But the Company of the Staple itself was not in a happy shape. There were divisions internally, especially over what was known as 'the Partition' arrangement for the sale of wool in Calais which, some historians have suggested, "plunged the wool trade into chaos and brought on a ten-year slump" and which seems to have come to an end in 1454. In 1448, there was a disputed election of the mayor of the Staple, and the government stepped in and imposed the unpopular duke of Suffolk as Governor on the Staple, although parliament in 1449 restored the Staple rules. And the government from time to

---

[54] Huizinga p 138; Sutton *Tates* p 71; Power 1926 p 29; see Harriss, Struggle; D Grummitt 2008 *The Calais Garrison: war and military service in England 1436-1558*, Boydell

[55] Steel *Exchequer* p 218; Carus-Wilson, Wash pp 195, 196, 200; keepers of the sea were appointed, *Rot Parl* v p 240, 244 5; 000 Harriss, Aids p 4; Griffiths *Henry VI* p 554; M M Postan 1933 Economic and political relations of England and the Hanse from 1400 to 1475, in Power and Postan pp 91-154; T H Lloyd 1991 *England and the German Hanse 1157-1611: a study of their trade and commercial diplomacy* Cambridge University Press

[56] Eileen Power perhaps exaggerates somewhat when she writes of the Company of the Staple, "so rich and so powerful that they became a constitutional menace, almost, it has been said, a fourth estate of the realm, with which His Majesty was wont to treat for grants apart from Parliament", *Medieval People* p 126

time placed an embargo on the export of wool in order to further its policy on the continent – for example, in 1428-9, 1438-9, and later in 1463 and 1485-6[57].

Thus the Staple Company – and William Browne as an active member of the Company - became heavily involved in the political and military controversies of the middle of the century. In December 1458, new ground was broken when Henry's government made a four-year agreement with the Company for a payment to the royal household of £4000 p.a. (to be paid quarterly) in return for a number of trading privileges: the limitation of licences to export wool by-passing the Staple, provisions against smuggling (which hit the Staple as well as the government), additional powers to control wool exports, and the appointment of envoys to the duke of Burgundy about trading infringements. To pay for the Calais garrison or indeed for the war in France was one thing; to contribute towards the regular costs of the administration, thus relieving the king of some of his appeals to parliament for taxes, was a different matter. But Calais was soon in the hands of the earl of Warwick on behalf of the Yorkists who were now in open rebellion against Henry VI's bankrupt government, and the government in the parliament of Coventry ordered the Staple to cease trading with Calais – an order which seems to have been ignored. So that it is not surprising that the Staple "began to invest in the alternative government offered by the party of the duke of York from 1456". "Because he [Edward IV] undertook to repay Henry VI's debts as well as his own", the fortunes of the new regime and the Staple Company were closely linked[58].

William Browne as wool trader

Despite all of this, the focus of the Browne brothers moved in the second half of the 1440s from cloth to wool. William Browne entered this world of wool trading wholeheartedly; his brother John was his close partner. But this does not mean that William and John gave up trading in cloth; William was exporting through London in 1477-8 and 1480-1[59]. Browne's wool hall would no doubt have many other goods in store. John's daughter married a draper.

---

[57] Under the Partition Ordinance of 1429, when the wool was sold in Calais to foreign merchants, the seller did not receive the sums due until all the wool had been sold and then the total proceeds were divided between all the Staple merchants. The details were revised several times as a result of dissension among the Staplers, but it remained an arrangement which many of the Staple merchants found objectionable and eventually managed to get abolished, so that they could sell their wool separately. See Power and Postan pp 82-90; Rich *Ordinance Book* pp 6, 21; Munro 1972 pp 84-92; Lloyd *Wool Trade* pp 257-269; Childs 1991 p 70

[58] Steel *Exchequer* pp 237-8; CPR 1452-61/500-1; Sutton, *Staple* pp 137-8

[59] PRO, E122/194/22; Cobb 1990 pp 110 (450), 114 (456), 166 (602); although there was another William Browne mercer of London at about this time, the editor ascribes this entry to William Browne of Stamford, and the presence of Christopher Browne and other Stamford merchants in

William Browne's role in the trade was as middleman and exporter. The trade was organised into *producers* (the sheep farmers and their landlords, laymen or monastic estates and clergy), *middlemen* (or 'broggers') who bought the wool from the producers and sold it to the merchants[60], and *merchants* who gathered the wool and skins and sold them either on the home market or abroad. It would seem that during the century, the middlemen were declining, producers selling more often direct to the merchants like William Browne.

Producing and purchasing: Although William Browne held much land, as we shall see, there are no signs that he developed his estates by enclosure for sheep; Browne probably did not produce any of his own wool. He bought wool from the producers (and presumably from other middlemen) and sold it both inside the country and abroad. We can see him at work as a middleman on one occasion early in his career: in 1441-2, he bought the whole of the wool production of the estates of the nunnery of St Michael by Stamford[61].

This is most likely to have been 'Kesteven wool'. Stamford stood at the centre of several different areas of wool growing; William Browne would have covered much territory to find wool. We know that he was in Lincoln in late 1450 (see above p 84), perhaps in search of wool fells after the autumn kill of sheep in the Lincolnshire wolds; Lyndsey wool was for many years among the best in England, commanding high prices, the chief export from the Wash ports. Nearer to hand were the middle grade Kesteven wools. The fenland areas produced a great deal of poorer quality short-haired wool. Inland, arable land was being converted to pastures for sheep. But the best were the wools of the Cotswolds and the Welsh marches[62]. Here, Browne's links with Coventry would have been important: for (as we shall see) William's sister Alice was married into leading Coventry families. With its connections with Southampton, the town stood at the centre of late medieval England's trading routes and opened the doors to the purchase of west midland and Cotswold wool to a merchant like William Browne (see below pp 259-60).

And Browne built another network which strengthened his trade, though it too had its political drawbacks. Sometime about 1457, William married his daughter

---

the same record suggests this attribution is correct. Browne used a number of factors and took the whole of one ship.

[60] Hanham *Celys*, Sutton *Tates* pp 65-68

[61] PRO, SC6/914/26 – 10 stones of wool for 33s 4d; the later accounts do not separate out the wool sales.

[62] *Rot Parl* v p 275; E B Fryde 1983 *Studies in Medieval Trade and Finance* Hambledon 1983 pp 3-31; Hanham, Wool p 143; Postan and Power pp 45-51; Power 1926 p 23; Lloyd *Wool Trade* p 310; Sutton *Tates* p 66

Elizabeth to John son of John Elmes of Henley on Thames, Calais Stapler. John was a middleman and wool merchant with substantial property in Oxfordshire. This alliance gave William Browne and his firm access not only to the Chiltern wool producers but above all to Southampton, where the Elmes' family had a wool house, and its trade with the Mediterranean, including wine and dyes. Browne's network stretched across the country[63]. But, although John Elmes senior was one of the largest traders with Italian merchants, William Browne must quickly have wondered about the wisdom of this alliance, for soon after the marriage, John Elmes the father was accused of illegal trading to the tune of 1200 marks (£800), a suit which, on his death, fell on William Browne's son-in-law, son and heir of John Elmes senior. The case continued in the reign of Edward IV, when the younger Elmes was accused of being a rebel, which he fiercely denied[64]. William Browne's family arrangements and his trading activities had their political risks.

It was the responsibility of the producer to get the wool to the market place, either to Browne's Stamford wool hall or direct to the port of shipment. Here would be William Browne's apprentices, learning their trade; here too would be the weighing beam for the payment of tronage (the tax on the wool weight). Here would be his wool packers[65]. Here the sarplars and pokes would be marked and despatched to the ships.

How much of William Browne's wool was destined for the home market and how much for markets abroad we don't know. Nor do we know which English fairs and markets he used in addition to Stamford. But, stamped with his distinctive merchant's mark (see below p 296), much of the wool went abroad.

---

[63] PRO, SC1/57/111. Peberdy 1994 p 181 suggests that John Elmes II was the adopted son of John Elmes I, but the transfer of property by deed from father to son could occur if the transfer were made during the lifetime of the father, if the son concerned were not the oldest son, or if the property were subject to special conditions such as borough English – as happened in the case of William Browne; and as we have seen, some sons of burgesses did pay an admission fine for entry to the freedom.

[64] PRO E159/235 Trin recorda m 7 ff; briefly noted in Childs 1991 pp 76, 83. In the summer of 1460, the crown accused JE senior of having in 1457 traded 120 sacks of wool at 10 marks per sack with an Italian merchant contrary to the statute of 8 Henry VI; the debts, amounting to more than £800, were to be paid over three years, 1458 to 1460. JE senior died and his son, heir and executor JE of Henley on Thames was sued in his place. He pleaded various pardons which he held (especially one dated 5 May 1462 with no less than seven designations), when he claimed he had not entered his inheritance and thus had not received any of the payments, "and he says that he is not, nor was he on 5 May, nor had he been at any other time a rebel". The judges apparently accepted that he had not been involved in the Italian sale in any way.

[65] Pipewell p 206; CPR 1476-85/321; Hanham, Wool p 146; for a London wool packer in Stamford in 1470, see CCR 1468-76/166 (630); for wool packers, see CPR 1494-1509/450; PRO, E213/107; Power 1926 p 25; Lloyd *Wool Trade*; Power and Postan pp 51-60; Kermode *Merchants* p 200

Exporting

Browne exported mainly from the ports of the Wash and East Anglia. These were witnessing a steady decline in their exports, in part due to silting up. Nevertheless, on the whole, the export trade from the Wash was still healthy during the fifteenth century, although concentrating on the export of less valuable wool. If the surviving customs accounts give us some indication of what is happening (there are gaps in these records), Boston was the chief port for wool; although there were short periods of boom in this port during the 1450s and 1470s, exports of wool declined substantially from the 1460s. Ipswich too exported quantities of wool; these fell off in the middle of the century but revived later. Lynn seems to have played a smaller part in the export of wool; it exported mainly cloth; its decline came from the late 1440s[66].

William Browne's first trading commitments were through Ipswich, where in 1449-50 he was a member of and later led a consortium of 28 Staplers which made a number of loans to the government and in return received licences to export wool free of or with reduced customs duties until the loan had been repaid. But when some of his licences were renewed in 1454, he had them changed to Boston. Decisions as to which port to use would depend on many factors – the source of the wool, the use of agents in the ports, the availability of shipping[67], and of course the licences to export.

Partnerships seem to have been particularly important in the wool trade: as one near contemporary noted, "Trade in companies is natural to Englishmen". Over the years, William Browne's partnerships seem to have become smaller and more focussed: in 1460 in a suit for debt, he headed a small group of Calais Staplers from York, Grantham, Gainsborough and Hagworthingham (Lincs). Two were clearly important and lasting. William and John Browne joined William Lewes of Oakham and Lynn in Ipswich in 1454, and they acted as executors for him in 1468. William and John also worked with Richard Sapcote of Stamford and

---

[66] Wren *Ports*, Carus-Wilson, Wash pp 185-9, 196-200; Hanham, Wool p 141; Power and Postan pp 41-43; Kowaleski 2000; Amor *Ipswich* p 21

[67] For shipping in the fifteenth century, see Mate 2006 pp 80-81; Rigby *Grimsby* p 135; G V Scammell 1962 Shipowning in England c1450-1550, *TRHS* 12 pp 105-122; M Kowaleski 2007 Warfare, shipping and crown patronage, in L Armstrong, I Elbl, M M Elbl (eds) 2007 *Money, Markets and Trade in late medieval Europe* Leiden: Brill pp 233-254; R Ward 2009 *The World of the Medieval Shipmaster: law, business and the sea c1350-1450* Boydell and Brewer. Shipping grew in the ports of Ipswich and Hull but declined in the other east coast ports, H D Burwash 1969 *English Merchant Shipping 1460-1540* Newton Abbott: David and Charles; Geoffrey Martin 1956 Shipments of wool from Ipswich to Calais, *Journal of Transport History* 2 pp 177-181

Rutland in 1454 and 1467; and Richard and his wife were members of William Browne's gild of St Katherine in Stamford[68].

We can see some of Browne's exports from Ipswich in 1449 and 1450, mainly with his brother John and William Lewes their partner, but at times with a larger group including Richard Sapcote. They shipped a total of 1330 sacks and 75,414 fells in these years; in 1455, the two Brownes and Lewes shipped 1161 sacks and 79,220 fells, by far the largest consignments from this port[69].

What can be seen of the Browne shipments from Boston in the 1460s were on a similar scale. Carried to the port mostly by water using the Welland and Nene-Ouse[70], the wool and sheepskins were sent abroad in ships coming (in this case) from places as far apart as Walberswick in Suffolk and Sandwich in Kent. The Browne family, like most merchants, split their goods between many ships to insure themselves against loss. Because of the dangers, the ships sailed in convoys. The wool fleets frequently left in August after the summer clip or in late autumn after the Martinmas kill of sheep[71]; but others left for Calais in May after the purchasing season.

The Brownes' shipments were winter and summer. In December 1463, William and John Browne had wool on three ships, William 55 sacks and John 33 sacks. In May 1466, William had some 20 sacks on five ships while John had 64 sacks spread between 12 ships. And on 18 May 1472, a fleet of 21 ships left Boston with William Browne's wool on 12 of these ships - 91 sacks of wool out of a total of 936 sacks, a tenth of all the shipments in that fleet. His were the largest shipments in each ship, sometimes by far. The Browne firm was a major player in Boston port on all three occasions[72].

---

[68] PRO CP40/796; John Notyngham Calais Stapler was suing William Browne of Stamford, Thomas Nelson of York. John Eldwet[?] of Grantham, William Kyng of Gainsborough and Richard Draper of Hagworthingham, all Calais Staplers, for debt. I owe this reference to Dr Nicholas Amor. Power *Medieval People* p 125; Postan 1973 pp 65-91; Power 1926 p 29. CPR 1446-52/ 315; 1452-61/210-2; CCR 1454-61/6, 13-16, 35; Rogers *Gild Book*; CPR 1452-61/210-1, 226; 1467-77/79, 213; CFR 1454-61/6, 14-15, 19; Simcoe 1038 M/T/9/2; Power and Postan p 237; for Sapcote glass in St George's church, see Peck xiv 43. *Rot Parl* v p 208; LAO, BHS 7/1/3. Other trading partners (Nicholas Mattok, John Turvey and William Selby in Ipswich in 1454 etc) are more obscure; they do not appear to be Stamford or Ipswich residents, so they may have been local to Ipswich ports or to the points of wool production or even to Calais. Mattok is sometimes written as Martok.

[69] PRO E356/19/125; E356/20/103, 105, 110.

[70] See Blair 2007 pp 15-18.

[71] Power *Medieval People* pp 148-9 for August fleets from London and Ipswich

[72] PRO, E122/10/4, 5, 17 ; I am grateful to Professor Rigby for help with this.

Membership of the Calais Staple seems to have carried with it not only trading privileges and financial responsibilities in the form of loans to the government and payments for the Calais garrison, but also some social cachet. For William, it clearly carried a lot of weight (see below p 314); membership of the Calais Staple was for him much more than symbolic capital; for he was a serious and serial trader in wool. Travel to Calais could not be avoided. His factor ("Brownes man of Stamford"[73]) looked after his interests in Calais, but that could not excuse the firm's principals from going there from time to time, and from Calais to neighbouring cities, especially Bruges and perhaps Antwerp. This would be how John Browne commissioned his Book of Hours; this may be where William Browne got his coconut cup which he passed on as a family heirloom (see below pp 294-5). It is certainly where William Browne got much of his wealth.

And this is surprising, for the troubles which characterised his early years as a wool merchant continued. The wars made trade uncertain at times, while in Flanders, a crisis led to revolts (1482-5 and 1488-92) and the collapse of the network of wool-buying and cloth-making towns. Pirates "who swarmed in the narrow seas between England and France", at times supported and even encouraged by both governments, continued to make shipping hazardous. The on-going feud with the Hanseatic league combined with the irresponsible behaviour of some of Edward IV's servants, paralleling the irresponsibility of Henry VI himself, rebounded on the wool trade. It was not a time for the faint hearted to try to make money; it needed a steady hand on the tiller. It has been suggested that profits from the export of wool, normally about 20% to 35%, were dropping during the later part of the fifteenth century[74]. Trade would need to be on a sufficiently large scale to ensure wealth.

In all these troubles, William Browne seems to have kept his head down. He partook in the general pardons which the Staple negotiated from the government. In April 1464, along with many other merchants of the Staple including John his brother, he received a pardon for all prior offences (as William Browne merchant of the Staple of Calais, alias William Browne 'of Staunford marchaunt'). In January 1472, although included in the general pardon to the mayor, constables and society of the merchants of the Staple of Calais, he and 24 other merchants took out a separate pardon; and he had a pardon as

---

[73] Hanham *Cely* pp 8, 155. See Power *Medieval People* p 149 for a description of the life of such an English factor in Calais, being overcharged for lodgings and having to find another set. For another factor in Calais, Thomas Kesteven, almost certainly from Stamford, see Rogers, Calais ; Hanham *Celys* pp 91-103

[74] Hanham, Wool p 145; Power and Postan pp 70-71. D Meier 2006 *Seafarers, Merchants and Pirates in the Middle Ages* Boydell; Power *Medieval People* pp 124, 149; Chaucer, *Canterbury Tales, Prologue*, line 148

William Browne merchant of the Staple of Calais in May 1480. His name and that of his brother (along with other Stamford merchants) are to be found in the comprehensive list of Staplers sent to the king in 1472[75].

He played no negligible part in the Staplers' affairs; he probably served as lieutenant of the Staple and was certainly on at least one occasion mayor of the Staple[76]. The duties of mayor were very extensive: elected probably late in March each year, he was senior Stapler, assisted by a court of assistants. He negotiated with king and council, dealt with disputes among members and with foreign merchants, and organised the accounts and the payment of the garrison in Calais. Much of the year would be spent travelling between Calais and London. He rendered accounts in the June after the end of his period of office.

And it is likely that William Browne served for a time as one of the 28 members of the council of the Staple[77], for from at least 1459 he was embroiled with other Staplers in a protracted dispute. Richard Heyron (or Heron) claimed that in 1459, he was in Calais trying to sell wool which at times he asserted was his own and at other times he said belonged to James earl of Wiltshire, Treasurer of England (1455, 1458-1460). But the wool was seized on the authority of John Proute the then mayor of the Calais Staple and six other staplers, John Walden, John Tate of London and Coventry, Roger Knyght of Lincoln, William Holte and Richard Cely both of London, and William Broun of Staunford. It sounds very much as if this is a formal group which gave support to the mayor of the Staple in the seizure. Heyron sued before the king's council in the dying years of the reign of Henry VI, but the king was deposed before any decision could be reached. How far William Browne was implicated in the later stages of this case which dragged on for a number of years is not known [78], but none of it seems to have been personal to William Browne. Nevertheless, it is a reminder that his

---

[75] CPR 1461-67/351; 1467-76/212-3, 315-6; 1476-85/243; PRO, SC1/57/111

[76] CPR 1476-85/118-9; in 1478 two soldiers retained to go to Calais in the company of William Browne mayor of the Staple were excused from going. There are few surviving records of the Calais Staple, so we do not know which year he was elected mayor, how long he served, or if he served more than once. Sutton *Tates* p 69 says the mayor was chosen from those who had served as lieutenant of the Staple, in which case William Browne also served in that capacity. In 1484, there were three candidates, Hanham *Cely Letters* p 204 (212). See Sutton, Staple pp 135-7.

[77] for the council of the Staple, see Hanham *Cely Letters* pp 147-8 (162)

[78] CPR 1461-67/275-6. Heyron, who was apparently a hatter (PRO C1/26/574), was something of a chancer; he took the case to the courts of the duke of Burgundy, the king of France, even to the papal court, failing on each occasion, and it became mixed up with other accusations; *Select Cases before the King's Council* Selden Soc 35 pp 110-4; Cal Pap Reg 1471-84/227-242, 252-3; see also Hanham *Celys* pp 104-7; *Rot Parl* vi pp 182-3; CPR 1452-61/209-11, 226; 1461-7/275-6; 1446-52/315, 323; Sutton *Tates* p 20; see P M Kendall 1962 *The Yorkist Age* Allen and Unwin pp 320-327 for a lengthy account of the incident. Heyron may have become a retainer of the duke of Clarence and served in Ireland, CPR 1467-77/468, 583, 596

role as Calais Stapler brought Browne into contact with royal officials and courts, with merchants of many cities both in England and on the continent, with the owners of large estates which produced the wool and their officials, with officers of state seeking loans, and with the king himself when he visited Stamford or in London. It gave Browne a good deal of influence and some power. He was up there, among the big men of his day.

Browne and Stamford

And he was big in Stamford; for 'merchants' formed the largest economic interest in the town. We know of at least 16 merchants in Stamford in the fifteenth century[79]; of these, nine served as Aldermen for a total of 24 occasions. In other words, the aldermanry was held by merchants for a quarter of all years during the century. Add to that the mercers and the drapers (see pp 64-66), and for two thirds (65 years) of the century, the cloth and wool trades dominated the town government. But 'merchants' do not appear among the lists of 'pagentes' (see above p 63)[80]. The drapers and mercers were linked together in one listing, while in the second list, drapers, hosiers and tailors were grouped, and mercers went with grocers and haberdashers. There is no mention of merchants.

Since William Browne 'merchant' and his council drew up these two lists, where did the 'merchants' fall? Several merchants were also mercers and some were drapers. But the Browne brothers did not use any other title than merchant; nor did several of their contemporaries. Were they powerful enough to exempt themselves from the urban ritual of the Corpus Christi plays and the regulatory machinery of the borough? What was their designation (and entry fine) on admission to the freedom[81]? Did their admission to the company of the Calais Staplers give them admission to the urban hierarchy?

We do not know how many of these merchants were Calais Staplers. John Colles and John Longe were 'woolmen', as was Thomas Bassett[82]. Thomas Kesteven draper[83], William Adam[84], William Colom[85] and Richard Sapcote were Staplers. It

[79] Apart from John and William Browne, there were Laurence Milton, George Chapman alias Orwyn, Richard Blogwyn, Richard or Robert Cok, John Longe, John Spycer, William Adam, William Colom, John Parker, Richard Sapcote, Christopher Browne, Thomas Bassett and Thomas Kesteven. List drawn from HB; Pardon Rolls; List of Aldermen; PRO, SC1/57/111; E210/2715; CPR 1467 77/212 3, 290 2; etc

[80] Hall Books i fol 2d-3d, pp 6-9; fol 5d-6, pp 13-15

[81] The only Stapler to be admitted under that title was in 1495, Richard Cannell from Louth who became Alderman in the next year; he paid 20s, the highest rate; see Rogers, Parl for his biography. In 1468, Richard Bonner was admitted to the freedom with a 20s entry fine, a sign of a mercer or merchant, HB i fol 11, p 28; he is not otherwise known in the town.

[82] PRO, C258/41/8; CPR 1436-41/113.

[83] CCR 1485-1500/9; CPR 1485-94/335; PRO, SC1/57/111

is possible that a local 'chapter' or syndicate of Staplers was formed similar to the Ipswich group of 1454; for in August 1470, soon after the battle of Loosecoat Field near Stamford, a group of 28 merchants of the Staple headed by William Cawode of Boston took out a general pardon. They included William and John Browne and William Colom of Stamford, Thomas Adam of Langham, William Wareyn (son in law of John Browne), John Kyrton, William Rose and William Trafford, all of Oakham, and merchants from Boston, Peterborough, Leicester (three), Loughborough, Broke in Rutland, Horncastle in Lincolnshire, Melton Mowbray, Market Harborough, and Grantham, and four 'of London' (including Robert and John Tate of Coventry) and two who gave their addresses as Calais. The highly focused nature of the group suggests some kind of regional affiliation[86].

Unfortunately we know little about William Browne's trading activities in his later years, except in London in the 1480s. There were severe disturbances in the Calais market in 1487-8[87], but by then William Browne was almost certainly out of the game. His predominant concerns lay elsewhere – with increasing and managing his estates, with his money-lending, with his town council and his gild activities, with service on local commissions in Stamford and the surrounding counties, and especially with his Hospital. His was a full life right to the end.

---

[84] PRO, E122/73/40; Hanham, *Cely Letters* 5-7, 9, 32, 166; for Thomas Adam Calais Stapler, see *Notes and Queries* 3rd series vol 5 (1864) p 239

[85] CPR 1476-85/266; PRO, C88/157/11; E179/67/12/501

[86] CPR 1467-77/213; is it possible that this group was the council of the Staple which consisted of 28 men? For Cawode, see his will of 1478 in *AASR Wills* pp 180-2 – he lists some of his wool debts

[87] Power 1926 pp 34-35

PART III: CHAPTER 3 MAKING MONEY: FROM MONEY LENDING

He is a marchande of gret powere

‑ ‑ ‑ ‑ ‑ ‑ ‑ ‑ ‑ ‑ ‑ ‑ ‑

Men owe hym mony a pounde[88]

William Browne's trade inevitably involved him in much credit and exchange. It has been suggested that at least 75% of any fifteenth century merchant's transactions would be in one or more forms of credit[89]. And such transactions could be made profitable to his personal interests. There were three areas where such dealings would enable him to make yet more money for his private fortune: the credit involved in his trading, loans to the government, and private money lending.

Trade credit

William Browne bought wool from the producers. In earlier periods, much of this was done on credit[90], but by the fifteenth century, it would seem that payment was made in full or in large part at the time of the purchase or at least on delivery to the wool store. So cash was needed up front. He had to pay the dressers and the packers whom he employed – and the wool packers were an aggressive element in the trade, at times holding the merchants to ransom for higher payments. He had to charter ships and pay to load them. He had to sell the wool in Calais – a complicated business. Payment for the wool was made by foreign merchants in foreign currency and had to be converted into English sterling; some of it was exchanged in Calais or elsewhere but part of it had to be taken to the Calais mint to be turned into English nobles. Then the money had to be got back to England – either in coins, in notes of exchange or in goods. And all this had to be done in an age when, although there was "an increase in the circulation of money", there was a shortage of coinage on the streets, especially in the 1440s and 1450s. And the coinage from time to time became debased, so that even in William Browne's lifetime, new issues of coinages were made several times, for example in 1412, in 1421-2 and 1464-5. It was not until

---

[88] C H Hartshorne (ed) 1829 *Ancient Metrical Tales* London: Pickering p 59

[89] Postan 1973 pp 1-27; C Briggs 2009 *Credit and village society in 14th century England* Oxford University Press; D Keene 2000 Changes in London's economic hinterland as indicated by debt cases in the Court of Common Pleas, in J A Galloway (ed) 2000 *Trade, Urban Hinterlands and Market Integration c1300-1600* London: Institute of Historical Research pp 59-81

[90] Pipewell; see Postan 1973 pp 161-2, 204-212; J Kermode 1994 Medieval indebtedness: the regions versus London, in N Rogers 1994 pp 72-88; Childs 1991.

the last three decades of the century that both trade and money supply to some extent revived[91].

Calais noble of the Annulet issue (1422-c.1430)
(Fitzwilliam Museum, Cambridge)

Much of this involved complicated exchange rates. The control of currency changes switched from time to time between the English merchants of the Staplers and the continental merchants. There were "elaborate calculations and constant disputes" over coinage and exchange rates which a merchant like Browne would have had to negotiate, but which, if managed well, could provide opportunities for profit: like Chaucer's merchant, "Wel koude he in eschaunge sheeldes selle"[92]. Since in this market, Browne would have acted as his own broker and banker, there were opportunities of making a profit from such exchanges; but in other arenas where alien merchants (mainly Italian) acted as bankers, exchange transfers could result in heavy losses.

William Browne then was intimately experienced in the various instruments of credit that were in use in lieu of coinage - bonds, bills of obligations, recognisances, and notes of exchange, all in different currencies. A variety of financial arrangements grew up, especially those developed by alien merchants. Browne would have been involved in complex relationships of trust which could lead to law suits over debt or non-delivery of goods and services. Wool

---

[91] For 'the great bullion famine' 1395-1415, and even lower supplies in the 1440s and 1450s, see Huizinga p 27; Kermode *Merchants* p 304; J Day 1987 The great bullion famine of the fifteenth century, in J Day (ed) 1987 *The Medieval Market Economy* Oxford pp 1-54; Childs 1991 pp 68-71; CLBL, Book L 1461-1509 p 54. Credit shrank in the same period, see Hatcher, Slump p 244; Nightingale 1990; P Spufford 1988 *Money and its uses in Medieval Europe* Cambridge, pp 363-77 and chapter 15; Kermode *Enterprise* pp xi, 6, 68, 72. The need for credit may have contracted as international trade contracted, Nightingale 2010; M Allen 2001 The volume of English currency 1158-1470, *Econ Hist Rev* 2s 54 pp 595-611; M Allen 2011 Silver production and the money supply in England and Wales 1086-c1500 *Econ Hist Rev* 2s 64 pp 114-31; N J Mayhew 2004 Coinage and money in England 1086-c1500, in Wood 2004 pp 72-86; P Nightingale 2004 Money and credit in the economy of late medieval England, in Wood 2004 pp 51-71; R H Britnell 2004 Uses of money in medieval England, in Wood 2004 pp 16-30

[92] Chaucer, *Canterbury Tales* Prologue lines 276-8; for bullion and list of currencies and exchange, Power *Medieval People* p 154.

merchants "might have to wait years for full payment, even if all of their own wool had been sold. Such delay was fatal to the small man, but those with capital behind them could afford to wait for higher prices, secure in the knowledge that the circle of suppliers was growing smaller". "It was the well-capitalized alone who could survive in a market characterized chiefly by large-scale exchanges" [93]. William Browne was among the bigger merchants and could afford to take such action as would enable him to profit from the system.

We have little evidence of such credit transactions in relation to his wool trade. It seems he paid the nuns of St Michael in cash for their wool. We rarely find him suing for debt; the suits to which he was a party tended to be concerned with property rather than the wool trade[94]. But that may simply be a matter of the survival of evidence; for without doubt William Browne and his brother and their factors would have engaged in credit transactions and bills of exchange on a daily basis. Services and goods were provided up front; the cash came in later.

Loans to the government

For this was how the country was run during the fifteenth century. The government took taxes from the country – but to ensure cash flow, it borrowed in advance of these taxes and gave pledges for repayment against future income. At times, the government turned directly to the people for a loan or special gift (an 'aid', a 'benevolence') which are today not always easily distinguishable: "it is often impossible to discover those conjunctions of loans and grants"[95] made to the government (nominally to the king, but for much of the reign of Henry VI, the council, the royal household or the duke of York as Protector wielded the real power in the king's name; Edward IV was different – for much of his reign, he paid close attention to government finances).

The Lancastrian government in the 1440s to the late 1450s was more or less bankrupt and had perforce to turn to loans, voluntary or forced. Indeed, loans

---

[93] Postan 1973 pp 1-27; A Hanham 1973 Foreign Exchange and the English wool merchant in the late fifteenth century, *BIHR* 46 pp 160-75; Lloyd *Wool Trade* p 266; Fairford pp 6-7

[94] A search in PRO, E34 (loans to the crown) and C131 and C241 (statutes staple) revealed no documentation of William Browne's loans. A possible but unlikely reference occurs in BL Harl 773 fol 36d item 134: **obligation of the staple:** WS alias WB nuper of S (Lincs) to Robert Q £20 sterling for merchandise bought in the staple of Westminster; shall pay to Robert or his attorney on showing this writing or to his heirs or executors at Christmas next; and if not done, I agree that the penalty of the statute of staple ordained for the recovery of debts shall be on me, my heirs and executors; dated in dicta stapula tricesimo die Octobris anno R R Henry VI 39: Certified in chancery of the king by Ralph Verney, 13 May 8 Edward IV; Scribatur hoc in dorso oblig' etc [abbreviations as in original. Q would seem to be Quatermain from the context].

[95] Loans p 53; see Gray, Benevolence p 112; Virgoe 1481 p 26; Harriss, Aids p 3; for 1441 loan, see BL, Cotton Cleo FVI fol 235; Browne sued a merchant in Boston for debt.

created one of the few occasions when a medieval king might have face to face discussions with some of his humbler subjects. Much would depend on the persuasiveness of the king's ministers and even on occasion of the king himself: Edward IV in 1473-5, when he asked for a gift from everyone with an income of £40 or more a year, a move which was widely seen as "a new and unheard-of imposition", was said to have "plucked out the feathers of his magpies without making them cry out", and on at least one occasion, to have obtained a loan in return for a kiss[96].

But there were rules governing such advances to the crown. The king had to plead his 'great necessity', mainly because of war but also royal ceremonies and especially marriages. When William Browne started out on his business career, Henry VI was asking for an aid to pay for his wedding to Margaret of Anjou, and in 1444 and again in 1446, he asked for help with his "viage for pees" with France. On the other hand, the people could not excuse themselves except in cases where such a loan or grant would destroy them and make them unable to make future payments[97].

Such advances to the government often took a long time to be repaid. There were different ways of repayment. One way was to obtain tallies (split wooden sticks with notches indicating the debt and ordering a taxation source, especially the customs at the ports, to make payment), but these were often dishonoured and returned to the royal Exchequer to be reissued – sometimes several times; so that some people discounted them, selling them on to a dealer at a lower value. Merchants could obtain a licence to export without paying all or some of the customs duties or with some other privilege. But such licences had their problems, for they might compel merchants to export goods at times when the prices or the supply were not advantageous. There were other kinds of rewards which would be agreed. On several occasions, the king himself pledged royal jewels against such loans[98].

William Browne was involved in government loans in two respects. First, for many years, the government had turned to the towns to help them out financially. As early as 1382, a special council of town representatives had been

---

[96] Pugh, York p 126; Harriss, Aids p 3; Gray, Benevolence pp 91-2; Loans pp 55, 64; Virgoe 1481 pp 26-33, 43

[97] Harriss, Aids pp 3, 16; CPR 1441-6/61-2; PRO, E34/1B contains a fragment of a return of refusals from Lincolnshire in 1436 giving the reasons for refusal; they are all in common form, probably indicating that by now the royal council had agreed a formula which expressed the commonly agreed reasons for inability to help the king.

[98] e.g. CCR 1468-76/287-8 (1053), 341 (1236); 1476-85/326-7 (1104); Steel *Exchequer* pp 220, 221, 238 etc

summoned to make a grant to the government, and later in his reign Richard II again turned to the towns. Some towns copied into their minute books letters which had been sent to them asking for their 'aid', but Stamford has no such record until 1465 when a new Minute Book was started which has survived. But in 1436, while William Browne was Alderman for the first time, the town gave the government of the day £40. Although technically a 'free gift', the government made an assessment of what each town could afford to pay without raising the hackles of jealousy. In the last year or so of his reign (1481), Edward IV made himself unpopular by writing to the towns demanding loans, and Stamford would undoubtedly have received such a demand. William Browne and his brother as leading citizens would have contributed their share to meeting such requests[99].

So William Browne knew about loans to the government from Stamford and perhaps personally. But his main role in this respect was as a Stapler – for the Staplers became the government's bankers after wealthy individuals like Cardinal Beaufort had departed the scene. In the fifteenth century, loans were more often coming from groups, from syndicates, and especially from the company of the Staple as a whole. "One of the few bodies able to raise a large sum at short notice", the company had been occasional lenders to the government during the fourteenth century, but company loans became more frequent and larger during the reign of Henry VI, and this continued under Edward IV. At first to meet crises such as the French attack on the English lands in Gascony in 1441-2 but later to pay more generally for the ongoing war, the merchants of the Staple (William and John Browne among them) lent huge sums to the government. No sooner had one been repaid than another was required of them. And soon it was for more domestic issues: Richard duke of York raised a loan from the Staplers in order to ensure his allies could gain entry to Calais which was being held against them[100].

Some of the Staple loans were very large, such as the 10,000 marks (£6,666 13s 4d) prior to 1435, and again in 1447-8, and the 7000 marks (£4666 13s 4d) prior to 1454[101]; Browne's involvement in these is not known. But there were a

[99] *Rot Parl* iii pp 122-3; Harriss, Aids pp 8, 11; Kermode *Merchants* p 219; POPC iv p 320; Virgoe 1481 pp 30-33, 43. For a loan from the towns in 1496, see H Kleineke 2008 Morton's Fork: Henry VII's 'forced loan' of 1496, *The Ricardian* 13 pp 315-327

[100] POPC v pp 414-8, 201; CPR 1441-6/61-2, 68, 92-3; Harriss, Aids p 4; Loans p 67; Lloyd *Wool Trade* p 275; CPR 1397-99/178-182; Steel *Exchequer* pp 205, 220, 225, 236-7, 265; some loans are not recorded on the Receipt Rolls, Steel *Exchequer* p 266; Haward 1933. Henry VII continued this – see CCR 1485-1500/2-3 (9); CCR 1500-9/250 (655)

[101] Steel *Exchequer* pp 208, 211, 230, 276; Loans p 67; CPR 1429-36/46; *Rot Parl* v p 208; CCR 1454-61/6-16; 1468-76/288 (1054). The first loan from the Staplers was to be repaid from clerical taxation, not wool exports; they are discussed in detail in Harris, Struggle

number of occasions in his early years (1449-1454) when he personally incurred substantial obligations. Indeed, these loans are the first we know of his membership of the Staple, so that it is possible that it was the banking aspect of membership which attracted him as much as the wool trading.

William was involved in four large loans from the Staplers to the government. The first was a total of £10,700 which the Staplers had "lent to the king at divers times" prior to 1447. No purpose is given for these loans[102]. Of this sum, William Browne and his firm consisting of John Browne his brother and William Lewes of Lynn had contributed £625 19s 2d. This was the third highest sum of those listed in the repayment schedules of October 1449 (the higher ones were £832 18s 10d and £639 15s 4d), so William Browne's group was among the highest lenders. Whether William Browne and his partners joined in the initial loan sometime before 1447 or whether they bought into someone else's loan (which was common practice) is not clear.

To get repayment, the firm was allowed to export wool with reduced customs to the value of four annual payments of £156 9s 9½d from Ipswich. William Browne and his partners would need to obtain writs of privy seal (which they did[103]), and the collectors of the customs in the port were to record the exports and report to the Exchequer. Like many other merchants, William's group was able to use three of the four instalments, but the last payment had not been made by 1454; and in that year, they with other Staplers obtained through parliament a renewal of their licence to continue exporting from Ipswich[104].

The second loan was made again some time before 1450, probably 1445-6. The mayor, constables and company of merchants of Staple of Calais had lent £2000 to pay the wages of Henry viscount Bourghchier and Ralph lord Sudeley and others to keep the castle of Calais and also Rysbank in the marches of Calais. A group of nine Ipswich Staplers, including William and John Browne and Richard Sapcote, had become responsible for 400 marks (£266 13s 4d) of this sum. For this, in March 1450, they were granted licences to export wools and fells from Ipswich to the full value of this sum. The other lenders were syndicates of 17 merchants in Boston, 15 merchants in Hull and 12 merchants in London. It is possible that this credit was sold on to London merchants, for the sum seems to have been repaid eventually in London and we do not hear of William Browne's involvement in it again[105].

---

[102] CPR 1446-52/314-6; 1452-61/209; this is unlikely to include the 10,000 marks loaned in December 1447, Steel *Exchequer* p 230

[103] Two of these writs survive as PRO, E122/224/87(1)

[104] *Rot Parl* v p 208; CPR 1446-52/314-5; 1452-61/209; CCR 1454-61/6

[105] CPR 1446-52/323; Haward 1933 pp 303-4. This may be the expedition which the council ordered to go to the marches of Calais in May 1441 and which lasted until 1448, Griffiths *Henry*

The third loan was different. It was part of the triangular warfare that was going on between Henry VI of England and his government, the Dauphin Charles, later king of France, and Philip duke of Burgundy who also ruled Flanders and thus was vital to the interests of the English traders. In a long-drawn-out dispute with Burgundy during which the goods of the Flemish merchants had been seized, the Staple paid on behalf of the English government 4000 marks (£2666.13s 4d) as compensation; this was regarded as a loan to the government. Again, an Ipswich grouping of Staplers (26 of them, headed by William Browne; John Browne is also included) agreed to find a quarter (1000 marks; £666 13s 4d) of this sum[106]; and the king in parliament in June 1451 agreed that this syndicate should be allowed to export wool to the value of 1000 marks. William Browne and his partners (this time John Selby and William Turvey; John Browne is not mentioned) were among those licensed to export wool and fells from Ipswich with reduced custom payments. But they were unable to obtain the whole sum from Ipswich, so the Staplers appealed to the parliament. As a result, in October 1454 many Staplers including William Browne and his partners had their licences renewed by parliament; but this time the Browne firm changed their export town from Ipswich to Boston for the outstanding sum of £49 10s 0½d[107].

The fourth such loan had also been made before June 1451. This time the Staple had lent 1000 marks (£666 13s 4d) for the costs of the royal household. The king had granted to the same syndicate of 26 merchants (again headed by William Browne) a licence to export wool and fells with reduced customs from various ports, but again they had been unable to export enough wool in the specified time to gain the full benefit of the licence. In the 1454 settlement by parliament of the Staplers' claims, William Browne and John Browne on their own obtained a licence for exports to the customs value of £162 10s 9½d, and again they switched the port from Ipswich to Boston. The Sapcote firm was also involved but they remained at Ipswich[108].

The change of pattern is interesting. In the first of these loans (c1447), the Browne firm was working on their own within a very large overall Staple loan to the government; in the second, William Browne and his brother were members of a group of nine Ipswich merchants. In the third and fourth (both c1450-1),

---

VI pp 460-461; Steel *Exchequer* p 225. It is not possible to tie all of these loans against those listed by Steel.

[106] A Hull syndicate found the remaining 3000 marks, CCR 1454-61/15

[107] CPR 1452-61/210-1; CCR 1454-61/13

[108] CPR 1452-61/226; CCR 1454-61/15

William Browne was leading a larger syndicate of 26 merchants[109] based in Ipswich, but by 1454, he had switched some of his exports to Boston.

Whether the loans that William Browne made to the government as part of the Staple Company loans made him a lot of profit is not clear. But four loans amounting to well over £1000 in the first few years of his activity as a Stapler, and the fact that he and his partners were among the largest lenders, speak highly of his affluence and influence so early in his career. However, the difficulties in obtaining repayment may have resulted in a more careful approach to royal loans either on his own, through the town of Stamford or through the company of the Staple. William Browne and his partners obtained measures for repayment in October 1449 when the government was under pressure from the duke of York, in March 1450 when York was abroad in Ireland, and in October 1454 through parliament. This last comprehensive settlement of the outstanding claims of the Staplers may have been due to the fact that the duke of York was temporarily in control of the government; but this does not mean that York exercised patronage over the Staplers. Rather, York was keen to secure the support of the Staplers in his dispute with the garrison at Calais who had not been paid their wages and had seized and sold the Staplers' wools in reprisal, so he needed to placate the aggrieved Staple members, just as they needed him to exert control over the unruly garrison and obtain effective repayments[110].

William Browne then had to negotiate not only with his trading creditors and debtors but also with the political system of the day which was becoming ever more complicated, with an unpredictable and wayward king swayed by favourites, a council of peers trying to ensure sound government, fractious nobles seeking what they believed to be their rightful place in government, all leading eventually to civil war and a change of regime. The new government of Edward IV adopted different approaches but it too sought large loans from the towns and Staplers, which would have faced William Browne with hard decisions. But through it all, he not only made his way but made a fortune. If only we had more surviving records (and we know he did keep careful records), we might be clearer how it was done.

---

[109] It is remarkable that provincial syndicates of Calais Staplers appear to have been of about the same size, 26 in Ipswich, 27 in Hull, 26 in Boston (all 1454) and 28 in the east Midlands in 1470 and 25 in 1472, CCR 1454-61/ 5, 13, 15, 17; CPR 1452-61/211, 226; 1467-77/213, 316. But there were smaller syndicates.

[110] Harriss, Struggle

Private money lending

But we can get one further glimpse of the man and his methods. For William Browne clearly still had surplus cash in hand, in an age when even the nobility found it difficult to find liquid assets. Ready cash to pay servants, hire horses or transport or to buy household provisions was often hard to come by. While servants could be paid by being granted annual pensions from the estates which the lord held and then left to go and collect the money, or by being given offices which they let out to others to perform in return for part of the income, real money was needed for daily purchases and costs. "Something could be done to ease liquidity from year to year by turning surpluses into plate which could be later sold or mortgaged in need, but ... the most usual resort was to borrow"[111]. Short term loans for cash flow, to be set against some form of pledge (land or jewels) were a normal part of everyday life.

This was the age when pawnbrokers emerged as a profession – *montes di pietas*, as they were called. "Money-lending, which had previously been widely dispersed among local people, was now becoming concentrated in the hands of a few wealthy professionals, especially in market towns and cities"[112]. And the rise of the mortgage, like pawn-broking, as a means of raising capital both for current expenditure and investment, was a significant feature of this period. Who better to turn to than rich landlords or merchants of one's acquaintance? William Fermur of Warmington asked his lord of the manor Sir William Stokes to tide him over and pledged his lands against a loan in cash – cash which Stokes kept stored in his local parish church. William Elmes provided the warden of the newly established Browne's Hospital with the sum of £20 in cash for immediate charges, either from his own resources or from the treasury of the gild of All Saints, leading to a disagreement as to whether this were a grant or a loan[113].

Wealthy William Browne of Stamford was well known to many of the nobility who had local connections. So that it is not surprising that we can from time to time catch glimpses of William Browne lending cash against land, pledges and sureties. His will (1489) speaks of his debts, but it appears to be formulaic:

I will that all my dettys which I owe to any person be weele and truly paid. Also I will that every man that sufficiently can prove that I have done any harme or wrongid in any wyse, he he restorid and satisfied as consciens will, though a part of my bequests be lessid and withdrawn.

---

[111] Carpenter, Stonor circle pp 188-9.
[112] Mollat pp 278-280; McIntosh 1986 p 222
[113] PRO, REQ 2/4/246; see Rogers, Fermur; PRO, C1/357/15; see Rogers and Hill, Browne's Hospital

Margaret's will, a few months later, is more detailed, for William Browne left her in charge of his affairs:

> *Item I wil that a pair of bayns of silver and gilt laied to myne husband to be restored to the Awners [owners], the money paied ageyn. Item I wil that vj peces of silver with a coveryng to the same and a gardevian pleggid to myne housband be restorid to the Awner, the money paied agein. And alle this plate pleged with alle other plegges to be in the keping of my brother maister Thomas Stok. Item I wil that a pyve [pyx] in the Almonshous having a coveryng to the same being in my Cuppebord in the parlour which was layed to wedde [i.e. pledge] to my housband for a certeyn money, Which Wed I wil that it be in the keping of my said brother, he to Restore it to the Awner, the money paied agayn.*

She thus passed the securities left with William Browne for loans to her brother and executor Thomas Stokes. And some of the same pledges turn up again in his will six years later, in part echoing the wording of her will:

> *Item I will that all pleggs and weddys which my brother William Brown and my sustre hys wif lent mony upon be restored to the owners, the mony that they hath fore paid that is to say, a paire of basyns gilt plegged by lord Souche lying for xx^{li} iiijs as appereth by my brothers own hand in his rede boke, vj pecys of silver with a covering plegges for viij ^{li} by Stones of Barnak. Item a pix of silver being in the almes house with a covering[114], a crosse in the top plegged by Vincent of Barnake for xxvjs viijd. Item a womans girdill gilt plegged by a woman of Spalding called [space] for xiijs iiijd. Item a standing pece of the old ffacion [fashion] plegged by Dalalaund for lxvjs viijd as it appereth by my brothers Browns boke.*

Here we see a fully fledged business with details contained in a 'red book' in his own handwriting. William Browne kept careful records.

And Margaret joined him in this business, as Thomas Stokes recognised – "which my brother William Brown and my sustre hys wif lent mony upon". This is confirmed by the will of Margaret:

> *Item I wil that my said brother Restore a Ringe to the son of William Brooke pleggid to me by his fader nowe deceassid, And if he cannot be founde thenne to yeve to prestis and poor people iijs iiijd to pray for the soule of the dede for a Recompense of the overpluse of the Wedde[115].*

The securities are mainly silver plate and jewellery – basins, unspecified silver, a pyx (which the Brownes felt free to use in their almshouse) and an old-fashioned

---

[114] this is the pyx mentioned in the will of Margaret Browne
[115] Rogers, Wills

standing piece which Stokes suggested should be melted down; a woman's girdle (for many women her most precious possession[116]) for 13s 4d – Stokes could not remember her name but she came from Spalding. Lord Zouche was a client, as were two men from Barnack, one of them a tenant of Browne. The de la Laund family who gave the old-fashioned silver cup as a pledge later gave land to the Hospital in return for being enrolled in the obit list. The sums varied – from 13s 4d to £20 4s 0d.

Such debts were common among fifteenth century merchants as well as the nobility. Robert Toppes of Norwich died with a long list of outstanding debts due to him[117], as did many other merchants of the day. Stamford would have been well acquainted with debts, for the time at which credit of all kinds was normally settled was at the great fairs like Stamford's[118]. Recognisances for debt were registered in the borough Hall Book, and suits about debt or about the refusal of holders of pledges and obligations to return them after the loan had allegedly been repaid are frequently recorded. Books listing outstanding debts are mentioned in other wills, as are pledges of plate and other items, even books[119].

St Katherine's gild

There is one other piece of evidence which is suggestive, William Browne's activities in relation to the gild of St Katherine in Stamford. There is a surviving Act Book of this gild from 1480 to 1534. The gild of St Katherine met in the chamber over the porch of the parish church of St Paul in Eastgate. Its origins are unknown, but it was in existence early in the fifteenth century[120]. But by 1480, it was in dire straits with only thirteen surviving members. It was refloated by William Browne its Alderman.

The relaunch in 1480 included the distribution of gild stock amounting to £10 among the surviving thirteen members of the gild except the anchoress. Under this arrangement, each stockholder paid an annual "increment" on the money they held, amounting to 7½% p.a.. Although this rate seems to be higher than the norm at the time[121], it is important to stress that this was not a high social class gild; it was – at least while William Browne was its Alderman – a town gild

---

[116] J Loengard 2008 'Which may be said to be her own': widows and goods in late medieval England, in Kowaleski and Goldberg 2008 p 176

[117] See Toppes. For lord Latimer, see Exeter-NRA 92/2. Lord Scrope in his will in February 1488 recorded that he owed William Browne mercer 50 marks, but this is likely to be the William Browne of London; CCR 1485-1500/88-9 (323)

[118] Obligations to repay at Stamford fair occur frequently on the Close Rolls

[119] for wills, see *AASR* Wills pp 179, 188, 189; Exeter-NRA 92/2.

[120] GCC 266/670; Rogers, *Gild Book*

[121] The rate in 1433-4 was about 5%, *Loans* p 62.

with a small number of local men and women of all classes among its members (see below p 225). In 1480, new members joined the gild and after a short gap some further stock was distributed to some of these members at the same increment. A careful record was made of all these transactions.

This lasted while William Browne was gild Alderman. He was personally involved as one of the gild members, holding 13s 4d (his sister-in-law Dame Agnes Broune widow of his brother John held 20s of this stock); it was clearly his initiative. There was reluctance on the part of some members – John Capron clerk and John Basse paid no increment all the time they held the sums against their names. This was clearly not from reasons of poverty, at least in the case of Basse, for he was exporting and importing cloth and wine through Lynn between 1455 and 1467[122]. And this reluctance must have become stronger; for the moment William Browne died, the payment of most annual 'increments' ceased, and those payments which continued were described as *ex devocione*, a 'gratuity', and they soon died out altogether.

The putting out of stock is of course known for gilds in other towns. But the insistence with which William Browne pursued this procedure in the case of the gild of St Katherine, the comprehensive nature of the distribution of the stock (to all existing members), and the regularity of the payments (annually at $7\frac{1}{2}\%$) as well as the immediate cessation of such payments on his death indicates that he saw the gild as part of an approach to money-making. The gild accumulated money out of the entry fees of new members and the annual payments by the gild members of 'waxshot' (the pennies collected at meetings to help maintain the gild lights), and this may have been a useful source for some local tradesmen to obtain scarce small change, just as in some countries beggars provide local shopkeepers with small coinage. For the gilds would have been one of the few centres of urban life where small coinage would be held in large quantities; each member paid 2d (a half groat) or 4d (a groat) on arrival at each gild meeting, and this was collected assiduously. The "lack of half pennies and silver farthings" was noted by parliament in 1445[123].

The accumulation of large numbers of small coins is revealed by the 'Stamford hoard' discovered in St George's churchyard in October 1866. This consisted of over 3000 coins. A small number dated back to the reigns of Edward III (1351-60 and 1360-69), Richard II and Henry IV; but the majority were from the reigns of Henry V and Henry VI, together with a significant number from the first

---

[122] PRO E122/96/37; E122/97/8
[123] *Rot Parl* v pp 108-9: "the poor common retailers of victuals and other necessities for lack of such coins ... often are unable to sell their victuals and items". See Fairford pp 6-7

years of the reign of Edward IV[124]. Here is a working collection of coins used in Stamford in the 1460s worth more than £50, a sizable sum even for William Browne to have had about his person, suggesting that it may have been some corporate body which had and hid these coins in the 1460s.

But the use of the gild's small change by traders cannot account for all the gild stock allocated to members such as Dame Agnes Browne. William Browne's treatment of the stock of the gild of St Katherine reflects, I think, his attitudes towards money lending. Money was meant to make more money; the gild stock must be put to work. Which raises the arguments about the medieval church's rules which forbad usury. Although royal loans, being obligatory, were regarded as different from usurious loans, there was still an official embargo on loans at interest[125]. However, whatever the legal situation, for the merchant engaged in long distance trade, lending and seeking rewards of some kind for such loans must have been commonplace and clearly open. Taking pledges of lands or plate would help – William Browne could charge a higher price for its return than he gave against its pledge. But a standard annual increment of 7½% was transparent and in an ecclesiastical context. Perhaps the *ex devocione* recorded was a sop to the religious lobby to assure them that this was not interest; but for William Browne, it can be argued that such devices would have sounded hollow. Good money needs a good increment if profits were to be made.

---

[124] It included both heavy and light coinage of Edward IV; most were from the London mint but some were from the Calais mint. See F. A. Walters, The Stamford find and supplementary notes on the coinage of Henry VI, *Numismatic Chronicle* vol. 11 (1911), pp. 153-175; J D A. Thompson 1956 *Inventory of British Coin Hoards 600-1500* London p 128. In another instance, a cash sum of £7 4s 4d was received in a mixture of "King Harry pence" (£1.11s), gold (£5) and groats and 2d pieces (13s 4d), *Stonor Letters* i 40; 15s was paid out in groats, £4 7s 6d in pence and twopence coins.

[125] Harriss, *Aids* pp 1-3. Robert B. Ekelund, Jr., Robert F. Hebert and Robert D. Tollison 1989 An Economic Model of the Medieval Church: Usury as a Form of Rent Seeking, *Journal of Law, Economics, and Organization* 5 2 pp. 307-331; Gwen Seabourne 1998 Controlling Commercial Morality in Late Medieval London: the usury trials of 1421, *Journal of Legal History* 192 pp. 116-142; Jaume Aurell 2001, Merchants' attitudes to work in the Barcelona of the later Middle Ages: organisation of working space, distribution of time and scope of investments *JMH* 27 3 pp 197-218

PART III: CHAPTER 4 MAKING MONEY: FROM PROPERTY

"...[merchants] do attain to great wealth and riches, which for the most part they do employ in purchasing land..."[126]

Like other merchants of his day, "a good portion of [William Browne's] mercantile profit ended up in real estate" – and in the process, he made another fortune. Rents formed an increasing part of his income; and if the profits of agriculture and urban rents fell during the century (which seems unlikely in Stamford), the loss could be made up by acquiring more property.[127] An active land market with some engrossment (the amalgamation of smaller properties into larger holdings) was a feature of the period here as elsewhere.

The evidence of title deeds

Most of the evidence we have for William Browne's acquisitions comes from surviving title deeds[128]. William Browne lived in an age when a number of changes were occurring in the literacy practices of the day. For one thing, the document recording the actual transfer of 'seisin' (possession) of property, which occurred sometimes as much as six years prior to the document, was coming to be seen more and more as coincidental with the transfer itself. Secondly, there was concern to ensure that all previous transactions were recorded and preserved. Thus transfers of property were usually accompanied by quantities of earlier deeds, and such documents were deposited in safe places such as (in Stamford) the nunnery of St Michael. Registration of deeds in the lord's court in Stamford castle for a fee occurred from time to time[129]. Recovery of "evidences" was a major cause of litigation in this period: Robert Hans was sued for detaining documents, John son of Nicholas Billesdon and John Busshe both sued for documents. John Richemounte claimed that all the evidences, charters, 'escriptes,

---

[126] Hooker, cited in Horrox, Gentry p 25

[127] Kermode, Oligarchies p 100; J Oldland 2010 Allocation of merchant capital in early Tudor London *Econ Hist Rev* 2s 63 p 1058; Butcher, Rent; Hatcher, Slump p 247; Dyer *Standards* p 195 says that "Merchant wealth declined in the middle of the fifteenth century as a pronounced overseas trading depression coincided with a decline in urban rents"; he follows Hilton, Urban property pp 100-1: "it would not seem that the net income from [urban] property would be very important to the individuals concerned .. one gets little evidence that any of them could have relied on their urban property holdings to give them an adequate income". But the evidence we have suggests this was not true for William Browne.

[128] See Rogers, Archives; and Rogers *Deeds*

[129] See M T Clanchy 1993 *From Memory to Written Record: England 1066-1307* Blackwell; NRS 2 *Pytcheley* p 33; PRO, C1/16/387; C1/24/90; C1/53/321; C1/58/328; C1/76/39; CAD iii pp 463, 502; Peck xiv 15-16; MCO 44.

scrows' and muniments relating to three tenements and land in Stamford "be commen unto the hands of oon John Elmes of Lilford, Northants, gent and lernyd in your Lawes. The nombre wherof he knowyth not or whether they be inclosed in bagge, box or chest lokked or sealed"; he wanted them back. Margaret Spenser, widow of a notary, in her long will of 1508, gave detailed instructions to her elder son about making releases to her younger son for the property which came to the latter, and ensuring that disputes over the wording of the title deeds should be settled by competent lawyers[130].

William Browne was on occasion engaged in such controversies. When Richard Cok sold him the Aungel in the parish of St Mary at the bridge and a messuage in Cornstall, Browne claimed that Cok had delivered all the deeds and evidences except the deed of sale. And William and Margaret his wife, executrix of Thomas Philipp of Stamford, sued Thomas Wille for an obligation which Wille was still detaining[131].

It is clear that, when he acquired any property, William insisted on obtaining the deeds which belonged to that property. Some 300 deeds from his collection survive, and estimates put the total at in excess of 2000. He kept them carefully filed and sorted; those which survive carry markings which indicate some kind of arrangement - it would be nice to think that some of these markings were made by William Browne in his own handwriting. When he split his estates between his Hospital and his daughter Elizabeth, he gave each of them the deeds relating to their properties.

Unfortunately, as we have seen (above p 22) later antiquarians plundered the Hospital deeds. William Forster, warden of Browne's Hospital, took all the deeds relating to properties in the town, and Peck acquired and published notes of some of these deeds up to 1461 in his book *Antiquarian Annals of Stanford* in 1727, but the deeds have vanished; there are many gaps and errors in the notes, and everything after the year 1461 has been lost[132].What Peck has preserved is useful and we should be grateful to him for this; but I must confess I wish Forster and Peck had left them alone, for most of the rest of the Hospital deeds have survived, and although some have become less legible over the intervening years, almost all are usable. Thus original deeds survive for less than a quarter of the properties Browne held at his death - all the Hospital estates outside of Stamford, as well as some notes on the Hospital urban properties up to 1461. A

---

[130] PRO, C1/111/37; C1/123/47; C1/189/8; REQ 2/4/77; PROB 11/16/118
[131] PRO, C1/26/443; C1/60/126
[132] Peck Preface p x. See Peck's letter printed in Rogers, Archives p 6. For Foster's contributions to the history of Stamford, see Peck Appendix.

few deeds for the properties which passed to Elizabeth Elmes, William's daughter, can also be traced[133].

These deeds can be supplemented with information from other sources, especially inquisitions post mortem and some smaller collections of deeds in the possession of other archives. And from all of this, we can see something of the estate that William Browne built up and was still building until just before his death in 1489[134].

We cannot do this for his brother John. His will has not turned up, nor is there any inquisition post mortem for him; and the title deeds he acquired would have passed down that branch of the family. He joined his brother in some transactions, but we rarely see him acting on his own. We know he purchased one property in Stamford, but certainly there were others. He held and probably lived in the house next door to the vicarage of All Saints[135], but there is as yet no sign of any property outside of Stamford.

William Browne and the land market

The title deeds reveal William and John acting in three capacities – as witness, as feoffee, and as party to some transaction – buying, selling, leasing etc.

Witnesses: As guarantors of the transaction, witnesses could be called upon to attest the validity of the title in court[136]. An example of the kind of dispute which could normally only be settled by witnesses is given by Peck. In 1442, John Smyth vicar of Wodestoke "stirred as he asserteth by his own conscience", confessed that he had sold a messuage in Stamford Baron to William Lewys of Oakham but that he (John Smyth) had no title to that property; it belonged to the occupier William Ledys of Stamford, who was now suing William Lewys, since, as Smyth agreed, "the charter and letter of attorney which he contrived and sealed with his own hand to be altogether unjust and by law invalid". William Browne would have been concerned, for only in the previous year he

---

[133] In Devon Record Office, Simcoe collection. There is in the Hospital archive one precious document which lists the Stamford property given by William Browne to his Hospital which escaped Forster's notice: it has been affected by damp but fortunately a full and accurate transcript of it was made in the nineteenth century and published in Wright's *Domus Dei* and is in the *Deeds* volume. The description of this document in the LAO list of Browne's Hospital Archives is incomplete and inaccurate.

[134] Especially the Stamford deeds in Magdalen College, Oxford. See Rogers *Deeds*

[135] PRO CP25/1/293/72/364; HB i fol 19d, pp 52-3

[136] Carrel 2000 p 283

had bought from the same John Smyth clerk, then priest of Burghley, a tenement in Stamford Baron. As we have seen, Lewys was a close family friend[137].

It is of course possible that this accusation and confession were part of a fictitious law suit designed to record a legitimate transaction – for such practices were common at the time. But the Smyth case does not read like a fictitious law suit; it sounds as if Ledys was able to produce witnesses that the property had been and remained his.

Witnesses then were important. They often included people who might at a later stage wish to make some kind of claim against the property, but normally they were relatives, friends or neighbours of one or other party to the transaction or they were local officials.

William Browne very rarely stood as witness – and that almost only in his early years (1443-1454). In 1443, he was a witness for the nuns of St Michael, and two years later for the Burle family of Burghley by Stamford; twice (1452, 1454) he was witness for Robert Browne, probably a relation. But other than that, it was as Alderman of the borough that he witnessed other people's transactions, and that relatively rarely[138].

Trusteeships: He was trustee for other people only marginally more often. Feoffeeships were used to transfer property to particular persons for particular purposes, especially to fulfil the provisions of the owner's will or to establish family trusts, so that those agreeing to undertake this often onerous task were invited because of their nearness in relationship or because of their eminence. We have seen how William acted for the Storeton family from the 1430s to the 1479s. In 1441, he acted as trustee for a neighbour in a transfer of what was until very recently the Half Moon inn on the corner of Star Lane and St Paul's Street; and he and John were feoffees for the Browe family in Rutland in 1450. Towards the end of his life, 1485, he was trustee for a Lincolnshire family, which included a draper of London, in two Lincolnshire estates, Hungerton and Wyville[139]. But records of such transactions will not normally appear in the family papers of the trustee but of the main family involved; so we will never know all the times Browne acted in such a capacity.

---

[137] Peck xiv 14-17; Simcoe 1038 M/T/9/2; see above pp 56. Smyth seems to have moved from Burghley to Woodstock in 1442, which may have occasioned the sale
[138] PRO, E315/42/148; Stamford Borough records, TH13/1/4; MCO 18, 38; Harvard Deed 343
[139] MCO 2, 10, 12, 16, 53; LAO Stamford parish records PG1/6, 7; ROLLR DE 1431/274; LAO 1 PG 1/43; see pp 57-8 for Storeton

William Browne and John Chevercourt

Acting as trustee could involve risk as well as opportunities for profit[140]. We can see this in a series of incidents which involved William Browne acting for John Chevercourt when the latter tried to raise money by disposing of property in the town. Chevercourt was a Kesteven gentleman who served on a number of commissions in that county; clerk of the peace in Kesteven 1428-1446, feoffee in Swinstead (Lincolnshire) 1425-1455 (a manor that came to Browne), he took his oath among the gentry of Kesteven in 1434. As John Chevercourt of Kesteven and Stamford, he was surety for the abbot of Bourne (1432), Sir Robert Roos sheriff of Lincolnshire, Sir Ralph Rocheford and others. He was granted the wardship of the Browne family friend, the young William Fairfax esquire of Deeping Gate, in 1435. His interests in Stamford were substantial. He farmed the Southorp lands in Stamford in the 1434, 1453 and 1464; in 1436, he was trustee for the gild of Corpus Christi in Stamford, and he held property in the town and in Stamford Baron. As John Chevercourt of Stamford, he received a pardon in 1452. His relations with the Browne family were not always hostile. He appointed Ralph lord Cromwell and John Stokke of Warmington, William Browne's father-in-law, as his feoffees some time before 1455[141].

William Browne found himself involved in two separate and long-running disputes in relation to Chevercourt. One came to the surface after the death of Chevercourt (about 1464). Browne asserted that Chevercourt had enfeoffed him and other trustees (all of whom were by that time dead) with property in Stamford (two houses in St George's parish, 9 acres of land and 3 gardens) to pass it on to Chevercourt's nominees. However, Chevercourt had been sentenced in the King's Bench to pay £14 13s 4d to a London merchant. He seems to have got into a panic about this sum. First, he made arrangements for John Wake of Northants to pay the fine and take all the property; but Wake did not pay. Then Chevercourt split the property into three and sold each part separately, aiming to use the money to pay the fine. According to Browne, he gave contradictory instructions to Browne to pass on the property to different persons. But Browne sat tight, so that all four sued for the property or parts of it. Browne agreed that Chevercourt had enfeoffed him with that and other property to perform Chevercourt's will, "but what will of John Chevercourt it is unknowen to the said William". He also pointed out that there were now four bills against him, and asked all parties to "enterplede upon on[e] of the said billes

---

[140] See for example, PRO, C1/17/27
[141] CPR 1429-36/382; CFR 1430-7/87, 198-9, 249, 265, 318; 1452-61/28; Rogers, Electors p 51; Rogers, Fairfax: PRO, E179/136/198; E179/276/44. For Southorp lands, see above, pp 112-3; PRO, C67/40; 1461-71/124; CCR 1454-61/35; PRO, CP25/1/145/160/33; see SC6/1260/18; C1/24/90

and the verrey true wille and entent of the said John Chevercourt". He "at all tymes shall bee redy for to [do] therin as lawe and concience will require and as the seid Court hym shall award or deeme ... [he] praith to be dismyssyd oute of the said Courte and for the premissez with his reasonable costez and damages to hym awarded for his wrongfull vexacion in that behalve according to the statute in suche case provided and ordeyned". How the matter ended we do not know but it seems to have dragged on for some time with counter-responses. Consultation took place between the plaintiffs, for the wording of the pleas was much the same, and the pledges provided were the same Londoners in several cases[142].

An earlier case involving Chevercourt concerned property which William Browne acquired for himself, and on this occasion William Browne sued Chevercourt. Thomas Basset[143] wool merchant of Stamford enfeoffed his property in Stamford for his will, asking the trustees to sell the property; Chevercourt was one of the feoffees. William Browne claimed that he had bought from Basset's executors the Swan in Stamford Baron and a messuage in the parish of St Michael the Greater; Chevercourt made a quitclaim to Browne in 1455. The two sets of parties, Basset's feoffees and Basset's executors, disagreed. It was perhaps to counter the opposition of the feoffees that William Browne enfeoffed these two messuages onto Ralph lord Cromwell, John Stokke esquire (William Browne's father-in-law) and Richard Lee wright of Stamford, a former

---

[142] PRO, C1/48/333-340: John Wake esquire of Northants sued for all the property which he claimed he had bought from John Chevercourt for cash, but William Browne refused to release the properties. William Wode claimed he had bought the land and gardens (not the two houses) from Chevercourt for money. The Alderman and gild of Corpus Christi and St Mary in Stamford claimed that Chevercourt had enfeoffed the house on the south side of the church to Browne ("now liffing") and others ("nowe dede"), and had ordered Browne to sell it to pay a debt of £26 which Chevercourt owed to the gild "as for duyte perteyning to them by reason of the seyd Guyld". But (said the gild) Chevercourt had also told John Wake that he could have that property if Wake would pay to John Godyn of London the sum of £14 13s 4d which had been imposed on Chevercourt by the King's Bench. The gild claimed that Wake did not pay Godyn but that Chevercourt paid Godyn in cash, and they therefore asked the court to force William Browne to sell the property and give the proceeds to the gild. John Nele's suit concerned a property north of the church. He said there were many communications between Chevercourt and William Browne to the effect that Wake should have this property if Wake paid Godyn the fine but if Wake did not do this, Browne should hand the property to other persons named by Chevercourt. Nele too claimed that Wake did not pay the fine, but that Chevercourt paid it. Chevercourt then sold this part of the property to Nele for "a certeyne summe of money byforhand paid". The same sureties acted for three of the parties, Henry Toky of London gent and John Barton of Stamford yeoman; Wake used John Broune and John Yerburgh, both of London gents
[143] for Bassett wollman, see PRO, C258/41/8; BL Harl 773 fol 39, 43d; CPR 1454-61/35; he was chief steward of the property of John de Veer earl of Oxford, and a tenant of Browne in N Luffenham, Bodl, Rawl B352; parishioner of St Mary's church, Leche accounts; feoffee with Alice his wife for Chevercourt, CPR 1436-41/113, 447; Exeter-NRA 8/56, 61

Alderman of the town, and for greater security he had this enfeoffment enrolled in chancery. William Browne asked the Basset feoffees to release the two properties to Cromwell and the other feoffees, and they all did except Chevercourt. So Browne sued Chevercourt.

Chevercourt responded that, under Basset's will, Basset's widow held these two messuages for her life, after which they were to go to John Merchaunt and William Palfrey of Stamford for the sum of £100; £49 had been paid, the rest would be spent to pay for a chantry priest for the Basset family. John Brygge, as executor, asked Chevercourt and the other co-feoffees to confirm this sale to Merchaunt and Palfrey. But Brygge "died sodeynly" and, Chevercourt alleged, the said William Browne "anone forthwith the same night bi torche light toke away all the myniments and evidences" concerning the said messuages and other property, and so against all faith and custom William Browne "ocupieth the said two messuages and kepith" the evidences, contrary to the will and sale of the reversion.

William Browne responded that no such will had been declared at the time of the feoffment and livery of seisin of the two messuages by Basset to his feoffees (including Chevercourt). There was no statement about the sale of the two messuages to Merchaunt and Palfrey; it was (he said) to the use of the gild of Corpus Christi in Stamford, "to which bargain and sale the brethren of the fraternity disagreed". Merchaunt and Palfrey did not pay £49 or any other sum; Brygge never charged Chevercourt to grant the reversion to Merchaunt and Palfrey. Rather Brygge (who was both feoffee and executor) sold the two messuages to William Browne; the other feoffees agreed, as is shown by their releases to Browne's feoffees. Browne took away "no manner muniments or evidences, nor the will of Thomas Basset". Browne is ready to prove all of this. To which Chevercourt replied "that the matiers specified in his seid answers been true like as he hath surmytted by his seid answers wych maters he is redy to verifye and prove true"[144].

Chevercourt made a quitclaim to Browne in 1455 and the Swan became part of the endowment of the Elmes family[145]. But the problem with feoffees was that the system could lead to uncertainty; there are occasions where feoffees entered an estate after the death of the owner, only to have their title challenged and for each of them to be accused of forcible entry.

---

[144] PRO, CP25/2/145/30; C1/24/90; CCR 1454-61/35
[145] PRO, C1/629/3, 6

William Browne's own trustees

In view of such incidents, William Browne chose his own feoffees carefully. In 1443 and again in 1454 when he was engaged in the Chevercourt dispute, he turned to Ralph lord Cromwell, sometime lord treasurer of England. Browne's links with Cromwell probably came from his father, for John Browne senior had been feoffee with Cromwell for the eminent Lincolnshire family of Mallory[146]. Cromwell had interests in Stamford, in part acquired from the earl of Suffolk's estate and apparently tied to Collyweston nearby which Cromwell bought in 1441. He is alleged to have founded a hospital in Stamford (St Helen's), and it is possible that for a time he acted as York's steward in the town, as his heir and successor Humphrey Bourghchier lord Cromwell did. But along with Cromwell, the other feoffees were Thomas Palmer, William Armeston, a slater or tiler of Stamford, and Browne's father-in-law John Stokke esquire of Warmington. William Browne did not set out to maintain social distinctions.

Browne used a number of local merchants as trustees in his transactions: William Storeton baker, Henry Cok stainer, one of William Browne's circle and a bailiff for the duke of York and for other estates in the town, Laurence Milton merchant, Thomas Kesteven draper and Calais stapler, William Colom mercer and Calais Stapler, and John Gregory of Stamford mercer, friend of William Browne's friends, the Fairfax family at Deeping Gate. Richard Lee wright councillor was used in 1445 and 1455 as well as in the Chevercourt dispute[147]. All were Aldermen of the town except Colom who was a councillor.

But as time went on, Browne's feoffees came mainly from two groups. One was family - his own and especially his wife's family, the Stokes of Warmington, Northants. John Browne his brother acted as feoffee for William from 1457 until his death in 1476[148]. Margaret's oldest brother William Stokes was used from time to time, but more frequently was her other brother Thomas Stokes clerk. He became executor for Margaret's will and the patron of Browne's Hospital after William Browne's death and drew up the statutes of the Hospital. From 1473, William Browne's son-in-law John Elmes merchant of the staple was a feoffee. Some of Margaret's other relatives, the Fazakerley family, also acted as feoffee for William Browne.

But the other group is also significant – secular clergy, especially parish clergy. Thomas Stokes was vicar of All Saints in the Market, Stamford, and rector of

---

[146] LAO, Stamford parish records PG/1/43; CCR 1454-61/35
[147] Simcoe 1038 M/T/13/6, 7, 122 ; LAO, BHS 7/9/115; CPR 1461-67/351; 1476-85/266; Rogers, Fairfax; Harvard Deed 343; CCR 1454-61/35; PRO, C1/24/90
[148] Rogers, Stokes

Easton on the Hill; he combined both categories. John Brampton, William Halle and Richard Halle were among the clerics who served William Browne as trustees[149]. Successive vicars of William Browne's church of All Saints in the Market, from John Hallyday who acted as attorney to deliver seisin of the family wool hall to William Browne from John Browne the father in 1433, to Henry Wykes who outlived William Browne, frequently acted as trustees, which makes one wonder if William Browne had a hand in selecting the holder of that benefice. In 1488 on his death bed, when William Browne established feoffees for his Hospital estates, he chose secular clergy and local merchants[150].

Acquiring property: The main purpose of all this activity was to acquire property – houses, shops and land in Stamford, manors and farms in the rural area around Stamford. I do not think this was intended to extend "urban control over rural landed property"[151], although it had that effect. But simply to say that William Browne invested his profits in landed estate is to paint only part of the picture.

One major concern which wealthy merchants had at that time was where to place their surplus cash so as to be ready at call. As we have seen (above p 151), jewels and plate were the obvious way, and I have no doubt that William Browne had such items in his strong room; Margaret Browne's will seems to indicate this. But there are few signs of this, for the Hospital was not generously endowed with such items. Another way of ensuring that cash could be found at relatively short notice was to acquire land and tenements, and to sell them or use them to raise loans as needed. Property, as one "element in a complex arrangement of cash, credit and investment", gave merchants "security to offer their creditors, increased their social status, and allowed them to provide for their wives and children and their own old age"[152]. The example of John Chevercourt reveals how property could be used to raise cash as needed.

The fact that merchants held property as security probably accounts for the fact that many of William Browne's acquisitions came from fellow merchants or from persons who seem to have required funds at certain times. Other people's

---

[149] One John Brampton sued John Browne father of William for assault some time between 1404 and 1426, PRO, C1/6/155; PRO, CP25/1/293/72/361; Hawlle was a feoffee of Browne, Stamford Borough records, TH13/1/4; MCO 18; Peck xiv 38; CPR 1452-61/210-12; CCR 1454-61/6, 14-15

[150] Peck xiv 12, 43; CPR 1485-94/294; CCR 1485-1500/121 (423); Simcoe 1038 M/T/13/6; PRO, CP25/1/294/79/37; CIPM Henry VII i 1485-96 p 230 (551); iii 1504-9 pp 508-9 (992); LAO, BHS 7/12/24. One name among this list is John Lylleford clerk used in Stretton in 1466, LAO, BHS 7/8/14; the other feoffees were John Bone merchant of Stamford, Mr Richard Halle clerk, Mr Thomas Stokkys clerk

[151] Dyer et al *Hilton* p 168

[152] Kermode *Merchants* pp 288-9; Nightingale 1990 p 569; see Postan, Credit

necessities were his opportunity. Land in Stretton was acquired from John Clipsham merchant. Property in Stamford came from Thomas Basset merchant and Richard Cok merchant, from William Dykeman mercer, William Storeton baker and William Hykeham baker. The manors of North Witham and Swayfield came from the Misterton family, formerly stewards to Ralph lord Cromwell; Browne advanced money to these when they needed it, perhaps by way of mortgage, and in return obtain some of their property – perhaps on occasion, like Cromwell, Sir William Stokes and others, taking advantage of the dependency of the mortgagor. With one exception, we do not know of the property which he himself sold, for little evidence of such sales survives; but in 1480, he sold half an acre in Pilsgate[153].

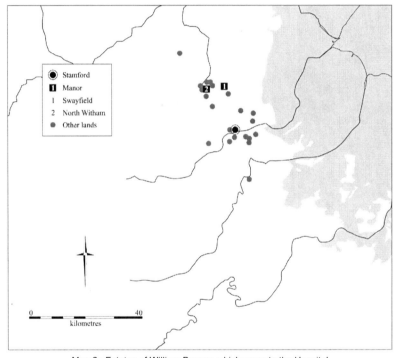

Map 6a Estates of William Browne which came to the Hospital

---

[153] BL Harl 773 fol 123; for mortgage abuses, see S J Payling 1995 A disputed mortgage, Ralph lord Cromwell, Sir John Gra and the manor of Multon Hall, in Archer and Walker 1995 pp 117-136; Rogers, Fermur. Burghley MSS MB8/65

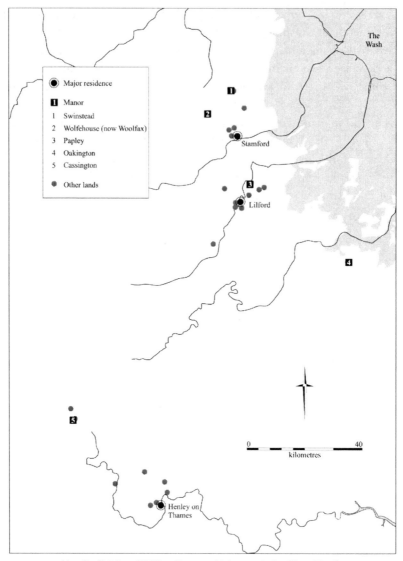

Major residence

■ Manor
1 Swinstead
2 Wolfehouse (now Woolfax)
3 Papley
4 Oakington
5 Cassington

● Other lands

The Wash

Stamford

Lilford

Henley on Thames

0 ———— 40
kilometres

Map 6b: Estates of William Browne which came to the Elmes' family
(the map also shows the estates of the Elmes family in Henley and Oxfordshire)

He started by taking over the woolshop and other premises in the town from his father, but we do not know for sure what William and his brother John acquired in this way. He also inherited some land outside Stamford from his father who had interests in Barholm and Wilsthorp (Lincs) and Marholm (perhaps from his mother), Warmington (Northants) and perhaps Elton (Hunts), to judge by his will. Warmington was clearly an important centre for him; not only did his father have interests there before he was born, but his wife came from there. The nuns of St Michael held a good deal of property in the parish, and some of Browne's closest associates such as Richard Sapcote had possessions there[154].

From this base, he built up his estate. The surviving deeds suggest that he first bought property around the perimeter of the town. At the time he took over the business, he bought the house next door to his own for his father and mother to live in. In 1437[155], he acquired property in Scotgate, in 1441 in Stamford Baron, and in 1447 in Bradcroft, all in the suburbs, while in 1443 he obtained two properties in the centre of the town (the parishes of All Saints in the Market and St Michael the Greater). He does not seem to have started his rural purchases until 1454, and for a short time he kept both town and country acquisitions going. Between 1467 and 1477, he bought the Bell on the west side of St Mary's Hill, and he acquired two more urban properties in 1478[156].

The larger acquisitions came mainly later in life. The manor of Papley, Northants was added by purchase to the lands which he already held in Warmington in 1456 and extended in 1457 for £40[157]. The acquisition of the manor of Lilford in Northants and Oakington, Cambridgeshire, is particularly revealing. Despite the execution in March 1470 of both Richard lord Welles and his son Sir Robert for their part in the Lincolnshire Rising, Richard's daughter Jane and her husband Sir Richard Hastings were allowed to enter the lands she was due to inherit from both her father and her brother (June 1470), including Lilford and Oakington. Soon after this, William Browne purchased the two manors from Hastings and his wife Jane. But since both manors were in danger of being included among the family estates forfeited to the crown, William Browne twice obtained from Parliament a statement that these two manors should be exempted, first from the act of attainder and secondly, when that act was reversed, from the act of restoration of the Welles inheritance; for greater security, he got these exemptions recorded on the patent rolls of chancery[158]. In that age of uncertainty, one could never be too sure.

---

[154] Peck xiii 7-8; an account for Warmington in BL Nero Cvii fol 85 mentions Sapcott, John Knivett, Richard Broun junior, etc; see RCHME *Northants* vi p 157; VCH *Northants* iii pp 113-122; BL Add Ch 738a, 738b; PRO, CP25/1/179/95/120; NRS 16 *Morton* pp 49-50, 53, 167; *Feudal Aids* iv 23, 28, 48; PRO, SC6/914/1.

[155] The dates of all these acquisitions are approximate, for they are the date of the title deed, not the actual acquisition.

[156] MCO 12, 16, 53; Peck xiv 13, 14, 15; LAO, Stamford parish records PG 1/6,7; Peck xiv 21; MCO 29, 32, 19, 34, 6, 11, 4, 50

[157] PRO, CP25/1/179/95/139, 146; Bridges *Northants* ii 478-483; VCH *Northants* iii pp 113-122. Papley was held by tenure of the royal household – serjeant of the butler of refectory, see NRS 2 *Pytcheley* pp 117-8

[158] *Rot Parl* vi pp 144-5, 287; CPR 1467-77/207, 213, 218, 508-9; 1485-94/294-5; see LAO, BHS 7/12/21; CCR 1485-1500/121 (423) . VCH *Cambs* ix p 198 says 1472, VCH *Northants* iii pp 227-231 gives 1473. For Hastings, see *Complete Peerage* vi p 385; Hastings married Joan daughter

In Lincolnshire, his interests developed from the 1460s, acquiring property in Swayfield from the Chevercourt family, and the manor of Swinstead from the Colville family in 1465 for a further £40. He bought the manor of Swayfield and its dependencies in Woolsthorp, South Witham, Corby (Glen) and Conithorp, Lincs, in 1480 from the Misterton family for £100, and in 1483, he acquired a manor in North Witham in Lincolnshire from the same family for £40[159].

North Luffenham farm (Rutland) in almost the same condition as when William Browne acquired it in 1482 (photo: Nick Hill)

Browne acquired his properties in various ways, although the use of feoffees sometimes hides the originator of the transaction. Some came by mortgage: as late as 1486, only three years before his death at a very advanced age, two tenements in the parish of St Mary at the bridge (one of them Le Cressaunt), a grange and a garden were pledged as surety for a loan of £32 to be repaid in eight annual payments; this property fell in to William's executors in July 1489, three months after Browne's death. It would seem that the acquisition of the manor of North Witham (Lincolnshire) from John Misterton of Nottinghamshire, son and heir of Nicholas Misterton, lord Cromwell's steward in some of his manors, who had fallen on hard times and had to sell some of his father's estates, followed a foreclosure in 1483. The Swayfield manor came to

---

and heir of Richard lord Welles and Willoughby in March 1470 but she died without heirs of her body before January 1475. See Bridges *Northants* ii 241-6; J R Lander 1961 Attainder and forfeiture 1453-1509 *Historical Journal* 4 pp 119-151

[159] LAO, BHS 7/7/8; 7/9/116-121; PRO, CP25/1/145/162/62, 12; CP 25/1/145/163/1. Since the deeds relating to the manor of Wolfehowse in Greetham (Rutland) went to the Elmes family, we do not know when and how this manor was acquired. VCH *Rutland* ii p 136 has no information on this manor between 1305 and 1495 when it was in the hands of Browne's feoffees.

him after a careful building up of small pieces of land in the parish, some from the Chevercourt family (1460) and others from the Misterton family (1471, 1475), until the manor fell in in 1480[160].

In only a few cases can we see the direct purchase of these estates by William Browne. The Barnack property came to him from a widow, Stretton from the executors of the merchant owner – he added another farm there in 1480. Tillysplace croft in Warmington with its extensive farmlands came on the death of Richard Pappeley in 1461, Wilsthorp on the death of Robert Woodman in 1465, Barholm on the death of John Freman in 1473. Most of these were simply indicated by releases to William Browne by the widows or heirs of the deceased. Some property Browne may have acquired by dubious methods; as we have seen, he was accused of underhand practices in the case of Thomas Basset.

It is possible that William Browne had a policy in regard to his acquisitions. Although he had opportunity to acquire property in Coventry, he did not do so; nor, so far as we know, did he buy property in Boston, Lynn, Ipswich or London where he traded. There are no signs he acquired property in Calais, as some English merchants did[161]. Apart from Lilford (16 miles or so) with its outlier of Oakington near Cambridge (some 32 miles away), all the properties lay within ten miles of Stamford, close to main roads; but Lilford, the Misterton lands and the various mortgage acquisitions remind us that the properties may have owed more to opportunism than policy - but not so far away as to be difficult to manage (this may be why Lilford became immediately the main residence of William Browne's daughter and son-in-law).

William Browne built his estate in the town as well as the countryside. But we should not draw too sharp a distinction between the urban properties and the rural, for most of the town properties brought with them land in the open fields and a share of the meadows; indeed, judging by a terrier drawn up in 1486, shortly before William Browne's death in 1489, Browne was named as the largest holder of strips in the town's common fields after the duchess of York. He may have farmed these himself (we know his wife had sheep and cattle) or let them out for rents, but their possession would mean that his concerns with the agricultural economic cycle would be keen (see p 34 above)[162].

---

[160] MCO 39, 37, 13, 26, 1, 3, 21, 43; LAO, BHS 7/7/8; see note 38 above
[161] Kermode *Merchants* p 169
[162] Stamford borough records TH 8A3/1. For the view that urban and rural were not so sharply divided, see below p 299

It was not of course unusual for substantial merchants to build up large urban estates. William Canynges of Bristol possessed no less than 55 urban messuages by 1474. In Stamford, other accumulations were known: John Whytside bought 10 tofts and 6 cottages in one transaction early in the century[163]. In all, William Browne came to own some thirty properties in Stamford and Stamford Baron (conceivably more), land in all three of the open fields and in the fields of Stamford Baron; and no less than seven substantial manors in the counties around, with properties in at least 29 other locations in the three counties around the town.

Despite the bad harvests of the 1480s, he does not seem to have improved these estates, as did his daughter and grandson at Lilford and his nephew at Tolthorpe, all three earning great unpopularity in the process, causing riots and a summons before the Star Chamber; the strips which William held in the Stamford open fields remained unconsolidated throughout his lifetime[164]. Nor did he consolidate his other holdings – where manors had outlying lands in other parishes, he retained these as sources of rents. He bought whole manors and let or put managers in them. Bartholomew Holmes was his agent in the south Lincolnshire estates, inherited from the Misterton family, Robert Beomond his man of business in Stamford and probably Northamptonshire. Stamford was a convenient centre from which to manage his estates.

These estates brought William Browne into contact with the estate officials of many of the greatest in the land. His links with Ralph lord Cromwell have already been noted. The de la Zouche family, friends and allies of William Browne, held property in Stamford and in North Luffenham where Browne acquired property. Browne held Witham manor of the de la Launde family, Swayfield and Swinstead of lord Grey of Castle Bytham. Barholm was held of the earl of Westmoreland, some Witham property of Lady Margaret Beaufort. Oakington was held of Ramsay abbey, while Wolfhowse manor in Rutland, held of Fineshade priory, lay within the orbit of the earl of Warwick's manor of Greetham, later held by the duke of Clarence; Stretton passed from Humphrey duke of Gloucester via the crown to the Hussey family[165]. Warmington and Papley were within a bow's shot of the York headquarters of Fotheringhay, and

---

163 W G Hoskins, English provincial towns in the early sixteenth century, in W G Hoskins (ed) 1965 *Provincial England* Macmillan pp 86-114; CIPM 23 1427-32 p 139; Butcher, Rent. John Huggeford esq of Coventry had 10 burgages, 8 messuages, 3 cottages, 2 barns, 2 gardens and 6 unoccupied sites. See Hilton Urban property.

164 VCH *Northants* iii pp 117-8; Stamford borough records, TH terrier 1495; Hatcher, Slump p 249

165 VCH *Rutland* ii pp 195-203; CIPM Henry VII iii 1504-9 p 230 (551); VCH *Rutland* ii pp 136, 146-7

the overlord was Peterborough abbey, while Lilford was held of the honor of Huntingdon. There are no signs that William Browne had a policy of buying within any lord's catchment area; he was no man's retainer.

By the time William Browne died, he was a very substantial landowner in and around Stamford. Faced with the fact that he had only a daughter to inherit his estate[166], William Browne chose to make a division of his property between Elizabeth (Elmes) and his Hospital. In 1488, he settled part of his property on feoffees for his Hospital, seven of them secular priests and four burgesses of Stamford, including Thomas Stokes the elderly brother of William's wife Margaret, and Henry Wykes from the well endowed family of Burghley by Stamford and the current vicar of All Saints. Thomas Hikeham rector of St Peter's church was related to William Hikeham baker, Alderman, restorer of the Corpus Christi chapel in St Mary's church. John Taillour clerk was William Browne's chaplain, a young Oxford scholar, supported by Thomas Stokes, who became the second warden of Browne's Hospital and later vicar of St Martin's church in Stamford. John Coton and William Haukins were the two current chaplains at the Hospital. David Malpas esq was a landed gentleman in Rutland, friend of Sir John Hussey steward of Stamford, and himself steward and bailiff for various estates in the Stamford area, MP for Stamford and sheriff of Rutland. Robert Fitzacreley was brother in law to Margaret Browne. John Gregory and Thomas Kesteven were substantial mercers and drapers in Stamford; Kesteven was a Calais stapler, and Gregory was in addition a friend of the Fairfax family of Deeping Gate. With perhaps the exception of Malpas, it was a group chosen for their closeness to the family rather than their position[167].

The enfeoffment to Elizabeth can only be seen by a settlement made in 1499 as the property was resettled. The feoffees on this occasion were of a different character: John Verney knt., Guy Wulston knt., Robert Harecourt knt., Robert Brudenell, John Danvers, Christopher Broun, John Burgoyn, William Coke, John Glynton, Thomas Mountegen, Nicholas Fazakyrley, John Colston, Walter Elmes and John Wylles. These were Northamptonshire gentlemen, friends of John Elmes of Lilford, Northants, esquire; William Browne's family had become gentrified by the second generation[168]. But on the death of John Elmes (William Browne's son-in-law) in 1491, Elizabeth his widow used her father's feoffees John Taillour and Henry Wykes clerks to settle William Browne's lands on

---

[166] See Payling, 1992; S Staves 1995 Resentment or resignation? dividing spoils among daughters and younger sons, in J Brewer and S Staves (eds) 1995 *Early Modern COonceptions of Property* Routledge pp 194-218. See Kermode *Enterprise* p x

[167] LAO, BHS 7/12/24

[168] According to Leland, Elmes had "an attractive manor house" at Lilford, John Chandler (ed) 1993 *John Leland's itinerary: travels in Tudor England* Sutton p 323.

William her son with remainder to John Elmes his brother. Among the witnesses were William Cook of Oundell merchant who had married a second daughter of John Browne and sister of Christopher Browne, and Robert Beomond, William Browne's man of business[169].

Because we do not have details of the Elmes' bequest, it is not clear if William Browne was following the tradition that one third of his estates should go to charity, two-thirds to his heirs. Two manors and lands in ten other villages in Lincolnshire, in four villages in Rutland and in six villages in Northants together with at least 16 houses or shops in Stamford as well as arable land and pasture in the town, went to the Hospital. The tenements lay all over Stamford – in Stamford Baron, St Peter's parish, All Saints, St Mary at the bridge, and St Michael the Greater. They were large and small, occupied by drapers and tailors, a shoemaker, a patinner and a sawyer - properties bought to increase rental income. Henry Wykes, vicar of All Saints church, William Browne's favourite feoffee, settled on the Elmes family the manors of Swinstead in Lincolnshire, Wolfehouse in Stretton, Rutland, Lilford and Papley-in-Warmington, and Oakington in Cambridgeshire together with lands in four villages in Lincolnshire and in eight villages in Northamptonshire. A number of properties in the town of Stamford came in this way to the Elmes family, such as the Bell inn and the Swan, with the proviso that if the family died out, the lands should revert to the Hospital; and for at least three generations, these lands were kept separately, being called "Browne's lands"[170]. The Browne family shared the desire of many others to keep family estates intact.

It is not possible to assess the value of William Browne's estate when he died, but there are some clues. Late in 1489, Margaret Browne died and we have a list of some of the property which she held for her life and which passed to the Elmes. The Lincolnshire lands amounted to £59 16s 8d p.a., Rutland lands to £2, and Northants lands with Oakington, Cambridgeshire to £27 – making a total of £88 16s 8d. Some fifteen tenements in Stamford provided £26 13s 4d of this total. But it is likely that these are assessments rather than revenues arising from the estate, and not all of the properties are listed in these inquisitions. When compared with the portion that went to the Hospital, we see a different

---

[169] Simcoe 1038 M/T/13/6-7. There was however still some tidying up to be done after the death of William Browne. In 1491, the Hospital obtained a quitclaim in North Luffenham; in 1497, one of the mortgages which William Browne had made in Stamford in his lifetime fell in, and the property came to the Hospital trustees; in 1502 and later, land in Carlby came to the Hospital; and in 1503, the Hospital made a final release to John Misterton, MCO 1, 3, 26; LAO, BHS 7/3/7-13; 7/12/28

[170] CCR 1485-1500/121 (423); CPR 1485-94/294-5; CIPM Henry VII iii 1504-9 p 594; VCH *Northants* iii pp113-122; Rogers, Wills; Simcoe 1038 MT/13/7

picture. The intention was to endow the Hospital with an annual income of 50 marks (£33 6s 8d). The property in Lincolnshire (including the Stamford property) was alleged to have amounted to £20 3s p.a., the Rutland lands to £2 p.a. and the Northamptonshire to £6 10s – a total income of £28 13s 0d per annum – but these figures are clearly an under-estimate of their value. The first accounts of the Hospital (1494-1496) show that the annual gross income to the Hospital from its endowments was over £71 (net £64) in the first year, and £62 (net £55) in the second year[171]. On this basis, Browne's yield from his estates was probably in excess of £150 p.a.

But the costs of maintaining this estate were large. The account book for the Hospital shows a remarkable picture of the Browne estate management system run from Stamford where William Browne lived. Every year extensive repairs were made to the tenants' properties on all the estates from a focal point of Browne's house and the adjacent Hospital grounds. The site was a veritable builder's yard with large quantities of nails, lime, sand, timber, slates etc stored in bulk and conveyed out to the various properties, and surplus materials brought back to the yard. This makes sense of the clause in Margaret Browne's will about building material to be used on the buildings now in the hands of her trustees (see below p 273). Every year the warden spent a large amount of time going round all the estates, inspecting and commissioning 'reparacions', and paying local wages. Manor courts had to be held, and rents and other dues paid. Distresses were taken by neighbouring landlords for failure of tenants to pay rents or to attend the local manor court, or for other offences, and these distresses had to be fought. 'Decays' of rents had to be chased up. It is clear that this was a system inherited from William Browne, that at least in his later years, Browne managed his estate to a large extent in person, although he may have trusted Holmes and Beomond more than the warden clearly did[172]. Having a large and scattered estate did not mean simply sitting and waiting for the rents to come in; a great deal of attention had to be paid to detail. The Hospital only had half the estate to deal with, but that was too much for the first warden; William Browne had the whole estate.

At the beginning of his journey, in 1436, William Browne was assessed to the income tax at only £18 p.a. Although the richest man in Stamford at that time, it was small beer compared with Philip Tylney of Boston who was assessed at £198

---

[171] CPR 1485-94/456-7; the valuation must be an under-estimate. CIPM Henry VII i 1485-96 p 230 (551); CIPM Henry VII iii 1504-9 pp 508-9 (992). Wright *Domus Dei* pp 496-500; Bodl, Rawl B352.

[172] Drawn from Bodl, Rawl B352; Holmes was sacked early on for maladministration.

p.a. from property in four counties[173]. But Tylney came from a long established family; Browne was just starting, though with some family assets. He built up his estates in one (admittedly long) lifetime, becoming very wealthy at least by local standards, a "merchant of a very wonderfulle richnesse" – and this may be why he felt the lack of a male heir so strongly that he built his Hospital to compensate.

---

[173] PRO, E179/136/198

APPENDIX: ESTATES OF WILLIAM BROWNE divided between Elizabeth Elmes daughter and heiress and Browne's Hospital (list compiled from title deeds and inquisitions post mortem):

1. Estates given to Browne's Hospital in 1488 by William Browne (LAO, BHS 7/12/24) supplemented by endowment made by Thomas Stokes in 1494 (CPR 1485-1494/456-7; CIPM Henry VII iii 1504-9 p 594)

Lincs
mSwayfield
mNorth Witham
Barholm
Carlby
Colsterworth
Counthorpe
Gunby
North Witham
South Witham
Stainby
Swayfield
Twyford
Wilsthorpe
Woolsthorpe (in Colsterworth)

Stamford:

Property	Parish	Tenant
Tenement	St Peter	William Buck
Tenement	St Peter Malory Bridge	Helen Bellamy
Tenement and 1½ acres meadow	St Peter	Thomas Peryman
Shop	ASM	William Bullok draper
Shop next door	ASM	William Barnard patynner
Tenement	ASM	Robert Johnson shoemaker
Two tenements together with grange in Scotgate c p	ASM	John Sabyn
Tenement	ASM	John Beevor tailor
Tenement	ASM	John Sherman at Malory Bridge
My tenement	St Michael the Greater	Richard Tailour
Tenement with 1 acre of meadow at small bridges	St Andrew	John Thistleton
Tenement or hospice called le Aungell	St Mary at the bridge	John Young tailor
Tenement (Est-by-the-water)	St Martin	John Barford junior
Tenement	St Martin	John Gybson
Tenement	St Martin	Robert Dudley sawyer
Garden	St Martin	Robert Lambe tailor

3 acres and 3 roods of meadow lying together which cannot be separated in Estmedewe at small bridges

(summarised as manors of Swafield and North Witham, 14 mess, 190 ac land, 20 ac meadow, 10 ac pasture in Stamford, Carlby, Wilthorp, Barholme, Lincs worth £20 3s p.a., CPR 1494/456-7)

Rutland
Bredcroft
North Luffenham
Sculthorpe
Stretton
(3 mess, 3 tofts, 2 dovecotes, 180 ac land, 20 ac meadow in Stretton, N Luffenham, Bredcroft by Stamford worth £2 pa, CPR 1494/456-7)

Northamptonshire
Bainton
Barnack
Easton by Stamford
Pilsgate
Stamford Baron
Walcot
Warmington
Wothorpe
(10 mess, 7 cottages, 3 tofts, 200 acres of land, 30 ac meadow in Easton, Warmington, Wothorp, Walcot, Pilsgate, Barnack and Stamford Baron worth 10 marks and 3s 6d p.a., CPR 1494/456-7)

2. Elmes list (from Devon RO Simcoe): (this includes lands of the Elmes family)

Lincs
mSwinstead,
Swinstead
Witham
Stamford
'Broadyng'

Rutland
mWolfehouse, ,
Bredcrofte,
Great Casterton
Little Casterton

Northants
mPapley (in Warmington)
mLilford
Warmington,
Papley,
Ogerston,
Polebrook
Irthlingborough
Wigsthorpe
Thorpe Achurch
Pylton
Benefeld

Cambs

mOakington, Cambs.,

Oxon

mCassington, Oxon.,
Henley on Thames,
Rotherfeld Grey,
Badgemore
Watlington Hill,
Worton (in Cassington),
Somerford (in Cassington)
Bladon

Berks

Wallingford

Bucks

Hambleden
Chyr Feld
Skirmett in Hambleden

3. Property in Lincolnshire held by Margaret on her death (CIPM Henry VII i 1485-96 p 230 (551))

Property	Lord and rents	value
manor of Swafield	Lord Grey of Castle Bytham rent £2 10s 4d	£10
manor North Witham	Thomas de la Laund	£4
Wilsthorpe tenements	Robert Eland of Wilsthorpe manor – rent cumin	13s 4d
Barholm tenements	Ralph earl of Westmorland - rent ½d	10s
Stamford 12 tenements, 60 acres land, 8 acres meadow	Cecily duchess of York	£13 6s 8d
manor of Swinstead	Lord Grey of Codnor	£11
North Witham 5 tenements	Lady Margaret Beaufort	£7
Stamford: Swan, Bell, Clement, 80s acres of land, 12 acres of meadow	Cecily duchess of York	£13 6s 8d

Total: £50 6s 8d [sic]

PART IV: WILLIAM BROWNE AND THE COMMUNITY

In this section, we look at three aspects of William Browne's involvement with his local community –

- *his participation in the local government of Stamford,*
- *his involvement in the town's religious practices,*
- *and his building activities*

PART IV: CHAPTER 1   LOCAL GOVERNMENT: WILLIAM BROWNE AND STAMFORD'S POLITICAL ELITE

"to make pees, unite and acord, poore and ryche to ben oon in herte, love and charite, nevermore fro this tyme forth to ben dissevered"[1].

William Browne came from a family with a long tradition of service. The Brownes provided Aldermen (i.e. mayors) of the town since the mid-fourteenth century, and had taken their turn as Stamford representative on commissions to collect royal taxes in Kesteven. William's father was Alderman three times; Robert Browne (almost certainly a relative) was also Alderman. So when William followed his father in his trade and in his roles as feoffee and witness, he also succeeded to his role in local government. He was on the First Twelve and became Alderman of the town for the first time at an exceptionally young age in 1435[2]. But the comprehensive exemption he obtained in 1439 implied that William was determined from the start to engage in such activities as and when it was convenient for himself[3]. He did not hold any offices of profit (such as steward or bailiff),but he fulfilled offices of public service at both county and local level which could yield benefits in the form of connections (social capital) as well as perquisites.

Public service

Despite his exemption, William undertook public service, although at first rarely; he was a Kesteven tax collector in 1442[4]. But from the 1460s, he became more heavily involved: he was appointed sheriff of Rutland 1466-7 and 1474-5, sheriff of Lincolnshire in 1477-8 (in view of the distance, he probably served that office largely through his under-sheriff[5]), sheriff of Rutland again in the year of dynastic crisis 1482-3[6] and again under Henry VII in 1486. Despite his age, he was appointed JP in Rutland in 1483 and again from 1487 until his death in 1489; and he was tax collector in that county in 1483 and again in 1488.

---

[1] Norwich city, 1415, W Hudson and J C Tingey, *Records of the City of Norwich* 1906 i p 94

[2] Kermode *Merchants* pp 38, 40, 45-6, 49, 68. One Raphe Browne Alderman in 1409 is almost certainly Ralph Bond who was prominent in the town at that time; no Ralph Browne is known; Rogers, Aldermen. For Robert Browne, see above pp 52-3

[3] CPR 1439-41/341; see above pp 59-60

[4] CPR 1441-6/61 ; he may have served on an embassy to the duke of Burgundy concerning trade in 1446, and on a commission concerning piracy in 1456, CPR 1446-52/140; 1452-61/306

[5] For the importance of the under-sheriff, see *Paston Letters* ii p 523 (877).

[6] November 1482 to November 1483: appointed by Edward IV, confirmed by Edward V's government and by Richard III

Such offices would have given scope for profit. The age was one of what today would be regarded as considerable corruption and venality; there were contemporary protests about fees and bribes. We have no evidence of such activity on the part of William or John Browne; but that they were careful to take out general pardons suggests that they feared pleas in relation to various offices as well as property transactions or wool trading. William took out three pardons in 1452, one in 1464, two in 1470 after the Lincolnshire Rising, one in 1472 and one in 1480 – apart from those in common with other Staplers. Occasionally we can see direct profits from his offices - in 1452, the goods in Stamford of a felon, and in 1482-3, a sum of £13 6s 8d paid for "the great losses, costs and charges to his grate hurt" incurred as sheriff of Rutland[7].

Office-holding both reflected and enhanced his influence. Although never an MP, he had command of parliamentary procedures: in the 1450s, he with fellow Staplers persuaded parliament to revise the terms of their repayments of loans made to the king; and he twice (1472-75) obtained the exemption of estates in Northamptonshire and Cambridgeshire from acts relating to the attainder of lord Welles and Willoughby[8].

Browne then did serve – when he wished. He was not named to the royal commission of gaol-delivery in Stamford in 1478 but was so named in 1484[9]. Such commissions were issued to those serving on the town council; and it was on the town government that William focused much of his attention for most of his life.

Serving the town – as Alderman

William Browne was Stamford's chief officer for a record of six times in his lifetime. Alderman a second time in 1444-5, he served again in 1449-50, just before the crisis of 1450-52; chosen as Alderman for the crisis year of 1460-61 (and thus almost certainly started the negotiation for the first royal charter of 1462), he was Alderman again in 1466 and during the third crisis year of 1470-

---

[7] see p84; PRO, SC6/1115/6: William Browne of Stamford *pro bonis et catallis cuiusdam Johannis Kyngespere felonis ad manus ipsius Willielmi devenient*'; E404/77/3/106. For corruption see Kermode *Merchants* p 57; Griffiths, Bureaucracies p 124; Loans p 52; Davies 1968 p 219; J Gower, Mirour de l'Omme, in G C Macauley 1899 *Complete Works of Gower* Oxford vol i pp 280-1

[8] See above p100

[9] In 1478, William Hussey and Reginald Gayton (lawyers) were named along with most of the members of the First Twelve but not William Browne; but in December 1484, William Browne was named to the commission of gaol delivery in Stamford along with the other First Twelve members; once again Hussey and Gayton were of the quorum; CPR 1476-85/144; PRO, C66/543 m 26d ; 558 m18d; I am grateful to the History of Parliament for this reference.

71[10]. It cannot have been accidental that he was called upon to steer the town through times of considerable potential trouble.

John Browne his brother served alongside him – Alderman in 1448-9 (William immediately succeeded him), 1453, immediately after the alleged assemblies in Stamford, and in 1462, just after William's fourth term of office. But John had no other public office except as Alderman[11].

The Alderman of the town was supreme; he 'was Stamford' for his term of office and spoke for the town. There are no signs in Stamford of the checks on his power seen in other towns[12]. Although we have the oaths of office of the other borough officials, we do not have the oath for the Alderman, so we cannot see his accountability; but he took an oath (during William's lifetime, in the town hall before his peers, presumably administered by the town clerk). "Ancient custom" stated that the Alderman should take his oath before the lord's steward but that practice seems to have fallen into disuse; when in 1488 Pontefract asked for the same customs as Stamford, they specified that the elected mayor should take his oath in the motehall before the co-burgesses[13].

He was chairman of the bench of justices of the peace and "chief overseer and ruler of this markate". He controlled the accounts of the other officers, had powers of arrest and control of the town gaol, held his own court and administered such charities as had been entrusted to the town council, such as the St Nicholas chantry in St Clement's church[14]. There is no sign in Stamford of an endowment or fee for the office.

The Alderman was 'elected' every year on the feast of St Jerome (30 September)[15], and affirmed by the whole body of freemen by raising of hands. In 1475, the procedure was changed; the First Twelve were to put forward three

---

[10] Rogers, Aldermen

[11] He had commissions to arrest and of gaol delivery as Alderrman

[12] See *Medieval Norwich* p 237. The Alderman was of the same status as 'mayor' in other towns: in 1464, a messenger was sent from Nottingham "to speke with the Maire…" of Stamford, *Records of Borough of Nottingham 1399-1485* Rolls Series, ii p 376. "Mayors were monarchs more absolute than the king, able to act almost without restraint", M Hicks 2002 *Political Culture in fifteenth century England* pp 81-2; see Fleming, Oligarchy p 181; Rigby, Oligarchy p 72. In many towns, he was seen as the king's representative, Horrox, Patronage pp 147, 160

[13] HB i fol 68 *secundum antiquam consuetudinem*, CPR 1485-1494/261 For the importance of oaths, see Attreed *King's Towns* p 45; J Lee 2007 'Ye shall disturbe noe mans right': oath-taking and oath-breaking in late medieval and early modern Bristol, *Urban History* 34 pp 27-39

[14] CCR 1381-5/64; PRO, C1/66/313; HB i 25d, p 69; CY *Visit* iii pp 73, 100, 506; *AASR* Chantry pp 247-9; for fee for office of mayor, see Kermode, Oligarchies p 100; Rigby *Grimsby* p 89

[15] There are no signs of contested elections with rival candidates in Stamford as elsewhere; for elections by secret ballot, see Kermode, Oligarchies pp 89-91. Grimsby had two candidates and majority voting, Rigby *Grimsby* p 89

names and the freemen chose one, a procedure followed from time to time in the sixteenth century[16]. In 1488, when the Alderman died in office, a meeting of eight of the First Twelve put forward the name of his successor for the remainder of the term of office, and the commons (i.e. the freemen) 'elected' him.

There appears to have been no *cursus honorum* before selection as Alderman except service on the Second and First Twelve[17]. The Alderman must come from the First Twelve ("so he be one of the first xij") but not all the First Twelve served as Alderman. It is not clear what exempted some members from service as Alderman; royal service may have been one reason, but this could not be pleaded by all those who did not serve as Alderman. There are few signs of reluctance to serve[18], though on occasion a member of the Second Twelve was promoted to the First Twelve and immediately became Alderman, even when there were members of the First Twelve who had not been Alderman.

No Alderman was continued in office beyond his one-year term, but many served more than once. As we have seen (above p 66), the occupations of the Alderman of Stamford show that there was no domination of the town by any economic or social interest group: in 1488, when the Alderman, a stainer, died in office, he was replaced by a fishmonger[19]. Although the cloth and wool trades (merchants, mercers, drapers) appeared more frequently than any others, the frequency of fishmongers, wrights and others showed that the office of Alderman was not in hock to any trading group. It is possible that (as elsewhere), there was a link between wealth and frequency of service[20], but more likely were personal capacities and willingness to serve. Until the 1480s, we cannot see any parties in Stamford.

The Alderman controlled admission of burgesses[21]. Here we can see some personal influence, but it seems to have been personal rather than economic or social interests. A fishmonger admitted 26 freemen in each of two of his four terms of office, a draper admitted 24, a stainer 22, a mercer 19; but a baker (6

---

[16] HB i fol 20, p 53

[17] See Kermode, Oligarchies p 97; D M Palliser 1979 *Tudor York* Oxford University Press. We have no names of chamberlains, bailiffs or constables before 1465.

[18] Rigby *Grimsby* pp 138-9, citing Dobson 1973, suggests that in declining towns, there was a good deal of evasion of office; but this does not appear in Stamford which again provides some indirect evidence that Stamford may not have felt like a declining town in this period.

[19] HB i fol 44, p 131; see Kermode, Oligarchies p 89

[20] R H Britnell 1986 *Growth and Decline in Colchester 1300-1525* Cambridge University Press p 235; Fleming, Oligarchy; Dyer et al *Hilton* pp 171-3, 178. Britnell, Elites suggests that men who served as Aldermen came from those who employed others to work for them which left them freer to undertake such offices.

[21] Cornwall *Wealth* p 9

admissions), a barber and a glover (5 each) show that these were not partisan admissions. William Browne was the lowest of all; in 1466-7, he admitted only four, and in 1470-1, no admissions at all. We might notice that during his term as Alderman of the gild of St Katherine, Browne admitted relatively few new members; after his death, membership soared (see p 225 below).

We have details of William Browne's last two years of office, 1466-7 and 1470-1 – but both years are sparsely recorded in the Hall Book. In 1466-7, he was also sheriff of Rutland and thus supervised two elections of MPs, what seems to have been the first parliamentary election for the borough, and one for the county. Under him, the town council legislated for dunghills (a significant issue for his later Hospital), and collections were taken from named citizens, mostly councillors, for the "reynuyng and making of the Westgates of the towne" and for a gift to "lord le Cromewell" (Humphrey Bourghchier). Courts were held for outlawry, admissions to the freedom, and sureties to keep the peace; among those fined were his fellow staplers, councillors and colleagues William Colom, Thomas Kesteven, Thomas Holton and William Sutton. The Hall Book also records two fines for "playing at dice illicitly by night". His second year of office (1470-1) was even more poorly recorded; there are only two entries, both undated, in the Hall Book. Collections were taken to cover the cost of troops riding to the conflicts of 1471 (see above p 100); unusually the names of those appointed to levy these sums are not recorded. 1470-71 was a year when recording the activities of the council was even more inadequate than normally[22].

But despite this paucity of records, it is clear that William Browne took his duties as Alderman seriously. In January 1467, the Hall Book records the appearance of an alleged offender before the Alderman: "he came before me" (*coram me*) and "he found for me sureties" (*invenit michi*) that he would appear "before me and my fellow JPs" (*coram me et sociis meis*). This is the only time in the Hall Book that these words appear; William Browne saw himself as the personification of the borough. In 1467, immediately after his fifth year of office, he gave a new set of fetters to the town gaol. In 1483-4, he advanced the expenses of the town's MPs, presumably to avoid a delay before they received their expenses through a town levy; he was reimbursed in 1485[23]. His commitment to the town's government was firm.

---

[22] HB i fol 6-8d, pp 16-23. The only other entry is four suits of citizens of Stamford against other persons, again for reasons unstated.

[23] HB i fol 8, p 22; fol 9,p 24; fol 38d, p 113

... - in other offices

Because of its history, Stamford had a full panoply of officers similar to those in 'king's towns' (mainly county towns) as distinct from seigneurial boroughs like Grantham. The hereditary 'reeve' of Stamford now belonged to the family which held Burghley (successively the Milton, Wykes and Williams families, all from Stamford Baron); and the 'lawmen' (see p 8) seem to have had no function[24]. The town had an Alderman, chamberlains, constables, a serjeant of the mace, a bailiff, a coroner and a town clerk - all appointed by the town council.

Two chamberlains were appointed from the First or Second Twelve. Each pair served a variable term, "from this dey unto the dey of a newe ellectyon" (sometimes as long as three years), accounting "within one moneth after the dyscharge" from office[25]. There is no pattern of one senior and one junior chamberlain. As the oath which they took shows, they collected rents and other dues to the town, made payments under the supervision of the Alderman, and were responsible for passing the sums raised in national taxes to the government collectors.

The serjeant at mace and the town bailiff were appointed for several years at a time: although salaried, the remuneration available would rarely cover their costs: "To make up the shortfall, [they might need to] draw on [their] own wealth", but they would expect preferential treatment when contracts and leases were available[26]. There was much interchange between these offices: William Taverner was serjeant, bailiff and then serjeant; Robert Dodale was bailiff, serjeant and (after a gap) serjeant again; John Syll ostler was serjeant (it seems) for eight years. Their oaths reveal their duties: the serjeant was to register "all manner straungers commyng in to the towne to inhabyte ..[with] ther names and ther occupacyones", collecting their fines for trading rights in the town; while the bailiff, the executive officer of the council ("to all manner commaundements of yow [the Alderman] and yowr bredern I shall be attendaunt and obedyent") and keeper of the town gaol, executed "all manner wrytts, warrants and precepts", collected "all manner escheytts, fynes and amercyaments with other dutyes to the towne perteynyng... [avoiding] all manner specyall favour", and handed them to the chamberlains, rendering account to the Alderman. It is not clear if he acquired more powers and duties during the century or if the bailiff lost power to the Alderman as elsewhere[27].

---

[24] Attreed *King's Towns*; see Shaw *Wells*, Kermode, Oligarchies p 88

[25] Hall Book i fol 11d,p 31

[26] Attreed *King's Towns* pp 46-7; the town serjeant and bailiff in Stamford were not of the category of esquire or 'gentleman' as in other towns,Horrox, Gentry pp 28

[27] e.g. CCR 1369-74/482; CFR 1337-47/497,501; LRS 36 p cviii; the names of the town bailiffs are rarely known until the surviving Hall Book commences. There are no signs that the outgoing

Three (occasionally four) 'king's constables'[28] were appointed for variable periods, sometimes for less than one year; continuity was sometimes provided by one constable being reappointed. Some were from the Second Twelve, and there was interchange between the offices of constable and chamberlain. They enforced the king's peace, while the town bailiff enforced the town by-laws.

Under the charter of 1462, a coroner was chosen, exempting the town from the Kesteven coroner. He was a member of the First Twelve and served until he resigned or died; John Murdok coroner 1481-5 was elected MP (1483) for the town[29]. But like some other towns, Stamford during the fifteenth century does not seem to have had a Recorder, an important office through which the king exercised influence[30]; William Hussey lawyer sat with the First Twelve twice in 1472-3, and John Walcote and William Elmes, both lawyers, alternated to sit with the council from 1490 onwards, presumably as retained counsel, until Elmes was formally appointed Recorder in 1502.

Two assessors and two collectors, "notable and substanciall persones" but not council members, were appointed for each parish; they took their oaths before the Alderman to make the assessment and collect the taxes without favour[31]. They were supervised by (usually four) nominated men drawn from the First or Second Twelve. Searchers of the market were chosen by the trade groups until 1478, when they were appointed by the council, mainly from the First and Second Twelve.

We have the name of the town clerk once in the fifteenth century, John Kirkby alias Fox; he was also a servant of the duke of York. John Goylyn may have

---

bailiff chose his successor as elsewhere, Kermode, *Oligarchies* p 90. For bailiff in action, see CPR 1452-61/553; 1494-1509/39; PRO, C1/28/435; SC6/914/1; SC1/47/197. See P Nightingale 2008 The intervention of the crown and the effectiveness of the sheriff in the execution of judicial writs, c.1355-1530 *EHR* 123 pp 1-34 for towns and return of writs; Shaw *Wells* pp 136, 169

[28] e.g. HB i fol 68d

[29] There are many references to the coroner in Stamford and in Kesteven, e.g. CCR 1288-96/230; LRS 36 p 138.

[30] HB i fol 17,p 46; fol 18,p 49; fol 69,fol 74-5; L and P Henry VIII 9 1535 p 79. For recorder, see Attreed *King's Towns* p 53. Horrox, Patronage pp 150-151, 160-1 discusses the shift from retained counsel to ad hoc payments to national figures. Hull first paid a recorder in 1440 but still had three retained counsel, ibid p 151. Later Grantham and Stamford shared a Recorder. Although officially the town's legal officer,increasingly the office of Recorder was coming under direct crown influence, J Lee 2003 Urban recorders and the crown in late medieval England, in Clark 2003 pp 163-177; Lee 2009.

[31] Virgoe 1450 p 130; Virgoe 1481 pp 31, 34

been clerk in 1495, he wrote a letter for the council. Nicholas Trygge public notary too may have been clerk[32].

We do not know if William or John Browne served in any offices prior to 1465 but after that date, they held no office other than Alderman; this looks like a deliberate decision on their part.

And William Browne also came to head up other organisations. He was the Alderman of the gild of St Katherine from at least 1480 until his death in 1489; Alderman of the gild of Holy Trinity in 1480, and of the wealthy and politically important gild of St Mary and Corpus Christi in 1485, as well as Alderman of the gild of All Saints for life. Such an accumulation of positions would give him undoubted dominance in the town's affairs – little could be done without consulting him. Outside the town, he became Alderman of the gild of Corpus Christi, Boston, in 1481-2; and as we have seen, mayor of the Calais staple in or sometime before 1478. His death would have left a major gap in the town's social structures.

The town council

Apart from his service as Alderman, William was a permanent member of the town council. Stamford was governed by twenty-five councillors, who were "to contynewe during ther lyves naturall". Vacancies would be filled by co-option.

Not all wealthy freemen served on the council; men like John Marchaunt mercer, William Spencer notary or the Leche family of goldsmiths who provided St Mary's church with their churchwarden, did not serve. The office of councillor was neither generally sought nor evaded; it seems to have been a matter of individual choice.

Government in Stamford was thus by a small group of laymen of the "better sort" who combined religious sanctions with the authority of charters; good rule was God's intention for towns like Stamford[33]. The 'commons' (i.e. the rest of the freemen) had only a small part to play: it was not until after William Browne's death that a Third Twelve (1489-90) appeared (briefly) to represent the

---

[32] Exeter-NRA 53/1; NRO Fitzwilliam (Milton) Charter 1632; PRO, E326/5553; SC6/1115/7; C67/40 m6; see above p 80; Kirkby drew up a new rental for the duke in 1441-2, PRO SC6/1115/7. John Kirkeby made a nil return to the income tax of 1450, PRO, E179/276/44. In some towns, the town clerk was an outside lawyer and acted as 'steward' for the town ensuring town courts were held, see Rigby *Grimsby* p 95. It is unlikely such a procedure operated in Stamford at this time, the Alderman seems to have been too powerful.

[33] See Rigby, Oligarchy p 64

rest of the freemen, and that *congregationes generales* were held from time to time[34]. Within the council, hierarchy played its part – a Second Twelve with its recognised 'leader', a First Twelve with its leader William Browne followed by the Alderman for the year. The larger number of people below the freemen[35] do not appear on the stage of Stamford's government - they are audience only, perhaps at times vocal but relatively powerless.

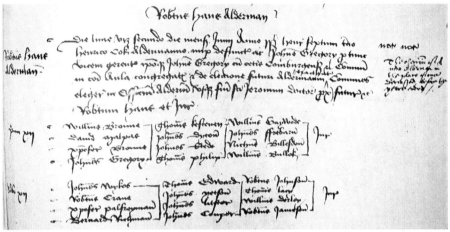

William Browne's name appears at the head of every list of councillors (above that of the outgoing Alderman) throughout the Hall Book until his death in 1489 (photo: Alan Rogers)

There is one hint that special status was given to past Aldermen among the members of the First Twelve, but they did not form a separate grouping on the town council with their own livery[36]. The two Twelves were self-perpetuating oligarchies; although membership was confirmed annually, dismissals and resignations were rare[37]. Women did not serve, and there are few signs of links between its members by marriage[38]. They enjoyed privileges of pasturage on the Meadows. They do not seem to have had constituencies: the early wards had

[34] HB i fol 23, p 60; fol 47, p 139; fol 68-68d; the council met with 'the major number of the community', 1494-5, and from 1500,common assemblies became more frequent, HB i fol 64d, 74d, 79d, 82d etc. These three - commonalty, Second Twelve and First Twelve - seem to have equated to the *inferiores*,the *mediocres* and the *potentiores* of Lynn; for senior and junior council, Lee 2009 p 82. See Kermode, Oligarchies p 89 for commonalty as all non-office-holding burgesses

[35] In other towns,the freemen comprised some one third to half of all households, Attreed *King's Towns* p 50; Amor *Ipswich* p 46; Exeter had only 21%, Kowaleski 1995 p 196; my guess is that they were less than one third in Stamford.

[36] HB i fol 30d, p 87; Past Aldermen were identified with the First Twelve: "Item, it is ordained that whoever has been in the office of Alderman shall have two liveried men and whoever are of the Second Twelve shall find one man similarly liveried to attend on the Alderman". Elsewhere, past mayors were not to be defamed, Attreed *King's Towns* p 48

[37] See Rigby *Grimsby* p 68; there is no known demand (as at Lynn) for annual elections to the council, see Dimmock 2001.

[38] There are no signs that a small group of "families welded together ...controlled most of the important offices in the town", as elsewhere, Rorig 1967 p 123

vanished, and the parish formed the unit for local administration. The members of the two Twelves represented the whole town community without economic sectoral or territorial interest. Despite a large clerical presence, "the sense of civic wholeness which in most towns ... depended on the Church depended [in Stamford, as in some other towns] upon the civic magistracy"[39].

The sixteenth century "common hall" over the north end of the bridge, probably on the site of medieval council chamber: when it was repaired in 1485, the council met in the gildhall of the Corpus Christi gild in St Mary's Place (from Peck)

These 25 men admitted others to the freedom of the town and collected their entry fines; they determined or authorised the groupings of the various crafts of the town into 'pagentes'. They registered apprentices, regulated trading in the town, forbidding trading on Sundays (except in August), forestalling and regrating. They had trouble with the butchers, and tried to control the town's refuse, keep the streets clean, paved and free from obstructions such as building timber and tethered horses on fair days. They maintained the West Gate and Scotgate but allowed wealthy residents to make doors through the town walls. They controlled the field system, the dates on which sheep and cattle could be allowed onto the common fields, and the herding of swine. The council held some land and leased it out[40]. They diverted the river Welland near St Leonard's priory and erected a mill there, probably to counter the power of the King's Mill

---

[39] HB i fol 20, pp 54-5; fol 26d,pp 72-3; fol 39, p 114 etc; Lee 2009 p 508; for the importance of parishes, see Kermode *Merchants* p 26

[40] HB i fol 4, pp 10-12; fol 12, p 32; fol 30d, pp 86-7; fol 38d, pp 113-4, etc; PRO, SC2/188/1-3; Stamford Borough records TH terrier 1485

further east,paying a rent to the priory. They set rules for fishing and for innkeepers and visitors. "Evil women", beggars, demobilised soldiers and shipmen occupied the town council; the playing of dice was banned in 1467 and again in 1478, and the carrying of weapons was restricted. Like other towns, they "asserted social order more vigorously" as national political order broke down; they dealt with "property, brawls, debt, petty theft and bonds for good behaviour" – but there are no signs of poor relief[41].

They tried to insist on the priority of the town's weekly Thursday court above other courts (they did not stick to Thursday for their meetings, despite their own ordinance). They collected fines for misdeeds, and bonds and recognisances for good behaviour. They legislated for attendance at council meetings; they twice forbad anyone to accept the livery or badge of any noble or gentleman (1469 and 1481). Moral (sexual) offences were interpreted as social crimes and therefore subject to lay courts like debt and contract disputes[42].

But involvement in the town's affairs reached beyond these 25 elite persons; others served in a variety of capacities. In the ten years between 1466-7 and 1475-76, at least 80 individuals from 73 families not on the council participated in the affairs of the borough in some official capacity, especially as taxers in the parishes – and there must have been more, for the borough records are not full. And service was not restricted to these appointments – there were many offices in the parish gilds as well. Under the Alderman, power was fairly widely distributed. We do not have details of the Stamford gilds (except St Katherine's gild from 1480), so it is impossible to say how far service in office or membership of the First or Second Twelve was related to gild membership[43]. But my impression is that, while there was no threat from these religious fraternities to the town council, equally there was no direct relationship between them and public office. The town council met in the gildhall of the gild of St Mary and Corpus Christi on occasion, and the church of St Mary at the bridge, in which

---

[41] Attreed *King's Towns* p 243; HB i fol 8d, p 23; fol 25d-26, pp 69-71; see Mate 2006 p 75; McIntosh 1998 p 165; McIntosh suggests that the main urban problems were "relief of the poor and maintenance of order", clean water and waste disposal, inns and alehouses; legislation against dice was passed in 1388 and 1409-10, but it was taken up by town courts from the 1460s,McIntosh 1986 pp 219, 227-8, 230, 232

[42] e.g. HB i fol 32, pp 92-3; fol 30d, p 87; see Horrox, Patronage pp 156-7. But equally ecclesiastical enclaves were intruding into secular justice, see e g C B Firth 1917 Benefit of clergy in the time of Edward IV *EHR* 32 pp 175-191

[43] For such links in other towns, see McRee 1987; B R McRee 1992 Religious gilds and civic order in late medieval England *Speculum* 67 1 pp 69-97; B R McCree 1993 Charity and gild solidarity in late medieval England *JBS* 32 pp 195-225; A G Rosser 1997 Crafts, gilds and the negotiation of work in the medieval town *Past and Present* 154 pp 3-31; P Nightingale 1989 Capitalists, crafts and constitutional change in late fourteenth century London *Past and Present* 124 pp 3-35; Giles p 58; Rubin *Corpus Christi* p 139

the gild chapel was situated, was the church of attendance of the Alderman and council. But it would seem that the gilds (with perhaps the exception of the Corpus Christi gild) and the town offices were separate fields of social practice. Although individuals would no doubt be actors in both fields, and although gilds exercised some role in the regulation of morals and public behaviour[44], as did the town council, there was no inherent link.

The council promoted the ceremonial round, including taking over the Corpus Christi pageants from the craft associations[45]. It has been suggested that Corpus Christi plays "provided a regular forum in which urban communities could engage with ideas about power and authority". In Stamford, the pageants, like the town council, provided an integrative counter-balance to the fragmentation of the parishes and parish gilds[46]; but as elsewhere they may have been unpopular because of their cost. In 1479, the full cycle of eleven pageants was challenged and in 1482, it was agreed that the eleven pageants should be divided into two parts, five in one year, with the other six in the following year[47]. The

---

[44] HB i fol 38d, p 112; fol 59; McRee 1987 pp 114-8; B A Hanawalt and B R McRee 1992 The guilds of *homo prudens* in late medieval England *Continuity and Change* 7 pp 163-179; R Tittler 1991 *Architecture and Power: the town hall and the English urban community c1500-1640* Oxford: Clarendon

[45] It is likely these pageants were plays rather than tableaux, for the churchwardens' accounts record *et in dat' histrionibus vjd*,BL, Cotton Vesp A24 fol 3d. For the relationships between plays and the trades' associations, see A F Johnston 1995 Traders and playmakers: English guildsmen and the Low Countries, in C Barron and N Saul (eds) 1995 *England and the Low Countries in the late Middle Ages* Sutton pp 99-114; James 1983; S Beckwith, Ritual, Church and Theatre: medieval dramas of the sacramental body, in D Aers 1992 *Culture and History: essays on English communities, identities and writing 1350-1600* Detroit: Wayne University Press pp 65-89. Pageants (tableaux) could also be occasional with political agendas,see Laynesmith 2003 for pageants at Coventry in the 1450s; Goldberg 1999; S Lindenbaum 1996 Rituals of exclusion: feasts and plays of English religious fraternities,in M Twycross (ed) *Festive Drama* pp 54-65; R Hutton 1996 *The Rise and Fall of Merry England: the ritual year 1400–1700*. Oxford University Press; Duffy *Stripping* pp 44, 66-68, 129; Giles pp 74, 76; Fleming, Oligarchy p 187. For civic ceremonial, see Phythian-Adams 1972; L C Attreed 1994 The politics of welcome: ceremonies and constitutional development in later medieval English towns, in B A Hanawalt and K L Reyerson 1994 *City and Spectacle in Medieval Europe* Minneapolis; S Anglo 1969 *Spectacle, Pageantry and Early Tudor Policy* Oxford; D Mills 1991 Chester ceremonial: re-creation and recreation in the English 'medieval' town, *Urban History Yearbook 1991* pp 4-5.

[46] James 1983; Kermode *Enterprise* p xii; Rubin 1991; see chap 1n31

[47] HB i fol 27d, pp 76-7; fol 33, p 96; fol 5d-6, pp 13-15; Leche accounts. In some towns, "cycles were not shown in full every year", Rubin *Corpus Christi* p 283; "relatively few communities mounted an entire cycle of plays",Duffy *Stripping* p 68. The feast of Corpus Christi was a relatively recent addition to the religious calendar; see S Beckwith 1993 *Christ's Body: identity, culture and society in late medieval writings* Routledge. The Corpus Christi procession "became the point of reference in relation to which the structure of precedence and authority in the town is made visually present", James 1983 p 5. "In urban parishes, Corpus Christi became a focus of elaborate ceremonial and lavish expenditure on banners, garlands, lights: the gilds, not the clerks,took over the management of the processions. These celebrations also became the principal occasions for the performance of cycles of devotional and didactic plays on the theme of salvation history, which in some places involved virtually the whole community", p 44. See A

council controlled the town minstrels; silver waits' badges were given to some of the councillors to distribute as items of patronage[48].

The council promulgated and tried to execute royal letters from time to time, including commissions of gaol delivery. They arranged for the collection of royal taxes; on at least one occasion, they supervised the tax collection in Stamford Baron which normally made its returns in Ness wapentake in Lincolnshire rather than in Stamford. The council mobilised the watch and troops as required.

They acted as arbiters in various disputes, even outside Stamford, and the resulting decisions were authenticated by the town seal[49]. In the late 1440s, Robert Browe the duke of York's steward was alleged to have dispossessed a tenant of the duke, giving the property to John Fox alias Kirkby (the town clerk); some eight or ten years later (1458), the Alderman and town council wrote to the duke over the town's seal seeking justice for the dispossessed. In 1470, a dispute between John Nettleham of Ryhall and Isabella widow of William Powell of Easton on the Hill and her feoffees was settled by a small committee, the indenture being witnessed by the Alderman, William and John Browne, Thomas and John Gregory and William Hikeham (all senior members of the council) and sealed with the town seal. In 1478, four men were appointed by the council to arbitrate in a local dispute. The seal was used in private matters also: in 1481, the council wrote to Northampton over the town seal to try to obtain the release of a Stamford citizen accused of the murder, and in 1495, William Wareyn (Christopher Browne's brother-in-law) used the town seal to validate a private letter[50].

Some of these were not enrolled in the Hall Book, bought in 1465. It consists of some 450 folios. It is not clear why so much paper was brought across from the

---

H Nelson 1974 *The Medieval English Stage: corpus Christi pageants and plays* University of Chicago Press; Laynesmith 2003

[48] HB i fol 29, p 80; fol 34d, p 100; fol 40d, p 119. The waits' collars are described in HB i fol 58d; David Cecil was given the badge held by John Dycon, his father-in-law and former Alderman and member of the First Twelve, HB i fol 59. See Justin Simpson 1885 The Stamford waits and their predecessors: an historical sketch, *The Reliquary* July 1885 pp 1-6. For pageants and *tableaux vivants*, see Huizinga pp 194, 198, 212; Kermode *Merchant* pp 33, 65; Phythian-Adams 1972; S J Kahrl 1974 *Records of plays and players in Lincolnshire, 1300-1585* Malone Society vol VIII (1974 for 1969) pp 87-89; James 1983

[49] HB i fol 24, pp 64-5. For arbitration, see Attreed 1992; Attreed *King's Towns* p 244; Shaw *Wells* pp 208-13; C Rawcliffe 1991 'That kindliness should be cherished more and discord driven out': the settlement of commercial disputes by arbitration in later medieval England, in Kermode *Enterprise* pp 99-117; M D Myers 2001 The failure of conflict resolution and the limits of arbitration in King's Lynn 1405-1416, in Biggs et al 2001 pp 81-108; S J Payling 1987 Law and arbitration in Nottinghamshire 1399-1461, in Rosenthal and Richmond 1987 pp 141-160

[50] Exeter-NRA 53/1; 1470, original letters patent in town hall collection on display among regalia; HB i fol 31d, pp 89-90; fol 63; for town seal, see below pp 203-4

continent for this purpose, for it must have been very awkward to write in when bound. The Hall Book during this period was badly kept; compared with other late medieval English boroughs[51], the records of Stamford town council are very poor. The number of meetings recorded is very few, an average of less than four per year, and the recorded business dealt with at each meeting is small; on several occasions, a heading for a meeting of the council has been written but nothing is recorded under that heading. The election of the town's first MPs, royal visits and other major events such as the funeral cortege of the duke of York in 1476 are not mentioned. There is a gap of two years, 1492-4. Only one list of pleas of debt heard by the council is included (8 pleas during the Aldermanry of William Browne in 1466-7); warrants of attachment for breach of the peace were apparently copied up from time to time from some other record[52]. Much must have been decided that has been left unrecorded. The minutes were at times written up some time after the event, with items or names added, in the wrong date order, copied or summarised from other records which have not survived[53].

The Charters

The Hall Book opens with an English summary of the charter of the borough's incorporation of February 1462. This was not of course the first charter it had received (see above pp 8-9), but this was the one which gave it incorporated status. The charter probably did not introduce major changes in the way the town council managed its affairs: it was apparently a "confirmation of previously achieved liberties"[54]. Indeed, the practices after 1462, as revealed in the Hall Book, did not exactly match the charter and probably reflect the practices in place before 1462.

A question arises as to why the charter of incorporation was so late. It seems that until 1461, the residents of Stamford did not feel the need for such a document. The sheriff of Lincolnshire was a long way away; and the attitude of the lords of the town was generally one of 'hands-off' administration, if not even supportive of local autonomy, so long as the income from the town continued through their

---

[51] It took almost 200 years (1657) to fill. The first few folios copy up entries going back to the charter of 1462. See Carrel 2000 p 282; Nottingham Borough Recorrds; Bateson, Leicestter Borough Records etc. Norwich lost some essential writs at this time which resulted in fines to the government, Attreed *King's Towns* p 76

[52] They are entered regularly from 1467 to 1472, an average of eight a year: but from 1472 to 1492, on only three occasions: 20 in 1476-7, 23 with 40 'corrections' (i.e. fines) in 1479-81, 55 in 1486-7.

[53] in 1476, for example, the name of Robert Skynner was inserted into the list of the First Twelve while it was still among the Second Twelve, and in 1470 the entry concerning troops sent to Warwick and Edward IV has clearly been written up after the event or added to, HB i fol 14d, pp 39-40; fol 22, pp 57-8; 49d, p 147,etc. Compare for example Grimsby (Rigby) and Ipswich (Amor); there may be some items among the archives at Burghley House.

[54] Attreed *King's Towns* p 35

officers. Richard duke of York was only 4 years old in 1415 when he inherited his title, and his estates, burdened with two dowries and a trust to pay for the over-elaborate plans for Fotheringhay, were managed for him; after 1433, while fighting in France, he continued to rely on his officials to run his affairs. The estate as a whole was administered through a court[55] run by a steward and/or a receiver or bailiff, with a deputy in Stamford[56]. Stamford was useful as a source of annuities to some servants, but there are no signs of recruitment into the lord's household or retinue from the town. Nor did York expand his holdings in the town even when other properties became available. Such a hands-off policy allowed the duke of Suffolk and then lord Cromwell to increase their interests in the town; the duke of York's officials seem to have had relatively little standing in the town[57]. The town had been able to "exercise some or all of those [urban] rights ... with or without specific royal permission"; it had not needed incorporated status to be flourishing[58].

But from 1461, the town's overlord (noted for his physical attractiveness, lasciviousness and "insatiable covetise") had become king, and thus it would be royal officials in future who engaged with the town. The town may not have

---

[55] Pugh York pp 110-1. For the nuns having business in the castle, see Sturman p 215. For courts, see CPR 1370-74/ 489; NRS 5 *Assize* pp 712, 905; J Bellamy 1973 *Crime and Public Order in England in the later middle ages* Routledge and Kegan Paul p 178; Platts *Medieval Lincolnshire* p 234; Selden Soc 46 ii p 42.

[56] For steward, see C Kelly 1986 The noble steward and late-feudal lordship *Huntington Library Quarterly* 49 pp 133-48. See above p 6. The local servants of Richard duke of York were relatively humble men; under Edward IV, their social standing rose substantially, CPR 1452-61/533, 553; CPR 1494-1509/39. More work is needed on the local administration of the York estates, but the names of some of the Yorkist household officials in Stamford are known: Henry Mulsho 1404; Thomas de Ufford; Sir John Tirrell; Sir Edward Mulso; Robert Browe until his death in 1451; Henry Bracy; Humphrey Bourghchier (later lord Cromwell) from 1451 until at least 1466; William Hussey of Sleaford. John Vincent was receiver of the estates in the late 1450s, BL Harl 773 fol 129; see Rogers, Stokes, for this office at the time of the attainder of the duke of York, 1459. The deputy bailiff in 1459-60 and 1466-7 was John Basse a mercer, PRO, SC6/1115/7, 9. The names of some of the bailiffs are known; John Northorp and John Botiler senior sometime before 1402, PRO, SC6/913/25; John Lumpney in Grantham and perhaps Stamford, 1400-1, SC6/913/25; Robert Garland (1434-5?), John Trunke 1444, 1466,CCR 1454-61/407; PRO, SC6/913/25; SC6/1115/6, 7, 9; John Bullok in 1450-52. Henry Cok stainer took over from Trunke as bailiff of Stamford and Deeping in 1466-7, and was in office in 1468-9 and in 1485-6, PRO, SC6/1115/9, 11, 13. The king had a bailiff (John Balle) in the town c1406 but that may have been while the estates of York were in the king's hands, CIPM 23 1427-32 p 139

[57] Richard duke of York did not take advantage of the fall of the house of Suffolk, 1388, to secure the substantial property which the de la Pole family had in Stamford and which must for a short time have been easy pickings when it was forfeited to the crown; CPR 1385-88/513; CIM v 1387-93 pp 66-7 (93), 91 (115); after the killing of Suffolk in 1450, the estates in Stamford or some of them passed into the hands of Ralph lord Cromwell.

[58] "Such documents added no privileges that the boroughs were not already exercising", but a charter was useful because "time-honored custom and the historic memory of such privileges were no longer enough"; in addition, a charter was "useful in giving the city what it could not take or evolve by itself", Attreed *King's Towns* pp 37-39

welcomed this change. It is true that in June 1461, Edward gave Stamford and Grantham to his mother Cecily duchess of York in dower, and on the whole, the hands-off policy continued; so that, even after the accession of Edward IV, Stamford did not share "the obsessive search" for patronage of other towns. There is only one recorded gift from the town (to Humphrey lord Cromwell) and that was small and for unspecified returns at a time of relative national calm (1467). Both Norwich and York wooed Cecily extensively with wine, cloth and other goods after 1461 to ensure her favours – but there are no signs Stamford attempted to placate her voraciousness. Nor in the last years of the century when Lady Margaret Beaufort sat powerfully close to the town can we see any attempts to court her with gifts[59].

Free fees in Stamford

But in 1461, it seems that it was not so much freedom from the overlord's courts and officials that was sought; more urgent was the role of the borough court, "the focus of town government", inside the town. Here trade disputes and breaches of the town's regulations were heard and business transactions could be registered. The profits of the court were considerable[60]; but its main attraction was the power which it gave to a group of leading citizens to control most of the town's affairs. The aim was that this court should cover all the residents and traders in the town. Two main issues were involved – money (tolls, royal taxes and payment of the town's fee farm) and jurisdiction. But as we have seen, several properties claimed to be free fees, exempt from the town's jurisdiction[61].

It is possible that the number of properties exempt from seigneurial and borough control in the town was increasing during the fifteenth century; in 1509, it was possible to talk about someone being 'a gentleman or a court-holder'. These were not coherent blocks of property but scattered holdings, a patchwork of jurisdictions and rights throughout the town. The strongest were ecclesiastical liberties, providing sanctuary to fugitives and criminals. In 1478, St Leonard's was claiming the goods of an outlaw as belonging to its jurisdiction; and this manor appointed its own constable and aletaster. Much monastic property such as that possessed by Sempringham and Thorney was held to be exempt; and the four orders of friars in Stamford claimed they should not be sued in the town courts even for debt. And in Stamford as elsewhere, the civic court was felt to be challenging the ecclesiastical courts on both social and moral grounds[62].

---

[59] CPR 1461-7/131; Virgoe 1481 p 25; Dobson 1977 p 15; see also Horrox, Patronage p 148

[60] HB i fol 40d, p 120; Rigby *Grimsby* p 41; see pp 111-2

[61] Attreed 1992; W O Ault 1923 *Private Jurisdiction in England* Yale; McIntosh 1998

[62] L and P Henry VIII 1 i 1509 438/4 mm 3,16, 21; HB i fol 25, p 68; CCR 1454/35; PRO, E118/1/22; see Carrel 2000 p 289

This kaleidoscope of lay fees, whose tenants had different rights and duties from those of other tenants, also seem to have been growing in assertiveness. The Pembroke fee in the hands of the dukes of York was kept separate in the accounts of the estate, and the manor of the de la Pole family, which came to lord Cromwell, seems have increased its independence. Smaller holdings too could give rise to complications of jurisdictions. As we have seen, a town like Stamford with extensive trading activities attracted local landholders to acquire property in the borough linked with manors outside the town. The major fees and some religious houses appointed their own bailiffs; Henry Cok and David Cecil made a living acting as bailiff for several fee-holders[63].

The largest exempt jurisdiction was that of the abbot of Peterborough. Mostly in Stamford Baron, the abbey also had properties north of the river, held by payment of a rent and (in some cases) two suits to the 'little courts'[64] every year. Although Stamford Baron was seigneurial, it seems to have had a good measure of self-government and at times could mount an effective campaign in its own interests. But Stamford Baron was special; it possessed territorial coherence. The bailiff of the Peterborough estates had much power; for the exemption of Stamford Baron from the town's authority created a sanctuary for those accused of ill-doing. In 1493-4, Sir John Hussey as sheriff of Lincolnshire justified himself to the king against accusations of "the misusing of your lawes":

> *"I took a thief and he told me about another thief who lived in Stamford but because it is half in Linc and half in Northts, he needs to be taken out of the franchise [Stamford Baron] by a trick; I got some mercery from Coventry and Robert Tovye and others toke him"*[65].

Relations between the residents and tradesmen of this suburb and 'Stamford in Lincolnshire' were always ambiguous, both in trading and law and order. The agreements made and remade between the inhabitants of Stamford Baron and the town council were complicated and constructed in each generation to suit the interests of the dominant group at the time. In 1491, Stamford north of the river imposed a boycott on Stamford Baron:

---

[63] See pp 20-21; for the use of such links, see HB i fol 27, p 74, an apprentice from Wakerley Cok was bailiff for the nunnery in 1473-4, PRO, SC6/914/1. For Cecil, see biography in Rogers, Parl.

[64] NRS 33 *Obedientiaries* p 132; NRS 12 *Peterborough Local Administration* p xlv; VCH *Northants* ii pp 522-28

[65] PRO, SC1/51/179 fol 206-7. NRS 5 *Assize* pp 116,157; NRS 2 *Pytcheley* p 88; *Chron Petrob*; Exeter-NRA 80/3; the bailiff administered the chantry for the Spenser family, Exeter-NRA 53/2. The office eventually came into the hands of the Cecil family.

> *... none inhabitaunt within this Burgh of Staunford after this day bye any vitailes or marchaundise in seynt martyn parissh of any dueller in the same parish nor any othyr thing wherfor they shall leve any of ther money ther. And also that no man inhabit within this burgh shall set any dueller within the parissh of seynt Martyn aforsaid in any occupacion and warke ... without any such person be suorne afor the Alderman.*

And in 1495, after having admitted a mason from Stamford Baron free of entry fine on the grounds of having been born in the town, this was rescinded and he had to pay his fine "because [he was born] in the parish of St Martin"[66]. But these may have been temporary controversies.

The council sought to enforce its jurisdiction over as many of the residents of the town, freemen and non-freemen, including the friars[67], as possible. Their aim was to control (in order to encourage) the trade of the whole town and any litigation which might arise out of that trade. This is not to say there was out and out warfare between these various jurisdictions; an equilibrium seems to have been reached by the fourteenth century, so far as we can see. There were matters in dispute, of course, over shared or common properties and rights[68]. In 1455-6, John Iccochester was unable to pay the duke's officials the rent of 3s p. a. for his lease of "one vacant toft on the east of the castle commonly called le Pynfold ... because, on account of the taking of the vacant plot by the community, the said John was injured so that his life was despaired of and there is no possibility of finding the culprits and their goods and chattels so that the rent can be distrained". The 'community' mentioned here is undoubtedly the town council. But issues were probably settled peacefully, mostly by arbitration. The council, claiming the right to a forfeiture from St Leonard's, eventually gave in; and the council supported the friars on matters relating to rubbish heaped up against their walls and to riotous attacks on their properties. While defending the principle of 'free fees', some friars used the secular courts for matters of debt[69].

The charter of 1462 then was a step in a long-running attempt by the town council to increase measures of self-government and control over the various interests inside the town; and to do this, some measure of freedom from outside interests such as the county sheriff and county JPs which could be used by the holders of free fees against the council was needed. This the charter gave them.

---

[66] HB i fol 18, p49; fol 49, p 146; fol 61

[67] CCR 1369-74/514-5; see CPR 1401-5/125 for the arrest of John Leycester friar of Stamford

[68] PRO,SC6/1115/7; "conflicts .. frequently centred upon areas used for common pasture, such as local meadows",Carrel 2000 p 284; Attreed *King's Towns* p 254; see Dyer C 1992; Dimmock 2001; S Dimmock 2007 English towns and the transition c1450-1550, in Dyer et al *Hilton* pp 270-285.

[69] PRO, SC6/1115/13; HB i fol 43d, p 130

The Charter of 1462

Town mace dating from fifteenth century (photo: John Hartley, with permission)

The new charter dealt with four main sets of matters. First, incorporation, giving it status to sue and be sued, with its own seal[70] and its own mace. Regalia was important for a town's dignity and the town began its excellent collection of plate. It was apparently at this time that the royal leopards were added to the borough's coat of arms[71]. Secondly, exemption from royal household officers, the marshalsea court, the sheriff of Lincolnshire, and the Kesteven JPs (members of the First Twelve now served as JPs for the town)[72]. The exclusion of the sheriff was of course only partial, for Stamford was not made into a separate county like Lincoln, Hull and Norwich[73]; the sheriff of Lincolnshire still had residual powers and duties in the town. But this was not a case of Stamford opting *out* of local government; rather it was opting *in* to play a full part, such as enforcing and returning writs, and assessing and collecting the king's taxes. Thirdly, the rules under which the council would operate – the election of the Alderman and the borough council, the Twelve (only one Twelve is mentioned), the office of serjeant at mace, and the Alderman's court. And finally, a range of privileges: power to control the markets and fair, and allocate the fines they collect; to elect their own coroner, be quit of trading tolls, and recruit their own watch and militia to keep order in the town and area around. None of these was unusual; indeed in 1488, Pontefract asked for the same charter privileges as Stamford had[74]. And it would seem that little changed in practice - the two Twelves continued, not just the one Twelve, as the charter indicated. But there

---

[70] C Ch R v pp 164-7. The town had a seal earlier than this, for the Alderman was a frequent witness to property deeds and this would have been confirmed by a town seal, not a personal seal. The arms of Warenne would have been on the seal.

[71] Attreed *King's Towns* pp 39, 73; for mace,see Horrox, Patronage p 146

[72] JPs for the town had been appointed in the 1350s for a short time, CPR 1350-54/90, 449, 451, but normally the JPs of Kesteven would have dealt with cases from Stamford. The 'town' cases and the crown cases can be distinguished in that the fines from the former went to the common chest or the hall,the fines for the second went to the king; see e.g. HB i fol 24, p 65

[73] Palliser 1994 p 144; Rigby, Oligarchy p 80. For the sheriff in Stamford in this century, see CCR 1405-9/147; 1409-13/77; CPR 1416-22/78; CPR 1452-61/124. At times his role was beneficent – he released some Stamford men imprisoned unjustly. In 1346, the sheriff of Rutland enforced a writ in Stamford, CPR 1345-8/232. See CIM vii 1399-1422 p 303 (535)

[74] CPR 1485-94/261.

was one major failure – the charter failed to specify the territory of the borough, so that the uncertain status of Stamford Baron remained[75]. Such sanctuaries continued to provide a thorn in the side of the council.

The borough seal with the royal arms and the arms of Warenne (from Peck).

The charter of 1481

A second charter in November 1481 did not resolve this issue. Who originated this charter and facilitated its passage at Westminster is not known. It is an anodyne affair, reiterating the exclusion of the sheriff of Lincolnshire and other officers from the town, and repeating the powers of the First Twelve to act as JPs for the town but including a requirement that a lawyer attend the sessions. It granted to the town two new fairs, at Corpus Christi (May-June) and the feast of Saints Simon and Jude (October), and a new Monday market, a gaol (which it already possessed)[76], and the Southorp properties which had been used to reward several royal servants and town MPs (see p 113).

---

[75] The borough extension into Rutland in the west was also not clarified, HB i fol 66

[76] CCh R vi pp 253-4. The position of the town gaol seems to be anomalous. Clearly, as the Hall Book indicates, the town had and ran a gaol in 1467. The town bailiff in his 1460s oath said that "All manner of prysoners commytt to my kepyng withowt any wyllfull eschape suerly I shall se to be kepte", HB i fol 11d, pp 30-31; and there are references to prisoners detained in prison in Stamford which clearly relate to the town gaol, see above pp 90-91. The town gaol was disputed by the lord's gaol in the castle, which was the subject of a gaol delivery commission in 1478, CPR 1476-85/144. The fact that the charter of 1481 gave the council permission to have its own gaol does not mean there was no town prison before 1481, only that the charter regularised the situation. See R B Pugh 1968 *Imprisonment in Medieval England* Cambridge; H Carrel 2009 The ideology of punishment in late medieval towns *Social History* 34 pp 301-20

William's last years: contestation in the town?

The Southorp grant may have been part of the changes which came over Stamford town government from the late 1470s onwards. These ante-date the accession of Henry Tudor in 1485, as well as the long-awaited change of lordship when Cecily dowager duchess of York at last died in 1495 and the lordship of Stamford reverted to Henry VII's queen Elizabeth.

In 1478-9, under Robert Skynner Alderman, a long-serving member of the First Twelve and former chamberlain, the town government was overhauled. All the officers were changed; the 'statutes, ordinances and articles' of the town were proclaimed again "by thauctorite of the kynges letters patentez' (i.e. the 1462 charter) and entered in the Hall Book. The town plays (over which there was some dispute) and the appointment of searchers of the markets were taken away from the craft associations and became the responsibility of the council. In the following year (1479-80), under William Hykeham, again a councillor of long standing, the officers' accounts were audited, and a stringent ordinance was passed against all forms of taking livery of any lord, although all councillors must wear their town livery when attending the Alderman[77].

Exactly what was going on is not clear; the inadequacies of the Hall Book obscure the picture. But two main changes in character of the political elite of the town can be seen. First, a number of county gentry, many of them having strong London links and some of them royal servants, were brought in. And secondly, a number of people (including most of the county gentry members) were 'fast-tracked' into office, coming onto the First Twelve without serving on the Second Twelve and becoming Alderman immediately[78]. In addition, there were controversies in the town, including a row within the council over the use of the town seal.

Influx of county gentry: There had been royal servants in Stamford prior to 1480, most of them initially associated with the York estate administration, but they were not county gentry; most of them were resident in the town. But in 1480, Richard Forster, a royal servant who had been living in and representing the town as MP since 1467, was belatedly admitted to the freedom without fee or pledge and was co-opted to the First Twelve, only (most unusually) to resign nine months later. At the same time, another royal servant and former MP, John

---

[77] HB i fol 30-31, pp 88-89. This was not unusual: virtually every town passed legislation against livery and maintenance, see Horrox, Patronage pp 156-7; Kermode *Merchants* p 37
[78] See Britnell, Elites; Horrox, Gentry; Kermode *Merchants* p 49; Shaw *Wells* p 156. The interaction of rural gentry and urban merchants is discussed in Dyer et al *Hilton* pp 50, 106. See Horrox, Gentry, for the London links of urban gentry

Murdoke junior, was elected directly to the First Twelve but with a caveat that he should "in no wise be burdened nor elected into the office of Alderman nor any other office to his own harm or detriment without the consent or will of the same John"[79]; he agreed to become coroner of the town at the same time, and he held both offices until he died late in 1485.

From 1482, however, new blood came onto the council and into office. David Malpas armiger, a royal servant from Cheshire and now of Pickworth, Rutland, was admitted to the freedom in March 1483 without fee, elected onto the First Twelve in June and became Alderman in September 1483. John Thurlby yeoman of Empingham was elected MP for Stamford in 1485 and again in 1487 and 1491-2, and became a member of the gild of St Katherine. In June 1487, John Frebarn yeoman of Easton on the Hill was admitted to the freedom, the same day elected to the Second Twelve, onto the First Twelve four months later, and Alderman one year later (September 1488)[80]. Richard Cannell mercer from Louth was admitted in December 1495, appointed to the First Twelve the same day, elected MP in December 1496 and made Alderman September 1497. William Radcliffe (later MP) from Yorkshire was admitted as 'gentleman' in 1489, appointed the same day to the Second Twelve, elevated to the First Twelve in February 1491 and made Alderman by 1495. David Cecil esquire from Herefordshire, yeoman of the guard to Henry VII, MP five times, was admitted to the freedom sometime between 1492 and 1494, marrying the daughter of the Alderman of the time, was on the First Twelve by 1504 and Alderman the same year. In September 1504, John Hardgrave of Rushden, Northants, was admitted, supported by David Cecil and William Radcliffe, and was immediately appointed to the Second Twelve; two months later (November), he was promoted to the First Twelve and made Alderman in 1508. Hardgrave was receiver of the duchy of Lancaster honor of Bolingbroke, Lincs; he was a young man at the start of his career (he did not die until 1547). He had no prior connection with Stamford and clearly was not in any significant way a trader or manufacturer in the town[81]. If we add to this David Cecil's patron, Sir David Phillips of Chenies, Bucks, sheriff of Bedfordshire and Buckinghamshire, soldier of Henry Tudor at

---

[79] HB i fol 31, p 88; we have no record of his admission to the freedom of Stamford. This is discussed in more detail in Rogers, Parl

[80] HB i fol 42, p 124; probably the son of the bailiff of Stamford (1453-4) and feoffee in 1451 with John Chevercourt and bailiff for Ralph lord Cromwell in Rutland, 1453-4, PRO, CP25/1/145/160/33; HMC de l'Isle i pp 216, 280. The son (John Frebarn junior) was taxed in Stamford Baron in 1450, PRO, E179/276/44. Margaret his wife was the daughter of William and Margaret Morewode; she had married William Wode as her first husband, Exeter-NRA 38/41-51; 90/1. He "dwells beside Collyweston" in 1460, HMC de l'Isle i 18, 187.

[81] HB i fol 81d, 87; Somerville Lancaster p 579; his son became Alderman in 1520 and 1528 and MP for Stamford in 1529, S T Bindoff 1982 House of Commons 1509-1558 Secker and Warburg vol i p 295; HB i fol 81d

Bosworth, squire of the body for Henry VII, keeper of Windsor Park and servant of Lady Margaret Beaufort, who died in 1506 and was buried in a chantry chapel in St Mary at the bridge, the influx of country gentry is clear.

Much the same can be seen of the town's MPs. From 1467 until 1481, all the town MPs were associated with the Southorp properties which were leased out by the government. Richard Forster of the royal household occupied one seat in every parliament, and he was accompanied mostly by other household servants who lived in the town or had very close connections with it. But from 1485, the persons elected were mostly landholders in Rutland and Northants with an occasional Stamford merchant among them[82].

The focus of this group was Christopher Browne. Christopher was the opposite of William Browne in many ways, a courtier merchant: Calais Stapler, at the court of Henry VII and later Henry VIII, councillor of Lady Margaret Beaufort. He took out a coat of arms, bought an estate in Rutland and became 'Christopher Browne esquire of Tolthorpe'. His commitment to Stamford was limited; when appointed Alderman in 1502, he accepted on condition that he serve by deputy (it may be significant that it was during his second term as Alderman, 1491-2, that the Hall Book ceased to record any entries until the election of a new Alderman in September 1494). Neither William Browne nor Margaret used him as feoffee or witness, or mentioned him in their wills; and Christopher was soon engaged in a bitter dispute with Browne's Hospital[83].

Christopher was admitted to the freedom in December 1481 without fee or pledge as one born in the town. To enable him to be elected as Alderman on 30 September 1482, he was appointed onto the First Twelve at a pre-election meeting on that same day. When William Browne died in 1489, Christopher claimed his place as the senior member of the Browne dynasty, including becoming Alderman of the St Katherine gild, and when William Elmes, grandson and heir of William Browne and his successor as Alderman of the gild of All Saints, died unexpectedly early in 1504, Christopher became Alderman of that gild.

Disputes and the town seal: It is in this context that signs of disputes in Stamford in the years 1479-1485 need to be seen. In May 1481, a small group of the First Twelve[84] led by William Browne locked the town seal in a chest and allowed it to

---

[82] More details are in Rogers, Parl
[83] Rogers and Hill forthcoming
[84] One additional name appears, Stephen Talbot esq, but I have not been able to trace him. For the importance of the town seal, see Shaw *Wells* pp 203-4; for the use of Stamford's seal, see above p 193

be used only under supervision. This situation continued until at least 1485 when, under the supervision of the sub-committee, the seal was used to authenticate the indenture of return for the election of the town MPs. In 1484, there are vague hints that Malpas's election as Alderman may have been contested, and in the summer of 1485, a number of sureties to keep the peace were taken and the king (Richard III) intervened to secure the release of a man who had been arrested[85]. One key figure seems to have been William Taverner, who in November 1480 had been appointed town bailiff in place of Thomas Parnell and who in March 1483 was himself displaced by Parnell again. The council renewed by-laws against anyone taking livery from outside lords, and insisting on attendance at meetings (which can be read as trying to stop meetings of smaller groups from being held). In 1489, a Third Twelve was summoned to help with an audit of the town officials.

Such disputes in towns were of course common[86], but exactly what was going on in Stamford is not clear. That Christopher Browne was at the heart of this can be seen in that Forster was admitted to the freedom at the same time as Christopher, that Malpas and Freebarn were admitted by Christopher, while Thurlby was MP with Christopher and became a member of St Katherine's gild sponsored by Christopher; most of the others were closely associated with Lady Margaret Beaufort's household.

There were also some long-standing citizens who in the 1480s were involved. Thomas Edwardes pewterer, admitted in 1472, constable in 1478-81, member of the Second Twelve in 1483 and the First Twelve in 1489, was MP alongside Christopher Browne in 1491 and Alderman in 1494. Nicholas Billesdon dyer, who was admitted in 1483, on the Second Twelve the next year, the First Twelve 1487 and Alderman in 1492, served as Christopher's deputy as Alderman. Thomas Philippe mercer, member of the Second Twelve since 1472, chamberlain and constable, was elevated along with Malpas to the First Twelve in June 1483 (an unusual date for such a promotion), was appointed to 'assist' Christopher if needed when Christopher represented the town in the royal council summoned for 1488, and in 1489 became Alderman of the town. John Stede, who had been admitted in 1465 and on the Second Twelve by 1474, was now (1485) elevated by Malpas to the First Twelve only a few days before he was elected as Alderman of the town.

---

[85] HB i fol 37d, p 109; the name of Torton may be significant, as it was the name of the Yorkshire family who in the 1450s came to Grantham to support the duke of York; see above p 81.

[86] e.g. in York; see Kermode, Oligarchies p 99; see Dyer 1992; Dimmock 2001; Yates 2007 pp 222-231; Kermode *Enterprise* pp xii, 8 etc

Fifteenth century chest in Town Hall, almost certainly the one used by Browne and his fellow councillors in 1481-5 (photo: Alan Rogers)

At the same time, some existing councillors resigned or were dismissed – it is hard to say which. There was an air of short-termism in the appointments: the small group of long-serving local "commercial mercantile elite" was being replaced or supplemented by a landed "urban gentry"[87]. It is tempting to see in this signs of the political tensions of the day, although the sequence of events goes back to the late 1470s. It is possible that Christopher and his friends were committed to the Tudor cause some time before it materialised; certainly Christopher was committed: his family claimed later that he joined Henry Tudor's invasion force in 1485. One possible interpretation of these events is that a party for the Tudor claimant was resisted by those who had so far tried to preserve neutrality from such commitments. But the evidence is thin for such a conclusion.

One factor in this may have been the Hussey family, stewards of Stamford for Cecily duchess of York. Sir William Hussey had built up an interest in Stamford over many years before he died in 1495. His son Sir John Hussey seems to have insisted on the election of the Alderman being confirmed by oath taken separately from the election process. This is first seen in 1484 with the

---

[87] Several of the new appointees served for a short time only. Christopher Browne was also of a resigning temperament. On the question of oligarchies in late medieval towns, see A B Hibbert 1978, The origins of the medieval town patriciate, in P Abrams and E A Wrigley (eds) 1978 *Towns in Societies: essays in economic history and historical sociology* Cambridge University Press pp 91-104; M Kowaleski 1984 The commercial dominance of a medieval provincial oligarchy: Exeter in the late fourteenth century, *Medieval Studies* 46 pp 355-384; Rigby, Oligarchy; Kermode, Oligarchies

newcomer Malpas (with whom Hussey held the manor of Pickworth in Rutland), and this is followed by the fast tracker Stede in 1485, by Cok in 1487 and then by Gaywode in 1490 and Christopher Browne in 1491. In these cases, the oath was administered in the common hall; but from 1495, after the death of Cecily duchess of York and a new administration in the town[88], we find the Alderman going to the castle some time after election to take his oath of office before a lawyer or the steward. A stronger control over the town was now in force.

For from 1489 (as we have seen, above p 105), a new force was growing, the household and council of Lady Margaret Beaufort from Collyweston. The town elites, men like Christopher Browne, David Cecil, William Radcliffe, were going to have to find ways of working with this new powerful focal point. But by then, William Browne was dead.

---

[88] For Hussey, see Ives *Lawyers* p 466. Reginald Bray became steward after the death of Cecily duchess of York (1495) when the estate came into the hands of Elizabeth of York queen to Henry VII; and Sir John Hussey, Thomas Manners earl of Rutland 1539 and Sir John Russell followed after Bray's early death in 1503. CPR 1485-94/370; 1494-1509/39; *Rot Parl* vi pp 460, 462; for a time, Stamford was seen as part of the endowment of the queen – Katharine of Aragon received it as part of her settlement, L and P Henry VIII 1 i 1509-13 p 49 (g94/35); HB i fol 65, 129, 137.

PART IV: CHAPTER 2   RELIGION: WILLIAM BROWNE AS 'GOD'S BAILIFF'

"ryche men whyche arn Goddis revys and Goddys baylys"[89]

A separate chapter on religion in a study of the late Middle Ages might seem superfluous, for religion was a fundamental component of the whole of life, economic, social, cultural and political: medieval men and women "turned daily activities into religious proclamations"[90].   William Browne's *habitus* was in essence religious.

We cannot look at Browne's religious identity without looking at the community in which he lived. It has been argued that late medieval religion was fundamentally communal – the whole community shared in expressing their religious and spiritual values[91]. But what strikes me most about late medieval Stamford is the diversity of religious expression in the town. True, we have to concentrate here mostly on religious institutions, for few wills survive to indicate personal and family pieties.   But a wide range of religious approaches were available to the inhabitants of the town. God was both remote and yet immanent, to be approached only through intermediaries and yet directly and personally, to be addressed through formulaic, extempore and/or silent prayer and meditation according to personal preference. Religion could be emotional and charismatic, or ritualistic and impersonal. Beliefs at the core of late medieval Christianity were questioned openly or discreetly; it was not only Lollards who challenged received doctrines. Papal authority was appealed to, as William Browne experienced in 1479, but at the same time this authority was challenged by local customs and laws. The individualist elements in religion were growing stronger, as Margery Kempe, Thomas a Kempis, Piers Plowman, the increase in religious literature and the many translations into English of older texts, show. Lady Margaret Beaufort's personal preference for monthly communion was said to be extraordinary, not to be emulated too widely[92]. It was growing individualism of belief and practice which fuelled the fear of Lollardy, for here personal expression went too far. Although much medieval religion was communal at heart and in practice, the social homogeneity of late medieval

---

[89] P H Barnum (ed) 1980 *Dives et Pauper* EETS vol 275 part ii p xvi
[90] Elisheva Baumgarten 2008 'A separate people': some directions for comparative research on medieval women *JMH* 34 (2) pp 212-228
[91] especially in the writings of S Duffy.
[92] Duffy *Stripping* p 93; S Powell 1998 Lady Margaret Beaufort and her books, *The Library* vol 20 (3)

religious practice was fractured[93]. William Browne's religious beliefs and practices were his own, selected from and influenced by those of his communities, the parish of All Saints in the Market, his gilds, the town of Stamford, the diocese, the nation and Rome.

Fifteenth-century Stamford was a visibly religious town: 13 parish churches[94] with multiple chapels, altars and images, three monasteries, four large and very active friaries, at least six parish gilds, at least four hospitals, several free chapels, monastic houses with holdings all over the town, some very significant like Thorney and Sempringham, two nationally known anchoresses - all for a population of some 2500-3000: " very few English towns could compete with Stamford in the number of religious houses"[95]. Durham and Peterborough owned large swathes of the town. The percentage of ecclesiastics among its residents was high. The opportunities for different forms of worship was considerable; the contrast between the 'dark' churches of St Mary and St John and the 'light' churches of All Saints in the Market and St Martin's can still be seen.

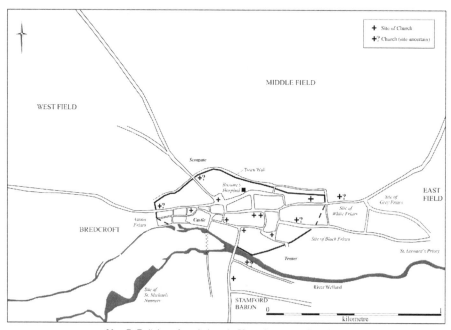

Map 7: Religious foundations in fifteenth century Stamford

---

[93] Tanner 1977; Duffy *Stripping* pp 7, 265.
[94] for list in 1428, see *Feudal Aids* iii 338-9; vi 364-5
[95] CY *Visit* ii p 118n

The parishes

The parishes were the hub for most of the laity: "the emotion that was evoked by religious teaching and festivals and neighbourhood loyalties, growing up around the parish churches, did much to keep friendships open between families that otherwise moved in different social spheres". "By the fifteenth century, the religion which was offered them in the parish church they participated in, they shared, even in some ways they created: it was popular religion. That, allied to intense local loyalties, meant the parish church was where their hearts were"[96].Thus when two suburban churches fell on hard times, the laity took steps to keep them going. Holy Trinity at Eastgate lost most of its population to the friaries, so a lay gild was formed and paid a chaplain to serve the parish church; St Clement at Northgate also declined, but an endowed chantry of St Nicholas with a warden and two chaplains provided the clergy[97]. When some parishes became unviable, they were amalgamated, St Mary Bynwerk with nearby St Peter's, and All Saints by the Water in Stamford Baron with St Martin's[98].

The multiple parishes, in contrast with the single parish of Melton Mowbray, Oakham, Grantham, and Boston, formed the basic unit of the town. This was not just a matter of social control, collecting taxes and regulating dunghills. Apart from its routine of Sunday mass and the newly popular Friday Jesus mass, each parish had its own calendar of festivals. Rich and poor met at parish events, although social hierarchies were confirmed; the procession for the offertory at the mass was "formed in order of seniority, wealth or worship"[99].

William and John Browne were brought up in St Paul's parish at the east end of the town [100], an area of mixed housing with larger merchants and smaller tradesmen and craftsmen living side by side. They knew from childhood the anchoress immured on the north side of their church; they saw the members of St Katherine's gild assemble every year in the room over the porch. When William Browne's family moved to All Saints in the Market, he retained links with St Paul's. But All Saints became his parish of choice. He became life

---

[96] Thrupp p 38; Richmond *Hopton* p 175
[97] St Clement: CCR 1381-85/64; "the chantry in the church inside the north gate of Stamford" was founded by Nicholas de Eston *alias* de Staunford 20 Edward III ; *Testamenta Eboracensia* vol iii Surtees Society vol 45 1864 p 24; *AASR* Chantry pp 247-9. CPR 1358-61/478; 1361-64/163; CPL 1471-84 pp 484, 562, 596, 680, 696 etc; for Holy Trinity see PRO, C143/421/4
[98] See above p 90. St Andrew and St Michael were united for tax collection from 1466, but remained separate for religious purposes until 1546. It appears that both churches and the parsonage of St Andrew's church stood in the one churchyard (now St Michael the Greater); see NRS 43 *Pilsgate* pp 91, 377; PRO E326/4736 speaks of the two churchyards; this revises the note in Hartley and Rogers p 22
[99] "Virtually every town had its Jesus Mass on Fridays",Duffy *Stripping* p 465; see Lutton 2006 p 69 for Lady Margaret Beaufort and the Jesus mass. Duffy *Stripping* p 125; Dyer *Standards* p 257;
[100] PRO, E179/135/76

Alderman of the parish gild; his brother-in-law, Thomas Stokes, became vicar there, and William used successive vicars as feoffees; and the vicarage (rebuilt during this period; this must have had his support) lay between William's house and John Browne's house.

Apart from the festivals of Christmas, Easter (with Palm Sunday, that "most elaborate and eloquent of the processions") and Corpus Christi with the town pageants, the different patronal festivals and the feasts of their parish gilds (not always the same – St Mary's church had the Corpus Christi gild; St John the Baptist church had the gild of St Julian) would have been celebrated. No month would go past without some local expression of devotion. This "duplication of festivals" led the parish clergy of Stamford to petition bishop Repingdon in 1412 to allow them to celebrate all patronal festivals on the same day, the first Monday after Relic Sunday (7 July)[101], but it is unlikely that this got off the ground. A calendar can be built up of all the festivals of these churches, their chapels and side altars, their chantries, gilds and images, showing that there were few periods of the year when such public events did not take place, with processions through the streets, each parish vying with its neighbour for greater glory. The timing of a new fair in 1481 to the end of October (SS Simon and Jude) may have been intended as much to fill a gap in the religious calendar as in the economic life of the town.

The groupings of crafts may also have celebrated[102]. And there were family devotional practices, obits and namesakes more than birthdays. In the Book of Hours which John Browne and Agnes commissioned from Flanders, the feast of St Agnes was made into a red letter day. The newly fashionable Gregory masses became a Browne family tradition, being mentioned in several wills of members of the family (see pp 233-4); and the family seem to have honoured St Thomas Becket also[103]. Here were other occasions for forms of devotion to be exercised.

The parish clergy played a large part. Many were graduates[104]. Some parish churches like St Mary's at the bridge and St Peter's changed their incumbents frequently, despite (or because of) being rich benefices[105],and were held with

---

[101] R Hutton 1996 *Rise and fall of merry England: the ritual year 1400-1700* Oxford University Press; LAO Reg Repingdon XV fol 67d; LRS 58 p 278 (*propter alia festa duplicia*) gives the date as 16 September (so Pounds 2000 pp 259-260) but the Salisbury rite changed the date of Relic Sunday in 1319 to July; in Lincoln diocese, this date may have been 10 July; see *Handbook of Dates* p 83.

[102] Goldberg 1999

[103] John and Agnes Browne were buried in the chapel of St Thomas of Canterbury in All Saints church, and it is noteworthy that the figure of St Thomas in the Book of Hours has not been defaced by later family members when other saints have been. See also Dinn 1992 p 164.

[104] CPL 1362-1404/510; CPL 1471-84 ii 484; see Davis 2002

[105] PRO E36/62; E179/136/315; E179/276/44

other churches in plurality; others like All Saints in the Market (three incumbents in ninety years) changed less frequently. They were knit together in a chapter under a dean of Stamford, an office that dated from a very early period[106]. How the deans were appointed and how long they served are not known, but the position did not go with the richest or most important benefices in the town: the rector of St Mary Bynwerk, a peripheral church deserted a few years later, was dean in 1414. The dean had many functions including making inquiries, arbitration and jurisdiction, the settling of disputes, and the probate of wills. The chapter served the parish clergy as a gild, with ceremonials on the obits of its members and memorial masses[107].

The parish incumbent (if resident) was ostensibly in charge of the ritual – even if at times he was hardly able to regulate the activities of all the other clergy who clustered in 'his' church or the wishes of laymen or women who insisted on special patterns of devotion and paid handsomely for glass, wall paintings, carvings in wood and stone, for tombs and brasses, painted figures and rood screens inside the church and vestments. Control of many public expressions of religion was increasingly with the laity[108], including the town council services, helping to assert the special dignity of council members by excluding those without the livery, while at the same time attracting spectators from out of town. Funeral processions, poor men with torches accompanying a coffin or draped hearse, were organised by lay gild officials[109]. Sir William Bruges gave a 'feretory'

---

[106] For dean, see CAD ii p 283; Clement dean 1239 HMC 4th Report p 145; *Taxatio Ecclesiastica* (Rec Comm) 1902) p 62; LRS 52 p 35; LRS 60 pp 32, 49, 70-71, 135, 154, 188, 194, 211; LRS 64 pp 95-6; BL Harl 45 F43; A Hamilton Thompson (ed) 1911 Register Gynewell 1347-1350, *Archaeological Journal* 68 pp 343-4. For the office of 'rural dean', see R N Swanson 2001 Peculiar practices: the jurisdictional jigsaw of the pre-Reformation church *Midland History* 26 pp 69-95. For probate before the dean of Stamford, see LRS 60 pp130-1; Simcoe 1038 M/T/9/2; Rogers, Wills; *Linc. Dioc. Docs* pp 162-3, 185; *AASR* Chantry p 7; CY *Visit* iii p 353; *Feudal Aids* vi 364; PRO, SC6/1260/12. How far outside the town the jurisdiction of the dean of Stamford extended is not clear, but deanery activities brought people from outside into the town; see LRS 78 p 815; in 1495, there is mention of the deanery of Ness and Stamford, CY 78 *Morton* p 138; for inquiry, CY *Chicheley* i pp 98-101

[107] CIM vii 1399-1422 p 303 (535) CPR 1416-22/99. See D Hickman (ed) 2001 *Lincoln Wills 1532-1534* LRS 89 p 438 for the lying of deceased clergy in St John's church "aftyr the laudable custome of the chapiter". In 1526, a total of 20 clergy were serving the parish churches which remained, Salter 1526 pp 60-61. No college of priests was established in Stamford unlike many other towns, see Clive Burgess and Martin Heale 2008 *The late medieval English college and its context* York Medieval Press

[108] R W Dunning 1981 Patronage and promotion in the late medieval church, in Griffiths *Patronage* "local laity were becoming more deeply involved in the affairs of their own churches", McIntosh 1986 p 225; also Rosser p 44; Davis 2002

[109] *AASR* Wills p 93; Rubin *Corpus Christi* pp 248, 263-4; Giles pp 76-77; Orme and Webster p 146; Goldberg 1999. Processions controlled by the "secular civic authorities ... expressed local political meanings". See Rubin 1991 pp 142-6. But these processions were still religious, not secular, see P D Clarke 2008 New evidence of noble and gentry piety in fifteenth-century England and Wales *JMH* 34 pp 23-35

of wood and silver and adorned with jewels surrounded by angels bearing emblems of the Passion, to carry the cup of communion in the Corpus Christi procession[110], and Agnes Browne gave a covering for the Palm Sunday processional pyx.

And inside the church, the laity controlled the fabric and much religious symbolism. Churches and chapels were rebuilt and bell towers erected; the sound of their bells would reverberate throughout the day and some of the night. Sir William Bruges provided for "the complesshyng and ending of the seyd chirch [St George] of Staunford; that is to understand, in coveryng with lede, glassing ... and a pleyn rodelofte, and in puyng [pewing] the seyd chirche, nourt curiously but pleynly; and in paving of the hole chirch, body and quere, with broad Holand tyle", the re-roofing of the nave and chancel, and the aisles with the chapels of the Blessed Virgin and St George were to be "closid with estrich boarde" replacing the "pleyn borde" around those chapels, "and clere storied"[111]. In return for rebuilding All Saints, William and John Browne appropriated the north chapel of St Thomas and the south Lady chapel for their family burials. Merchants helped rebuild St John's church and installed glass there; and a merchant re-roofed the Corpus Christi chapel in St Mary's church. Sir David Phillipps endowed a chantry there[112]. Margaret Spenser's will (1509)[113] instructed her executors to set up in St Martin's church four 'tabernacles'

---

[110] Peck xiv 25-26; Bruges also gave "a solempnite of Array for the fest of Corpus Christi, oon partie wrought in the plate of sylver and overgilt and that other in tymbre to be borne betwene the Decon and Subdecon; the tymber is peynted and overgilt with fyne gold". See Rubin *Corpus Christi* p 252

[111] *Test Vet* i pp 266-270; Peck xiv 20; Salzman 1967 p 409; see H S London 1970 *Life of William Bruges* Harl. Soc. vols 111, 112, esp pp 111-2; F P Barnard 1925 (reprint 1975) *Edward IV's Expedition of 1475* Sutton p 130; BL Add Mss 6323 fol 2; Stowe 594; Pugh York pp 118, 136-38; he was a retainer of the bishop of Winchester, see G L Harriss 1988 *Cardinal Beaufort: a study of Lancastrian ascendancy and decline* Clarendon; F P Barnard 1925 (reprinted 1975) *Edward IV's French Expedition of 1475* Sutton. He placed portraits of himself, his wife and three daughters in the windows of the church, H Collins 2000 *The Order of the Garter 1348-1461* Clarendon pp 32, 228, 231, 252; John Smert married Katherine daughter of Sir William Bruges and became the next Garter King of Arms with interests in Stamford. Churches were being pewed in the fifteenth century, see Duffy *Stripping* p 332. Why Bruges chose St George's church Stamford for his memorial church is not known; he may have been connected with William de la Pole duke of Suffolk, for "Between 1440 and 1450, admission to the fraternity [of the Garter] was restricted almost exclusively to members of the king's household", controlled at that stage by Suffolk, H E L Collins 1996 The order of the Garter 1348-1461: chivalry and politics in later medieval England, in D S Dunn (ed) 1996 *Courts, Counties and the Capital* Sutton p 174

[112] CPR 1494-1509/515

[113] PRO, PROB 11/16 fol 118; Robert Spenser prebendary of Lincoln, clerk or gentleman, one of her sons, was executor, L and P Henry VIII 1 i 1509-13 p 268

in the whiche shall stande an ymage of Sainte Dorothe and next that over the Northside a Tabernacle with an ymage of Sainte Margaret and upon the North side of the said churche towards the Chauncell a Tabernacle with an ymage of Sainte Kateryne and the iiij[th] ymage with the tabernacle shall stonde in the North Ile next to sainte Kateryn and an ymage of Saint Barbara in the same.

The church building was looked after by laymen - churchwardens and parish clerk. The accounts of John Leche goldsmith, churchwarden at St Mary's at the bridge in 1427-8, shows him dealing with repairs to the bells, bell ropes and bell shaft, and purchases of bell ropes, timber, iron, wax, glue, lead, string, canvas, towels and vestments, and leather. Payments were made to the (parish) players and for the repair of the parish books, "viewing the rodelofte" and the repair of the church windows. Many people, seeking an outlet for their devotion, focused on their parish church. Gifts of furniture, plate and vestments in varying colours and cloth for the many clerics in each church, feature in surviving wills[114].

But some public expressions of religion transcended the parish. While the funeral processions of the gilds, especially of well-known figures in the town ("I will that four men of my mystery to bear my body to the church"[115]) were focused on the parish church in which the burial would take place, open penances and abjurations, like that of Richard Gray in 1442, condemned to being whipped round St Mary's church on four Sundays or feast days and in the market on four Fridays for having seduced one of the nuns of Stamford, or that of friar John Russell in 1424 who had preached to the Corpus Christi crowds that a priest could marry and have sex, and pinned this on the door of St Mary's church, were more public[116].

Other religious institutions

Russell's preaching reminds us that there were other religious institutions in Stamford. There were 'free and private chapels' in the castle, in the suburbs of Bradcroft, Burghley and beyond Eastgate, and in some of the larger properties in the town like the Luterel manor[117]. There were hospitals - the *domus dei* in St Paul's Street, St Giles' hospital in Stamford Baron, and especially the pilgrim

---

[114] BL Cotton Vesp A24 fol 3d; not St Thomas at the bridge as in NRS 16 *Morton* pp 4-5; Thomas Glasyer was paid for the windows. See Duffy *Stripping* p 146. For furnishings in a church in Stamford, see L and P Henry VIII 9 1536 p 587

[115] *AASR* Wills p 93

[116] CY *Visit* i p lx; in fact Gray appears to have got out of his sentence. There seems to be some uncertainty as to whether Russell was a White friar or a Grey friar; Peck xiv pp 2-3; OHS 20 p 257 and Owen p 89,following Harrod i 28, say that his name was William Russell,that he was a Grey friar and that he also preached against tithes. See Appendix to this chapter

[117] I note the bequest to "every church in Staunford where daily mass is said", implying there were churches which did not have a daily mass,*Calendar Wills Husting* ii p 234

centre of St John the Baptist and St Thomas the martyr at the bridge, endowed and maintaining its own cadre of priests. The Hospital of St Helen was founded in the 1450s by Ralph lord Cromwell, and Browne's Hospital in 1475[118]. There were almost certainly shrines in some of the streets, some attended by priests or quasi-priests, others unattended but still the object of veneration by men and women leaving offerings - all providing opportunities for the devout to pray and for the less devout to pay their way to eternal bliss.

The most important were the friaries "whose influence on urban religion in particular was profound throughout the later Middle Ages"[119]. It is impossible to exaggerate the significance of these institutions in this town. Few Stamfordians failed to leave them a bequest in their wills – although William Browne did not[120]. Although they drew much of their membership from the locality, the Stamford houses were of wider significance: they linked Stamford into the national and international scene. Visitors arrived for them, sometimes in great numbers. As we have seen, the king lodged at the friaries[121].

Primarily academic bodies, with schools, theologians and student-novices in attendance, they were among the largest and most eminent of their orders in the country. The White Friars and Grey Friars held provincial councils in Stamford during William Browne's lifetime, as did the Premonstratensian canons in the 1470s. Richard II's patronage resulted in the Stamford Franciscans supporting Richard after his deposition in 1399. The Austin Friars were expanding during the fifteenth century, resulting in several disputes over property, and the White Friars also may have been rebuilding[122]. The friaries had their own services, and their bells competed with the bells of the parish churches. White, Black, Grey and Austin Friars could all be distinguished in the streets. The White Friars provided a school in the town. Friars sometimes served in the parish churches and acted as confessors; they often preached in the streets of the town as they

[118] CY *Visit* ii pp 116-20; LAO RAI IV/96; Exeter-NRA 31/59; 33/4; 53/3-9; 76/72; CY *Visit* iii p liii. The "free chapel of St John the Baptist" was described as "upon the Hill in Stamford" which suggests it stood at the south end of Stamford Baron, L and P Henry VIII 16 1540-1 pp 573-4. For St Helen, CPR 1547-8/23; 1553-57/182

[119] See Duffy *Stripping* p xv; Kermode *Merchants* pp 123, 125 suggests their influence was declining in the late fifteenth century

[120] Not only from Stamford but also from Lincoln, Grantham, Sleaford, London etc: see *AASR* Wills pp 62, 74, 104; NRS 42 *Northampton Wills* pp 85-6; LRS 5 pp 33, 46; *Cal Wills Husting* ii pp 234, 326-7; Gibbons *Wills* pp 22, 80, 83, 168; LRS 57 pp 24-5, 147, 151, 190, 192; LRS 58 pp 244, 275-6; CPR 1385-88/188; *Linc. Dioc.Docs* p 266

[121] See p 27; VCH *Lincs* ii pp 225-6; CCR 1468-76/318-20 (1164). Names like Deping, Grauntham and Swafeld are among the Stamford friars,see CPR 1429-36/447

[122] VCH *Lincs* ii pp 227-230; H Colvin 1951 The *White Canons in England* Clarendon p 235; the Franciscans were holding general chapters of the order in Stamford in the 1520s, L and P Henry VIII 3 1519-1521 p 1541. See *Test Vet* i p 14; E F Jacobs 1961 *The Fifteenth Century* Oxford University Press p 29; CPR 1385-88/188.

"espoused a more personal and informal pattern of worship". Even without going out of town to seek devotion in pilgrimages (which seem to have been declining in popularity at this time), the choice of churchmanship open to the religious minded of medieval Stamford was probably as wide as it is to the modern resident[123].

And here the excitement of danger entered religion. For open air preaching was a particular pastime of the period, and at times waves of revivalist enthusiasm swept parts of the country. When one listened to a street preacher, one never knew if there might not be a public instance of heresy, for the range of openly expressed views in the late Middle Ages was actually very wide, despite attempts to contain them. The town would not have forgotten the council held in 1392 to condemn false teaching about the friars associated with John Wycliff. Stamford friaries were alleged to have been involved in a plot against Henry IV; John Leycester, Grey Friar, was arrested and executed for treason in 1402. A friar of Stamford was said to have preached sedition in 1451; and towards the end of the century, one of the Black Friars would be accused of conducting a false marriage in the town. John Russell Greyfriar and Thomas Winterton Austin friar were both accused of heresy but not of Lollardy[124], but the people of Stamford would have listened avidly – perhaps in the hopes of a burning.

Which of course gave an excuse for friction between the town and the friaries. When the Despensers gave part of their estate to the Grey Friars, some in Stamford objected strongly, for (they claimed) the land included some common grazing. In 1416, two friars were attacked in the town, and the town council had to order people to stop throwing their dung under the Black Friary walls. But the town council exerted some authority over the friars; they were sued for debt, and two friars were fined in the borough court in 1486-7[125].

The monks and nuns were less controversial. Three houses stood in Stamford. St Leonard's Priory (a cell of Durham) was a large complex of buildings with a very small (two monks in 1440) housling population who were not local people. It

---

[123] G W Bernnard 1998 Vitality and vulnerability in the late medieval church: pilgrimage on the eve of the break with Rome, in Watts 1998 pp 199-234; Fleming, Charity pp 43, 48. For choice,see A D Brown 1995 *Popular Piety in Late Medieval England: the diocese of Salisbury 1250-1550* Oxford University Press

[124] CCR 1402 5/389; CPR 1401-5/125. See I Forrest 2003 Anti-Lollard polemic and practice in late medieval England, in Clark 2003 pp 63-74; M Jurkowski 2007 Lollardy and social status in east Anglia *Speculum* 82 pp 120-152; F Somerset, J C Havens and D G Pitard (eds) 2003 *Lollards and their Influence in late medieval England* Boydell.; Lutton 2006. By the early 1530s, strong reforming views were expressed in Stamford at street level, see L and P Henry VIII 5 1531-2 p 1309; L and P Henry VIII 9 1535 p 611

[125] CCR 1369-74/514-5; HB i fol 43d, p 130; CPR 1367-70/121; 1370-74/95, 140; PRO, C143/357/19; CIM vii 1399-1422 p 303 (535)

was suggested that the prior (usually a highly educated monk) did not stay long at any time because of the poverty of the house. But it had a prominent place as a school and as a landlord, defending its sanctuary in St Cuthbert's fee; and senior ecclesiastical and noble visitors stayed there. It obtained local patronage: for example, Elizabeth lady Grey of Castle Bytham and Stamford wrote to Durham asking that one of the monks there be made prior: "I withe othur lordes ladys and gentils in these parties have gode love and effection" for him and would be "gode and tendur lady unto the saide place" if he were appointed; Sir John Basing and lord Zouche wrote similar letters – but it seems without effect[126]. Nearby was Newstead priory which hosted several general chapters of the Austin canons during the fourteenth century, but by 1440, it had four canons, of whom one was too ill to appear before the bishop at the time of visitation, and one was absent[127].

The nunnery of St Michael south of the river would have been more visible. It ran a boarding school: in the 1440s, there were 7-8 pupils from some of the more prestigious families in the town. Throughout the century, the number of nuns fell from 19 (1379-80) to 9 (1487); by 1508, there were only seven nuns, and by the dissolution only four[128]. Its prioress was usually a member of a prominent family, but the poverty of the house probably put these families off sending their daughters to it long-term. Some bequests are known; the wealthy merchant and official Sir Roger Flore of Oakham left 13s 4d, and Margaret Spencer in 1508 6s 8d. But apart from Lady Margaret Beaufort in 1508, the days of legacies from nobles such as Blanche of Lancaster (6s 8d to each nun and twice that amount to the prioress) or merchants like William Stacy of Stamford in 1410 (6d to each of the sisters and novices and 12d to the prioress) were past[129].

The poverty of the house was well known and of long standing. It may well have been poverty which caused the nuns in 1447 and in 1528 to revive the claim that it was Cistercian, not Benedictine like its patron Peterborough Abbey, a claim originating in the 1260s-1270s and supported by the king but rejected by the

---

[126] Two monks in 1377, 3 in 1381, see LRS 81 pp 12, 106, 167. BL Add 41063 fol 75; for its value in 1450, see PRO, E36/62; SC2/188/1-3; C143/133/14; CCR 1402-5/166-7; LRS 60 p 154; LRS 21 p 346. Heale *Priories* p 199. BL Stowe 141 is a survey of Stamford monastic establishments c1538.

[127] *Alnwick Visit* ii pp 346-7; Harvard deed 343; see HMC 8th Report Appendix I p 265; *AASR* Wills p 68; CY *Visit* ii p 240.; by the fifteenth century, it was in practice a cell of Belvoir, HMC 4th Report p 145

[128] PRO, E179/238/77; 12 nuns and two novices (1407); 8 nuns and 3 novices (1440-5); 11 nuns (1482); 9 nuns and five novices (1487); see Sturman pp 174, 201.

[129] Gibbons *Wills* pp 83, 138; PRO PROB 11/16 fol 118; Jones and Underwood pp 132-3. Thomas Holland duke of Exeter and Sir Roger Flore petitioned on behalf of the nuns in 1426, Sturman p 86.

officials, designed to exempt the house from various forms of taxes[130]. Part of this distress was caused by falling incomes from rents and farms, part by incompetence in the management of their estates and keeping accounts. During the fourteenth century, the bishop of Lincoln appointed a prior to handle some of these matters, but by the fifteenth century much of the estate management was done by the nuns. Like other houses, the nuns leased out more and more of their income sources in return for fixed sums; but income fell during the century as the leases became longer and longer, up to eighty and even one hundred years. The bishops did not like this practice but reluctantly agreed: in 1457-8, the bishop of Lincoln gave the nuns licence to lease out their parish churches. The leases were often made to local people, perhaps for more than business reasons: in 1482, William Morewode of Peakirk and his wife leased a large part of the estates for ten years, at the same time as one of the novices who was given special privileges was Margery Morewode[131]. The bishop of Lincoln made three visitations of the house between 1440 and 1445 to try to sort out the administrative mess the house had got itself into.

And the scandals; for the nunnery had its share of troubles. In the 1440s, one of the nuns slipped away from the monastery, first with an Austin friar and later with a harp-player. In 1442, a nun became pregnant by a lay corrodian[132]. In this, the nunnery of St Michael was not very different from other small nunneries, but such matters as well as its poverty and mismanagement would have damaged the convent in the town's eyes.

For the house was meshed into Stamford closely. The surnames of the nuns indicate that most of the nuns came from local families, and visits home were permissible under their rule[133]. Most of the prioresses during the century were

---

[130] The nuns' income in 1450 in the dioceses of Lincoln was stated as 100 marks; Peterborough drew only £14 5s 10d from Stamford, PRO E36/62. For the Cistercian claim, see PRO, E326/6819, 10567-8, 11356; E135/6/48; C V Graves 1979 English Cistercian nuns in Lincolnshire *Speculum* 54 pp 492-99; E Freeman 2005 Male and female Cistercians and their gendered experiences of the margins, the wilderness and the periphery, in L H McAvoy and M Hughes-Edwards 2005 *Anchorites, Wombs and Tombs: intersections of gender and enclosure in the Middle Ages* Cardiff: University of Wales Press pp 68-70.

[131] T Madox *Formulare Anglicanum* (Rec Comm) p 333; PRO,LR 14/917; Exeter-NRA 31/56

[132] *Alnwick Visit* ii pp 348-350; see LAO Reg Dalderby III fols 180, 228; VCH *Northants* ii pp 95-102

[133] Maltby, Alyngton, Blisworth, Swinstede, Welton, Purley, Manton, Grantham, Spalding, Wrangle, Tattershall, Tallington and Halington all appear; LRS 57 p 90; later names of the nuns included local places like Wyteryng, Croylande, Multone, Normanton, Warmington, Seaton and (further away) Haxey and the family names of Willoughby,fitz Alan, Marmyon and Hotot, PRO, E179/238/77. It may be that the nuns took new names when they professed but this strengthens their local origins. In a list of nuns c1402-3, PRO,SC6/1260/14,there were fewer local placenames: the surnames of Eylesworth, Swynster, Marmyon, Lecke, Weldon, May and

drawn from local families such as Leche, Copuldyk and Weldon; two Isabel Savages held that office, one in the 1480s and the other in the 1530s. The convent's circle had shrunk from the days when it took daughters of noble families such as the Mortimers[134].

The house possessed land, tenements, shops, and several churches in Lincolnshire, Rutland, Leicestershire and Northamptonshire as well as in Stamford - St Martin, All Saints by the Water in Stamford Baron and All Saints in the Market, and the tithes of St Andrew and St Clement, the last of which led to a long running dispute with the rector of St Peter. Local clergy such as the vicar of St Andrew's parish acted as confessor to the nuns. The house needed servants, at times more servants than nuns, and long-term and seasonal farm workers for their home farm; they hired carts and carriages and horses when they travelled. They used Stamford men like John Arketil carpenter[135], John Bytham slater and John Broun glasyer for the repair of their buildings. They chased recalcitrant tenants for their outstanding rents; they borrowed money from local merchants such as Robert Loksmyth (although some of these 'loans' may be unpaid bills due to the tradesmen). They bought goods from local merchants like John Browne the father draper and John Glasyer fishmonger; they supplied corrodies (board and lodging) to some local residents such as Richard Page and his wife. They had a good deal of business with the steward of the lord of Stamford, to whom they paid an annual rent; on one occasion, some of their servants were imprisoned in the castle. They had a keen interest in who visited the town, for some of the richer might be touched for a donation: Henry Beaufort bishop of Winchester, in Stamford in 1429 with the king, gave them an indulgence, Edward IV on visits to the town renewed their charters in 1464 and gave them alms in 1480-1. A small and poor nunnery needed good lordship: thus they appealed to the duke of Exeter in 1426 and to Henry earl of Northumberland later in the century, and to local eminences like Sir Roger Flore of Oakham to help them in their poverty[136].

Redyng occur. See also E King et al (ed) 1983 *Northamptonshire Miscellany* NRS 32 p 6; Gibbons *Wills* p 138; G A J Hodgett (ed) *State of the Ex-Religious 1547-1574* LRS 53 p 100.

[134] PRO, E329/66, 211; SC11/420; E314/76; E326/5111; SC11/421,422; SC6/914/3; VCH *Northants* ii pp 100-101; Alice Copuldyk came from a family which furnished Lincolnshire with sheriffs and escheators. CUL Mss MM 1 38 fol 373. Margaret Mortimer in 1440 came from Thornhaugh by Stamford, CY *Visit* ii pp lvii, 349. But it still had something of a wider circle of interest: in 1425,for instance, the nuns subscribed to mortuary roll of bishop Wakeryng of Norwich; in 1399, some of them attended the funeral of the duke of Lancaster, Sturman; BL Cotton ii 17

[135] He was a frequent witness for the nuns, and his daughter Margery was one of the nuns, Sturman pp 326-8.

[136] PRO, E210/1529; SC6/1260/4; 913/26; CY *Visit* i pp 166-7; CPR 1461-67/296; the nuns secured regular confirmations of their charters, e.g. L and P Henry VIII 2 i 1515-1516 p 1037

Agnes Leche illustrates this link with the town. She came from a long-standing local family, known in both Grantham and Stamford since the middle of the fourteenth century. John Leche (perhaps her father or brother) was the goldsmith churchwarden of St Mary's church (1427-8). Agnes became treasuress of the nunnery, and (from at least 1409) prioress; she was a person of business apparently, for between 1423 and 1426, she took over all the accounts of the other nuns and engaged in a fierce bout of travelling to inspect the convent's property and further its interests. She retired as prioress in 1429, not perhaps because of incompetence as has been suggested but perhaps because of unpopularity with the other nuns. A later Agnes Leche became anchoress at St Paul's church in 1496[137].

Apart from buying the wool from the nuns' estates, William Browne would have dealt with the nuns over presentations to the church of All Saints in the Market and its rebuilding to which the nuns would have been unable to give any considerable financial support; over the church of St Clement to which the town Alderman acted as patron; and over tithes in Swayfield and Corby, part of William Browne's estates. Henry Cok, one of William's friends and feoffees, was bailiff to the nuns.

Apart from these three houses, there was, as we have seen, throughout the town a great deal of monastic property. At least 33 houses are known to have had possessions in the town at one time or another, serving perhaps as recruiting centres, providing access to Stamford fairs and markets, run perhaps by a single monk or lay brother. Some of them too served as schools. Even local parish clergy like Pickworth had a house in the town[138].

Personal piety

Anchoresses: The religion of parish and regular clergy was supplemented in fifteenth century Stamford with a more personal lay piety. Recluses were at one and the same time both deeply personal and yet social in nature; cut off, yet they related to the society around them. A common feature of lay piety in fifteenth century England, supported in many cases by the wealthy, they were typified by Julian of Norwich, the most notable of many in that town[139]. Men and women

---

[137] BL Add Mss 25288 fol 141; VCH Northants ii p 100; for Leche, see p 43
[138] Hartley and Rogers; see Owen p 68; for monastic town houses, see Giles p 57; Wilkins 2007 p 180; CAD iii p 461
[139] For lay piety, see Lutton 2006; Lutton and Salter; R Gilchrist 1995 *Contemplation and Action; the other monasticism* London; Warren *Anchorites*; Clay; Idris Foster 1950 The Book of the anchorite *Proc Brit Acad* 36 pp 197-226; Miri Rubin 2001 An English anchorite: the making, unmaking and remaking of Christine Carpenter, in R Horrox and S R Jones 2001 *Pragmatic Utopias: ideas and communities 1200-1630* Cambridge University Press pp 204-223; A N Galpern 1976 *Religions of the*

who lived a life of contemplation were highly revered in both social and religious terms: revelations might be vouchsafed to "a woman solitary and recluse", and prayers which had been composed in hermitages were esteemed. Stamford had its share: bequests were made in 1380 by Blanche lady Wake of Lancaster to each recluse in Stamford, and "the hermits and anchorites in or near Stamford" were mentioned in 1383: these included a long standing anchorage at Ryhall. It is possible that 'Peter Goldenarme goldsmyth alias heremyte' mentioned in Stamford in 1452 was a solitary[140].

Most of these would seem to have been occasional recluses. But the anchorage between St Paul's church and the town wall was long standing, and some of its successive occupants are known – they all appear to be relatively local.

The ruins of St Paul's church – the anchorage would be on the north side between the church and the town walls; no picture remains of that part of the building. What remained of the church was later used for the grammar school, now part of Stamford School (from Drakard).

Geoffrey le Scrope canon of Lincoln (1382) and Henry lord Scrope (1415) both supported the anchoress "in the parish church of Stamford"; Ellen Empingham (1398) and Emma Tong of Bourne (1435) were immured in a chamber on the north side of the church of St Paul. The anchoress listed as a member of St Katherine's gild in St Paul's church from 1480 to 1491, and legatee of William Browne in 1489, was probably Margaret Jeralde, perhaps related to dom William

---

People in 16th Century Champagne Cambridge, Mass; N Tanner 2004 Religious Practice, in *Medieval Norwich* p 139; Tanner 1977; L H McEvoy (ed) 2010 *The Anchoritic Tradition in Medieval Europe* Boydell

[140] Huizinga p 195; see Duffy *Stripping* pp 191, 218, 249, 254; *Cal Wills Husting* ii p 234; VCH *Rutland* ii p 274; PRO, C237/43/222; BL Harl 773 fol 36d; *AASR* Wills p 208; Hughes 1988 p 68

Jeralde vicar of St Paul's 1458-64; she died soon after William Browne. In 1496, Dame Agnes Leche anchoress was admitted to the gild, and continued by name as a member until 1509 after which 'the anchoress' (unnamed) continued in membership until the record ends in 1534[141].

There was a second anchoress in the town: in 1504, "Dame Margaret White anchoress at the Nuns" was admitted to the gild. Lady Margaret Beaufort brought her from Kent, set her up in "iiij littil Chambres ... at the nunnrey at staunfford", and paid for her "ffyndyng" and her "profession" in that same year. Later, she granted this anchoress an annuity (1506) and the cost of a maid servant (1508). But Lady Margaret also supported the St Paul's anchoress, in 1505 rebuilding the house "adjoining the church of St Paul", providing furnishings, wall-hangings and bed linen, "makyng a dower [door] in the towne walle in the bake side of the ancrese hous" for her convenience, and in November 1504, "paying her an afternoon visit bringing apples and wine for a little refreshment". She left bequests to both anchoresses in her will of 1508, as did Margaret Spencer in 1509:

> *I bequeth to the ankerys in Polls Church in Staunford aforsaid vjs viijd. Also I bequeth to the Ankerys at the Nonnys of Saint Mighell aforsaid iijs iiijd*[142].

In addition, there were *vowesses*, women, mainly widows, who took a vow of chastity and sometimes some form of profession. Lady Margaret Beaufort took such a vow in 1499. Some "retired into religious seclusion after their husband's death", but others remained in the secular world, distinguished by their dress and their demeanour. Roger Flore of Oakham made provision for his wife in his will (1424) "if she take the mantel and the ryng and avowe chastite". John Browne on his brass enjoins his wife to become a vowess ("After me, may you be a bride of Christ"), which she probably did[143]. Churchleaders had hesitations about

---

[141] *Foedera* ix pp 275-6; LAO Reg Beaufort XIII fol 5; LRS 57 p 51; LRS 5 pp 17, 44?; CY *Visit* ii p 113; LAO Reg Gray XVII fol 187; Clay p 228; NRO Prob B12; *AASR* Wills p 209; LAO Reg Burghersh V fol 412. A bequest to "the ancrysse of poulys" was made as late as 1533, *Linc Dioc Docs* p 163.

[142] GCC MSS 266/670 fol 53; Rogers *Gild Book* p 144; see Jones and Underwood pp 132-3, 142-4. LRS 5 pp 17, 44, 102; LRS 57 p 51; HMC vol 78 Hastings i pp 307-8. William Elmes, John Fermur of Market Deeping and the widow of lord Hastings left bequests to the anchoress in St Paul's. Catherine of Aragon, on her death in 1536, left 20s to the anchoress of Stamford, L and P Henry VIII 4 ii 1526-28 p 2732 ; see Warren *Anchorites* p 185. Margaret White disappeared from the gild record between 1527 and 1532 but Agnes Leche was still recorded when the record ceased in 1534.

[143] *AASR* Wills p 81; see PRO PROB 11/16 fol 118; Innes-Parker 2002 p 5; M C Erler 1994 Three fifteenth-century vowesses, in C M Barron and A F Sutton (eds) 1994 *Medieval London Widows 1300-1500* Hambledon Press pp 165-183; M C Erler 1995 English vowed women at the end of the Middle Ages *Medieval Studies* 57 pp 155-201; *Gothic* p 277; BL Add 32490 W14. See P H

personal vows, sometimes taken rashly: the bishop of Lincoln once commissioned a friar of Stamford to try to dissuade a woman from a vow of fasting which had made her ill[144].

Religion, piety and social life

Parish clergy, chaplains, curates, monks, nuns, friars of various orders, pardoners and lay brethren, anchorites and vowesses, novices and students - all of these were an everyday part of the Stamford townscape. Clericalism was the very air breathed in the town. My guess is that, except in the markets, probably one out of every three persons on the streets of Stamford was a 'religious' person of one sort or another, maintained in some sense by ecclesiastical bodies. They were not all united – when have religious persons ever been united? Hostility was open between the different religious cultures as with denominations later.

But it would be a mistake to divide up the population of William Browne's town into secular and religious. For the sacred and the profane were mixed in every person in different quantities; clerks can be called 'gentlemen'. The organisations of the town used religion to justify their decisions: as the borough council said in 1469, in introducing their new ordinance about tapsters and bar maids:

> *itt is by the said Alderman and his comburges ordeynyd for as myche as the grett pleasure of God is any persone or persones suspect in lyvyng to be putt in correccyon and the greatt occasyon of synn and mysruell to avoyd and perfittlye to redresse and amend,...[145].*

The councillors were implementing God's will as much as any priest. The Corpus Christi pageants were to be staged "for the honour of God and the reformation of the faith", and the officers and councillors were sworn with a religious oath maintained by attendance at church. The Alderman's dedicatory service in St Mary's church during the mid-Lent fair, which every councillor was forced to attend on penalty of a fine, is an example of this. So it is not surprising that William Browne was one of those called upon to witness the confession and public humiliation of a simoniac clergyman in a consistory court in St Mary's church[146].

Cullum 1996 *Vowesses and veiled widows: medieval female piety in the province of York Northern History* 32 pp 21-41; Rosenthal 2001 p 13

[144] LRS 64 p 59

[145] HB i fol 13d,p 36

[146] HB i fol 30d, p 87; see LRS 86 p 157; CY *Chicheley* i pp 98-101; iii pp 91-99; LRS 74 p 146 (269); see NRS 16 *Morton* p 43; *Linc Dioc Docs* pp 114-6

Gilds

The gilds are typical of this intermingling: in these "lay religious organizations", the ceremonies were religious (even the feast) but the gild clergy were appointed by laymen, subordinate servants of the gild[147].

There are no known craft gilds in medieval Stamford, only 'pious confraternities' - "providers of essential personal, familial, religious, economic and political services .. providing security in some essential areas of life". They were not built up "in animosity of parochial religion" but in active support of parish church life, increasing the diversity of religious experience. Perhaps to compensate for some decline in the parish populations, virtually every parish church in the town had a gild, some more than one. They provided social capital and an opportunity for feasting and trading – the Rotary of their day[148].

Most of them reached out beyond their parish base. Sir William Bruges left plate to the gild of Corpus Christi (in St Mary's church) to be held in his parish church of St George unless his executors decided "it would be safer in the church of Our Lady of Stamford" where the gild met[149]. Membership was either by choice or by invitation; it was not exclusive, so people had opportunities to attend the rituals of different gilds. Gilds provided lights at altars in the parish church, burial services for their members and their families, attendance at which was a requirement, and an annual feast, exhibiting "sociability and charity". Some required special livery or hoods but this was apparently on the decline in the fifteenth century. Some gilds had banking functions or entrepreneurial activities through the use of the gild's stock, as well as religious observances. Not all the

---

[147] A G Rosser 1988 Communities of parish and guild in the late middle ages, in Wright 1988 pp 29-55; P R Hoffman 2007 Early modern guilds *Urban History* 34 1 pp 76-88; Duffy *Stripping* pp 142-152, 220; Giles 2000; Toulmin Smith; Westlake *Gilds*; Rubin 1991. See LRS 74 p 110 for gilds of Holy Trinity, St John and All Saints; Cox 1913 p 406 for gild priest in 1546 (Sir Thomas Beckett). Salter *1526* pp 60-61; as time went on, however, several gilds in Stamford allowed the appointment of gild priests to lapse.

[148] Fraternities "provided funerary services and relief to members and their dependents, and organised feasts and dinners; some provided legal support, and all indulged in para-liturgical activities, those religious practices which went beyond basic parochial requirements",Rubin *Corpus Christi* p 234; see p 233; McIntosh 1986 p 228. The combined gild of St Mary and Corpus Christi met in the parish church of St Mary at the bridge. All Saints gild was based in All Saints in the Market, St Katherine's gild in St Paul's church, while St John's church had the gild of St John and St Julian. St Peter's church had a gild of that name, St Clements a gild of St Nicholas, and the gild of Holy Trinity kept the parish church of St Stephens going. St George's church had a gild; so did St Michael the Greater. St Martin's parish had the gild of St Martin and the gild of St Mary Magdalene; PRO E179/136/315; E 179/276/44; E36/62. See S Brigden 1984 Religion and social obligation in early sixteenth centuiry London *Past and Present* 103 p 95

[149] *Test. Vet.* p 266

gilds were orthodox, as can be seen from Leicester. Like the parishes, they had patron saints and festivals; and several had their own gildhalls[150].

The Stamford town cycle of pageants staged in the streets every year at the feast of Corpus Christi was the responsibility of trade groupings set up by the town council rather than the parish gilds; from at least 1479, the town council assumed greater responsibility for the pageants. Were these the town's annual carnival or its celebration of the story of redemption? Or both one and the same? Similarly, was the annual bull baiting for which the gild of St Martin was responsible[151] a religious as much as a secular occasion?

Just as the gilds of Stamford drew members from outside the town, so Stamford men and women were not limited to gilds in their own town. In 1474-5, Thomas Decon of Stamford pewterer gave seven "dysshes of pewter and ten sawcers of pewter" to the gild of Holy Cross, the Blessed Virgin Mary and St John the Baptist in Stratford upon Avon in return for prayers for his soul. Several Stamford citizens joined the Holy Trinity gild of Coventry[152].

William was admitted to the Corpus Christi gild in Boston – but the circumstances suggest that such enrolment outside of the town was for him unusual. In March 1476, John Browne his brother died; in May 1476, William Browne, Margaret and Agnes Browne widow of John, all joined the gild at Boston. That William, who had done most of his trading through Boston for much his life[153], had not felt the need to join the gild earlier and that he now joined with his wife and his brother's widow, Margaret's sister, suggests that the impulse for this came from the women at a time of distress. They sought religious capital rather than social capital, for the distance and travel conditions would make participation in the fraternity activities difficult for them. But William combined different purposes; five years later, he served the Boston gild as Alderman.

William Browne thus participated in the "planning, attention, common sense and mutual bargaining which made fraternities flourish" at this period, serving as

---

[150] Hartley and Rogers; Rubin 1991 p 145; G Rosser 1994 Going to the fraternity feast: commensality and social relations in late medieval England *JBS* 33 pp 430-446; Duffy *Stripping* pp 142-3, 148, 151

[151] HB i fol 27d, pp 76-7; fol 33, p 96; Westlake *Gilds p 34*; Toulmin Smith *Gilds* p 192; for the Old Bull Pitt in High Street, see CIPM 21 1418-22 p 62 (216); Bullrynge,PRO, SC6/1115/7

[152] J Harvey Bloom (ed) 1907 *The Gild of the Holy Cross, the Blessed Mary and St John the Baptist of Stratford upon Avon* Phillimore p 161; *Coventry, Holy Trinity Guild*

[153] He also had other dealings in Boston,see CPR 1476-85/266

Alderman of the gilds of Holy Trinity, All Saints, St Katherine, and the combined gild of St Mary and Corpus Christi[154].

The gild of which we have most information is that of St Katherine based in St Paul's church. This gild dates from at least the beginning of the century[155]. As we have seen, William Browne as its Alderman saved it from extinction in 1480, bringing in new members from the town and setting up a money lending programme using the gild stock. It would seem that one of its main functions was to support the anchoress at St Paul's church; she was a member, attended gild activities consistently and made donations to the gild. The money-lending scheme came to an end after William's death (1489), when Christopher Browne became its Alderman for a short time; he resigned in 1496 and Thomas Philippe merchant of Stamford became Alderman for life. After William Browne's death, more and more members were admitted, mostly from outside Stamford and of a superior social status, including Lady Margaret Beaufort, mother of Henry VII, from Collyweston. It was never a very large gild; the number of members rose from about 30 in the time of William Browne to some 120, but it became Stamford's premier social gild in the early sixteenth century, very different from William Browne's vision of the gild[156].

William's personal piety

William Browne seems to have had an antipathy for the regular clergy. He did not leave the friars anything in his will. As Alderman of the gild of St Katherine, he admitted a few secular clergy as members, but no monks or friars; after his death they enrolled in substantial numbers. He was one of those merchants who had "close and friendly relations on an individual basis with priests or retained their own chaplains .. and had close involvement and pride in their parish churches". He had a chapel in his house and his own chaplain, and he used parish clergy frequently in his property transactions. William probably shared the views of others like Pierre d'Ailly, that the mendicant friars were taking the bread

---

[154] Rubin *Corpus Christi* p 233; see p 192

[155] see pp 153-4. There was a cult of St Katherine in Stamford: special prayers to St Katherine and her altar in the church of St Paul are mentioned from about 1400; an alliterative poem to her gild was composed. There is a window portrait of St Katherine in St George's church (perhaps associated with Sir William Bruges' daughter Katherine) and what is probably a head of St Katherine in the glass of Browne's Hospital; see F A Greenhill 1986 *Monumental Incised slabs in the County of Lincolnshire* Newport Pagnell: Francis Coales Charitable Trust; B I Deed 1954 *History of Stamford School* Stamford p 79; Huizinga p 169; Kennedy 2003. It may not be entirely coincidental that there was a gild of St Katherine in Warmington church where the Browne families had a strong base, see R M Serjeantson and H Isham Longden 1913 Parish churches and religious houses of Northamptonshire, their dedications, altars, images and lights *Archaeological Journal* 70 p 425

[156] Rogers, *Gild Book*. The gild of St Mary and St John the Baptist, Lichfield, had between 200 and 1000 members, Rosser, Lichfield

out of the mouths of the poor and the sick. It is unlikely that he shared d'Ailly's hostility to "the ever-increasing number of churches, of festivals, of saints, of holy-days, ... the multitude of images and paintings", but he may well have desired "to impose restrictions on the mendicant orders whose social utility he questions: they live to the detriment of the inmates of leper houses and hospitals, and other really poor and wretched people"[157].

What probably moved him and his family at this time was a sense of mortality (in 1475, he would have been about 65 years old) and the dangers of purgatory, a doctrine which was gaining strength at this time[158]. William and Margaret's young grand-daughter died in 1471, and John his brother died five years later. It was, I think, a growing sense of mortality that moved William Browne to found his Hospital as both a gild hospital and as a private chantry-hospital. The gild of All Saints was the main gild of the parish; it met in William Browne's new almshouse, and William was the gild Alderman. To see the Hospital as in any way a rival to William's commitment to his parish church would be a mistake. His building work at the parish church would have ensured his place on the parish bederoll; and the parish vicar was closely involved in the Hospital. The Hospital was an extension of the parish.

But William does not appear as anxious about his soul as many others; his will suggests confidence that he had done enough. I cannot see William Browne consulting his anchoress before making trading decisions or setting out on journeys, let alone petitioning images as others were doing. And, unlike most rich merchants of his day, "heavy purchasers of soul-masses", but like an earlier bishop Philip Repingdon, "his will ... contains not a word about masses for his soul after death, gave not a mite to any religious order or foundation"; his legacy to the anchoress does not require her prayers. His obits of one week, one month and one year were to be marked by the distribution of alms to the poor rather than by instructions for masses to be said. Unusually, there is no date of death or *orate pro anima* clause on his brass[159]. It is only in his Hospital that prayers for

---

[157] Cited in Huizinga pp 155, 179-80. See for example LRS 74 pp 8, 73, 110,232, 285-6; Kermode *Merchants* pp 129, 155

[158] P Aries *The Hour of Our Death* (Engl transl London 1981); Burgess 1988

[159] See Saul, Brass p 171: "a request for prayers was invariably included in the epitaphs"; p 187.: "It was almost de rigeur for the date of death to be included, to allow the anniversary to be marked". See also Norris, Brasses p 184: "the primary purpose of securing prayers for souls departed". But in Kent, "there seems to have been less emphasis placed on prayer towards the end of our period, with an ... increasing number whose only provision was a request for their executors to attend to the health of their soul",Fleming, Charity p 40. Fairford p 11; M Aston 1984 'Caim's castle': poverty, politics and disendowment, in B Dobson 1984 *Church, Politics and Patronage in the fifteenth century* Sutton p 66

himself and his family in perpetuity are required; and (and apart from the *orate* clause in the glass) these were stipulated by others after his death in 1489.

The glass in the windows of Browne's Hospital, the "most complete glazing of all the charitable foundations preserved", is fragmentary and the dating of it uncertain. Most of it post-dates the death of William Browne, but there are some elements which may date from his lifetime[160]. There appears to be a head of St Katherine. The scheme in the Audit Chamber must of course have been chosen with the gild in mind, for the bedesmen had their own hall in the buildings behind the Hospital. In different windows, there are figures with inscriptions to St David and St Paul. St Paul may represent the patron saint of the family from their days in the parish of St Paul; but St Paul was also the lawgiver – like Seneca who (with Solomon) also features in these windows twice.[161] And Seneca is more likely to have appealed to the classically educated Thomas Stokes or the lawyer William Elmes than to William Browne.

I am not sure how far we can see the Hospital as a sign of his concern for poverty in the town. I do not think it was poverty which attracted him to the anchoress at St Paul's church, for she was not what d'Ailly called 'the true poor'. She came from a well-to-do family with a member who was a graduate and beneficed priest; hers was the chosen apostolic poverty. She attended St Katherine's gild for most of the feasts, paying her own dues; and she gave the gild a golden cup which perhaps someone had bestowed upon her. Nor do I think that the founding of Browne's Hospital was intended as a contribution to the relief of the poor in the town, viewing poverty as a social evil; his almsmen were the respectable old, not the 'poor and wretched'. They were bedesmen, prayer-men; the prayers of the poor were especially efficacious. In this respect, his was a practical religion: to use his wealth to secure his soul by employing others (clerical and lay) to work for him and secure a memorial to his family in

---

[160] R Marks 1993 *Stained Glass in England during the Middle Ages* Routledge p 102; CMVA; P Hebgin-Barnes 2009 *The Medieval Stained Glass of the county of Lincolnshire* Oxford University Press for British Academy. It has been suggested that William Browne had a special devotion to the Virgin Mary, since a head in the glass has been read as showing the image of 'the Virgin through the glass'; see C Rawcliffe 2008 Christ the Physician walks the wards: celestial therapeutics in the medieval *hospital*, in M Davies and A Prescott (eds) 2008 *London and the Kingdom* p 86, citing A Breeze 1999 The Blessed Virgin and the sunbeam through glass, *Celtica* 33 pp 19-29. But there is nothing in William's life to indicate any special veneration of the Virgin; the only dedication of the hospital chapel which dates from William's own life time was to All Saints (St Mary was added after his death); and the dedication of his burial chapel to the Virgin was made before he took it over.

[161] Henry VIII took up St David, the poet king, as his special symbol; P Tudor-Craig 1989 Henry VIII and King David, in Williams 1989 pp 183-205. See Rosie Mills in CMVA *Vidimus* 18 (May 2008) *Panel of the Month;* David and Solomon were being put up in King's College windows at this time

perpetuity. The anchoress and the bedesmen served the same purpose – but poverty (whether chosen or unintended) as such had relatively little to do with it. Nevertheless, he gave a substantial sum (£20) to the 'true poor' in his will[162].

In summary, we can suggest that William Browne was concerned not solely with the future of his soul in another world but with his reputation in this world both while he was in it and in particular when he would not be in it. He wanted to know that others would remember him with respect.

The evidence of wills

Something of the religious views of Browne and his family can be seen in their wills. The few wills which survive from late medieval Stamford, the only personal statements from the period[163], tell us something about personal piety. Drawn up when facing a journey or at times of illness, especially on one's deathbed, they reveal a range of concerns which go beyond everyday concerns. They were not only a statement at the time of expected death but also a plan of action for continuing the life of the deceased after his or her death. The provisions of the will were not always implemented, but they indicate the testator's desires and intentions[164].

John Browne the father's will[165], proved before the dean of Stamford, was written in 1433 but he survived until 1442. In Latin, the will is short and standardised. He left bequests to the parish churches of Warmington, Elton and 'Tischenters' [?], and to the free chapel in Warmington parish. He made

---

[162] Duffy *Stripping* pp 360-61. For alms for the afterlife, see Fleming, Charity p 44: "Men don mest comounly her elmsse in hope to ben thankyd and rewardyd therfor at the laste dom". William and Margaret had been supporting bedesmen in his almshouse during their lifetimes – what has been called "alms at the doorstep", Shaw *Wells* p 292.

[163] For wills, see Duffy *Stripping* pp 303, 315, 322-3, 355-6. See Dinn 1992; P Maddern,Friends of the Dead: executors, wills and family strategy in fifteenth century Norfolk, in Archer and Walker 1995 pp 155-174; Salter 2006 *passim*; Fleming, Charity; M Zell 1979 Fifteenth and sixteenth century wills as historical sources *Archives* 14 pp 67-74; M M Sheehan *The Will in Medieval England* Toronto 1963; P Heath 1984 Urban piety in the later Middle Ages: the evidence of Hull wills, in R B Dobson (ed) 1984 *The Church, Politics and Patronage in the fifteenth century* Sutton pp 209-234; C Burgess 1990 Late medieval wills and pious convention: testamentary evidence reconsidered, in Hicks 1990 pp 14-33; J S Loengard 2008 Plate, good stuff and household things': husbands, wives and chattels in England at the end of the Middle Ages *Ricardian* 13 pp 328-340. The lack of wills from Stamford is noted in LRS 89 p xx.

[164] Wills made on starting a journey, *AASR* Wills p 90; lying in his "deth bedde", PRO, C1/111/37. Warnings about the interpretation of wills have been given: "The frequently simplistic view of the Canonical will taken by many historians and then reduction of information derived from wills into a statistical form has sometimes led to the distortion and misuse of evidence which this abundant documentary source may contain"; Judith Ford PhD thesis 1992, cited in Salter 2006 p 175

[165] see above p 52

payments to those clergy who attended his funeral and to thirteen[166] poor men to carry torches at his interment; he left money for two priests to pray for him in the chapel for one year after his death. He left a bequest to Vaudey Abbey, a wool-producing monastery. His executors included a local rector[167].

Of John Browne the brother (d 1476) and his wife Agnes (d c 1484-5), we know rather less. His will has not been found; some inaccurate notes are all that survive of her will[168]. These mention vestments given to All Saints church and to the chapel in which she wished to be buried alongside her husband; the very large sum of £75 for a priest to sing for her soul for fifteen years. She gave

> *a cloth of silk and gold with a valence of the same to be borne with four petyt staves over the sacrament on Palm Sunday ... and ... the painting of the Tabernacle in the Corpus Christi chapel in St Mary's church in Stanford.*

There are some indications here of greater devotion and greater acquaintance with the ritual of the church; her education at the nunnery and her joining the gilds of St Katherine, and Corpus Christi, Boston, together with the injunction of her husband for her to become a vowess all point to a substantial if traditional commitment. This is confirmed by the Flemish Book of Hours which John Browne and Agnes owned. Handsomely bound in engraved leather, it contains an illustration showing John and Agnes witnessing the miracle of Pope Gregory (the family saint)[169]; it has been personalised by the inclusion of the feast of St Agnes among the red letter days, and the Browne merchant mark appears in an illustration and on the gilt clasps which have been added to it[170].

---

[166] Thirteen or twelve were favourite numbers in the later Middle Ages for such bequests; see the number of inmates planned for Browne's Hospital. It seems to have come from the Last Supper, Duffy *Stripping* p 362.

[167] The will survives in a copy only and is damaged: Simcoe M/T/1038/9/2; for transcript, see Rogers, Wills. For Vaudey, see PRO, SC1/38/159

[168] Made by Blore from the original at Tolthorpe manor; Blore's *History of the County of Rutland* 1811 p 94; Blore dates the will to 1470 but in it she is described as 'widow' of John Browne, so it must be after 1476 when her husband died. She died c1484.

[169] For merchants and Books of Hours, see Kermode *Merchants* p 153; Duffy *Marking*, P Saenger 1988 Books of Hours and reading habits in the later middle ages, in R Chartier (ed) (transl 1988) *Culture of Print: power and the uses of print in early modern Europe* Princeton University Press pp 141-73. Although unauthorised, the Papal Trental of St Gregory is mentioned in many fifteenth and early sixteenth century wills; see E Male *Religious Art* pp 94-100; R W Pfaff 1974 The English Devotion of St Gregory's Trental, *Speculum* 49 pp 75-90; Duffy *Stripping* pp 43, 103, 108, 238, 293-4, 353, 370-5.

[170] *Gothic* p 278. Nicholas Rogers talks of "gaudy miniatures by two mediocre Bruges miniaturists", made memorable by its binding and its gilt clasps, and Duffy *Marking* p 29, describes it as "a gaudy example of the books mass-produced for the English market". See Nicholas J. Rogers 2002 'Patrons and Purchasers: Evidence for the Original Owners of Books of Hours Produced in the Low Countries for the English Market', in B Cardon, J Van der Stock and D.

William Browne's will is even shorter. Made only two months before he died, we do not of course know if it replaced earlier wills. Unlike his father's, it is in English. It does not waste time on exhortations or excessive piety; it is above all business-like. It lays out with precision the location of his own grave (for which he had already purchased his brass). He then settles his debts:

> *I will that all my dettys which I owe to any person be weele and truly paid. Also I will that every man that sufficiently can prove that I have done any harme or wronge in any wyse he be restorid and satisffied as consciens will, though a part of my bequests be lesse and withdrawn. Also I will that every man that hath offendid unto me in word or in dede have forgevenesse therof and I pray god forgeve them and in likewise I pray god and them forgeve me.*

He gave sets of vestments to the parish church – a fine and very expensive black velvet to the parish priest and cheaper ones to other clergy -

> *iij coopis, a vestment and ij tonacles with the albes and other thingis therto belonging, price lxvj li xiijs iiijd. ... White sylke for our Ladies chapell in the parissh church of Alhalowue aforseid, price vj li. And also to the same chapell a course vestiment, price xxvjs viijd. And also in like wyse ij vestimentis for the chapell in my almes howse, price of the oone iiij marc, and of the other xxvjs viijd.*

He split £10 between all his servants[171]. He made his wife sole executor and appointed to support her Thomas Stokes clerk her brother, John Elmes his son in law and William Elmes his young grandson, a lawyer in training; and he both signed and sealed the will. Here is a man going to his God with the books made up, signed off with both a seal and a signature. Religion and economic matters were not separate but combined. We can see an example of this in the matter of a pix, given to William Browne as a pledge for a loan - he used it in the chapel of his almshouse while it was in his possession; it was at one and the same time a pawnbroker's pledge and a sacramental vessel in use.

There is no sign here of that preoccupation with death which it has been said was characteristic of the age; he eschewed the contemporary fashion of a cadaver on his brass or tomb. The family motto '+ me spede' which appears on his church and his brass and in the glass at his Hospital is as much the "formula of

---

Vanwijnsberghe (eds) 2002 *'Als ich can': Liber Amicorum in Memory of Professor Dr. Maurits Smeyers* 2 vols, Leuven, vol. ii, pp. 1165-81

[171] He left 40s to Thomas Howys and his wife; Howys was not a servant but a local trader; this is probably a late debt.

daily speech" as a specific petition, whereas the plea of his wife, 'Dere Lady help in need', is clearer[172].

The only personalised feature of the will is the bequest to the anchoress of St Paul:

> *I bequeith to the ancresse in Staunford aforseid xxs, and x yere after my decese if eny be there closid, every yere xxs.*

Here is a personal commitment – not simply to the anchoress but to her successors; it was her office as much as her person which he set out to support. There is other evidence that his personal religion included a reclusive element. As Alderman of the gild of St Katherine, he was proactive in support of the anchoress; and an English translation of a manual for would-be hermits, the *Myrour of Recluses*, is known to have been in his household[173]. While it is not certain that William Browne himself possessed this book, his adherence to the anchoress was not a last minute whim; it was part of his personalised religion.

Here then was no general anti-clericalism, nor an "individual piety" accompanied by "hostility to the institutionalised church", and certainly none of "those vehement outbursts of fervour and penitence which stamped so powerfully the religious life of the fifteenth century". The use of English religious texts does not imply that William Browne held heterodox or vernacular theology, for the English language had "extended to all religious fundamentals ... long before the Reformation". Nor does support for anchoresses mean support for heresy; it probably however does imply some measure of self-determination in matters theological[174]. Did William's international travels and connections bring him into contact with the disciplined religious life of the Netherlands? If only we had knowledge of what other books he had in his collection.

---

[172] Rosenthal 2001 p 15; Duffy *Stripping* p 301

[173] BL Harl 2372; see below p 270. For this book, see E A Jones 1999 A new look into the Speculum Inclusorum, in M Glasscoe (ed) 1999 *The Medieval Mystical Tradition, England, Ireland and Wales* Brewer pp 123-145; M P Harley 1995 *Myrour of Recluses, a middle English translation of the Speculum Inclusorum*, Fairleigh Dickinson University Press; Harley describes the book as mid-fifteenth century and locates its origin in Hertfordshire. For other English versions of rules for hermits, see D Pezzini 2009 An edition of three late middle English versions of a fourteenth-century *Regula Heremitarum, Leeds Studies in English* 40 pp -103.

[174] Griffiths *Henry VI* p 568; Duffy *Stripping* pp xxiv,80; K B McFarlane 1972 edn *Wycliffe and English Nonconformity* Penguin p 12: anchoresses at Leicester and Northampton were accused of being Lollards. While there are signs of anticlericalism earlier in Stamford (LRS 64 p 125; LRS 52 p 82; LRS 60 pp 142, 183 etc),there are few signs of it in the fifteenth century except against the friars.

231

For William Browne was among those fifteenth-century laymen who had direct access to devotional books in English. There was a growing demand for English devotional texts: "those who could read, primarily nuns, were generally assumed to be literate in the vernacular only, especially by the end of the Middle Ages ... [many] women could not read Latin and therefore created a demand for religious texts in English". The only book which can be traced to St Michael's nunnery is an English translation of the rule of St Benedict. However, "texts which were originally addressed to female audiences rapidly found their way into the hands of a wide range of readers, who included both men and women and ranged from secluded anchoresses to lay persons who were very much involved in the social and political climate of their day" [175].

Margaret Browne's long and much rewritten will (1489) shows more personal concern and warmth[176]. "Item I geve to the supprioresse of the Nonnes my mantell that I was professed in" suggests that she had been schooled in the nunnery of St Michael. She makes bequests to all the parish churches of the town and to her family church of Warmington, to the gild of All Saints and to the four orders of friars in the town; she gives bread to the poor at her funeral and at her later obits. Her executors were her brother Thomas Stokes, her son-in-law John Elmes and grandson William Elmes; her witnesses were the vicar of All Saints, the two clergymen in the almshouse, John Coton and William Hawkins, and her man of business Robert Beomond. Among a long list of goods are some which hint at the religious element in her life. The vicar of All Saints (Henry Wykes) gets "a Cusshyne of carpet werk with the name of Jhn theruppon[177]"; Isabell Fitzacreley, her sister, was to have "a hede of seint John [the Baptist], and my best prymer covered with velvet";

> *I geve a Ringe of fyne goold of the salutacion of our lady to be offered aftir my decesse to our lady of Walsingham ... Item I geve to the churche of all halowes ij cusshins to the presbiterye wretin in theym 'O mater dei', a whyte torche to our ladyes auter wher mym husband lyeth, xx li of wax to fynde the ij lyghtis in the qwere, ij lightis in the Chapelle, one before seint Anne, one before seint Margaret, one before seint Crasine, thise lights to be founde in festivall dayes....*

Throughout the house, religious symbolism was everywhere.

---

[175] Innes-Parker p 1; Ker *Libraries* p 182; J W Adamson 1930 The extent of literacy in England in the fifteenth and sixteenth centuries: notes and conjectures *Library* 4th ser 10 1930 pp 162-193
[176] PRO, PROB 11/8; Rogers, Wills
[177] It is possible that the inscription should read 'Jhu' and is a sign of the growing cult of the Holy Name of Jesus, see Duffy *Stripping* p 93; and above p 209

But masses for her soul hardly appear – presumably the almshouse was to take care of that. Much the same is true of her brother's will: Thomas Stokes rector of Easton in his will of 1494 did leave some money for a priest "to sing at Eston to pray for me, my brother Brown and Dame Margaret his wif, oure progenitours and frendes and for all Cristen soules". His will opens with a long (and exceedingly abstruse) peroration about the fall of man and original sin, but the feeling here, as with his poetry, is that he is trying to be clever rather than pious, and he soon gives up the Latin and turns to English. He mentions his "englissh bokes" and a *Polychronicon* but no religious items. There is little here to indicate great piety.

But the wills of later members of the family show a clear difference. Elizabeth Elmes, William and Margaret's daughter, in 1511[178] gives detailed instructions about the masses to be said for her soul: she left money to several parish priests,

> *praying theym of theire charitie and every of theym to saye a trentall of seynt Gregory for the welth of my husbonds soule, my soule and all cristen soules. Also I will that on the day of my buriall the xxxth day and my xijth moneths daye and in every of theym be song with note iiij masses with dirige, laudes and commendacion; ffirst masse of our ladye, second of the holygost, iiijrde of Requiem, And every secular preest beyng at the said iiij masses the said three daies and saying masse ther present shallhave for every day of the said iiij daies vjd.*

After further bequests of bread to the "poor and needy", she continues:

> *Also I will that Immediatly aftir decesse contynuyng xl daies besides my burying daye and my xxx^{ti} daye, that ther be song xl^{ti} masseȝ with note in that churche where it shall please god me to be buryed, that is to say xxx^{ti} masses off seynt gregorys trentall with placebo, dirige and commendacion all with note[179]. Also other x to complishe the said xl as thus iij of Alhalowes, iij of the v wounds, iij of Requiem and oon of the Angelys with all offices and other mysters as in the daies of the said fests is used and solempnysed; ... Also I will that there be said iij trentalls of seynt Gregory with dirige, lauds and commendacion within the said churche where it shall please god me to be buried in also goodely hast as may convenyently aftir the said xl daies ... And I will thies be doon for the helthe of my husbonds soule, my soule, my fader and moders soules and all cristen soules.*

After bequests to four orders of friars in Henley, she continues:

> *And if it please god to call me at Stamford or there aboute, then I will the said xs to every of the iiij orders of freers of Stamford, And they to say the said trentalls under the said maner.*

---

[178] PRO, PROB 11/22; Rogers, Wills
[179] *Placebo* is vespers; *dirige* is matins

Also I will that thos said places of freers to whom my legacies shall come Immediatly aftir shall syng in their places oon masse of Requiem with placebo, dirige, lauds and commendacion. Also I geve and bequeth to the freers of Redyng xs, and they to say in their place a trentall of seynt gregory with placebo, dirige and commendacion in due maner. Also I will that aftir the forsaid xl daies that myn obite be kept in the churche where it shall please god me to be buried moneth aftir moneth unto the tyme of my xij moneths mynde, that is to saye, unto thende of the hole yere Immediatly aftir my decesse with iij solempne massez.

She leaves instructions about the poor men who are to accompany her body with torches and who are to hold torches at the later obits; when she makes her bequests, she ends each with the words "and godds blessyng and myn"; and at the end of a long will, she cannot rest assured until she has added once more:

Also I will that my preest that shall happen to be with me the tyme of my departyng kepyng hymself so in honesty shall contynew to syng and rede for my husbonds soule my soule and all cristen soules within the church where it shall please god me to be buried by the space of oon yere fully to be completid aftir my decesse and he to have for his stipend and wages by the hands of myn executours ix marcs. And the saide preest to fynde hymself brede wyne and wax the said yere during.

The tone could hardly be more different from that of her father and mother.

Elizabeth had a long widowhood; her son, William Elmes, died before she did, a young man with a young family. A lawyer, his will shows concern for the disposal of his property. The religious provisions are relatively few: a legacy to the anchoress for the next four years (William Browne's 20s a year for twenty years would soon come to an end, and William Elmes is keeping it going for another four years). Like his mother, he asks for a trental of St Gregory to be said for him. But he is more concerned to give money to church building, monasteries and the poor than to clergy to say masses. Like his grandfather, his is a practical will.

But the will of John Elmes III, his son, in 1543[180] is very long, and his anxiety for the safety of his soul very apparent. He spent at least £80 on bequests directly linked to masses for his soul in which he insisted he be mentioned by name; some of these were to last for eighteen to twenty years. The church where he was to be buried must pray for him every Friday for seven years; all his servants were to be given a black gown on condition they pray for his soul. He passed on a great cup which had come down to him from William Browne, again on condition that prayers be said for his soul. The feeling is almost paranoia – and

---

[180] PRO, PROB 11/30; Rogers, Wills

since he had been accused of enclosing land at great cost to his tenants and others, there may have been cause for this.

Conclusion

There would have been in William Browne's town among laity and clergy a wide range of attitudes, combining at one and the same time enthusiasm for and distrust of religion, with perhaps most people having both of these attitudes at the same time in different mixes. And the choice of religious practice available would have been wide. The commitment to one's parish church was counter-balanced by the greater voluntaryism of the gilds which, even though tied to the parish churches, drew their membership from all over the town and outside. Religion in late medieval Stamford was like a curry; it was the precise spices used and the amounts of each involved which gave the particular product its unique flavour. For some, it would be the fervour and public penitence of Margery Kempe, for others the withdrawn contemplative mysticism of Julian of Norwich, for yet others the restrained discipline in the world of the *devotio moderna* of Thomas a Kempis[181].

But the over-riding impression given of most people (except William and Margaret Browne) is of concern about the soul after death, the search for someone to continue to pray for one after entry into the very real next world[182]. The most extreme case of this is in the will of John Elmes III. As the reformed doctrines spread, this family clung to the old religion: it is possible that their adherence to the mass of Pope Gregory was seen as a defence of the doctrine of transubstantiation against the reformers.

---

[181] Huizinga pp 193, 226
[182] See Burgess 1988

APPENDIX: HERESY IN STAMFORD: First Sunday in Advent 1424

For asmuche as I Frere John Russell Religious man and prest upon Corporis Christi day in this toun of Staunford taught and openly preched evel and wykkedly this errour, that a Religious Man may flesshly medele and comune with a womman and not synne deedly; and afterward wrot this conclusion in latyn, and soo hit was sette up on this churche dore, the whiche sayng was and is wikked, erronyous, sclandrous and troublyng mennys consciences and ledyng un to deedly synne, I was charged by oure moost Reverent fader my lord of Canterbury for to apere byfore the worshipfull' Convocacion of the Clergye next after folowyng. Byfore whech' convocacion I confessed my trespas axyng forgevenesse and promyttyng to revoke myn errour in this place. And soo I the saide frere John not wyllyng to geve any crysten body occasion' of errour but submyttyng me to al the worshipfull' Convocacion' of the Clergie at this tyme and all' times I revokyd and revoke myn errour byforesaid; reqyreng that no man ner woman hold hit ner defende hit here after. And inasmuche as I gaf occasion' of errour and of synne,I axe yow all forgevenesse, for I purpose and make full' promesse never to teche hold hit ner defende hit, but with all my pouer under peyne of fauterie of errour promisse to holde and defende that what ever Religious man flesshly medel or comune with a womon synneth deedly and shalbe dampned therefore but if he amende hym.

Canterbury and York Society, *Register of Henry Chicheley archbishop of Canterbury* vol iii p 91

PART IV: CHAPTER 3 WILLIAM BROWNE AS BUILDER AND PATRON: BROWNE'S HOSPITAL

Many [merchants] be good and worshipful also,
And many charitable dedis they do,
Byld Churchys and amend the hyeways,
Make almyshowsys and help many decays[183]

William Browne, like other merchants, spent a good deal of the money he made on building. We need to put this work into context.

Building in Stamford in the fifteenth century

We have already seen that fifteenth century Stamford was characterised by much building activity (pages 116-128). The friaries received legacies that led to the building of tombs and chapels; the Austin friary and White Friars were expanding. The nunnery of St Michael, despite its poverty, saw development of its buildings. All the medieval parish churches that survive were wholly or substantially rebuilt with improved towers and wider spaces for liturgical ceremonies; such rebuilding often took a long time to complete. It is likely that the other parish churches and the hospitals in the town saw some rebuilding work. Several of the gilds improved the facilities available to them; the gilds of All Saints (1475), St Katherine (1480s), and Corpus Christi (1484) had new gildhalls and/or chapels during the century[184]. The town hall was the subject of reconstruction. In all parts of the town, larger stone and timber-framed domestic and/or commercial buildings were being erected where formerly two or more smaller properties stood; empty places were being filled and chimneys added to existing buildings. The council complained of obstructions in many streets.

Such activities must have strengthened some sectors of the economy. Local quarries and timber suppliers must have benefited. A high quality glass workshop based in Stamford undertook work in many churches in and around the town including Peterborough Abbey. In addition to the glass in Browne's Hospital (1490s), elaborate glass was placed in St George's church (an extensive display of the legend of St George and the history of the Garter, c1450) and St John's

---

[183] A C Partridge and F P Wilson (eds) 1949-50 J Haywood, *Gentleness and Nobility* (Malone Society) vol ii lines 671-4

[184] Giles pp 58, 85 suggests that gildhalls were newly built or rebuilt at times of major change in the gilds or to boost identity during a recession; this may not always be the case but can be seen in the case of the gild of St Katherine.

church (1451)[185]. But the building trades do not appear to have had significant political importance in the town. Among those Aldermen whose occupations are recorded, one wright was elected (four times) and one 'stainer' (twice). A glazier was a member of the Second Twelve for a short time (1476-84); no other member of the building trades was among the urban political elite. Relatively few glaziers, masons, carvers, joiners, plasterers and slaters were admitted as freemen: in the 1490s, only three building tradesmen appeared among 25 new freemen, and 2 out of 19 in a second list. Building tradesmen were split between two groups of trades: "All manner handecrafts: ... every ironmonger, hamerman, weyver, walker, slater or any other handyecraft .." for whom freedom would cost 2s, while masons are placed even lower: "Laborers: every common laborer before nott rehersid, servyngman, wryght, mason or any other handycrafte .." admitted for 1s, the lowest in the town. When dividing up the trades for the town 'pagentes', again they were combined with other trades - carpenters, masons and slaters, with scriveners, glaziers, painters, stainers, barbers and chandlers; other building workers were placed with the ironmongers, smiths, saddlers and bottlemakers[186]. The building trades did not form a significant element in the town's formal economy or in the borough consciousness. Presumably much of the elaborate building work was done by persons who had not taken out freedom to trade in the town; some may not have been permanently resident in the town.

William Browne's buildings

William Browne played his part in this activity, in both his private and official capacities. The first account book of the Hospital shows that he engaged in extensive maintenance and some redevelopment of his rural estates and the houses, inns and shops in Stamford which he owned, using the site of his house and the Hospital as a builder's yard. In 1473-4, land in Stamford Baron stood

---

[185] NRS 9 *Peterborough Local Administration* p 12: "payd to the Glaseyer of Staunford for mendyng the wyndowse of the Chyrch vjs" (1472-3). See R Marks 2007 A late medieval glass-painting workshop in the region of Stamford and Peterborough, in R Marks 2007 *Studies in Medieval Stained Glass* Pindar Press; R Marks 1982 A Late Medieval Glass-Painting Workshop in the Region of Stamford and Peterborough, in Peter Moore (ed) 1982 *Crown in Glory*, Norwich pp 29-39; LRS 55 p 77; HMC de L'Isle i p 199; Peck xiv 23-24, 35-38. The glass in St George's church relating to the order of St George was very elaborate and has been extensively documented; BL Dugdale 71474 Book of Monuments; A R Wagner 1956 *Heralds and Heraldry in the Middle Ages* Oxford University Press p 116; S Riches 2000 *St George: hero, martyr and myth* Sutton; W A Rees-Jones 1937 *Saint George, the Order of St George and the church of St George in Stamford* London: Churchman Publishing; S Riches 2001 The lost St George cycle of St George's church, Stamford: an examination of iconography and context, in C Richmond and E Scarff (eds) 2001 *St George's Chapel, Windsor, in the late middle ages* Windsor: Dean and Canons of Windsor, pp 135-150; J Good 2008 *The Cult of St George in medieval England* Boydell

[186] HB i fol 3, p 8; fol 5d, pp 13-14; see above pp 63-4. In York, the groupings of the building industry were carpenters, masons, plasterers and tilers, Giles p 61

"opposite the land which William Browne has newly built". In 1474-5, in his capacity as Alderman of the gild of Corpus Christi, he took a lease of "a vacant place containing 6 feet in length and ½ foot in width" for erecting a chimney in Briggestreete. During his term as Alderman of the gild of St Katherine, a cottage on Cleymont was rebuilt as "a messuage called Saint Kateryns hall" or "the geld halle"[187]. He did not rebuild his own residence in a more modern style (see below p 309), but he did rebuild his parish church of All Saints in the Market and build his Hospital.

All Saints in the Market

Contributing to the building of churches was a characteristic of many fifteenth century wool merchants and others, especially the newly rich, in both rural and urban contexts. It has been noted that, when raising a perpetual memorial for oneself and one's family, the parish church was the obvious object of such devotion; the rebuilding of All Saints in the Market was part of William's design for his commemoration. The cost and perhaps the direction of the work were apparently shared with his brother John, for All Saints was the 'tomb-church' of the family[188]. John their father was buried in the chapel of St Thomas at the east end of the north aisle, where John the brother and his wife, and Christopher, John's son, were also buried and commemorated by brasses. William adopted the chapel of St Mary at the east end of the south aisle. Here he gave precise instructions for his burial and set brasses for himself and his wife, Margaret Elmes his grand-daughter, and Alice Bradmedewe his sister.

The rebuilding of All Saints church by the Brownes[189] is seen from their merchant's mark carved on both the exterior and interior; two bosses have Margaret's rebus of the stork and the motto '+ me spede', both of which are on the brass of William Browne and Margaret. There are two early bells named John and Margaret but it is uncertain whether these date from the fifteenth century[190].

---

[187] PRO, SC6/1115/13; GCC 266/670 fols 4d, 62, 73; Rogers, *Gild Book* pp 23-24

[188] Duffy *Stripping* p 302; see Fairford p 7

[189] Tradition from early years ascribed the work to the Browne brothers, although later antiquarians disputed over whether one or other brother did it alone. Butcher says William built the steeple because of the merchant's mark on it; Peck says John Browne (esq!) built it; see Butcher 1727 p 22.

[190] Butcher 1717 p 18; LRS 1 *Holles Church Notes* p 200 records a brass on the north wall: *Hic jacet J Browne mercator stapulae Calesie et benefactor huius ecclesie qui obiit 26 die Julii A D 1545 cuius anime etc*. This is a misreading of the brass of John Browne the father, *mercatoris Stapule Calisie et Margerie uxoris eius; qui quidem Johannes obiit xxvi die mensis Julii A D 1442*. There was no John Browne of 1545, and no mention of benefactor of the church.

The south view of All Saints in the Market, Stamford, after the rebuilding by the Browne brothers. The chapel on the south side of the chancel is the burial chapel of William Browne and his immediate family (Buckler 1811, British Library Board Add Mss 36369 fol 123)

Their work was not as extensive as many have made out, but it was clearly costly. Characterised by "architectural elaboration and by some degree of fantasy"[191] on the exterior, the interior was not substantially altered; the original arcades were retained (only the south arcade slightly reconstructed at the west end). It was the exterior which was largely rebuilt. The plan and dimensions of the original building were retained; the existing church was pulled down to the height of the window sills (the blank arcading below these sills is thirteenth century) and rebuilt with a raised roof, clerestory, new chancel arch and larger windows. William Browne's burial chapel was rebuilt. A tower with spire was built at the north west corner of the church, with a clock face, described as 'new-fangled'. But the rebuilt church is not as imposing as some of the Staple churches of the Cotswolds which seem to be more urban in scale, perhaps owing to the restricted site of the original church; and it lacks the cohesion of St John's church or St Martin's. One would like to know how long the rebuilding took and whether John, Margaret and Agnes were closely involved or not; the rebuilding was not apparently completed when William Browne died in 1489, for William Elmes in his will (1504) gave to "the reparacions of the lady chapell within the parish church of allhalow in Staunforth xiijs iiijd and to the reparacions of the body of the same church xxs"[192].

---

[191] RCHME *Stamford* p 9
[192] Rogers, Wills

This was William's parish church; and three successive vicars (John Halyday, Thomas Stokes his brother-in-law and executor, and Henry Wykes) who served the parish for 90 years (1419-1508) became close friends, acting for William in various property transactions. The vicarage house of All Saints was rebuilt during the late fifteenth century in a somewhat old-fashioned style[193], probably when Thomas Stokes was vicar of All Saints (1468-79); and since the Browne brothers owned the property immediately on both sides of the vicarage, it is hard to believe they were not involved in that building alongside their work on the parish church, with financial support, if nothing else. It may well be substantially another of William's buildings. Thomas Stokes was almost certainly responsible for the building of the so-called priest's house at his parish of Easton on the Hill three miles south west of Stamford, which betrays some affinities with the vicarage of All Saints, just as the rebuilt tower of Easton on the Hill seems to have copied the new tower of St John the Baptist in Stamford.

The same may be true of the contemporary rebuilding of the church at Warmington in Northamptonshire, the family home of Margaret Browne and the village where the Browne family had substantial long-standing properties. John Browne the father left a bequest to Warmington church, as did Margaret and other members of the family. Here however the hands of the Stokes family may have been at work; a late fifteenth century chest tomb in that church from which the brass or inscriptions have now vanished may have belonged to Sir William Stokes, lord of the main manor and brother of Margaret Browne and of Thomas Stokes[194].

---

[193] CPR 1358-61/342; see Surtees Society 76 p 324; for the building of ASM vicarage, see Owen pp 136-7.

[194] RCHME *Northants* vi p 157.

THE BUILDING OF BROWNE'S HOSPITAL, STAMFORD

By far the biggest project William Browne undertook was the building and endowment of the Hospital that goes under his name – Browne's Hospital, a remarkably complete late medieval hospital of a high standard. The story is complicated and relies on both documentary and architectural evidence[195].

The architectural and archaeological evidence, at first sight, has suggested to some that the Hospital was built as a single story building and converted later into the existing two story building. But closer inspection of the fabric suggests a different picture. The south facade (facing the road) has clearly been built all in one stage, indicating a building which was built in one stage, but which experienced changes in design during building and indeed botched work. Some elements such as the glazing in the windows were clearly delayed until later but the two-storied building as it substantially remains (other than the changes of the 1870s) was of one build.

The documents reveal that William Browne built a hospital, called Claymont Hospital after the market area on which it stood, in 1475. The immediate trigger may have been a recent family bereavement: in 1471, William's eldest grand-daughter, Margaret Elmes, died, and William and Margaret Browne were so moved that they erected a brass in her memory in their family chapel in the parish church; she could not have been more than nine and was probably considerably younger. This must have brought home to William that he had no surviving son to perpetuate the family name; his line would die out. It may have been at this time that the idea of erecting and endowing a family memorial came to the couple.

But they combined this with a hall for the parish gild of All Saints, of which William Browne was Alderman. This was to be both gild hall and family chantry to pray for the souls of William and Margaret Browne and their clan family. The first floor was built as a gildhall on an elaborate scale; here the gild met, held their annual feast and stored their possessions. But it was William Browne, not the gild, who bought the site and paid for the erection of the buildings; and he and Margaret paid all its costs while they lived.

---

[195] This section is based on a detailed study of the origins of Browne's Hospital in which all the documentation and archaeology is cited, shortly to be published. I am grateful to many people, especially Andrew Butcher, John Schofield, Linda Monckton and above all Nick Hill for help with the archaeology and reconstruction, and to the trustees for their help and interest. But they are not responsible for the views expressed here.

Interior of Audit Room of Browne's Hospital, the gildhall of All Saints Gild (photo: Nick Hill)

Confirmation of this comes from two sources. First, in April 1475:

> *On this day was granted to William Browne a postern gate to be made by him on the boundary wall at the north end of a new place [loci] between the places [placea] of the same William Browne and Robert Hans; and the aforesaid William Browne, his heirs, executors and assigns shall fully and sufficiently repair, sustain and maintain the aforesaid boundary wall there in everything as it was in ancient times etc on pain of forfeiture of the aforesaid postern.*

Browne's Hospital showing William Browne's house to the west (Buckler 1011 in British Library Board Add Mss 36369 fol 14v)

243

William and his heirs (not the gild) were charged to maintain this gate in future[196]. It was alleged that the site was originally a 'vile dunghill' which William Browne, as Alderman of Stamford, had relocated in 1466, along with the other town refuse heaps. It was the highest point within the town walls, visible from many miles away. But above all, it was next door to Browne's own house. The Hospital occupied the full frontage of the plot, so that the entry passage for the gild to access the stairs to the gildhall encroached on his garden next door. The irregular boundary between the Hospital and Browne's house to the west and this encroachment on his garden of the original access to the stairs indicate the personal nature of the relationship between Browne and the Hospital.

Secondly, in 1479, the rector of St Michael the Greater was suing Thomas Stokes, vicar of All Saints in the Market, alleging that Stokes was saying mass in the newly erected Claymont Hospital, the chapel of which lay in the parish of St Michael, depriving the rector of some of his fees. This, said the rector, had been going on for at least three years (i.e. back to at least 1476). The plea must have been made to the bishop of Lincoln; Stokes took his defence to the archbishop of Canterbury, so the rector took his plea to the papal court in Rome. The suit was not settled until a month or two before William Browne died. The rector was suing the vicar of All Saints, not the gild; and it was William Browne who made the final settlement.

It was then William Browne's own foundation; nevertheless, the gild of which Browne was Alderman held that it was in effect a gild hospital.

Hospitals and concern for the poor

Browne's Hospital housed ten poor men and two poor women[197]. Religion and social concerns came together in the founding of late medieval hospitals. Belief in the efficacy of prayers (even of lay people) for the deceased led to the establishment of private or corporate chantries, sometimes served by small lay communities. But by the second half of the fifteenth century, government was more opposed to the perpetual alienation of properties for the purpose of establishing chantries. It was thus easier to obtain licences for the creation of hospitals; and founding hospitals for the poor and old was in accordance with the concerns of the time[198]. Support for the poor was a religious duty and

---

[196] This refers to Browne's Hospital in building – hence the 'new place, HB i fol 19d, p 53. The gate (rebuilt) still stands.

[197] Fotheringhay was founding a hospital for ten inmates at the same time; this may have provided a model.

[198] "Alienation of land to the church - in mortmain – was only possible by special licence from the king, which did not come cheaply",Fleming, Charity p 39; most chantries in the later 15th century had almshouses,hospitals or schools attached, McIntosh 1988 p 225. See Duffy *Stripping*

brought with it religious benefits, especially in the afterlife. Other forms of public service were of course followed, especially the financing of public works – repair of roads and bridges, cleaning of streets, and construction of water supplies and new gildhalls. But the large numbers of persons living at or near subsistence in both town and village, although largely hidden from historians, were all too apparent to contemporaries. Thus the fifteenth century saw an increase of disquiet about, and help offered to, the poor by the wealthier members of society[199].

Two main groups of 'poor' were identified – the *pauperes*, those born into perpetual dearth, and the *indigentes*, those who through (sometimes temporary) accident have fallen into poverty (that could include competent tradesmen and craftsmen as well as widows or the sick). Most poor relief measures were aimed at the *indigentes* to help them endure their reduced circumstances and if possible to restore some dignity ('worship'): thus when in 1440 Henry VI nominated his first 'poor' scholar at Eton, he came from the *indigentes*, not the *pauperes*[200]. But, in England as elsewhere, such attitudes were being challenged: the evidence of suffering was too great. The towns were particularly affected by rural poor seeking refuge from "successive harvest failures". Faced with the undeniable signs of increasing poverty arising from the great slump and with increasing fear of the soldiers and others returning from the continent as the wars there progressively failed, there were two main reactions: legislation (including urban regulations) concerning itinerants and beggars, and what has been called 'discriminatory charity' focussing aid on the "genuinely indigent", the deserving poor, especially of the local community (often the parish), not on 'sturdy beggars'. Both gilds and rich merchants responded, since "Charite is the good marchaunt that overal wynneth and never leseth"[201]. Exhorted to give to charity one third of the possessions they left, those wealthy enough often left money for

---

p 510; Dobson 1967; Dobson 1992; S Raban 1982 *Mortmain legislation and the English church 1279-1500* Oxford

[199] e.g. Duffy *Stripping* p 367; Giles p 77: "those on the margins of urban society such as the indigent poor appear as absent from this discursive construction of the civic community as they do from its political reality" – see above pp 35-6. See Dyer *Standards;* on charity, see W K Jordan 1959 *Philanthropy in England 1480-1640: a study of the changing pattern of English social aspirations* Allen and Unwin ; W G Brittle and R Todd Lane 1976 Inflation and philanthropy in England: a reassessment of W K Jordan's data, *Econ Hist Rev 2c* 29 pp 203 210; 31 (1978) pp 105-128; Gilchrist p 101; Miri Rubin 1987 *Charity and Community in Medieval Cambridge* Cambridge University Press

[200] See Rogers, Stokes

[201] W N Francis (ed) 1968 *Book of Vices and Virtues* EETS 217 p 89. See Mollat 1978; Giles pp 68, 86; for growing "suspicion of poverty and homelessness", see Attreed *King's Towns* p 299; McIntosh 1986 p 228; for the growth of a "corrective attitude towards poverty", see Dyer, *Capitalists* p 20

the founding of almshouses and hospitals. A number of gilds provided and ran hospitals for the poor and sick, often from their own mystery or locality[202].

Stamford shared in these values and practices. Bylaws against 'vagabonds' and 'strangers' occur throughout the Hall Book, especially in 1469, 1479 and 1482:

> *And that no maner of straunger unknawn and no vacabounde ne others callyng them self shipmen ne no comyn beggers, straungers abide or contynue in this toune over a day and a nyght as for the beythyng. And yif thei abide or contynue longar, thei shall have corporall punysshment accordyng to the statute therfor provided.*

Several 'strangers' were fined. At the same time, the local poor were sometimes cared for: a will of 1410 left 10 marks to all the bedridden poor in Stamford, and the wills of John Browne the father, William and Margaret Browne, Christopher Browne, and William, Elizabeth and John Elmes[203] all made provision for the poor at the time of their death. So that the provision of a hospital fits in with contemporary understandings of poor relief.

The term 'hospital' in late medieval England had several meanings – a medical centre such as a leper hospital for the care of the sick; an almshouse or bedehouse for the long-term care of the more able-bodied poor; or a wayside stopping place for travellers, especially pilgrims[204]. The Hospital founded by William Browne was not for the sick: "no leprous man or woman be admitted ... if any one of the aforesaid Almshouse, after admission thereto, shall become leprous or infected by any other infirmity repulsively noisome to his or her fellows, he or she ought to be removed" – presumably to one of the other hospitals in the town, St Giles leper hospital, St John with St Thomas the martyr, the Goddeshows or *maison dieu* in Eastgate, or other[205]. Browne's Hospital was an

---

[202] See p 308; Kermode *Merchants* pp 127-8, 147; Goldberg 2004 p 111. For hospitals, see Orme and Webster; Clay; W H Godfrey 1955 *The English Almshouse* London; J Rowe 1958 The medieval hospitals of Bury St Edmunds *Medical History* 2 pp 253-263; M Carlin 1989 Medieval English hospitals, in Granshaw and Porter 1989 pp 21-39; M Rubin 1989 Development and change in English hospitals 1100-1500, in Granshaw and Porter 1989 pp 41-59; C Rawcliffe 1999 *Medicine for the soul: life, death and resurrection of an English medieval hospital, St Giles's, Norwich c1249-1550* Sutton; S Sweetinburgh 2004 *The role of the hospital in medieval England: gift-giving and the spiritual economy* Dublin; C Rawcliffe 2008 *Dives Redeemed? The Guild Almshouses of Later Medieval England*, in Clark 2008 pp 1-27; Duffy *Stripping* p 510; Giles p 90; Sutton *Tates* p 5

[203] HB i fol 26, p 71; for strangers, HB i pp 30, 36, 42, 60, 70-1, 78, 79, 80, 83, 99; LRS 57 p 190; see Rogers, Wills

[204] Gilchrist pp 102-3. For God's House, Giles pp 68-69; Salter 2006 p 13; Cullum, Vowesses; M Davies 1995 The Tailors of London: corporate charity in the late medieval town in Archer 1995 pp 161-190. Cullum 1994 suggests that *maisons dieu* were usually very small, usually unendowed and often temporary almshouses.

[205] See Hartley and Rogers pp 48-53; above p 28

almshouse where relatively healthy local poor persons received accommodation and a subsistence allowance for the remainder of their lives.

A private foundation

Despite the evidence of the gild association with the Hospital, later accounts state that William Browne, supported by Margaret his wife, maintained Claymont Hospital without any support or oversight from any other source. It was a private chantry: '*Orate pro animabus Willielmi Browne et Margarete uxoris sue*', proclaimed a window in the chapel. The inmates had a duty of prayers in the chapel every morning and evening and three times during the day; at these, a senior bedesman "shall say openly in English: 'God have mercy upon the souls of William Browne of Stamford and Dame Margaret his wife, and ... on the soul of Mr Thomas Stokk, founder of this Almshouse, the souls of their fathers and mothers, and all Christian souls". This would account for Browne's insistence in his later foundation documents that the Hospital would not be called the Hospital of All Saints but 'the Hospital of William Browne of Stamford'. It was the preservation of his name which he sought as much as the relief of the poor or the salvation of his soul.

But there arose the problem of how to endow the Hospital so that it could continue to be supported after the death of William and Margaret. The gild did not have the resources to fund the Hospital; this would have to come from Brownes' estate. Three routes were open to them. They could give the endowments to some existing established and enduring organisation, such as the gild or the town council. The gild later claimed that since it was unincorporated, it could not hold property; and for reasons which cannot now be determined, Browne decided not to go down the town council route, despite (or perhaps because of) the fact that the council was already acting as patron for St Nicholas chantry in St Clement's church. Secondly, they could have established a permanent board of feoffees, as did other contemporary donors such as Jenkyn Smythe of Bury St Edmunds in 1481[206]. Thirdly, they could incorporate and endow the Hospital itself and make its personnel the trustees. This was the route they decided to follow.

Sometime between 1475 and 1483, William Browne drafted a petition to Edward IV for a licence to convert the 'chapel and other buildings' known as Claymont Hospital, which he had recently built, into a perpetual Hospital, to incorporate it

---

[206] "Almshouses established after 1450 were operated usually by lay feoffees and were nearly all intended for local old people", McIntosh 1988 p 229; see Margaret Statham and Sally Badham 2011 Jankyn Smith of Bury St Edmunds and his brass, *Transactions of the Monumental Brass Society* XVIII (Part3) pp 227-250

(in terms of the warden, confraters and 12 inmates), to establish within it a chantry for him and his family and others (including the king and queen), and to endow it directly. It was now to be called 'the Hospital of William Browne of Stamford'. There is no mention of the gild. This petition may not have been presented before Edward IV died in March 1483. In 1484-5, Browne drafted a revised petition for such a licence, and the chantry beneficiaries were to include Richard III and his queen. This was successful; in January 1485, "William Browne of Staunford hath a licence to founde an almonye House there for ever" for the substantial fee of 200 marks (£133. 6s 8d)[207]. But Richard III too died, killed at Bosworth field in August 1485.

William Browne acted upon the January 1485 licence. In July 1488, clearly knowing he was in his last months, he divided his extensive estates, appointing feoffees to pass,after the death of his wife, one group of estates to his daughter Elizabeth wife of John Elmes, and another set of feoffees to pass the rest of his estates to the Hospital. In February 1489, a settlement was made by the bishop of Lincoln in the dispute between the rector of St Michael the Greater and the vicar of All Saints; although not a party to the suit, William Browne granted to the rector an annual rent from one of his properties (the Angel in the Hoop). Two months later, William Browne died.

William's executor was his wife Margaret. Immediately after his death, a new petition to Henry VII for a licence to endow the Hospital was drafted, replacing Richard III and his queen with Henry VII and his queen and other members of the royal household among the beneficiaries. The support of Sir Reginald Bray, the king's confidant and constable of Oakham, was obtained to facilitate this petition. But Margaret Browne died in October 1489, leaving to her brother Thomas Stokes, executor of her will, the final stages of establishing the Hospital on its new footing, which he accomplished by 1494. Stokes had been an active associate in the foundation from the start[208].

The new licence of 1493 was held up because the clerks of the chancery demanded a fee despite the fact that the licence stated that since 200 marks had been paid in 1485, no further fee was needed. In fact, Stokes paid a further £50 to get this licence. In 1494, Stokes finished drafting statutes for the Hospital and promulgated them in 1495, a few days before his death. In December 1494, he appointed (or re-appointed) the warden, confrater, ten poor men and two poor women, and the estates were passed over to the warden and confrater. And on

---

[207] BL Harl 433 fol 93; Horrox and Hammond i p 254; CPR 1476-85/505

[208] Condon 1990; Richard III's grants were not recognised in the early years of Henry VII; see P Tudor-Craig 1995 Margaret queen of Scotland in Grantham 8-9July 1503, in B Thompson (ed) 1995 *The Reign of Henry VII* Stamford: Watkins pp 273-4

22 December 1494 the ageing bishop of Lincoln (only eight days before his own death) re-dedicated the chapel. William Browne's memorial Hospital was well and truly launched. Just in time – for in October 1495, Thomas Stokes too died, and it was left to his executor, William Elmes, to finish things off by granting the Hospital a seal and completing the glazing in the Hospital. In 1497, a brass plaque was erected at the bottom of the stairs to the upper chamber announcing the completion of the building (see p 298) – Browne's Hospital's own 'topping out ceremony'.

This throws some light on the glazing of the Audit Room, which was the gild's hall. The schema relates to the gild, not to the Hospital; the bedesmen had their own hall in the rear buildings. Although William Browne and his wife may have had a hand in choosing the subjects (the use of his merchant's mark and her rebus of the stork in the upper windows suggests this), the arms used indicate that the final work was done by William Elmes who also put his arms on the seal he gave to the Hospital[209]. A date of 1494-1497 may now be given to the glass in the Audit Room; the glass in the chapel may be earlier.

One of the two David and Paul windows showing the Browne merchant mark and stork above (photo: Alan Rogers)

---

[209] There are no arms of the Stokes family in the glass despite several statements by later writers to the contrary.

Seal of Browne's Hospital
(from Wright) [210]

The building

The re-dedication of the chapel in December 1494 indicates the end of the conversion of the Hospital from the gildhall of All Saints gild; the dedication became Our Lady as well as All Saints. The design of the Hospital was somewhat old-fashioned for the period. The ten bedesmen were housed in cubicles on the ground floor in an infirmary-type room rather than in separate cells around a courtyard as was more normal for the period[211]. The large and elaborate first floor room with fireplace, and the pantry and buttery and access to the kitchens, were used as the gildhall; a separate hall was provided for the bedesmen behind the main building. A chapel occupied the east end through both floors. The upper room, with its separate staircase at the west end, and the chapel with a separate door from the street, could be used without the gild members having to go through the dormitory. There were extensive outbuildings with accommodation for the warden and the two serving women, service rooms and a schoolroom.

The Hospital was endowed with something approaching half of William Browne's estates. William's licence was to grant it an income of 50 marks (£33 6s 8d) p.a.. In order to obtain that net income, estates worth over £60 p.a. were needed, for the regular outgoings from these estates amounted to over £8 p.a., decay of rents lost the Hospital another £3 to £8 each year, repairs to the estate ranged from £12 to £17 p.a. (20-25% of the income), and other costs, purchases and agents' fees took up more of the income, so that the Hospital was hard pressed to find £30 to pay the paupers and the clergy each year. Initially payments to the inmates were 8d per week, but this was quickly reduced to 7d

---

[210] The Hospital seal (now alas missing) is exceptional in that it carries a rare representation of 'the bosom of Abraham Trinity', for which see P Sheingorn 1989 The Bosom of Abraham Trinity: a late medieval All Saints image, in Williams 1989 pp 273-295; see Rogers and Hill (forthcoming)

[211] e.g. Dyer *Standards* p 244: "often living in separate rooms arranged in a row or around a quadrangle"; Gilchrist p 103

per week as provided by the statutes[212]. The auditor who was to be paid a fee of 5 marks if the expenses allowed it, only received that sum in the first year of the Hospital.

The history of the Hospital after the death of Thomas Stokes is very revealing. William Elmes was Alderman of the gild of All Saints in succession to William Browne, and took over from Thomas Stokes as 'patron' of the Hospital. He provided the warden with ready money to cover day to day expenses. When John Coton died (1496), William Elmes appointed John Taylor as warden. Although Taylor had been one of William Browne's feoffees, and was a protégé of Thomas Stokes, this was a surprising appointment, for Taylor was a young scholar from Oxford, and for a time he combined the position with his fellowship at Oriel College, Oxford. In 1498, a further substantial donation came to the Hospital from the de la Launde family of North Witham, Lincolnshire, a family that had been among the leaders of the rebellion which led to the battle of Loosecoat Field in 1470.

In the documentation concerning the re-founding of the Hospital, the gild of All Saints was carefully excluded, although it continued to meet in the Hospital while William Elmes was alive. But in 1504, the warden John Taylor left to become vicar of St Martin's Stamford, and Elmes appointed his successor William Sharp. Then Elmes died, apparently unexpectedly and at a young age. Christopher Browne now became Alderman of the gild of All Saints – but not patron of the Hospital. Until now, the Alderman of the gild had been the patron; now the link was broken. It was the vicar of All Saints who appointed new staff and inmates, and who audited the accounts of the Hospital, not the Alderman of the gild.

Immediately a bitter dispute broke out. A quarrel between the warden and Christopher Browne had been going on since at least 1502, while William Elmes was alive, over unpaid rent from land in Lincolnshire. This now developed into a major dispute between the gild and the Hospital. The gild claimed that William Browne as Alderman had made provision for the gild to use the building as their gild hall, and that this access had continued since the early years of the Hospital; but the warden had excluded them from the Hospital buildings for their feast. Christopher as Alderman of the gild also called upon the warden to account for the money which (said Christopher) William Elmes had loaned, not given, to the Hospital from the gild treasury. John Taylor, who clearly supported the new warden strongly, wrote a long account of the foundation of the Hospital in his account book, and copied up all the accounts of John Coton and of himself,

---

[212] It is possible that 8d was the rate paid to the inmates by William and Margaret Browne while they lived.

getting the vicar of All Saints to audit every page carefully, so that the exclusion of the gild would be demonstrated.

The gild responded vigorously. Since (it was claimed) the gild was unincorporated, Christopher Browne as Alderman pursued the suit in his own right; thus private and gild matters became intertwined. Christopher claimed that William Browne had built the Hospital as a gild hall, and that William in his will had given the gild the right to hold their meetings in the building[213]. The warden replied that the gild's activities there were simply by grace and favour; William and Margaret Browne had built and supported Claymont Hospital without any other body being involved, and endowed it from their own resources, accounting to nobody. The statutes broke the link between the gild and the Hospital – and this implied that the gild members were no longer eligible for the religious and secular benefits of the Hospital.

The warden appealed to the council of Lady Margaret Beaufort at Collyweston and Christopher was ordered "to desist". But Christopher (a member of Lady Margaret's council) took the case to chancery and then to the relatively new Court of Requests. The warden went to London several times on this suit but a verdict was given against the Hospital; late in 1506 under the eyes of the town Alderman and members of the council, the padlock on the pantry was cut off and the goods of the gild were inventoried. But the case dragged on for some time more.

What then are we to make of this saga? It seems that William Browne, with the support of his wife Margaret who is named in most of the documents as a co-founder of the Hospital, built a Hospital on the plot of ground next door to their own house; it was then called Claymont Hospital. William was Alderman of the gild of All Saints, and the Hospital included a gildhall. The double function of the building is revealed in the quality of the upper room with its fireplace, elaborate 'high table' area and hangings, and perhaps also the quality of the chapel, its stalls and its fine glass. The gild and the Hospital cohabited for some years. But when it came to be endowed, William Browne did this from his own resources, changing the name of the Hospital. Thomas Stokes finalised the arrangements for the incorporated and endowed Hospital, carefully excluding the gild and changing the dedication. On Stokes' death, William Elmes (now Alderman of the gild) became patron, and a clear distinction between his role as patron and as Alderman was not maintained. Until the death of William Elmes,

---

[213] There is no such provision in the written will but William Browne may have made an oral will; see Fleming Charity p 55 n 11

relations between the gild and the Hospital remained amicable; but after Christopher Browne became Alderman of the gild (who again did not distinguish clearly between his individual interests and those of the gild), the statutes were used to challenge the gild's presence in the building. In part, the hostility seems to have been of a personal nature between Taylor and Christopher Browne. But what had started out as a gild-almshouse had now become the private almshouse-cum-chantry of the Brownes and their extended family. The gild may have continued to use the Hospital, but it seems to have withered away, for there is no certificate for its dissolution.

Conclusion

William Browne's building at the Hospital, church and elsewhere was on a grand scale. We have no idea what it must have cost. The buildings, especially the stonework required from both local quarries and further afield, must have called for large resources. It is likely that this work took over as William Browne's primary concern in his later years, though both of his wool trade and money lending continued to occupy him to the end.

PART V: IDENTITIES AND CULTURE

This part looks at who William and Margaret Browne were –

- *at their identities as family members and as friends within the context of fifteenth century Stamford*

- *at Margaret Browne's role among the diversity of women in Stamford at the time,*

- *and finally at the material culture of the family reflecting these multiple and changing identities.*

PART V: CHAPTER 1 FAMILY, HOUSE HOLD AND FRIENDS

"....my brother Brown and Dame Margaret his wif, oure progenitours and frendes"; will of Thomas Stokes, 1494[1].

Of all the social units of the period, the town, the parishes, the gilds, the craft associations, it was the family with its various extensions which was the most influential. Throughout the country, mementoes (real or fabricated) of family were being collected and recorded in glass and other forms[2].

William Browne's family was important to him. The impression is of a close group, held together by multiple bonds, social, economic, cultural and religious as well as kinship. It was not one simple nuclear family but a network drawn from members of three families, the Brownes, the Stokes and the Elmes – a 'kinship' or 'clan family'[3]; and although focused on the town, it extended beyond the walls. William Browne actively formed his kinship network which was both inclusive and exclusive.

The family – nuclear and extended

When considering late medieval families, it is important to recognise that we rarely know how many children each medieval family unit had. Many children died young, leaving no record. The Fairfax family of Deeping Gate near Stamford, who were close friends of the Brownes, listed fourteen births spread over a period of 27 years from 1445 to 1472; without that list, we would know about only three of the children[4]. The brass of Thomas Stokes of Ashby St Ledgers, Northamptonshire, (1416) shows sixteen children, most of whom died in infancy. Sir Henry Colet, mercer and lord mayor of London, is reputed to have had twenty or more children, of whom only one survived (Dr John Colet dean of St Paul's). Thus any family could have had many children who had died young; and the chronological gap between those who survived could be as much as 20-25 years.

---

[1] PRO, PROB 11/10; see Rogers, Wills

[2] See Payling 1995; Kermode *Merchants* p 70; Duby 1988; Salter 2006 pp 51-2; Grace 2009; Fleming Charity p 51, M Kowalski 1988 History of urban families in medieval England *JMH* 14 pp 47 63

[3] Fleming Charity p 36

[4] Bodl Mss Lit Latin e10, Book of Hours of Fairfax family of Deeping St James, fifteenth century; Rogers, Fairfax; for other such records, see Duffy *Marking.* For infant mortality in towns, see Thrupp pp 202-3; J Hatcher 1986 Mortality in the fifteenth century *Econ Hist Rev* 2s 39 pp 19-38

The death of Margaret Elmes in 1471, recorded solely in the brass in All Saints church, shows this in William Browne's own family; without that, we would not have added her to the children of William's daughter Elizabeth. So that when we speak of William Browne as having an only daughter Elizabeth, we must insist that we do not know how many other children there may have been.

Naming customs may help. The Fairfax children show that names were chosen carefully to commemorate or please previous family members as well as godparents. The Browne-Stokes-Elmes families clearly followed traditional naming customs. Every head of the Browne family had been John from at least the 1360s to the 1440s, some five or six generations. So that when we find William being the oldest surviving son and John the younger son, this suggests that there had been an older son named John who died in childhood and that a younger son was later named John to ensure the family still had a child of that name. The only surviving son of John Browne the brother was called Christopher, again indicating that there had almost certainly been earlier sons, that Christopher was not the first-born child[5]. Similarly the Browne family followed a pattern of naming girls after the mother or grandmother. Thus John Browne the brother had a daughter named Agnes, the third Agnes in succession after John's mother-in-law and his wife. Elizabeth (found in William's family and in John's family) broke this sequence and suggests there were likely to have been earlier daughters. The fact that the only known sister of William Browne was called Alice rather than Margery again suggests that there may have been earlier sisters who died young.

Both the Stokes family and the Elmes family seem to have shared the same practice. John, William and Thomas are repeated in the Stokes family, and John was given to at least four successive generations of Elmes. All three families, Brownes, Stokes and Elmes, passed family names down in a hierarchy of value. Christopher seems to have broken this; he drew the names of his surviving sons (Francis and Edmund), perhaps from his friends at court.

I am therefore suggesting that William and Margaret Browne had more offspring than the sole daughter who survived, as did John Browne the father and John Browne the brother. And that such family losses were not taken as a matter of course but were felt deeply and affected patterns of behaviour. The family mattered to the Brownes.

---

[5] This may help to account for the 'lost years' which Christopher's biography suggests. "It was not unusual to give two sons the same name", Kermode 1982 p 16

Certainly all the Brownes, with one exception, worked closely together. John Browne the father and William Browne, separately and together, acted as feoffee and witness for Robert Browne, glover and husbandman and Alderman of Stamford (1441-2), who was probably a member of the same family[6]. In 1433, John Browne the father passed his business to William his eldest surviving son, taking steps to avoid the limitations of borough English which would have passed the property to the youngest surviving son; William was executor of his father's will with John's wife Margery. In return, William purchased a house standing between William's house and the vicarage of All Saints, in which his father could retire. It seems clear that William looked after his mother in her eighteen-year long widowhood, and he ordered the two brasses to commemorate his parents. He took care of his brother's widow Agnes during her widowhood.

Alice Bradmedewe and Coventry

The most striking example of this is the care he and his brother John gave to their sister Alice. Alice was married to a merchant in Coventry. That the Browne family should have interests in Coventry should not surprise us, for (as we have seen) Coventry was at the centre of the Midlands trading community, especially the wool and cloth trades. It stood close to the Cotswold sheep rearing area, and its road and river communication systems were well maintained; its economic and political significance remained high throughout the century. It is likely that the initial Browne connections were through William's trading interests.

Such connections did not take place in a vacuum. There were long-standing links between Stamford and Coventry. The gild of Holy Trinity, St Mary, St John the Baptist and St Katherine in Coventry included several members from Stamford, including two successive rectors of St Michael the Greater in Stamford. Trading between the two towns was frequent; Coventry merchants had debts in Stamford, and Stamford traders paid debts in Coventry. Merchants of Stamford teamed up with merchants of Coventry: Thomas Philippe of Stamford and William Ford of Coventry acted as joint executors for a fellow merchant in 1483-5. The priory of Coventry owned property in Stamford. The road between the two towns was well trodden, so that Roger Flore of Oakham, through which that road went, could in successive items in his will of 1424 give legacies to the friars of Stamford and to the Charterhouse of Coventry. In 1450, the two towns were linked politically in that both were seen as needing to be warned by the Lancastrian regime. The sheriff of Lincolnshire could trap a thief in Stamford by telling him of goods brought from Coventry for sale[7].

---

[6] See above pp 52-3

[7] *AASR* Wills pp 74-5, 79; *Coventry, Holy Trinity Guild* pp 12, 29, 71, 78: "Lincolnshire villages and towns furnish many members" p xx. See Phythian-Adams *Desolation* p 28; PRO, C1/65/183;

Alice Browne first married Richard Botener of Coventry fishmonger[8]. It may
seem surprising for a family of drapers and woolmerchants to marry into a
fishmonger family, but Calais Staplers often had more than one occupation –
fishmongers such as Richard Yorke, John Betson and John Reynewell, skinners
like John Buknell, farmers and landholders like Thomas Adam of Langham,
Rutland, officials like Roger Flore of Oakham, country gentlemen, even senior
clergymen like Cardinal Beaufort, "the greatest merchant of wools", were
Staplers[9]. And the Botoner family was an established and wealthy family in
Coventry, reputed to have been the builders of St Michael's church. Richard
Botoner was bailiff of the town in the 1430s. In about 1432, he settled some
property on Alice his wife, using William and John Browne, brothers of Alice, as
his feoffees[10].

Richard died before Alice, and Alice married Robert Bradmedewe draper of
Coventry (by 1453) and brother of the more active and prominent Thomas
Bradmedewe draper and hosier[11]. Although relative newcomers into Coventry,
the two brothers soon came to occupy every major position in the town –
mayor, chamberlains, bailiffs, sheriffs, city wardens and JPs, and masters of the
gild of Holy Trinity[12].

On her second marriage, the two Browne brothers were holding the Botoner
property for the life of Alice their sister; in 1453, they settled this property on
Robert Bradmedewe and Alice for the life of Alice. Robert Bradmedewe added
to Alice's holdings, granting to William Browne property which had come from
his mother as part of the marriage settlement. In 1475, William and John Browne
quitclaimed Alice's property to Robert Bradmedewe and Alice with the proviso

---

E315/41/117; parts of the body of the executed Frammesley were sent to Stamford and
Coventry, see above pp 77, 135. The Browne family itself may have had links with the area
earlier, for a John Browne clothseller is known to have acted in the Coventry area in 1397 and
1403.

[8] CRO, DR429/32; PA14/1/48

[9] Lloyd *Wool Trade* p 265; Tooley p 16; Hanham *Cely Letters* p 288 note 20; Kermode *Merchants* p
169; Gray, Benevolence pp 12-16; Power *Medieval People* p 157; Loans p 62. Power 1926 p 34
suggests that side trading was unusual but it appears frequently. See e.g. CPR 1494-1509/450

[10] Shakespeare Birthplace Trust Records Office DR10/371, 376; PRO, C1/5/49; CRO,
DR429/32; BA/B/17/7/1; PA468/5/3/32/21; PA100/25/7; BA/B/16/164/7

[11] CRO, BA/H/8/372/1; PA468/5/3/44/13; BA/H/8/293/13; Botoner ceased to be a member
of the Holy Trinity gild in 1451, *Coventry Leet Book* p 266

[12] G Templeman 1944 *The Records of the Guild of the Holy Trinity, St. Mary, St. John the Baptist and St.
Katherine of Coventry* Dugdale Society 19 ii p 68; Robert was mayor of Coventry in 1457, CPR
1452-61/410

that after the death of Alice, it should go to the right heirs of Robert Bradmedewe, thereby cutting out the Botoner remainder[13].

Alice not only held property in and around Coventry, but she appears to have had business of her own: at some date after 1453, Alice Bradmedewe formerly Alice Botoner was being sued in the king's courts for withholding some possessions of a Coventry fishmonger. William Browne and his brother continued to hold property in the name of their sister; in 1477, William was selling part of her lands. This may have been necessary, for it appears that Robert ran into financial difficulties, and in 1482, he and his son and heir John had to turn over some of his property to his brother Thomas[14].

Robert Bradmedewe died between 1482 and 1484[15]. John son and heir of Robert Bradmedewe and of Alice his wife sold some of his parents' property (1484), after which nothing further is heard of him; he probably died early, for the bulk of the property of Robert Bradmedewe seems to have passed by 1491 to Thomas Bradmedewe the brother of Robert[16].

William Browne's interests in Coventry were in support of his sister Alice.[17] The main concern of William and his brother was to secure the interests of their sister Alice, obtaining from her first husband a marriage settlement which she took with her to her second marriage, and obtaining a share of her second

---

[13] CRO BA/B/16/239/7; BA/B/16/239/9; BA/H/8/293/13; the notes of one of the deeds refer to *Richard* Bradmedewe and his brother Thomas but this is an error, as CRO PA468/5/3/44/13 shows; CRO PA1577/1

[14] CRO, BA/B/16/239/9; BA/H/8/297/1; BA/H/8/293/12 1/1480; PRO, C1/26/176; CRO, BA/B/16/304/4, undated but prior to 1476 when John Browne died; there is one transaction which appears to suggest that William and his brother John acted as feoffees for others in Coventry than their sister, but this seems unlikely; see BA/H/8/372/1-2 and other deeds in this collection.

[15] Alice formerly wife of Robert Bradmedewe and John son and heir of Robert came into the manor court of Humphrey Talbot knight and surrendered copyhold land, including some of the Botoner land; they also sold some freehold land at this time; CRO, BA/H/8/372/1; BA/A/2/60/1-2; BA/B/16/424/3

[16] CRO, BA/H/8/372/2, BA/A/2/60/1; is he the John Bradmedewe who founded a chantry in Holy Trinity church, Coventry? CRO, PA468/5/3/69/8. It is possible that this John was the son of an earlier marriage rather than the son of Alice Browne; the wording of other deeds suggests this; see CRO, BA/A/2/60/1-2 and BA/B/16/424/3 - the reference to 'sons' in the plural is surely an error?

[17] The William Browne draper and Margery his wife admitted to the gild of Holy Trinity (no dates are given in this register) are unlikely to have been our William Browne; he is not the William Browne who with his wife Alice was suing John, master of St. John's Hospital, Coventry, for a box of deeds which had been entrusted to the Master's predecessor by Richard Walkele and Margaret his wife, mother of the said Alice; CPR 1467-76/167, 174 - probably of London as well as Coventry, PRO, C 1/16/387

husband's property to add to her initial endowment. But in the end, the family disengaged themselves from Coventry. The widowed Alice moved back to Stamford where she joined the gild of St Katherine in 1484, and lived until her death in 1492 when a brass was erected in the Browne's family chapel in the church of All Saints in the Market:

> *Pray for the soul of Alice Bradmeydew late sister of William Browne who died and was buried under this stone 10 February 1491[/2], may God have mercy on her soul. AMEN.*

Her commemoration as "sister of William Browne", and not as husband of Robert Bradmedewe of Coventry, suggests an attempt to forget Coventry. The wording repeats the deeds in Coventry where she is consistently described as sister of William Browne, while both William and John Browne of Stamford are described as brothers of Alice Botoner and Alice Bradmedewe. The birth family took precedence over the marriage family in her case[18].

The family then hung together. William and his brother John II worked very closely together, sharing the same merchant's mark; although they each put their own name against the wool exports, it is clear that for many purposes they formed one firm. They acted as feoffees for each other in their various purchases.

And the same is true of his two marriage alliances, his own to the Stokes family and his daughter's into the Elmes family, despite the fact that both of these nearly landed him in political trouble. The Browne-Stokes-Elmes families made a very close-knit entity.

The Stokes family[19]

The same was true of the Stokes family – they and the Brownes clung together.

When William married Margaret Stokes in the 1430s and his brother married Agnes her sister, they joined forces with a whole family. John Stokes esquire the father was a member of a far-flung family of Stokes with strong connections in Oxfordshire; he married an heiress in Warmington, Northants, but his main connections were at court. Serjeant usher of the royal household, he received in

---

[18] Her will is not to be found in the Prerogative Court of Canterbury which suggests that she had disposed of all her property (including dower) in Coventry.

[19] This section is based on Rogers, Stokes, where full references may be found; see Bridges *Northants* ii 478-483; S J Reynolds 1956 Master Thomas Stokke of Easton-on-the-Hill: a fifteenth century Northamptonshire parson, *Northants Past and Present* vol ii pp 147-153.

1439-40 a number of grants which indicate his closeness to Henry VI himself. He was able to transfer a grant of forfeited lands in Warmington to his eldest son John with a very substantially reduced rent, and he passed a royal corrody from Peterborough Abbey to his second son William. William Stokes, at that time aged only 13-14, despite his income, was named by the king as the first 'poor scholar' in the foundation charter of Eton College; he attended Eton, closely followed by his younger brother Thomas, and then both proceeded to the new royal foundation Kings College, Cambridge. Meanwhile, the older brother John, having served for a few years in the same royal household office as his father, usher of the gate, became usher at Kings College - but he died young. William Stokes took his place as usher of the gate in the royal household after Cambridge. The various grants to the Stokes family were exempted from the Acts of Resumption. These are signs of considerable personal interest by Henry VI.

Both families were committed to education, for girls as well as boys. John Browne the father ensured that William and John Browne were well educated, literate in more than one language; the family's merchant mark includes the letter 'B', and the family motto was "+ me Spede"[20]. John Stokes educated two of his daughters, probably all three; and he sent William and Thomas Stokes to Eton and Cambridge. The will of Thomas with its references to books and a grant to a young scholar at Oxford shows the influence of schooling on him. William Browne ensured that Elizabeth his daughter was educated, as her will shows, and a school was included in his Hospital. He sent William Elmes, his grandson and heir to half his estates, to Inner Temple. William's extended family had come to terms with a culture which called for new skills and a wider range of knowledge. In this, it may be that the chivalric Christopher Browne, with his search for acceptance among the county gentry and courtiers of his age by obtaining a coat of arms and a country estate, was the traditionalist rather than William Browne who could see the necessity for modern skills in a new age.

John Stokes' court attendance led to other connections. In 1433, he was surety for Ralph lord Cromwell, Treasurer of England, and this link lasted throughout Cromwell's life; in the 1450s, Stokes and Cromwell were trustees for William Browne in a long-running dispute. By 1457, both William Stokes and the younger brother Thomas had become regular feoffees for William Browne. But loyalty to Henry VI nearly caused the family a disaster William Stokes seems to have married into the family of Darcy of Yorkshire, and (as we have seen) in the civil war of 1460-61, he fought for Henry VI, was knighted (presumably on the field), and remained loyal to the deposed king until 1468, when he surrendered,

---

[20] Huizinga pp 233-4

was attainted and sent to the Tower of London. He was pardoned in 1469 and his attainder was reversed by Parliament, and he resumed his place in Northamptonshire county society, receiving royal grants in Rockingham Forest, serving as JP and trustee (including for William Browne again), and defrauding at least one of his neighbours (William Fermur) of his inheritance. He died in October 1485 and seems to have left two illegitimate children.

For William and Margaret Browne, the youngest brother Thomas was their closest friend. He was a clerk, rector of Easton on the Hill (near Stamford) for life; he became canon of York and was described as chaplain to the chancellor of England. His links with the Browne family were very close indeed. A feoffee in almost all the important settlements made by William Browne, he became vicar of All Saints in the Market, Stamford (William Browne's church) in 1468, living in the vicarage next door to the Brownes. When he resigned in 1479, he obtained from the patrons (the nuns of St Michael, Stamford) the next presentation and appointed to the benefice another friend of William Browne, Henry Wykes. He helped with the foundation of the Hospital, became executor to both William Browne and Margaret his sister. He drew up the statutes of the Hospital, settled its endowments and arranged for its dedication. Like William Browne, he worked on the details of the Hospital until just before his death in 1495. He may have been responsible for some of the iconography in the glass, and he certainly wrote some tortuous Latin poetry and prose; his will mentions Latin and English books. He probably built both the vicarage house in Stamford and the so-called 'Priest's House' in Easton on the Hill; a building account of his survives[21].

Like the Brownes, the Stokes' family was tight-knit. William Browne used members of the family of the third sister Isabel (Fitzacreley) as trustees, and Elizabeth Elmes became close to her aunt Isabel Fitzacreley and inherited some of her land.

The Elmes

In the late 1450s, William Browne married his daughter Elizabeth into the Elmes family of Henley on Thames, wool merchants and landholders in Oxfordshire. Here the links seem to have been trade more than personal as with the Stokes, for the Elmes family had extensive trading interests with a wool hall in Southampton. John Elmes, father-in-law to Elizabeth, was a major trader, particularly with Italian merchants, and his credit was very substantial. His

---

[21] PRO, SP 46/123/fol 57; a later Thomas Stokes clerk and gentleman, the illegitimate son and heir of Sir William Stokes, became clerk of the treasurer in the Exchequer and prominent in London; he joined the gild of St Nicholas in London in 1492, *St Nicholas Gild*. A file of his papers as teller in the royal exchequer survives, PRO SP 46/123

connections with the Stonors of Oxfordshire were close – his brother Walter was their receiver or steward, a post which caused him much worry: "By my trouth I kowde not slepe for sorowe thus nygth" because of the extravagance of his patrons Dame Elizabeth (Riches) and Sir William Stonor. Walter and William Elmes acted for Elizabeth Elmes in various land transactions in 1488-9[22].

The Elmes were big players in Henley on Thames; as with Alice in Coventry whose second husband with his brother occupied all the major offices of that city, Elizabeth was married into a family with civic power. Her father-in-law was bridgewarden of Henley for 31 years. He passed to John Elmes his son in 1458 (about the time the latter married Elizabeth Browne) a very large inheritance in Henley on Thames (at least 22 tenements and other property), Southampton, Wallingford and Oxfordshire including the manor of Cassington; he died about 1460[23].

Elizabeth's husband John was also a Calais Stapler who succeeded his father as bailiff, burgess and bridgewarden of Henley; like his father-in-law, he bought an exemption from office early in his career (1443). However, William Browne used him only occasionally as a feoffee, although he was executor for Margaret Browne. He inherited from his father not only a fortune and a trading firm but also a court case and an accusation of being a rebel against Edward IV. Later in life, he had problems with credibility. In 1477, Elizabeth Stonor wrote ironically to William Stonor, "And as towchyng John Elmys, truly, syre, he is a marvelus man"; and in a letter of 1474, Elmes himself referred to his failure to keep his promises: "suche promys as I have made on to yow and to Maister Fowler y shall trewly kepe hyt". But Elizabeth Stonor went on:

I conseyve be my son that he [John Elmes] wold goo from his promesse that he made to you and to hym of his woll [wool] that hyt suchld aryse as good in poking thys yere as hyt dyd the last yere: and that I consyve he cannot make good but never the lesse I dout not but that you and my son Betson wyll handyll the matyrs well I-nowe: ffore blessyd be God ye be on the surere side: ffore all the sayde woll I have ress[eyved] hyte and fayer howsyd hyt. And yyt

---

[22] Walter Elmes: Simcoe collection passim; PRO, C1/211/13; C1/139/7; C1/196/86; see brass in Harpeden church; BL Add 32489 cc6; 32490 s12; BL Sloane 1429 fol 110. John Elmes senior of Henley was trading with Genoese merchants (well over £800 credit) in 1457, Childs 1991 pp 76, 83; W C Metcalfe 1887 *Visitation of Northants 1564 and 1618-19* p 19; *Stonor Letters* i pp xl-xli; ii 22, and Stonor Supplement pp 1-26; Carpenter, Stonor circle p 181. There was a younger William Elmes, see Emden Oxon

[23] See Peberdy; CIPM Henry VII i 1495-96 pp 243, 254; VCH *Cambs* ix p 198

ffore all that I wot well that you and my son wylnot dele with hym othyrewyse than right and consyes [conscience] wyll require, and that is best[24].

John and Elizabeth Elmes had at least two sons, William and John, and three surviving daughters, all apparently married, who were listed in the will of Elizabeth as Kateryn Conryke, Jane wife of Peter Turnour of London and Isabell Stonysby. John Elmes however died soon after William Browne, in 1491, and for the twenty years of her widowhood, Elizabeth settled mainly in Henley on Thames with visits to Lilford, Northants, while William Elmes their son remained in the family home in Stamford[25].

William Elmes was born about 1465 and was clearly a favourite of his grandfather William Browne. Care was taken over his education - after initial school, he was sent for training to the Inner Temple. In 1488, despite his youth, he represented Henley on Thames in the Great Council of Henry VII, and he was burgess there by 1490 and warden from 1492 to 1496[26]. But his field was primarily Stamford. In 1489, as *literatus*, he was appointed by William Browne one of his trustees to endow the Hospital, and was nominated with his uncle Thomas Stokes to assist Margaret Browne with William's will. He succeeded his grandfather as Alderman of the gild of All Saints, closely tied to the Hospital being founded at the same time. He was executor and residuary legatee for Margaret later that same year, and was living in William Browne's house in Stamford. By 1494, he was a fully fledged lawyer (*legis peritus*) and executor for Thomas Stokes, named as patron of the Hospital in the statutes. In 1495, he became MP for Stamford and by 1502 was Recorder of the borough. He acted as feoffee on several occasions, and served on several commissions in Oxfordshire and in Stamford, Kesteven and Rutland; he was JP in Leicestershire, Lincolnshire, Northants, Oxfordshire and Rutland from 1500[27]. He was closely tied to Lady Margaret Beaufort's circle and became a member of the gild of St Katherine at the same time as she did. He married Elizabeth the daughter and coheir of John Iwardeby esquire of Great Missenden and they had two surviving sons, John Elmes and Thomas, and at least two daughters Elizabeth and Joan.

---

[24] *Stonor Letters* i p 53; ii pp 18, 22; PRO, E321/15/7; CPR 1441-46/169; A R Maddison (ed) 1902 *Lincs Pedigrees* Harl Soc 50 vol i p 328 calls him Sir John Elmes; he was never knighted. Elmes had a dispute with the wife of Thomas Sackville and sister of Thomas Stonor, Carpenter, *Stonor circle* p 190. For biography, see Rogers, *Parl*.

[25] CFR 1485-1509/137; CIPM Henry VII i 1485-96 p 254

[26] Ives *Lawyers* p 473; Holmes 1986

[27] e.g. PRO, CP25/1/145/160/59; C1/196/86; CPR 1494-1509/294; *Rot Parl* vi p 540

He was clearly marked out as a potential force in the neighbourhood; but he died young (probably of the sweating sickness) in 1504[28].

The later Elmes seem to have been a litigious group. Elizabeth Elmes was accused of enclosure on her estates in Warmington and Lilford; John Elmes her second son was involved in a number of suits in Chancery, Star Chamber and Court of Requests. He sued for the Swan in Stamford which had come to his younger brother Thomas by borough English[29]. John Elmes of Lilford and of 'the Swanne', Stamford, who married the daughter of lord Mordaunt of Turvey, was noted for his enclosures, causing riots in the area; and his conscience clearly troubled him, for in his will (1540) he wrote

Item I wyll that yf any man can lay to my charge truly of any wrongfull doing or taking awey or wytholding any lands or rents from any creature that of right I ought not to doo or take and the same by wyttnes or better proved and my executours showe not sufficient matter by myn evidences and writings or by other lawfull weyes to discharge my conscience, that my executours after due examinacyon make large amends of the rents and revenues of all my londs that ys sett to the performaunce of this my last wyll. And yf the sayd lands cannot paye yt, Then of suche goodes cattelles and money that I have or any man to my use hathe that may be goten while yt lasteth and to aske god and them forgyvenes that I have so committed ayenst. And I wyll that knowledge be given of this one article of my wyll aboute Oundell and Stamford where I shall be most defamyd[30].

Christopher Browne

The family of William and Margaret Browne and their relations, the Stokes and Elmes, formed a strong and close network of kinship and support, built by William Browne and maintained by Margaret - all except Christopher Browne, son and heir of John Browne the brother. There are some anomalies about his career which are hard to explain. As we have seen, he first appears in Stamford in 1480, four years after the death of his father[31]. He applied for a coat of arms as 'Christopher Browne of Lincolnshire gentleman', and in November 1480, his name was added to the new members of St Katherine's gild, although that does not imply that he was present at that meeting. It was not until December 1481

---

[28] PRO, C1/1217/11; Ives *Lawyers* p 473; Rogers, Wills; PRO, PROB 11/14; VCH *Cambs* ix 192ff says he died in 1505, but probate was 21 June 1504. After his death, his widow married another lawyer, Thomas Pygot of Whaddon, Bucks, and she outlived him, dying in 1526.

[29] PRO, C1/ 696/69; C1/784/1-5; C1/981/33-39; C4/147/96; REQ 2/4/77; LR 15/141; STAC 2/14; 11/199; C1/629/3, 6; Thomas his brother left a son John, at Cambridge University, PRO, C1/706/20

[30] PRO, PROB 11/30 fol 21; Rogers, Wills

[31] He did not join the Boston gild with his mother and William and Margaret Browne in 1476. See Rogers, Parl for full biography

that he was admitted to the freedom of the borough, and at the following election day, September 1482, he was appointed directly onto the First Twelve, and on the same day was made Alderman of the town. From then on, his name came second in the list of the First Twelve after that of William Browne.

Christopher thus came onto the public stage of Stamford at a later stage in life than might have been expected. He may have been serving in Calais: for in 1476, "Kyrstower Brun ys man" brought a letter of Thomas Kesteven from Calais to London; and in May 1482, Richard Cely wrote that "howr brother Wylliam Dawltton schaull be maryd to who of the nexte kynyswhomen that Kyrstowyr Brown has". Christopher had two sisters, Agnes who married William Wareyn, Calais stapler of Oakham, and Elizabeth who married William Cooke, draper of Oundle. Christopher acted as executor for Cooke, and William Browne also had links with Cooke and Wareyn[32].

Christopher was a Stapler and a Merchant Adventurer; but the missing years were not all served in trade. In 1480, when he applied for his coat of arms, he claimed that he had "for a long time followed feats of arms". Later, his family said that he had joined the invasion force of Henry Tudor in 1485, for which the family was rewarded with honours at court[33].

Christopher then was a courtier, a cut above a royal household servant[34]. He was present in 1500 when Henry VII met with Archduke Philip of Austria. He attended the royal council in 1488 on behalf of the town of Stamford, and served as one of the borough's MPs three times between 1485 and 1495. In 1499, he started to purchase an estate outside of Stamford and went to live on his manor of Tolthorpe in Rutland, although he kept a residence in the town and continued to trade in wool and other exports. He was JP in Holland, in Kesteven and in Rutland where he also served as sheriff[35]. In Stamford, he clearly took his place

---

[32] L and P Henry VIII 1 i 1509-13 p 243; PRO, SC1/57/111; E122/73/40

[33] L and P Henry VIII 1 i 1509-13 p 506; W A Littledale (ed) 1925 *Miscellaneous Grants of Arms* vol i Harl Soc 76 pp 41-42; W H Rylands and W B Bannerman 1922 *Visitation of the County of Rutland 1681-2* Harl Soc vol 73 p 8. Francis his son claimed that he could go into the king's presence wearing a cap or hat because of the privilege given to his father by Henry VII for his support in coming from Brittany, James Wright 1684 (reprint 1973) *History and Antiquities of Rutland* London pp 129-130

[34] See R Horrox 1995 Caterpillars of the commonwealth? courtiers in late medieval England, in Archer and Walker 1995 pp 1-16

[35] Holmes 1986; J Gairdner (ed) 1861-3 *Letters and Papers illustrative of Richard III and Henry VII* Rolls Series vol 24, part ii p 91. He traded through London in the 1480s and joined the St Nicholas gild in London in 1507, *St Nicholas Gild*; for his seal with his arms on a title deed, see Simcoe 1038 M/T/13/6. L and P Henry VIII 1 i 1509-13 p 124; he served on several commissions of inquiry in these counties, ibid. pp 64, 996

(after William Browne) as the senior representative of the most important family in the town. He served on the town council and when (1502) he was elected again as Alderman, he pleaded that since he was a member of the council of Lady Margaret Beaufort, he needed to be allowed to serve that office by deputy. He became Alderman of the gild of St Katherine on the death of William Browne (1489), serving for six years before resigning, the only Alderman to do so. On the death of William Elmes in 1504, Christopher took his place as Alderman of the gild of All Saints.

There are no signs that Christopher and William Browne ever worked together in the years they overlapped. William Browne does not mention him in his will, nor more strikingly does Margaret Browne who names everyone else in the extended family; and his name is missing from the list of heirs of Thomas Stokes, his uncle. I do not wish to exaggerate from the evidence available, but it would seem that the whole approach of the two men was different. Perhaps it was in part a generation thing, for Christopher worked with William Elmes after the death of William Browne and was feoffee for Elizabeth Elmes; but he was apparently excluded from the older Browne-Stokes circle[36]. Indeed, there may have been some hostility between the two branches of the family, for Christopher Browne was involved in a bitter dispute with the Hospital by 1502 which ran on for several years.

Household

Surrounding the immediate family lay the *familiares*, the household. We have little evidence of the household of William Browne. It has been suggested that the larger households were predominantly male, with relatively few female servants; while that may have been true of royal and noble households[37], it does not seem to have been true of the more domestic urban households. William Browne does not mention his servants by name in his will:

> *Also that ther be destribute among my seruauntes x ᶦⁱ of money, so that every man and woman of them have a part like after ther continuaunce and desert by the discrecion of myn executrice.*

He seems to have left servant matters to Margaret. There would probably have been little distinction made between the male household servants and those

---

[36] This may have been a matter of ensuring security of tenure by having Christopher inside the list of feoffees, Simcoe 1038 M/T/7/13/6; CIPM Henry VII ii 1497-1509 p 742.

[37] See R G K A Mertes 1987 The household as a religious community, in Rosenthal and Richmond 1987 pp 123-40; P W Fleming 1989 Household servants of the Yorkist and early Tudor gentry, in Williams 1989 pp 19-36; Grace 2009; Shaw *Wells* p 145

employed in the wool house. The house William lived in was large and would have housed several resident household members; other workers would have been non-resident. Robert Beomond was apparently William's man of business in Stamford and carried on working closely with Margaret, William's widow, and her successors, including the Hospital: he was mentioned in Margaret's will and was one of the executors for Thomas Stokes and received a large legacy.

In her will, Margaret lists five women, most if not all of whom were probably domestic servants, but their names do not reveal whether they were local or not. And like other households, she made a modest provision for them to be retained after her death:

> *Item I will that my said brother [her executor] kepe alle my servaunts to gedir in houshold as many as will abyde the space of a quarter of a yer Immediatly aftre my deceasse uppon my charge and coost, mete drynke and wages, he to have the Rewle and providing of theym and noon other.*

Thomas Stokes took some of them on, since he mentions in his will Agnes Sklater who is also remembered in Margaret's will. Elizabeth Elmes also made provision for her servants:

> *Also I geve to every of my servaunts that shall happen to dwell with me in my house the tyme of my departing xs besides their wages and clothyng behynde if any bee, soo that they may have cause to remembre and pray for my soule.*

Length of service and devotion would be rewarded with the provision of funds and/or time to find another job[38].

Most households of this status would contain a priest. William Browne we know had his own chaplain, John Trus, who gave the *Myrour of Recluses* to Browne's Hospital, as the inscription inside the book shows:

> *Thys ys a good bok ffor holy men or women the whyche bok bylongeth to the almes howse off wyllam Brown in Stawnford in the dycesse off lyncoln By the gyft off S John Trus chapleyn to the seyd Wyllam Brown sumtyme and prest in the seyd beyd howse*

It is possible that John Trus (who is otherwise unknown) is the John Taylor clerk who was feoffee for William Browne in 1488, protégé of Thomas Stokes, scholar of Oxford, and who became the second warden of the Hospital from 1496 to

---

[38] See C M Woolgar 2010 Food and the middle ages *JMH* 36 1 p 17

1504[39]. If so, John Taylor was William Browne's private chaplain in 1488. Elizabeth Elmes too retained a priest, perhaps more than one, depending on whether she was living in Henley on Thames or Lilford at the time:

> *Also I will that my preest that shall happen to be with me the tyme of my departyng kepyng hymself so in honesty shall contynew to syng and rede for my husbonds soule my soule and all cristen soules within the church where it shall please god me to be buried by the space of oon yere fully to be completid aftir my decesse and he to have for his stipend and wages by the hands of myn executours ix marcs.*

Family friends

Beyond the family of the Brownes-Stokes-Elmes lay a circle of friends, such as the Fairfax family. In 1445, Elena wife of William Fairfax esquire of Deeping Gate by Maxey, while staying in Stamford, gave birth to a daughter; she was baptised in St George's church, Stamford. The child's godmothers were Edith St John daughter of Margaret (Beauchamp) duchess of Somerset of Maxey castle near Deeping (after whom the child was called Margaret) and Elizabeth daughter of lord Grey de Codnor of Castle Bytham, Lincs, wife of John lord Zouche of Harringworth Northants; both Grey and Zouche were resident in Stamford. The godfather was the abbot of Peterborough, and Margaret wife of William Browne was the sponsor. William Fairfax and his successive wives had another thirteen children, and the Browne family acted as godparents again for two of these (1462 and 1470)[40]. This was a long lasting friendship which brought Margaret and her husband into contact with many leading nobles and clergy of the area.

Such god-children extended the family connections. Elizabeth Elmes lists a number of 'god-doughters' in her will, among them a girl from the family into which the widow of William Elmes was later to marry. And beyond such relationships lay trading partners, often of long standing, like the Lewes family of Oakham and Lynn; William Lewes was executor for John Browne the father and a trading partner of William, and John Browne and William were executors for him. The circle included the Sapcotes of Rutland and Stamford, especially

---

39 This inscription was written by John Taylor, as a comparison of the handwriting of Taylor in Bodl, Rawl B352 and the writing in the book shows; while this does not prove that Trus and Taylor are the same person, Taylor, like Trus, was chaplain to Browne in the 1480s and priest in the almshouse. Taylor may be related to Laurence Mylton alias Taillour, a friend of Wllllam Browne and Alderman of Stamford; see e.g. Exeter-NRA 22/2; PRO C67/40

40 See Rogers, Fairfax; CIPM Henry VII ii 1504-9 p 77; VCH *Northants* ii pp 502-4. See P Maddern 1994 'Best trusted friends': concepts and practices of friendship among fifteenth-century Norfolk gentry, in N Rogers (ed) 1994 *England in the Fifteenth Century* Stamford: Watkins pp 100-117; J R Lander 1986 Family, 'friends' and politics in fifteenth-century England, in R A Griffiths and J Sherborne (eds) 1986 *Kings and Nobles in the later middle ages* Sutton pp 27-40

Richard Sapcote and Joan his wife (members of the St Katherine gild) and a Richard who traded alongside William Browne. The Zouche family keep turning up in the Browne circle, as do William Stourton baker, Henry Cok stainer and bailiff, and members of the Wykes family of Burghley near Stamford. The Knyvetts and Cheynes were numbered among those for whom the Brownes, Stokes and Elmes acted as feoffees[41].

One indication of the kind of social networks which William built up comes from the gild register of St Katherine. As the Alderman of the gild who refounded it in 1480, he would have greatly influenced its membership. William Browne kept it small, no more than fifty members; after his death, numbers rose rapidly to more than 120 members. As we have already seen, no monks or friars were admitted under William Browne, only secular clergy (and mainly minor clergy at that); after his death, regular clergy flooded in. William's members were not confined to the upper ranks of the trades in Stamford: the gild drew in rich and poorer members of the community – shoemakers, glovers, labourers, bakers, weavers, candelers, smiths, tailors, mercers, lawyers and at least one doctor, a broad section of the parishioners of St Paul's parish where the gild met - except of course the very poor. Later the gild took a distinct turn towards social elitism in its membership, including Lady Margaret Beaufort the mother of Henry VII - but that was well after William Browne had died.

---

[41] For Lewes of Oakham and Ipswich, see above pp 137-8

PART V: CHAPTER 2   MARGARET BROWNE AND WOMEN IN LATE MEDIEVAL STAMFORD

"... *because she was a woman*" (petition of Joan Veske, Stamford, c1456)[42]

Margaret was William Browne's partner for fifty years and more. It is clear that she joined him in many of his activities; her death just six months after his is probably an indication of their closeness.

The daughter of a royal household servant from a Northamptonshire village where the Browne family also held land, she and her sister were almost certainly educated in the school run by the nuns of St Michael, Stamford. The bequest in her will, "Item I geve to the supprioresse of the Nonnes my mantell that I was professed in", probably refers to this period. Christopher Browne on his return to Stamford in 1480-1 made a gift to the nuns to commemorate his mother Agnes and her sister Margaret, which again suggests some pre-existing link with the nunnery[43].

Although we have no indication of her involvement in William's wool trade, Margaret almost certainly was able to hold the fort when he was away on business or for other reasons; for "many merchants' wives did ... become reasonably familiar with the mysteries of commercial practice"[44]. She was a money lender on her own account: the will of Thomas Stokes refers to "all pleggs and weddys which my brother William Brown and my sustre hys wif lent mony upon", and she speaks of items which were "pleggid to me". She engaged in agriculture and in her husband's building activities: she bequeathed to her niece "alle my Nete [cattle] and Swyne unto hir mariage", and ordained "that alle my tymbre, borde, Iryn, stone, lede, Nayle, Lath and alle other stuf perteynyng to bilding or Reparacion being within my place or els where be preserved and kept to my said brother [her executor] for the Reparacions of the tenementis that stonden in feoffees handes". On at least two occasions, she is stated as being co-founder with William of Browne's Hospital. She sued for debt in the Alderman's court, and was executrix for Thomas Philippe merchant and Alderman of the town[45]. She must have been a formidable lady in her own right.

---

[42] PRO, C1/26/236, petition of Joan Veske of Stamford

[43] PRO, SC6/914/3; PROB 11/18; see Rogers, Wills.

[44] *Tooley* pp 12-13

[45] HB i fol 24, p 64; PRO, C1/60/126

William clearly treated her as equal. The brass he ordered showed her rebus of the stork standing on his woolsack; and the glass in the Hospital shows her stork alongside his merchant mark. On his death, she carried on his activities; she took over his money-lending pledges and added them to her own. She and Thomas Stokes drafted a new petition for licence to complete the foundation of the Hospital, and she granted it some woodland.

Her distinctive role as builder of social capital is clear; she kept the family network together. It was Margaret rather than William who was the focus of the link with the Fairfax family at Deeping Gate: she acted as godparent twice, while he was called upon once to act in that capacity. She and her sister Agnes joined William when they were admitted as members of the gild of Corpus Christi in Boston, just after the death of John Browne. Her long will, written with several codicils, reveals her concerns and warmth. Unlike that of William which is short and business-like, leaving everything not already placed in the hands of feoffees to Margaret his wife as sole executrix, Margaret's will is long and detailed, anxious lest any member of the family or any servant should be omitted; she mentions almost all living members of her extended family, down to "Lytill William Stok". Full of housekeeping details, it shows her as in charge of a large household of outdoor and indoor servants. Unlike her husband, she names the women servants who were each given a legacy[46]. Judging by this will, women were served largely by women servants; for (apart from the nunnery) domestic service was clearly the major outlet for the economic and social energies of many women, giving them some measure of independence.

It is unlikely that Margaret's religion was very different from that of her husband. She had more than one Book of Hours, for she left her best primer to her younger sister Isabel Fitzacreley[47]. Religious symbols abound on various items of furniture (see above pp 232-3), but the only hanging known had a secular subject, the story of the patience of Griselda. She made bequests to every parish church in the town, gave lights to three images in All Saints church, and, unlike her husband, she made customary bequests to each of the four orders of friars in Stamford, perhaps an example of what has been seen elsewhere, that women

---

[46] Jonett Bone, Agnes Sclater, Mawde Huntley, Alice Clopton and Jonett Walker, together with her man of business Robert Beomond; Rogers, Wills

[47] For women and literacy, see Salter 2006 pp 136-70; S G Bell 1988 Medieval Women Book Owners: arbiters of lay piety and ambassadors of culture, in M C Erler and M Kowaleski 1988 *Women and Power in the middle ages* University of Georgia Press pp 149-187; R Krug 2002 *Reading families, women's literacy practices in late medieval England* Cornell

seemed to prefer friars[48]. There is nothing to suggest anything other than traditional religious commitment; her warmth is for the family.

Margaret was a widow only for six months; she died in October 1489. As a landholder, inquisitions were held about her lands and estates. Elizabeth her daughter was stated to be her heir[49].

Margery, William's mother, outlived her husband John Browne by eighteen years, dying in 1460. In 1450, we see her paying tax on her property in Stamford valued at 20s, only a fraction of the property of William (£18)[50].

Elizabeth Browne-Elmes, like her mother and grand-mother, lived a long life: she was probably in her seventies when she died. Born about 1441 or earlier, her will suggests that she was educated (she refers to writings inside various items of furniture to indicate their ownership), and she shows a greater concern for religious duties than her mother. She was married to John Elmes of Henley on Thames about 1457 and bore at least seven children, including Margaret who died in 1471 at a young age.

Elizabeth inherited her estates on the death of her mother in 1489. In 1495, when she inherited further properties from her uncle Thomas Stokes, Elizabeth Elmes settled substantial lands mainly from the Browne inheritance on William her son, and in 1499 revised this settlement, using as her feoffees Christopher Browne, Walter Elmes (probably her husband's uncle) and others[51]. After the death of her husband in 1491, she remained single for twenty years; there is no mention of her husband in her will – she is clearly accustomed to being independent. With her aunt Isabel Fazakerley, sister of Margaret Browne, she inherited some of the lands of Sir William Stokes, and she continued the law suit against the Fermur family in Warmington. Later, she acquired some of Isabel's lands. She was accused in 1499 of enclosing land for sheep at Papley and Warmington. She died in 1511[52].

---

[48] Goldberg 1988 p 111; for Griselda story, see N N Sidhu 2008 Weeping for the Virtuous Wife: Laymen, Affective Piety, and Chaucer's Griselda, in Kowaleski and Goldberg 2008 pp 177-208

[49] CFR 1485-1509/88; PRO, PROB 11/18; CIPM Henry VII i 1485-9 pp 219, 230 (551)

[50] PRO, E179/276/11

[51] PRO, CP25/1/294/79/52; Simcoe 1038 M/T/13/6-7: John Verney knt, Guy Wulston knt, Robert Harecourt knt, Robert Brudenell, John Danvers, Christopher Broun, John Burgoyn, William Coke, John Glynton, Thomas Mountegen, Nicholas Fazakyrley, John Colston, John Wylles and John Taylor and Henry Wykes clerks.

[52] PRO, C1/328/58; Rogers, Fermur; Allison et al, *Deserted Villages;* Rogers, Wills; VCH *Northants* i p 108

Of *Agnes Browne* sister of Margaret and wife of John Browne, most of what we know is religious in nature. Almost certainly educated in the same nunnery school as Margaret her sister, she had links with the nunnery sufficient for the nuns to owe her money[53]. It was her saint – St Agnes – who was specially commemorated in the Flemish Book of Hours she and her husband owned. On his death in 1476, she was exhorted to become a vowess; she joined the gild of Corpus Christi in Boston with William and Margaret, and the gild of St Katherine in Stamford when it was re-formed in 1480, and received the largest share of the gild stock (20s) for which she paid her increment regularly until she died in about 1484/5. Some fragmentary notes of her will show her to have been a highly religious person, with bequests to the four orders of friars and her parish church, and instructions for the purchase of a Palm Sunday processional cloth and for the painting of the [Easter] tabernacle in the chapel of Corpus Christi in St Mary's church (which may indicate membership of the Corpus Christi gild like William Browne). Taken with her devotion to St Gregory the Pope, we see religious commitment beyond that displayed by either Margaret or William Browne.

Women and Stamford in the fifteenth century.

The Browne family provides a useful introduction to a discussion of the role of women in late medieval Stamford. Medieval society was of course gendered – assumptions were made about the different roles of men and women in almost all social practices of the period, religion, education, trade and industry, the law, marketing, culture, household management or warfare. Not everyone shared the same assumptions and values, and contemporary assumptions could be and were at times challenged. Margaret Browne probably challenged some assumptions by engaging directly in money lending by pledge[54].

It is not easy to see those assumptions at this distance of time; indeed, many would have been hidden from contemporaries. The documents which survive

---

[53] PRO, SC6/1115/6; SC6/914/1, 3

[54] See for example, P J P Goldberg 1992 *Women, Work, and Life Cycle in a Medieval Economy: Women in York and Yorkshire c.1300-1520* Oxford University Press; P J P Goldberg (ed) 1992 *Woman is a Worthy Wight: Women in English society c1200-1500* Sutton; Elisheva Baumgarten 2008 'A separate people': some directions for comparative research on medieval women, *JMH* 34 2 pp 212-228; S Bardsley 2008 *Women's Roles in the Middle Ages* Greenwood; Helen M Jewell 2007 *Women in Late Medieval and Reformation Europe 1200-1550* Palgrave; J Ward 2006 *Women in England in the Middle Ages* Hambledon; Wilkins 2007; C Briggs 2004 Empowered or marginalized? rural women and credit in later thirteenth and fourteenth century England *Continuity and Change* 19 pp 13-43. For women in urban communities, see Jewell op cit pp 60-83; Shaw *Wells* pp 146-7, 248-253; Kermode 1982 p 39. For women and religion, see Rosenthal 2001; Goldberg 1988; Cullum *Vowesses*; K L French 2008 *The good women of the parish: gender and religion after the Black Death* University of Pennsylvania Press

are normally designed (almost always unconsciously) to airbrush women out of the picture. Women in many cases are treated as if they were the invisible accessories to men, unless they were anchoresses, vowesses or other widows, especially of social standing. Thus, as we have seen, we know very little about Agnes Browne (nee Stokes). This is not to say that she was inactive; it is simply that few records relating to women (especially married women) were probably created and fewer survive.

The religious life offered to contemporaries some guidance as to the roles many people expected women to play. The majority of the saints adored and most of the images before which lights were maintained, were women[55]. Margaret Browne supported lights to the saints Anne, Margaret and 'Crasine' (?Christina?) in All Saints church; Margaret Spenser (1509) helped to restore the images of saints Dorothy, Barbara, Margaret and Katherine in St Martin's church; the cult of St Katherine was strong in the town. There were of course exceptions: the images in the glass in the gildhall of Browne's Hospital were predominantly male. But in the parish churches, representations of the ideal would have helped to create for many women a culture of patience in the face of suffering, reinforced by secular images like Browne's tapestry of Griselda.

This is of course not true of all women in Stamford's social network. Women above a certain degree were accorded status and power. Lady Margaret Beaufort at Collyweston clearly exercised a great influence on the town, even at times over-riding that of the lord of the town, Cecily duchess of York. Highly pious, nevertheless Lady Margaret was a schemer: she plotted while her son Henry Tudor was in exile; she plotted to maintain him when he assumed the throne. She surrounded herself with officers and a council which would execute her orders; and her council came to hold a position of authority in the region, sufficient for the royal council to send local disputes to it for settlement, and sufficient for the parties to other disputes to appeal spontaneously to her council for an enforceable verdict (see pp 105, 206).

Equally, Cecily duchess of York was no easy pushover. Noted for her life of extravagance and (at the same time) of piety[56], she too is alleged to have worked

---

[55] On the importance of images for women in late medieval England, see Renana Bartal 2011 The Pepys Apocalypse (Cambridge, Magdalene College, MS Pepys 1803) and the readership of religious women *JMH* 37 pp 358-77; C Hill 2010 *Women and Religion in late medieval Norwich* Boydell

[56] C A J Armstrong 1983 The piety of Cecily duchess of York, in C A J Armstrong (ed) 1983 *England, France and Burgundy in the fifteenth century* Hambledon pp 135-156; R E Archer 2003 Piety in question: noblewomen and religion in the later Middle Ages, in Wood 2003 pp 118-40; Ramsay i p 364, 370. Her will is in J G Nichols and J Bruce 1863 *Wills from Doctors' Commons* Camden Society 1 series 83 pp 1-8; see Alison J Spedding 2010 'At the King's Pleasure': the

tirelessly on behalf of her sons, helping to restore Edward in 1471 and bringing Clarence and the king together on at least two occasions, having "great influence over [her] son", as the papal legate was informed. Her closeness to her son Richard III is shown by his presence in her house Baynard's Castle in October 1483 when he appointed John bishop of Lincoln as Chancellor of England[57]. Some historians have suggested that the apparent religious devotion was public display rather than personal commitment and that the stories of reconciliation are apocryphal, but the circulation of such stories at the time confirmed her role model. She does not seem to have had as much interest in the concerns of the locality as did Margaret Beaufort who sought to stamp her authority on the region through her servants; Cecily's relationships with Norwich and York were closer than with Stamford. But she added to the general climate about powerful elite women.

But to the majority of women in late medieval Stamford, such women were above imitation. We must never, in making our generalities about gender, forget the wide diversity among women. But on the whole, the records of the period reflect a widespread attitude that most women were subsumed in the activities of men. Legally, despite increasing concern to give wives a secure title and the right to leave property according to their will, husbands were still responsible for the debts of married women, and needed to give permission for them to make a will, although in practice such rules did not always apply[58]. Women were meant to be helpmeets to men – a cultural practice which accounts for the fact that the two poor women included in Browne's Hospital were there to serve the ten bedesmen. Despite the involvement of Margaret Browne in the foundation, the Hospital was for poor *men*, not women; when the inmates are referred to in the statutes, they were usually seen as the men, not the women[59].

Independence (apart from breaking the rules extravagantly) could normally only be found in the religious life – in the nunnery or as an anchoress[60]. The two anchoresses in Stamford clearly enjoyed a relatively high style of life supported by many people including the nobility; paradoxically, submission to a rule gave

---

testament of Cecily Neville, *Midland History* 35 pp 256-72; K Jambeck 1996 Patterns of women's literary patronage: England 1200-c1475, in J H McCash (ed) 1996 *The Cultural Patronage of Medieval Women* University of Georgia Press; C Harpur-Bill in ODNB under Cecily; and Jones and Underwood. See above p96

[57] CCR 1476-85/346 (1170)

[58] Goldberg 1988 p 107; Kermode *Enterprise* p x

[59] The women were to say prayers but not as many prayers as the men since it was not the main duty of the women as it was of the men, Wright, *Domus Dei* pp 41, 47

[60] C Beattie 2006 *Medieval Single Women: the politics of social classification in late medieval England* Oxford University Press

them freedom. The nuns also enjoyed some measure of freedom; they could at times leave the house to make visits locally. Widows who took vows of chastity could again escape from male oversight so long as they conformed to the norms of such a status, usually in terms of dress. But normally a woman needed a man to establish her credentials and enable her personal activities.

One example of this tendency to subsume women in the record of men can be seen in the legacies or donations to churches to pray for the souls of the donor and his family. Occasionally a woman is mentioned (rarely by name) – e.g. "to pray for the souls of my father and mother", but in most cases only the name of the male partner is mentioned, prayers for the woman being assumed: John Elmes asked for prayers "for my fathers soule, my soule and all christen soules"[61]. The register of St Katherine's gild shows this tendency plainly. The statutes mention the 'sisters' of the gild very rarely and only in association with the 'bredern'. The lists contained in the register are even more revealing. Of the 44 persons (alive and dead) listed as the existing members at the time of the refounding of the gild in 1480, only five were women in their own right – the wives of male members are not mentioned although they were clearly members from the start. A few women were nominated to the gild in their own right, almost without exception of a higher social grouping. When a new member of "the brethren" was admitted, his wife was often mentioned, either by name ("George Chapman and Elizabeth his wife", 1481) or without the name of the wife ("Robert Beaumonde and his wife", 1497); but there are entries which consist of the name of the husband without any mention of his wife, the wife being assumed as also admitted; payments of waxshot at the married rate of 4d instead of 2d for the single person shows that a wife was included although not specified. Thereafter the wife simply disappears from the record. In a number of cases when a male gild member married again, his new wife was admitted by name, but then she vanishes from the records until she in turn became a widow. Thus, William Freman and Isabell his wife were admitted in 1488; the name of William Freman occurs without any mention of Isabell until 1496, when "Alice [clearly the new] wife of William Freman was admitted into the confraternity of the gild and will pay for her entry according to the discretion of the Alderman and the brethren ijs" (Freman was an official of the gild; her entry fine of 3s 4d was reduced in this case because of his position). Alice is listed by name among the entry fines not paid, but not among the attending members; only the name of her husband is so listed until 1502 when "Alice formerly wife [i.e. by now widow] of William Freman" appears as attending, and thereafter she is listed as the (unnamed) "former wife of William Freman" until she too vanishes from the lists.

---

[61] Rogers, Wills

If the husband died before his wife, her name appears in the list of members until she marries again, when it vanishes. Thus Richard Herte was admitted in 1482 with no mention of his wife; in 1486, his name is designated '*mort*', and the next year "Margaret former wife of Richard Herte" paid the waxshot for one year only; she may have died, left the gild (unlikely) or remarried. In 1480, John Pykerell was admitted to the gild without mention of a wife; in 1482, "Alice relict of John Pykerell" appears among the members and for several years she is "Alice formerly wife of John Pykerell" before becoming simply "Alice Pykerell". While a few *femmes sole* may appear in the lists, most women only appear when they are widows. In 1498, out of 82 listed members, only eight women are named although the amounts paid indicate that some 46 of the men were accompanied by their wives[62].

It is thus only as widows that women emerge from the (documentary) shadows: all we know about Margery, William Browne's mother, are that she was executor for her husband John Browne, paid tax in 1450 and outlived him by eighteen years. It was expected that widows would marry again, which is why many men made provision if their widows did marry again, and why some widows took a vow of chastity to evade pressing suitors. The story of Alice Bradmedewe points in both directions at the same time. She needs the help of her brothers to defend her estate interests, and she returns to Stamford in her widowhood to be close to her immediate family; but at the same time she is enabled by that same assistance to preserve her property and engage in business on her own behalf.

Most records of the period then hide women from view. When we find some record, it is usually in a negative frame of reference. The nuns of St Michael, when they appear in the bishop's visitations, are accused of breaches of the norms or needing assistance and regulation. Yet, as their account rolls show, most of these nuns had administrative duties which brought them into a position of authority in relation to some men. But apart from their household servants, most of whom are women, they tended to rely on men; the title deeds show that they leased their property to men[63]. The William Morewode and Margaret his wife, who took a long lease of a large part of the nuns' estates, were apparently related to one of the leading nuns of the house, but most of the leases made were to men alone.

---

[62] Under the gild statutes, men with their wives paid 4d p.a. but single men and independent women paid 2d; we can I think safely assume those men who paid 4d were accompanied by their wives, those men who paid 2d were unaccompanied.

[63] PRO, SC 6/914/1-4;1260/1-24; see Rogers *Deeds*

The borough Hall Book provides further evidence. Women were not town councillors or admitted as freemen (in other towns, this was possible). They did not register apprentices except with their husbands (George Chapman mercer and Elizabeth his wife took an apprentice in 1482[64]); they were not called upon to act as sureties; they were not appointed to any of the duties of the town such as searchers of the market or collectors of taxes. When they do appear, it is usually as trouble-makers or as victims, especially women servants; at least ten women were fined for unspecified offences. Attacks on women appear often: John Barlowe of Newstead by Stamford was charged not to harm Elizabeth Dawson widow (1480). At the same time, women could be accused of affray: out of 49 fines levied in 1486-7, mostly for disorder, nine were levied on women. In the bylaws passed by the borough council, women were classed with tapsters, innkeepers, strangers and vagabonds to be kept under scrutiny to ensure they kept the peace and obeyed the town's ordinances. The frequent iteration of such rules indicate that they were broken from time to time: at least two women were fined for being vagabonds[65]. But they also reinforced the stereotypes.

Throughout the country, there are signs of forced marriages and of abuse, violence and rape. It is possible that these were less in towns than in rural areas, and that there were more effective means of redress in the towns, for on the whole the law courts managed to treat women with some measure of consideration. Thus the Alderman's court at Stamford was used by women to defend their rights – like Margaret Browne's plea for debt. In 1467, Robert Braybroke alias Bottesford found himself sued by Joan his wife for what today would be called domestic violence ("any hurt or harm to Joan his wife whether in drawing of blood or else in breaking [of limbs] as a result of which the same Joan shall despair of her life in any way"), and a restraining order was issued to ensure that Robert "shall not hold in favour a certain Margaret Borugh or shall have any carnal copulation with her in the aforesaid town or elsewhere or ... exercise continual association with her which can be proved by trustworthy persons"[66]; Joan was clearly a determined woman.

Although no doubt unusual in her determination and success, Joan Braybrooke was not alone. Alice Ankes persisted in pursuing her case against the violence of even Leo lord Welles, husband of Lady Margaret Beauchamp of Maxey through many courts over many years[67]. Other women chased men who offended physically as well as through the courts:

---

[64] HB i fol 33d, p 96

[65] HB i fol 28, p 78; fol 28d, p 80; Goldberg 1988 p 118

[66] HB i fol 8, pp 21-23

[67] Mackman 2008

Elizabeth formerly the wife of JS[68] in her own person appealed Robert Lyndsesey formerly of Staunford Lincs servant of the same man [i.e. JS] because the said John at 8 p.m. in the feast Purification of the Blessed Virgin Mary in the 28th year of the present king [i.e. 2 February 1450] at Staunford Lincs came there in the peace of God and of the king; and against the peace of the crown and the dignity of the king in the said year, hour and place Robert Lindsay lay in wait to kill the said John and he insulted the same John and he then and there with one dagger feloniously killed him against the king's peace .... And immediately the said Robert felon fled; the same Elizabeth seeing Robert killed, chased him from village to village through four neighbouring villages until the same Robert was captured at the suit of the same Elizabeth.

Other women left their husbands; some even (like Margaret Welby who with John Smith of Pinchbeck labourer in April 1452 slew Thomas Welby "in his bed with a sword") killed their husbands and eloped with a lover[69].

And some women, like Margaret Browne, were able to fulfil a range of roles. Margaret the wife of William Spenser notary was a woman of business who controlled her sons closely; she carried out the wishes of her husband in his nuncupative will, including an annual requiem in five churches in the town. She purchased property in Witham and Irnham, Lincs. Other women were active in the town's world of business, as the borough records show. One woman was not frightened to sue Thomas Kesteven of the First Twelve and Alderman[70]. Women were not named among those accused in 1450-1452 of making assembly in Stamford on behalf of the duke of York; but several women were among those who took out pardons in 1452 and subsequent years. These and other women were negotiating their way through the labyrinthine customs and taboos which hedged them about, so as to achieve their own goals. Below the horizon provided by most of the documents lies a vigorous life, largely hidden, but occasionally revealed[71].

Joan Veske

The case of Joan Veske shows this tension between prevalent attitudes which limited women and the way some women managed to break through these successfully. In 1444, Joan and her husband Robert Caylflete of Easton, gent, rented from the nuns a tavern with two shops; after Caylflete's death, Joan married John Veske an innkeeper who was accused of repeated violence during

---

[68] BL Harl 773 fol 36; the document does not expand these initials

[69] PRO, KB9/65A/14,22

[70] PRO, PROB 11/16 fol 118; CP25/1/145/164/35; Exeter-NRA 53/2; HB i fol 8d, p23

[71] From time to time, women did act as feoffees and as executors, Goldberg 1988 p 116

the alleged Yorkist assemblies of the 1450s. But Joan was trading on her own account. Sometime about 1450, she made an agreement with Ralph lord Cromwell under which she was to rent his inn called the Tabard[72] in Stamford and 24 acres of meadow "with a tenement adjoyning to the same In[n] on the south side of the gate in which William Smyth now dwells and another tenement adjoyning the said Inn on the north side of the gate in which John Cook now dwells" for 20 years at a rent of £20 p.a.. At the conclusion of that period, she was to leave "in the said Inn at the end as much stuff of bedding and other things necessary to be occupied in an Inn as will amount to the value of 20 marks ... And for this accord to be had and performed, Joan Veske gave to Ralph lord Cromwell as a fine 20 marks *of her own proper goods* [i.e. not from her husband] and the said yearly fine of £20" [73].

But Ralph lord Cromwell would not engross this agreement between him and Joan Veske, as her petition (written in English) states, "*because she was a woman*". Therefore Joan (the words "of gret trust" are inserted into her petition) asked William Storeton of Stamford baker to enter into an indenture with lord Cromwell "to her use and behofe". Whereupon the said lord Cromwell "lete and toke to ferme the said Inne with the medewe and two tenements aforesaid to the said William Stourton for the terme of 20 years paying therefore yearly to Ralph lord Cromwell and his assigns £20 with the other covenants contained in the indenture". Joan Veske gave sureties to Storeton to save him harmless against Ralph lord Cromwell for the final covenants. Thus Joan "by virtue of the said accord has held and occupied the Inn with meadow and two tenements peacibly almost five years and paid the rent of £20 well and truly".

Joan Veske found a way round the obstacle which lord Cromwell put in her way. But the arrangement came unstuck when Cromwell died (1455).

> *Now cometh William Stourton because the said Ralph Cromwell is dede, proposing and ymagynyng to defraude and put oute the said Joan Veske of the farm and to enter it to his owne avantage, he has warned and charged her to voyde and departe oute therof. And he has taken and let the Inn, meadow and two tenements to one Rob Rypshawe of Stamford for certeyn yeres without any restitution made to the said Joan of the said 20 marks so by her payd to Ralph Cromwell aforehande and without any surety finding to Joan Veske for her discharge of the stuff that she should leave in the said Inn at the end of the said time to the value of 20 marks to the great and importable loss and undoing of the said Joan and against all truth and conscience.*

---

[72] There seem to have been two Tabards in Stamford at this time, one by the churchyard of St Michael the Greater and the other on St Mary's Hill.

[73] PRO, C1/26/236 (my italics); C67/40; KB9/65A/36; E210/8897

Joan did not take this to the Alderman's court but to the court of chancery, using two London sureties.

The case reveals some of the barriers operating against some women (I cannot imagine Ralph lord Cromwell insisting on the same arrangement with Margaret Browne). But it also reveals some of the strategies adopted to overcome them. Joan Veske was not unused to law suits: as executor for her first husband, she had been sued for debt, and again with her second husband John Veske, from which she escaped outlawry in 1457[74]. And for every case which went wrong, like Joan Veske's, there must have been cases which operated satisfactorily. Some women did run their own businesses, and those not just widows who carried on their husband's trading after his death like Elizabeth Reede and Joan Fowler who exported wool alongside William Browne from Boston and London. Margaret Croke and Margery Tate were described as Calais Staplers; Dionisia Holme of Hull traded in her own right.[75] Malting and hostelry were among the business concerns of women in Stamford in the fifteenth century. Walter Laurance of West Walton sued Anneys Marchaunt of Stamford widow for not fulfilling his order for 100 qrs of malt he had already paid her for: she only delivered 45 qrs "because that derthe rose in the cuntre there ate the tyme". Women borrowed money: a woman's girdle is listed among the pledges made to Margaret Browne[76].

And women like Elizabeth Elmes (nee Browne) held property in their own right, kept separate throughout all their marriages. Elizabeth Kyrkeby who was widowed in 1414 as a young woman, married and widowed again by 1470, held property in Eastgate throughout all this period; William Browne was one of her feoffees[77]. Indeed, it was the practice of multiple marriages which ensured that property which came to the woman was kept distinct so that it could be passed to the right heirs. Alice Browne built up a sizeable property portfolio in Coventry from her marriages to Richard Botoner and Robert Bradmedewe, but she took the help of her brothers to ensure that the feoffees of that property were adequate to cope with claims and counter-claims. When women held property in widowhood, they seem to have had full control over it; one widow let a property become so ruinous that the executors of her late husband's will petitioned her to

---

[74] CPR 1452-61/322-3

[75] Sutton *Tates* p 37; PRO, E122/10/17; E122/73/40. For Elizabeth Reede, see her will in *AASR Wills* pp 196-200; see also Anne F Sutton 2012 Agnes Don-Bretton, merchant stapler, widow and matriarch of Southampton and London c1450-1516, *The Ricardian* XXII pp59-93

[76] e.g. PRO, C1/45/306; CY Visit iii p 348; see above p 153

[77] MCO 23, 7, 12, 16, 2

get it repaired[78]. Women rented land and leased it, sometimes to other women[79]; the gardens and orchards of late medieval Stamford were most frequently held and run by women.

How many women outlived their husbands like Alice Browne we cannot tell, but several had long lives. All the Browne women were long lived. Margery, William's mother, died eighteen years after her husband and was certainly in her late sixties or even older. Margaret Browne died in 1489, probably in her seventies. Agnes outlived her husband John Browne by eight to nine years; and Elizabeth, William's daughter, outlived both her husband by some twenty years and her eldest son William Elmes by seven years, and died at the age of about seventy. William Elmes's wife outlived him by twenty two years and her second husband by six years. And there were others - Elizabeth Kirkeby, widowed by 1414 but still alive in 1470, Margaret Spencer widow of the notary William Spencer, Isabel Fazakerley. These are some of those we know about who seem to have lived long and relatively fulfilled lives. Many women died young in childbirth like William Fairfax's first wife; but his second wife bore him twelve children over a period of twenty or so years. The picture is many-hued.

These were however among the more favoured members of the society. Other women were bound into harder conditions: those hired by the nunnery of St Michael to cope with the harvest were mainly women, reaping and thrashing. The majority of women in late medieval Stamford are invisible to us, just like most of the poor. Some would occupy the time between childhood and marriage in their own home or working as servants in the homes of others. Some would engage in occupations such as sewing and brewing as well as retailing[80], but once again we have little evidence of this in Stamford. Agnes Tapstere was running the Tabard in 1442, and as we have seen, Joan Veske ran it in the 1450s; women were the butter-makers of the town. And of course women were active in Stamford in prostitution which caused concern in many towns in the late fifteenth century[81], although in Stamford this too is absent from the records.

The lack of wills from Stamford means that the role of women in maintaining networks of friends is hidden, although Margaret Browne's friendship with the Fairfax family and her long and detailed will provide us with one example of this.

---

[78] NRO FitzWilliam Ch 498; see above p 114

[79] PRO, C1/7/202 – "Jane, when single, enfeoffed ..." ; Stamford Borough records, TH terrier 8A/3/1; LAO Stamford parish records, PG2/1

[80] See Judith Bennett 1996 *Ale, Beer and Brewsters in England: women's work in a changing world 1300-1600* Oxford University Press

[81] Goldberg 1988 p 121; CY *Visit* i p 109

Women were as real parts of the town as the men – it is the records made and controlled by men which largely hide them from our view. It is possible that some women had become more oppressed by the late fifteenth century: in Stamford, 20 women (10%) out of 215 tax payers were recorded in 1333, whereas by 1524, only eleven women taxpayers (5%) were listed among 240 taxpayers[82]. But a number of women were able still to find fulfilment within their ascribed and chosen roles.

---

[82] PRO, E179/135/15; E179/136/315; Rogers, Fairfax; Goldberg 1988 pp 109, 122

PART V: CHAPTER 3 THE BROWNES' MATERIAL CULTURE

... the elevation of the inferior people in these days in their possessions and apparel in various costumes has shot up and grown, so that it is barely possible to discern one person from another because of the splendour of their dress and possessions[83]

The fifteenth century has been described as an age of growing consumer culture, especially among elites who demanded imported luxuries: "Contemporaries tended to assess a townsman's wealth in terms of the value of his goods and chattels"[84]. "The appetites of those in the upper and middle strata of society spanned the whole range of commodities available in fifteenth-century England, from wooden trenchers to gold dishes, from blanket cloth to embroidered silks..." [85]. The artefacts which William Browne created or surrounded himself with would have said much to his contemporaries.

We need to remember that consumption meant production, and some of that production would have been local. And we also need to remember that artefacts were also performances, displays to others, remembrancers to oneself: that "culture is a verb", in which the values and belief systems were acted out on the local stage of household, parish, and town. There was no one culture of Stamford in the fifteenth century; there were many collaborating and competing cultures in the town. Nor does it seem that any one culture was dominant; even within his family, the culture of William (and Margaret) Browne was different from that of Margaret's brother Sir William Stokes and William's brother's son Christopher Browne. Nor was it fixed: it would have changed over time. All we can get are a few glimpses of his culture from some artefacts possessed towards the end of his life.

But they are limited. We do not have anything which he wrote - so far as we know. Some endorsements on his title deeds and some entries in the Hall Book may be in his hand: "... came before me and gave surety to me". The first pages

---

[83] *Knighton* p 299: *Nam tanta elatio in inferiori populo illis diebus in habitu et apparatu in diversis guysis pullulabat et crevit, quod vix quis de populo dinosceretur ab alio per splendorem vestitus aut apparatus*

[84] Dyer C 1989; Dyer *Standards* pp 193, 205; M Kowaleski 2006 A consumer economy, in Horrox and Ormrod 2006 pp 238-259. "This was after all a world in which appearances mattered", *Medieval Norwich* p 243; Hicks 2001

[85] Hatcher, Slump, p 264. On merchants' material culture, see Kermode 1982 p 31; du Boulay 1970; C M Woolgar 2005 *Senses in late medieval England* Yale; R Radulescu and A Truelove (eds) 2005 *Gentry Culture in late medieval England* Manchester University Press; Horrox, *Patronage*; D A Hinton 2005 *Gold and gilt, pots and pans: possessions and people in medieval Britain* Oxford University Press; Oldland 2010; Salter 2006 pp 75-94, 159-62

of the St Katherine gild book may be in his handwriting, for he took the initiative in reforming that gild. But there are no letters or accounts, only a copy of his short will.

But his title deeds[86] and the records of debts due to him tell us that he was meticulous, business-like, and (if his will is any guide) a man of few words. His will was in English, not Latin, and he probably possessed an English translation of the Book of Recluses. His Latin would have enabled him to cope with estate records, trading records such as customs accounts, and of course the common form ecclesiastical Latin to help him through the church services.

There was a culture of books in his circle. Margaret possessed more than one Book of Hours; John and Agnes commissioned a Book of Hours from Flanders. If we compare the plainness of the *Myrour of Recluses* with this more elaborate volume, it may suggest a more prosaic attitude or a more religious than artistic concern. Thomas Stokes spoke of his English books and his *politroni* (i.e. the *polychronicon*, probably a Latin version). William Elmes as a lawyer had law books; Elizabeth Elmes too had books. This was a group which felt comfortable with books.

So much for texts: what about artefacts – coats of arms, high-value possessions, furniture, chests etc – whether intended for social display or not[87]?

The most imposing object created by William Browne was of course his Hospital; idiosyncratic, it was unlike most other Hospitals of that date and must have come from his personal inspiration - a combination of gildhall and kitchens for the feast, with a personal/family chantry chapel supported by a resident group of bedesmen and women and two priests, and with a schoolhouse. The ill-defined boundary between his house and the Hospital shows that the Hospital was part of his personal possessions. The design seems to have been deliberately old-fashioned at that date[88]. But the quality of the building, especially the street frontage facade, the elaborate gildhall with its fittings, and the chapel with its screen and stalls with their misericords, is very high indeed, as is the quality of the surviving glass. The iconography of some of the glass may have sprung from his imagination, although a large part of the design came after his death, some from Thomas Stokes and some from William Elmes. The glass was probably made in the local workshops in Stamford and Peterborough.

---

[86] Rogers, *Archives*.

[87] for "social display", see Coss 2007 pp 34-52.

[88] E Prescott 1992 *The English Medieval Hospital c1050-1640* London: Seaby pp 23-71

The chest in the Hospital, almost certainly one in which William Browne stored his archives; we can picture him delving into its depths and poring over items drawn from it . (photo: Alan Rogers)

The parish church of All Saints is another memorial of William Browne and his brother John - they facilitated a substantial rebuilding. The fact that, apart from the tower, the initial plan of the church was preserved may suggest a deliberate decision to retain much from the past but to build substantially something modern and seemingly more spacious The comparison of the light in the church of All Saints with the relative darkness of the neighbouring churches of St John the Baptist and St Mary at the bridge which were also undergoing restoration at the time is suggestive of different traditions of churchmanship; the chapel in the Hospital too is light, if confined in space. As with the Hospital, it is probable that work on the church was not completed by the death of William Browne. The merchant's mark and family mottos on the building, the arms of the borough of Stamford and of the Calais Staple in the west windows, and the clock in the tower are suggestive of being modern but yet loyal to tradition.

Brasses

With the brasses in the church, we come closer to William Browne[89]. In 1442, he purchased a brass to his father without inscription; in or about 1460, on the death of his mother, he erected an inscription to his father and mother, with its post-mortem emphasis on the Calais Staple. William's own brass was apparently ordered in about 1465, more than twenty years before he died. It depicted himself and his wife in full urban glory, William standing on two woolsacks,

---

[89] For brasses, see Norris, *Brasses*; R Emerson 1978 Monumental brasses, London design c1420-1485, *JBAA*131 pp 50-78; Duffy *Stripping* pp 326-28; Salter 2006 pp 124-5; "brasses were crucial to the strategies of legitimation by which families drew attention to their status and affirmed their position in the elite. ... fashioning and manipulating the family's self-image", Nigel Saul 2001 *Death, art, and memory in medieval England : the Cobham family and their monuments, 1300-1500* Oxford University Press pp 1-9; M Stephenson 1938 *List of Monumental Brasses in the British Isles* Monumental Brass Society p 292

Margaret with a small dog at her feet, and the two family mottoes - '+ me spede', and 'Der Lady help in need'. The wool sack with cross stitching and corner ties, and the robes and pointed shoes, at that time the height of fashion, indicate a prosperous merchant. A lengthy Latin inscription in two columns is divided by a joint rebus of a (rather crude) stork standing on a woolsack repeated twice; the stork indicates the closeness of Margaret his wife. But the inscription is almost incomprehensible – no doubt the work of Thomas Stokes. No date of death is given, for the brass was commissioned before his demise, in keeping with a man who ordered his own burial to the extent of indicating in his will precisely where he should be laid in his burial chapel ("my sinfull body to be buryed and leyd within the chapell of our Lady on the south side within the church of Alhalowue in the markett stede of Staunford aforesaid before, my feete betwene the water [holy water stoup] and the wall there"). He thought everything through in detail[90].

Brass of William and Margaret Browne
(All Saints church, Stamford) (from Peck)

In 1471 is the emotive brass to Margaret Elmes grand-daughter of William and Margaret Browne. It is small, fit for a child of nine years or less, but with a full

[90] For his brass, see BL Add 34806 A12. See Fairford p 26. For holy water stoups, see Duffy *Stripping* p 583

length portrait rather than the half effigy which would have been expected for a young person, perhaps indicating the importance of this death to William and Margaret Browne. The inscription (unlike the other brasses) is plain: "Here lies Margaret Elmes daughter of John Elmes and Elizabeth his wife of Henley on Thames who died 1 August AD 1471 – may God have mercy on her soul". It is striking that the relationship with the Brownes is not made clear, as it is in the case of Alice Bradmedewe.

In 1476 came the brass of John Browne his brother; elaborate, with a black letter inscription of some convolution, the heavily ecclesiological wording is probably that of Thomas Stokes but inscribing the desire of John Browne himself that his wife remain unmarried for the remainder of her life. It was erected soon after the death of John, leaving the date of her death (1484) to be filled in later. Finally there came the brass of Alice Bradmedewe, William's sister, who died in 1492 (see above pp 259-62). If William ordered this brass, it must have been commissioned and perhaps paid for before his death but was not completed until the date of Alice's death was known.

None of the brasses contained any coats of arms; apart from the effigies, William and Margaret's alone had symbols, the woolsack and the stork. Such a collection of brasses indicates the importance of these memorials to William Browne. One or two could be seen as a normal part of the procedures of death of a typical wool merchant of the day; but such a sequence indicate that they not only "provided a focus for the rituals of regular commemoration of the deceased", but "were integral to the strategies of legitimation by which families affirmed their position in the elite". All were ordered from two workshops in London – and these not the best workmanship in town. This was a deliberate choice, since there were other well-known workshops much closer in towns which William frequented, including Boston, Lynn, and Coventry as well as in Bury St Edmunds, Norwich and Cambridge. Some measure of loyalty to known producers is shown. "In general, only clients with strong metropolitan links, such as the gentry and higher clergy, continued to patronize the London workshops in preference to the regionally-based alternatives"; in this, William Browne was claiming his place among the 'gentry and higher clergy'[91]. That William Browne himself ordered these brasses, including his own, implies that he was determined not to be "dependent on others for the carrying out of his wishes"[92], which is confirmed by his precise commands about his burial place in his chapel. The collection also indicates the importance of the family to William Browne – his

---

[91] Saul, Brass pp 170-1; Norris, Brasses p 198. Some of these workshops used stone from the Stamford area to mount their brasses, Norris, Brasses p 189.

[92] Emerson, Brasses; Saul, Brass p 179.

father, his brother and his brother's wife, sister to his own wife, his sister whose Browne connections were seen as more important than her marital relationships, and his grand-daughter. Christopher Browne continued the tradition.

The fact that William Browne and his family concentrated on brasses for their memorials, however, may indicate that William drew a distinction between himself and the more prominent gentry families. He did not aspire to a chest tomb like Sir David Phillips in St Mary's church. His daughter Elizabeth Elmes, the next generation of merchant-cum-gentry, ordered a more elaborate memorial: "I will myn executours doo ordeyn and laye a stone of marbull with my armys and scriptur according to theire discrecion." She felt she had moved up one grade in the social order.

Property

As we have seen, William Browne acquired seven manors with substantial outlying estates, all occupied by tenants; he built up a network of patronage. He owned some 30 properties in Stamford[93], some large establishments such as the Bell, the Moon and Stars, the Angel, the Cressaunt, the Crane. He owned a large woolhall in the centre of the town.

His own house was part of his business interests. He first lived close to All Saints vicarage but later moved to a house on Claymont from which he ran his estate. Although large, it was not a courtyard house; it stood gable end to the street in a traditional form rather than parallel to the street as the more recent houses of fifteenth century Stamford were built. It seems to have been an older property, much changed over the years, with flexible living and working space. It had a hall with dais, behind which hung the tapestry of Griselda, a parlour and chamber, a "chapel chamber", kitchen, brewhouse and "iyle howse" (oil house?). Margaret had her own parlour, chamber with closet and private solar[94]; and her grandson William Elmes also had a chamber in the house. There were almost certainly more rooms than this[95]. William thus lived in a large old house which probably grew with his growing wealth, status and activities; he did not rebuild as many of his contemporaries did.

---

[93] See above pp 175-77

[94] See P J P Goldberg 2011 Space and gender in the later medieval English house *Viator* 42.2.

[95] The house survived until at least 1727, by which time it had been divided into two houses for major merchants of the town. Part of it can be seen in a later painting now hanging in the Town Hall. It was replaced in the late eighteenth century but some 15th century fragments appear to have been incorporated into the later building; RCHME *Stamford* p 73

Furnishings

Fifteenth century alabaster Head of St John the Baptist from east Midlands (University of Victoria, Canada)

Margaret Browne's will lists furniture, clothing, bedding, textiles, silver and other metalware and some jewellery in the house, room by room, sharing out the contents among members of her extended family. But there is some uncertainty about such legacies. We know that some legacies were not in fact paid[96], while others did not came from the house itself; the large number of church vestments listed in some wills must have been purchased by the executors. Thus, when six members of the family were all given a bed, two sheets, two pillows, a coverlet of various kinds, and two blankets, it is not clear whether these items were to be purchased or were all to come from the existing stock in the house. Again, when eight others, most of them servants, were to be given a mattress, a pair of sheets, a coverlet, tablecloths, towels, silver spoons and (at least 5 of them) a set of 12 pewter vessels, were all of these already in the household stock or was this a standard package which the executors were required to obtain for them? For no less than 30 sheets, 24 coverlets and 66 pewter vessels, apart from 7 beds and another 8 mattresses are listed. The silver plate included a standing cup, 5 salts (two of them old), six bowls, 46 silver spoons, 4 basins, 5 ewers, 2 silver pots, 2 candlesticks, and there were brass, latten and pewter vessels, and two large chafers, one for coal and one for water. Is it possible that we have here some of the contents of their trading premises? Personal items are more limited - testers, hangings, tapestries and two items of jewellery – a ring with a blue stone and a gold 'salutation' ring. There is a head of St John the Baptist[97].

---

[96] see, for example, *Tooley* pp 11-12

[97] For head of John the Baptist, Goldberg 1988 p 110

Of the furniture, Margaret gave away the great chest in the parlour, at least eight other chests or coffers, a casket, and three chairs; but two counters, a spruce chest and a cupboard, two hangings (including Griselda), a settle and two chairs, some vessels and two candlesticks, one of four lights and one of five lights, were to remain in the house. Some of the furnishings were decorated. The fourteen cushions mentioned included one with pelicans, "red cusshines with roses", "cusshins of violet with ymagis", cushions "wretin in theym 'O mater dei'", and one with the name of John [the Baptist] on it. The spoons had leopard heads and strawberry knops. Some latten basins had roses on them. Tablecloths were of fine diaper. Chests were painted. Her best "prymer" was covered with velvet. This was not just a relatively rich household but one in which symbols played a large part. How far this sprang from William as well as Margaret is hard to say, but it cannot have been displeasing to him.

There is one item which stands out, a coconut cup. William states simply that Margaret is to have all his plate. Margaret writes: "Item I wil that my brother [her executor] deliver or cause to be deliveryd my beste Nutte [cup] at the day of mariage of William Elmes to his wife which I geve to hir to remember me by". John Elmes of Lilford, Margaret Browne's great-grandson, in 1540 speaks in his will of his "grete nutt and cover ... the sayd nutt wyth the cover whiche I wyll shall remayne to the said Edmond and to his heyres and to the heires of my graunt father Wyllyam Browne of Stamford for ever"[98]. The cup was to descend along the line of William Browne's heirs.

Coconut shells polished and mounted in silver had become valued in the fifteenth centuries as a relatively rare item. Most of those which have survived remain in formal establishments such as colleges, suggesting that they were characteristic of such establishments. But these tend to survive because they had relatively little silver in them, so that the encouragement to sell them or melt them down at time of need was small. Some were made in England and these tended to be plain and polished. Others from the continent were often carved in relief, some having a prayer on them[99]. We do not know what kind of cup this one was or where it came from, but for William and Margaret to have had more than one (Margaret speaks of her 'best' Nut) and to pass it on as a family heirloom would suggest a family which was conscious of status symbols. The concept of heirlooms was growing at this time: David Cecil ordered that the furniture in his house in St George's Square, in the "hall ... greit parlure and in

---

[98] PRO, PROB 11/30, fol 21

[99] T Schroder 1988 *English Domestic Silver 1500-1900* Penguin p 44; C Oman 1965 *English Silversmiths' Work* HMSO plates 25, 41; C Oman 1947 *English Domestic Silver* London: Black p 27.

my gallery on the south side of my house do contynewe as they are and also do remayne theyr as standerds or heyre lomes"[100].

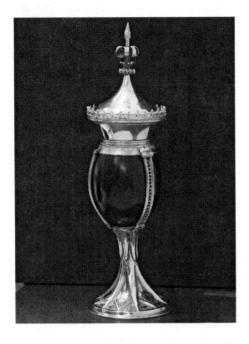

Coconut cup from Gonville and Caius College, Cambridge, of similar date to William Browne's cup (photo: Professor W Yao Liang)

Merchant's mark and coats of arms

But William's key status symbol was his merchant's mark. He used it in his trading. He put it on his church and it appears in the glass of Browne's Hospital. John used it in his Book of Hours. It seems they made a difference of it, with two 'wings' attached to the upright stem[101]. This to the two brothers was the equivalent of a coat of arms.

---

[100] PRO, PROB 11/29; BL Cott Ch iv 29. John Lee of Stamford requested "that tabyll and formes with bedstedes in the chambers stond as cyrelomys", *Linc Dioc Docs* p 163 See Salter 2006 p 39: "specifically chosen silverware as one category of heirloom"; see pp 76, 84

[101] Although used by both brothers, the two-winged version of the merchant's mark does not appear in the glass at the Hospital or in the church, suggesting that the symbol without wings is the mark of the whole family. The mark without difference appears on the brass which William bought for his father.

For there are no signs of any arms of William Browne during his lifetime. Christopher Browne asserted in 1480 that his family did not possess any arms. Arms depicting three hammers or mallets appear in Browne's Hospital and are attributed to the Browne family. The arms of the Brownes of Tolthorpe recorded by the heralds in the seventeenth century show the descendants of John Browne the brother as quartering four arms: two from Browne, one from Stoke and one from Pinchbeck, Christopher Browne's first wife. One of the quarters contains the three mallets of William Browne.

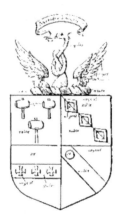

Arms of Browne family in sixteenth century including the arms of the Stokes family, the alleged arms of the Browne family (three mallets) and the arms awarded to Christopher Browne in 1480

The arms of Elmes and the alleged arms of Browne in the glass of Browne's Hospital (photo: Alan Rogers)

Neither Thomas Stokes nor Margaret Browne ever used the Stokes' arms, so far as I have been able to establish, although they were presumably entitled to do so. They used the rebus of a stork, sometimes on a nest but normally simply standing – it appears on the brass of William and Margaret Browne and frequently in the glass of Browne's Hospital.

The stork, motto and woolsack from the brass of William and Margaret Browne (photo: John Hartley)

John Elmes was also entitled to bear arms, but there are no signs he quartered any Browne arms. His son William Elmes, William Browne's grandson and heir, did quarter the alleged Browne arms with his own; he also quartered the Elmes arms with those of his wife Iwardeby as shown in the glass of Browne's Hospital.

How then do we account for the arms attributed to William Browne – arms which appear several times in the glass at Browne's Hospital and on the brass plaque at the bottom of the stairs of the Hospital? There the arms of three mallets have been squeezed onto the plaque rather than having been intended from the start[102].

The plaque with its dreadful Latin verses was erected in 1497, eight years after the death of William Browne: for in the Browne's Hospital account book[103], there appears the following item:

Item I payd to the marbuler for the plate off laton that stands at the grese fote in the cloyster of thalmoshows with the gravyng bygynnyg thus H[ec] nova structura   iijs iiijd

It must have been placed there by William Elmes, patron of the Hospital, and by the Oxford fellow John Taylor, the then warden[104].

---

[102] One corner bolt has clearly been relocated to avoid the arms.

[103] Bodl, Rawl B352

[104] John Taylor may have written the verses.

Plaque (1497) in Browne's Hospital showing arms inserted causing dislocation of fastening pin (photo: Alan Rogers)

The arms were then invented and ascribed to William Browne posthumously – an activity known from other families at this period[105]. It was, I think, William Elmes who created these arms for William Browne in about 1497. Why Elmes chose to put his own arms on the Hospital seal rather than the Stokes' arms or the alleged Browne arms, and why when creating new arms for Browne he hit upon three mallets cannot now be answered[106].

This is one of the surviving impressions of William Browne's seal on a title deed (PRO E326/5553); William Browne's seal is pressed very deeply into the wax, whereas all the other eleven seals on this deed have made superficial impressions on the wax. A man of determination. (photo Public Record Office)

William Browne's seal bore a merchant's mark, not a coat of arms; probably, like his father, he had more than one seal[107]. According to the surviving impressions, he tended to use it with vigour, thrusting the cylindrical die deep into the wax.

---

[105] See for example the Tame family in Fairford p 41

[106] The three hammers were alleged by Holles to have stood in the glass of Swinstead church, LRS 1 p 206; Swinstead was one of Browne's Hospital manors

[107] John the father left a gold seal and belt to his second son John. For seals, see A Weiner 1992 *Inalienable Possessions: the paradox of keeping-while-giving* University of Calidornia Press; Thrupp p 255

William Browne used his seal to lock away the borough seal in 1481 during a dispute inside the town council; the chest in the Town Hall is almost certainly the one in which the town seal was locked under three sets of keys. The very fine fifteenth century mace in the Town Hall was ordered probably immediately after the grant of the charter of incorporation in 1462 and was undoubtedly borne before William Browne more than once. Browne gave fetters to the town in 1467:

> *William Browne of Staunford merchaunt late beyng Alderman the xvij dey of December in the year of the reigne of kyng Edward the fourth the vij yeer hat graunt and geven to the commonialtye of the said towne certen instruments and necessarye thyngs by hym made in the prison and gayle ther as itt appearyth and shewyth under wrytten.*

> *In primis, iiij collers of yron with cheyns and staples festnyd to one pece of tymber*
> *Item one hamour of iren, one chysell, one pounch, on bolster, iiij payr of gyffes for leggs, one pair of long gyffes for hands, ij greatt lokks and one peyr of cheyns of the townes of xv lynkys etc[108].*

Such a donation displays a concern for law and order as well as for the authority of the town council.

Conclusion

What the material culture of William Browne and his wife suggests is a couple very close to each other, although different in character. A family that was deeply embedded in the culture of their day. We do not need to see this as urban in contrast to rural, for the contrast has been overstated; many merchants lived in urban style in rural areas[109]. They were secure, surrounded by comfortable furniture in a large household establishment, full of both religious and secular symbolism, educated, cultured, with wide interests but a strong focus on the family, fond of the good things of life and rich enough to enjoy them. Deeply committed to their local community and conscious of their status as Calais Staplers, theirs was not a culture of conspicuous symbolism, designed first and foremost to make an impression; rather it was the unconscious acquisition and

---

[108] HB i fol 9, p24. It is too much to hope that some of the prison irons surviving today in the Town Hall date from this period.

[109] Kermode *Merchants* p 49; R H Hilton 1982 Towns in Societies – medieval England *Urban History Yearbook* 1982 pp 7-13; M Rubin 2002 Religious culture in town and country: reflections on a great divide, in D Abulafia, M J. Franklin, M Rubin (eds) 2002 *Church and City, 1000-1500: essays in honour of Christopher Brooke* Cambridge University Press pp 3-22; Pounds 2000 p 134. See above p 171. William Ellys of Great Ponton near Grantham had an urban type house in this small village.

use of items which appeared to be 'normal' for a family of that status. William Browne and Margaret were living to the full the life to which they had been called and to which they felt entitled; they did not have to make grand statements to ensure their position in society. They were traditionally modern.

CONCLUSION: *NOBILIS MERCATOR*: IDENTITIES AND IDEOLOGIES

For, as I suppose, no man in this world hath lived better than I have done, to achieve that I have done[1]

What kind of a person was William Browne?

William Browne had many identities - wool merchant, member of the Company of the Staple of Calais; property owner, farmer and money lender; Stamfordian, town councillor, and local government official (sheriff, JP and commissioner). He was a parishioner and a gildsman; a builder, and founder and patron of an almshouse. He was a family man; he was a rich man with a position and status to maintain. His aim in all of these and many other identities was to shape and fulfil them fully.

He was not unusual in this: all those he met had multiple and flexible identities. It is important that we do not see William Browne as occupying one fixed identity. Identities are multiple and fluid; they are subject to constant (re-) construction and (re-)negotiation. Identities are relational, and consist of different performances and discourses in different social contexts. William Browne was constantly creating and enacting different identities in the town council, the gilds, the market places, the shire halls of Lincolnshire and Rutland, the streets, and especially the churches – for 'in the articulation and construction of the multiple identities which constituted that divided society, religion unquestionably had an intimate, even a dominant role – or rather, range of roles"[2].

But at the same time, William Browne was exceptional, even in his own day. This is not just a matter that "the surviving records only reveal the atypical assertive individuals and not the other folk"[3]. In his own society of Stamford and the Calais Staple, William Browne must have stood out. Medieval historians tend to look for what is typical in their biographies, what light one career can shed on others. Perhaps we should instead focus on the idiosyncratic, the differences – what made William Browne different.

---

[1] *Morte d'Arthur* xvii 16.

[2] Duffy, *Stripping* p xix

[3] Kermode *Enterprise* p xii

But we must also admit right from the beginning the lack of direct evidence for such pronouncements. We don't even know what William Browne looked like, whether he were tall or short, lean or well built, bearded or shaven. There is a detached head in the glass at Browne's Hospital which is usually identified as a stereotypical head of an unknown saint (or perhaps more likely a prophet, since there is no nimbus) - except that we can see a head with a similar shaped hat on a carved corbel in All Saints church, along with another bearded head on another corbel, which show a remarkable similarity of approach[4]. The temptation to suggest that here we may have some kind of portrait is strong, but temptation must be resisted.

Two of the fifteenth century bosses from All Saints church, Stamford (photos: Rob Foulkes)

Head in glass in Browne's Hospital (photo: Alan Rogers)

---

[4] I owe this identification to John Hartley.

But that he had a striking appearance, someone you would remember if you met in the streets, is, I think, shown by the comment of Leland some fifty years after Browne's death: "So that sum men be alive that have seene hym"[5]. Clearly he impressed these men as young children in and around the town.

The person who wrote up the Fairfax family record of the births of their fourteen children described William Browne as *nobilis mercator*, noble merchant[6]. Had this occurred once in this record, I would have taken it to be purely descriptive, the word 'noble' a simple adjective. But the fact that it is used twice, and that it was written up in the 1470s while Browne was still alive and active, indicate, I think, that it was a title either taken and used by William Browne or ascribed by others to him. It is, I am sure, a title which Browne would have appreciated and accepted for himself.

He certainly took the title of merchant – such titles had become important since Parliament legislated in 1413 that descriptors of residence, "estate, degree or mystery" should be used[7]. 'Merchant' is what he used universally from the late 1440s after dropping the word 'draper'. In all of his pardons, he was merchant – of Stamford or of the Calais staple; in the Hall Book, he is always 'merchant'. He is an example of the 'self-conscious merchant'; he displays all the characteristics of an 'entrepreneur'[8]. He used no other title; nor in his own lifetime was any other title used of him. When appointed sheriff of Rutland, despite the lands he held in that county, he was 'William Browne of Stamford' (which lay in Lincolnshire, not Rutland)[9].

If a coat of arms was a necessary criterion of gentility, he did not seek nobility: "All through Europe, ... the greater merchants sought to impress their importance on the noncommercial world and, perhaps, to heighten their standing in their own communities by borrowing the symbolic code that was used by noblemen and gentlemen, the language of heraldry"[10]. But as we have seen, there are no signs of any coat of arms of William Browne. He and his brother used their merchant mark; on his brass, William used the woolsack for

---

[5] Leland v p 89

[6] Rogers, Fairfax

[7] Gray 1436 p 625.

[8] Kermode *Enterprise* p xii, "Intrinsic to entrepreneurship was an ability to negotiate deals, to calculate exchange rates and prices in distant markets, and the temperament to venture your own (or someone else's) capital/credit in a range of enterprises". Kermode is less sure about how self-conscious merchants were.

[9] The occasional appearance of the term 'esquire' or 'armiger' in connection with William Browne are all late, secondary and baseless.

[10] Thrupp pp 306, 249.

himself and the stork for his wife. When Browne needed coats of arms, he used those of the borough or of the Calais staple.

This despite the fact that there was at the time (as we have seen, above p 257) an emphasis on family history. Many families put up in glass or in stone long arrays of the emblems of various parts of their family stretching back over many generations. William Elmes did this in the glass at Browne's Hospital, inventing in the process arms for William Browne. Christopher Browne incorporated in his family arms the alleged arms of William Browne, the arms of his mother Agnes Stokes and the arms of his wife. Perhaps in this William Elmes and Christopher Browne, despite their 'modern' approaches, with their focus on their family tree as expressed in coats of arms, were more traditional than William Browne.

My guess is that William Browne would have objected to the ascription of arms to him. If he accepted the title of 'noble merchant', it was not that he was emulating the nobility, adopting the trappings of arms and chivalry[11], but rather asserting that the occupation of being a merchant could be regarded in itself as 'noble', that a merchant's mark could be just as worthy as a coat of arms. He was not a gentleman but in his own field, he was as good as a gentleman.

The same is true of his chosen residence. William Browne was not one of the urban merchants seen moving out of the town into the countryside[12]. "When wealthy merchants invested in land, they often did so for short-term gains of security or speculative profit"; but equally some merchants had social pretensions when they bought rural estates. Merchants who did not move out of town have been accused of "failing to achieve the complete transformation they sought" – but not all merchants had such ambitions. Migrations from towns into the neighbouring countryside were common in the sixteenth century, but in the fifteenth century, there is "little evidence of many merchants accumulating sufficient land or rents to achieve gentrification"[13]. William Browne however clearly had acquired enough to become a country gentleman, but he showed no signs of retiring to his rural retreats, unlike his nephew Christopher Browne. William represented those merchant families who remained 'in trade', who seem to have preferred town life, Christopher those merchants who used their assets

---

[11] The sumptuary legislation of the period was in large part intended to clamp down on this: see Cornwall *Wealth* pp 11, 29

[12] Horrox, *Gentry*; Thrupp pp 279 ff

[13] Britnell, *Elites*; W T MacCaffrey 1975 *Exeter 1540-1640: the growth of an English county town* Harvard p 261; see also Mate 2006 p 100; Kermode 1982 p 37; Kermode *Merchants* p 288; for the contrary view, see Thrupp pp 279-282

to become gentry. Like some other merchants of his day[14], William's loyalty to his birthplace, Stamford, its gilds and its borough council, shines through his whole life.

He had opportunities to buy estates elsewhere, especially in Coventry where for a time he held property in the name of his sister Alice, but he chose not to do so; he sold her property there when she moved back to Stamford. William Browne was a traveller: his business concerns took him to other parts of the realm and to the continent. He acted as feoffee in Coventry and no doubt bought wool there, as well as north Lincolnshire. He traded through Ipswich and Boston and was a gild member in Boston; he had many links with London and exported wool and cloth through that port. His Staple offices took him to Calais and no doubt he visited places in France and the Low Countries. It was merchants like Browne who kept the international dimension in Stamford alive – there were very few 'alien merchants' in that town in the fifteenth century, unlike the thirteenth and early fourteenth century. He no doubt had command of several languages and experience of several different currencies. He would have been literate in English, French and Latin. But just as he was not a noble, William Browne was not a scholar.

Uncertain categories

But the near-century of William Browne's life saw much confusion about social categories. It was not just that society was changing; the discourses relating to these groupings, the ways people talked about them, were also changing. When Thomas Stokes junior, clerk of the Exchequer, could be described as 'commonly called gentleman', or Robert Spenser (probably the son and certainly the executor of Margaret Spenser in 1509) prebend of Milton in Lincoln cathedral was at times 'clerk' and at times 'gentleman', when one could be called 'yeoman or holywater clerk', it is clear that social categories and ascriptions were changing[15].

In 1433, just as William Browne was commencing his career, bishop Stafford gave a sermon to parliament describing

---

[14] see John Aunsell of Ashwell, Herts, in Salter 2006 p 32; Sutton *Tates* p 65; Horrox, Gentry p 26; Horrox, Patronage p 156

[15] This Thomas Stokes was probably an illegitimate son of Sir William Stokes, see above p 264, and Rogers, Stokes; he was one of those 'legal intermediaries' noticed by other historians, C W Smith 1987 A conflict of interest? Chancery clerks in private service, in Rosenthal and Richmond 1987 pp 176-192; N Ramsay 1991 Scriveners and notaries as legal intermediaries in later medieval England, in Kermode *Enterprise* pp 118-131. For Spenser, see will of Margaret Spenser PRO, PROB 11/16 fol 118; L and P Henry VIII i 1509-13 p 268 (438)

the three-fold status in the realm .. namely the prelates, nobles and magnates; secondly the knights, esquires and merchants; and then the people, farmers, craftsmen and the common throng[16].

His analysis of the class structure reflected the traditional division society between the magnates, the *mediocres* and *vulgares*. This is different from the earlier division between those who fought, those who prayed and those who worked: "There be in this world thre maner of men, clerkes, knygthis and commynalte"; "men of holychurche, gentilmen, and the commoune pepylle" (only men of course counted). In 1483, bishop Russell confirmed the lords spiritual, lords temporal and "the commens"; and within a year or so of William Browne's death, Edmund Dudley reiterated the traditional categories: the chivalry, the church and the commonalty. Unlike Stafford, Dudley included merchants in 'the commonalty' – they were not to be regarded as chivalry, nor as church. But, like some others, he drew a distinction between the large majority of merchants and those 'substantial merchants' who traded overseas[17], and although he recognised that the gulf between the merchants and the artisans was very wide, nevertheless, he felt that each person must keep within his own category.

But, despite this reiteration, perceptions of the traditional divisions of medieval society between those who laboured, those who prayed and those who fought and ruled, had broken down; there was no longer any "strict order of society", if there had ever been one. But the prejudices still remained among some of the elites. As Chastellain writing in the 1460s pointed out, "Coming to the third estate, making up the kingdom as a whole, it is the estate of good towns, of merchants and of labouring men, of whom it is not becoming to give such a long exposition as of the others [the clergy and the nobles], because it is hardly possible to attribute great qualities to them, as they are of a servile degree"[18].

Attitudes towards merchants however seem to have been changing – from one which "singled out the merchant as the type of avarice and ambition, narrowly absorbed in the pursuit of money and power, in contrast to the noble who, in the romantic world, made life an art", towards one which saw in the merchant one

---

[16] *Rot Parl* v 419; see J P Cooper 1983 Ideas of gentility in early modern England, in J P Cooper 1983 *Land, Men and Beliefs: studies in early modern history* Hambledon p 49

[17] Cornwall *Wealth* p 29; Giles p 75; W O Ross (ed) 1940 *Middle English Sermons* EETS 209 pp 237, 254-5; J G Nichols (ed) 1854 *Grants from the Crown, Edward V* Camden Society 1 series vol 60 pp lvii-lix; E Dudley, *Tree of Commonwealth* edited by D M Brodie, Cambridge University Press 1948; see Cornwall *Wealth* pp 8, 65. The Italian Relation spoke of "three estates in England, the popular, the military and the ecclesiastical", C A Sneyd (ed) 1847 *Italian Relation* Camden Society, original series vol 37 p 34.

[18] Huizinga p 60; see F D Matthew 1880 *English Works of Wyclif* EETS original series vol 74 pp 13, 439; Huizinga p 55

"in whom was wont to be the substance of the riches of alle the land". "Yt ys all wayes sene now a days/ That money makythe the man". Wealth as much as birth helped to create distinctions; gentility was coming to be seen to lie as much in behaviour as in birth-status; younger sons and Wycliffe's "porwe gentil men", forced to earn a living in war or trade or household service, needed to behave to earn the title of gentle: "manners makythe the man". In one sense, William Browne's life was challenging – in regarding the occupation of merchant as something noble in itself, full of worship[19].

In so far as he followed such categories, then, William Browne identified himself with his contemporary 'nobles'. I do not wish to suggest this was new to his age – the careers of William de la Pole and others show much the same ambition in the fourteenth century. But de la Pole set out to *join* the nobility. William Browne did not set out on this course, either for himself or for his successors. He sent his grandson and heir to the Inns of Court rather than to the royal or some noble household like his wife's father and brothers, or like his nephew Christopher Browne. His identification was with both the (upper) merchant category and the nobility.

There was still of course some general deference to nobility, but beyond that, it is not easy to see, even in such expressive letters as those of the Paston family, the range of contemporary attitudes towards the nobles. William Browne's values were probably influenced by the violent politics of the time and by lordly debts. There were rules to be followed, of course: "Life is regulated like a noble game"[20]. And there were required displays. But the traditional position of the nobility had been and was being confronted by men like William Browne. I do not think that it was true of him that he "could not understand that the real moving powers of political and social evolution might be looked for anywhere else than in the doings of a warlike or courtly nobility". His actions in relation to St Katherine's gild suggest that he did not regard "the nobility as the foremost of social forces", that he did not attribute "a very exaggerated importance to it, undervaluing ... the social significance of the lower classes"[21].

Christine de Pisan earlier in the century had a somewhat different analysis of society: the princes (rulers), the nobility, and the people (workers, among whom

---

[19] Thrupp p 315; *Engl Chron* p 31; BL Reg Ms 17B XLVII, cited in Thrupp p 317

[20] Huizinga p 39. See P Coss 2006 An age of deference, in Horrox and Ormrod 2006 pp 31-73; Britnell, *Closing* pp 189-207; R Horrox (ed) 1994 *Fifteenth century attitudes: perceptions of society in late medieval England*, Cambridge University Press; Thornton 2000; Hicks 2001; Payling, 1992; Duby 1988

[21] Huizinga pp 56-57.

she included the clergy)[22]. She distributed the merchants across two of these categories, distinguishing the burghers, the well-off and powerful merchants, from the more ordinary merchants and artisans. For her, there was a distinction between those who wielded power and judgment in some field or other and those who obeyed. Thus "the chief of theis folkes, as the substantiall merchants", were seen as being in the 'noble' class, among those who ruled. It was not wealth that set them apart so much as authority, their right to occupy positions of leadership.

A second attribute of nobility as set out at the time was that of providing a role model. Christine could speak of the "landowning class, nobility and gentry, the leaders of the community whose duty it was to set a good example to the rest". Indeed, a different attribute was being identified to mark off this class of those merchants who could be trusted to rule – thrift. It was 'knights, squires and thrifty men' above the rank of yeomen who were to come from the shires to the king's parliament and impose taxes on their localities, who would rule in the shires – and in parliament, the chief merchants met, debated and acted with the gentility[23].

But apart from the noble entitlement to rule and their obligation to provide a role model, a third aspect of the chivalrous class which both Christine and Dudley stressed would have found agreement with men like William Browne – their duties of care and guidance towards both the church and the commonalty. William felt himself to be among, 'the helpers and relevers of poore tenantes, and also … the maynteynors and supporters of all poore folkes', who ought to follow "the custom of setting aside at least a third of a man's movables, including the value of merchandise and debts, as a kind of voluntary death duty for pious and charitable purposes"[24]. In endowing his almshouse for poor men and women from his town or his estates, William Browne (like others of his kind) was acting as a 'noble merchant'.

Attitudes towards the clergy of course varied. Although William inevitably had close dealings with monks, nuns and friars of various orders, his sympathies (so far as they can be discerned) lay with the parochial clergy, especially with his own parish of All Saints in the Market where the vicars became partners in his various enterprises. Beyond this, his religious horizons were filled with the reclusive

---

[22] Tracy Adam 2009 Political significance of Christine de Pisan's third estate in the *Livre du corps de policie*, *JMH* 35 4 pp 385-398

[23] Edmund Dudley *The Tree of the Common Wealth; a treatise by E D Written by him while a prisoner in the Tower, in the years 1509 and 1510, and under sentence of death for High Treason* Manchester: Privately printed, 1859 pp 19-20; Loans p 56; Harriss, Aids p 2

[24] Cornwall *Wealth* 8; Thrupp p 312

nature of the occupants of the anchorage who were not 'poor' in the economic sense; but while some nobles took vows in later life, William Browne apparently did not.

His attitudes towards those who laboured with their hands are not clear. The records of St Katherine's gild suggest he had no 'side', that he mixed well with rich and not so rich from the parish in which the gild was situated. He was surety for the admission to the freedom of Stamford of a tailor and an innholder among others[25]. But to him, the merchant class was something different from 'those who laboured'.

How then can this merchant be called 'noble'? How far can he fulfil what Chastellain considered to be God's mission for the nobility – "that they should cultivate virtue and maintain justice, so that the deeds and the morals of these fine personages might be a pattern to others"? Or how far can he be seen as "the wealthy patrician encroaching upon the power of the nobleman"?[26]

He had many of the elements of display required for nobility. As we have seen, he had a large house, old, not newly built as elsewhere in the town. It had a chapel served at least for a time by William's own private chaplain, like most knightly families of the time. He had a household, although the number of his and Margaret's servants cannot now be estimated; Margaret had at least five women servants.

He had livery. William's display included his gild memberships and offices, both in Stamford and in Boston; there were probably others. It included his Aldermanry of Stamford on six occasions, with the livery of office; his shrievalty of two counties; his office as county JP as well as town JP and councillor, again with livery.

There were his building works – the rebuilding and extension of his parish church of All Saints in the Market with its tower and clock; a gildhall for St Katherine's gild, and a gildhall for All Saints gild; and other more domestic buildings. Brasses were the appropriate medium for noble merchants to display their position. And he founded his almshouse. The gentry founded chantries, merchants founded schools or almshouses. Browne's foundation was at one and the same time a gildhall, a chantry, an almshouse and a school.

---

25 HB i fol 5, p 12; fol 19d, p 52; fol 32, p 92

26 Huizinga p 59

In all of this, William Browne was not seeking to emulate others, whether nobles or rich merchants in other places. He was simply being himself, fulfilling with honour the role into which God had called him. There was no "numerous train of faithful followers", no pomp, no magnificence as he walked the streets of Stamford – but display enough in dress and gait. He sought no knighthood, as did his brother-in-law Sir William Stokes. He sought no courtiership, as did his nephew Christopher Browne. He remained true to his vocation, a merchant.

What I think distinguished William Browne was his propensity for leadership. He rose to the top of every organisation he joined. During his lifetime, he came first in every list of the town council which exists. As we have seen (p 188), he was Alderman of the gilds of St Katherine, All Saints for life, St Mary and Corpus Christi, and Holy Trinity in Stamford, and of the Boston gild of Corpus Christi; he became mayor of the Calais Staple, and led syndicates of Calais merchants in Ipswich and Boston. I do not believe this was a question of money, although of course that helped. It was, I think, a matter of pre-eminence being inherent in his person, a trait he shared with the noble.

And it would seem that he drew no distinction between himself and the offices he held, between the public and private spaces he managed. The gildhall/hospital which he built as Alderman of the gild of All Saints was still his personal property, on his site, built and maintained with his money, to be disposed of as he willed[27], just as Christopher Browne 'con-fused' his role as Alderman of that same gild with his personal interests. It was William Browne of whom it was written in the Hall Book that a local tradesman 'came before me' and 'gave to me' his recognizance – he was William Browne the Alderman and all that he did was performed 'in his own person'.

One thing that does come through from his law suits and his will, as well as his actions, is his total self-confidence. He was in charge of himself and his context; he could manage whatever happened around him. The pardons he purchased are not to be seen as a sign of weakness but as a strategy towards advancing his interests. He was probably arrogant; he was almost certainly at times duplicitous like his friend and trustee Ralph lord Cromwell and his brothers-in-law Sir William and Thomas Stokes. He may have been extortionate, exploitative, even at times corrupt by later standards. He followed vendettas, as for example against John Chevercourt. He took advantage of ambiguous situations as in the case of Thomas Bassett, and of the difficulties others found themselves in, such as the family of lord Welles. His personal, family and business interests came first. But he had a concern for his name and his family's name, as his brasses

---

[27] See Rogers and Hill forthcoming

show. His Hospital must be called by the name of William Browne. His sister Alice was to be buried in his family chapel in Stamford in the name of 'Alice Bradmedewe sister of William Browne', not as 'late the wife of Robert Bradmedewe mayor of Coventry'.

How was he regarded by his contemporaries and neighbours? He was rich certainly – well ahead of any other contemporary in the town in an age when £5 p.a. was seen as "a feyre lyvynge for a yeoman" and when his father-in-law as a royal household official would be receiving about £20 p.a.. And people might well believe a merchant to be "miche riccher than in tyrouthe he is"[28]. So was he richer than contemporaries in other towns? He was very unlikely to have approached the wealth of Thomas Spring of Lavenham or Reginald Bray; but when we consider the merchants of his lifetime such as William Cawode of Boston who reveals his wealth (and his learning) in his will of 1478, or Robert Toppes of Norwich who left extensive debts on his death in 1468, many still outstanding in 1492, or James Terumber of Trowbridge who built an almshouse and "a fair house" for himself and died in 1488, or Thomas Paycocke of Coggeshall, John Clopton of Long Melford, John Ashfield of Chipping Norton, William Grevel of Chipping Camden, John Smallwood of Newbury, John Barton of Holme by Newark (d 1491), John Baret (d 1467) or Jenkyn Smithe (d 1481) of Bury St Edmunds, the Tames of Fairford, the Canynges of Bristol, Thomas Kitson of Hengrave, John Tooley of Ipswich, William Browne of Stamford must rank along with them - although it is unfortunately impossible to say where he stood in these rankings[29]. There are no signs in William Browne's life of that "hatred of rich people, especially the new rich", which others have found[30]. I don't think he was ostentatious but we don't have enough evidence to rule that out.

Others have seen in this age "the strangely troubled life, the endless succession of evils, the sombre melancholy, contempt for this life which is dominated by fear of weariness and of sorrow, of disease and of old age, [which] is by an asceticism of the blase, born of disillusion and of satiety"[31]. This does not seem to me to sum up William Browne. His was not of course a smooth furrow, a calm existence. He and Margaret had family tragedies; and in the troubles of the period, he had ever to be watchful, to keep his head down and avoid confrontation. The risks inherent in overseas trade were exacerbated by warfare.

---

[28] Gray 1436 p 629; J Fortescue and C Plummer 1999 edn *The Governance of England* Clarendon p 151; Thrupp p 239

[29] Condon 1990; Oldland 2010 pp 1058-9, 1076; Toppes; *AASR* Wills pp 180-2; Yates 2007

[30] Huizinga p 28

[31] Huizinga p 36; Huizinga's account of the period is marked by his own pessimism.

But at the same time he was bold enough to take risks and exploit new situations as they arose. Although he took an interest in the contemplative life, he did not say with Deschamps

Si ce temps tient, je deviendray hermite.

This was no busy merchant hankering after the contemplative life[32]. Perhaps his sponsorship of the anchoress was a proxy for his own lack of contemplation.

He did not withdraw, being busy right up to the end; the fourteen year dispute over the parish boundaries which crossed his new foundation was not settled until two months before he died; his refoundation of the Hospital was not complete when he died - perhaps he was continually tinkering, continually dissatisfied with what he had done. Margaret too, despite being surrounded by vowesses including her own sister, remained engaged to the end; she signed a long codicil to her will only four days before she died. They did not seek to recreate the world in imagery; nor did they simply endure[33]. They tried to ameliorate the world within their own lights – through the gild of St Katherine and no doubt the other gilds; to improve law and order through the town council and the giving of implements for the town gaol; to help some poor through Browne's Hospital. They did not forsake the world or simply seek their well-being in the next life; rather they sought to perpetuate their presence in this world, concerned with their reputation after their death.

His death was no doubt marked by a spectacular funeral with all the town and other gilds involved. Ceremonies, solemn pomp and civic rituals such as the gild meals which became entertainments, and gild participation in funerals and obits helped to soften the harshness of life and of the many family deaths. Gild membership and their oaths, like the oaths of civic office, had to some people become the merchant equivalent of the orders of chivalry. But I cannot see William Browne engaging in "savage exuberance of grief", or following the "primitive custom demanding that the dead should be publicly and loudly lamented [which] still survived in considerable strength in the fifteenth century"[34]; his would have been a very restrained grief.

It has been suggested that "in the middle and lower classes, the chief motive of conduct is self-interest. With an aristocracy the mainspring is pride". If there is

---

[32] E Richards 2007 Writing and silence: transitions between the contemplative and the active life, in Lutton and Salter pp 163-179

[33] Huizinga p 37; Rogers, Wills

[34] Huizinga p 51; Huizinga as usual exaggerates.

any truth in this, then William Browne may be seen as a 'noble merchant'. He had both pride in his name as well as self-interest; he was concerned to build his wealth and yet be well regarded. But he was not "always striving to imitate the forms of the noble life ... the forms and the tone of the nobility"[35]. What he did had an integrity of its own: 'this is what I do and this is what it means to be living the life of a merchant to the full'.

Social capital

William Browne did not live a life apart from others. There are many signs that William's identity was bound up with that of his wife Margaret – they lived and died together. His immediate family was clearly very important – his father and mother, his brother John and John's wife, the sister of Margaret Browne, Alice his sister away in Coventry, Margaret his dearly loved young grand-daughter, and William his eldest grandson. His family extended to his wife's relations, the Stokes brothers; and when his daughter married into the family of Elmes in Oxfordshire, her husband's family as well as her immediate offspring came to share William's social space. And the Elmes, like the Stokes, brought with them clusters of relations and connections[36].

All this was expressed in a physical form. The rebuilt church of All Saints formed a focal point for his personal and family life; two chapels were appropriated by the Browne family. William was lifetime Alderman of the All Saints parish gild and was followed in this by his heir William Elmes and then Christopher Browne; his brother-in-law Thomas Stokes was vicar there for eleven years. At the east end of the church stood a group of properties in which from the north there lived John Browne, Thomas Stokes (in the rebuilt vicarage), William Browne's parents while they were alive, and then William Browne (before he moved round the corner into Claymont). Across the road stood their woolhall. The presence of the Browne family could be felt in Stamford.

But what strikes me most about William's identity is that – although it is built up around his immediate family - it takes as much, if not more, from his various communities. They also created his *habitus*: the town and his various offices in the area, his religious associations, the Staple. The key feature of his social environment was its inter-connectedness. Communities of interest were created and dispersed over time; as long as they served a purpose, they would endure, but no longer[37]. William found his identities not only in his family (that would

---

[35] Huizinga p 130

[36] See E Noble 2009 *The World of the Stonors* Boydell p 190

[37] For a different discussion of community, see C Carpenter 1994 Gentry and community in medieval England *JBS* 33 pp 340-380.

end with him and his name would only be kept alive through his Hospital), but also within his 'natural' community, the town and region in which he was born, worked, lived and died – and in his trading community which stretched beyond the walls of Stamford.

In the west windows of the parish church of All Saints in the Market, William set two coats of arms, those of the borough of Stamford and those of the Calais Staple[38]. With the parish church, they represent the focal points of William Browne's life and identities, key elements of his *habitus* which created his values and his practices. He was a Stamford man through and through, councillor, Alderman, gildsman, property-owner, for the whole of his long life. And he was a trader in wool, a Calais Stapler, the status of which clearly meant more to him than simply making money; hence his ascription of that same status to his father. Around these points, William's life centred, and from these, he drew the strength to build another focus, his family's Hospital in the town.

Arms of the borough of Stamford and of the Calais Staple, institutions which helped to make William Browne's identified habitus; he put these arms in the west window of his church of All Saints in the Market.

Stamford certainly was William's main arena. But beyond that lay his estates in the counties around the town, Stamford's region. As we have seen, Stamford was - and has always been – a border town, straddling three counties, Lincolnshire, Northamptonshire and Rutland. The town looked to the east and north-east through its trade links with Boston, Lynn and Ipswich and its drainage responsibilities in the wetlands. It looked to the north – at least as far as Grantham; its interactions with Kesteven, in travel, taxes, trade and justice (until 1462, the bench of Kesteven JPs oversaw local justice in the town) were significant. But in practice, Northamptonshire (and the counties immediately beyond) and Rutland became Stamford's primary stage of action. Thus although

---

[38] Butcher 1717 p 18; now missing; the current display comes from America and is recent.

Browne bought lands there and was sheriff for that county once, Lincolnshire I think held little for William Browne except some trade in the wolds and through Boston. His main focus was towards Northamptonshire and Rutland. William and John drew their brides from and focused their land holdings in Rutland and Northants, especially Warmington and Lilford. William chose his son-in-law from further away, Henley on Thames (Oxfordshire), and the wife of William Elmes came from Buckinghamshire (Great Missenden). William was sheriff and commissioner in Rutland frequently in his later years. Christopher Browne too related to Rutland and Northamptonshire, though his wife came from Pinchbeck; his sisters' husbands from Oakham and Oundle, and he went to live in Rutland[39]. Apart from the Browne family, many of Stamford's leading citizens had close links with Rutland or Northamptonshire; the gentry who moved into the town from the 1480s all came from Northamptonshire or Rutland, only one merchant came from Lincolnshire. Very few Stamfordians of the day looked into Lincolnshire, none, so far as we can see, moved northwards. The only connection with Bourne came late with David Cecil's daughter-in-law. The drift was southwards and south-west; Grantham men moved to Stamford. Stamford in the fifteenth century was conscious of what went on behind its back, but it faced towards the south and west. And that was also true of William Browne.

Contrasting ideologies

In William Browne and his wife Margaret we have, I think, an expression of one of two contesting dominant world views of his day. There was in the fifteenth century "no clearly thought-out theory of an individual's place in the universe"; but two world pictures contested for space. In one, birth more than wealth or influence determined one's position: "let us not change of our estatis". Wealth or lack of it alone should not bring about change: "poor gentry should not have to compete with men of lower birth, nor should they seek to exceed in power the better-born". Contemporary sermons laid "stress upon an individual's obligations to perform his allotted duties and to obey his superiors"[40]. This is not a passive 'stay as you are'. Rather it was a mission to work within that position to which God has called one, to fulfil whatever role one has been born into fully, to preserve and exploit it as far as it would go, not to use it to move into a different position within society. This would involve a communal element; a town like Stamford was where they were to be found and within which they would work.

---

[39] Christopher's second wife came from Norfolk.

[40] Thrupp pp 315, 288

Christopher Browne represents the alternative world view. He was not content to stay within his allocated social or physical space. He acquired a coat of arms and called himself 'esquire'. He moved out to Tolthorpe in rural Rutland; he attended the royal court and became a member of the council of Lady Margaret Beaufort, the king's mother. He almost certainly changed his costume from the merchant's robe. He was less communal in his concerns – when elected Alderman of Stamford as befitted his position, he insisted on serving in that post by deputy because he had other priorities; and he resigned his gild Aldermanship. His was a more personally motivated life: he engaged in a great deal of enclosure on his Rutland estates. William Browne's successors too followed that route after his death – Elizabeth his daughter and her husband lived as county gentry at Lilford and Henley on Thames and were noted for enclosures; William Elmes served as Recorder and MP of Stamford but also held offices in Henley on Thames, and was JP in five counties. The contrasts tend to emphasise William Browne's personal commitments to his urban community as well as to his immediate family.

Here then we see the confusion between the different interpretations of what it meant to be both traditional and modern at the same time. This was not a simple matter of social mobility (Christopher Browne) against 'inherent status' (William Browne). Both combined their own interpretations of change and stability in different ways[41]. Some expected people to fulfil with honour the degree or rank into which they had been born; exceptions to this might come about through 'calling' (mainly calling by God but also calling by sovereigns). This is why de la Pole was accused of betraying his initial status of 'wool merchant of Hull', why Richard II, Henry VI and Edward IV were accused of 'calling' to themselves favourites drawn from those categories who were not expected to occupy such positions of power and influence in society. Change beyond one's original status was not to be encouraged; the honourable thing was to live life to the full within one's birth-category. William Browne was born to be a merchant; he would thus fulfil that role nobly. Christopher Browne saw the world differently. For him, his birth status of urban merchant was not enough. He aspired to become a county gentleman and courtier; but his interpretation of what a county gentleman was was traditional; like his brother-in-law Sir William Stokes, his model was chivalric in nature.

William Browne needed no title of esquire, armiger, gentleman, knight or lord. He saw being a 'merchant' as his calling, something he was good at, something noble. "Gentrification was far from being a universal goal. ... for some

---

[41] Palliser 1994; Thrupp pp 300-302, 310-3. For a revision of the traditional approaches to social mobility in late medieval England, see Salter 2006 pp 51-57

townsmen, gentle status was earned by an elite role or professional occupation within urban society"[42]. William Browne achieved gentle status by being a fully formed merchant.

We cannot of course see how William Browne changed over such a long lifetime. My impression is that in his early years, he was primarily a trader, in his middle years, he was councillor and later local government commissioner, and finally he seems to have concentrated on his Hospital. But that is an impression given by what evidence we have. He seems to have been somewhat old-fashioned for his day. He did not modernise his own house; he did not found a college of priests but a Hospital which was decidedly old-fashioned in its style; the parish church he rebuilt retained its basic shape. He seems to have defended the tradition of the Alderman being sworn before his peers in the council chamber on election – it was after his death that the charter provisions of taking the oath before the steward of the lord of the town in the castle at some date subsequent to the election was enforced. But that does not mean that he did not change. Like Christopher Browne who adapted to his changing world in a different way, William Browne did not just trade, build up a portfolio of properties, engage in money-lending, and exercise power through many offices; he was modern enough to recognise the needs of the new age for professionalism in trade and estate management and send his grandson to the Inns of Court to learn the legal niceties required of the new economy of his time. William was a business man – but a late medieval business man. Tolthorpe belonged to Christopher Browne; but All Saints in the Market and Browne's Hospital survive today as testimonies to a 'noble merchant', a "merchant of a very wonderfulle richenesse"[43].

---

[42] Britnell, Elites. I have come across one occasion when the honorific '*Master* William Browne' was used, by the nuns in 1489-90, perhaps immediately after his death early in 1489, PRO, SC11/422. He never called himself or was called 'gentleman', as other wealthy merchants did.

[43] Leland v p 89

ABBREVIATIONS AND REFERENCES

This bibliography only includes items referred to in the footnotes by abbreviation; all other sources are cited in full there.

AASR: Reports and Papers of Associated Architectural and Archaeological Societies

AASR Chantry: C W Foster and A Hamilton Thompson 1922-5, 1930 The chantry certificates for Lincoln and Lincolnshire, 1548 *AASR* 36 (1), 37 (1 and 2) pp 100-106, 247-251

AASR Wills: C W Foster 1934 Lincolnshire wills proved in Prerogative Court of Canterbury, *AASR* 41 (1 and 2) pp 61-114, 179-218

Add Ch: Additional Charters, British Library

Add Mss: Additional Manuscripts, British Library

Allison et al 1966 K J Allison, M W Beresford, J G Hurst, *Deserted Villages of Northamptonshire* Leicester University Press

Alnwick Visitation, see LRS 14 and 21

Amor *Ipswich:* N Amor, *Late Medieval Ipswich, trade and industry* 2011 Boydell

Archer R E (ed) 1995 *Crown, Government and People in the fifteenth century* Sutton

Archer R E and Walker S (eds) 1995 *Rulers and Ruled in Late Medieval England*, Hambledon

Attreed L C 1992, Arbitration and the growth of urban liberties in late medieval England *JBS* 31 pp 205-235;

Attreed L C 2001 *The King's Towns: identity and survival in late medieval English boroughs* New York: Peter Lang

Bassett S 1992 *Death in Towns: urban responses to the dying and the dead 100-1600* Leicester

Bateson M *Records of Borough of Leicester* (Rolls Series) 3 vols 1899-1901

BHS: Browne's Hospital, Stamford, records, deposited in Lincoln Archives Office

Biggs D, Michalove S D and Compton Reeves A 2001 *Traditions and Transformations in Late Medieval England* Leiden: Brill

BIHR: Bulletin of Institute of Historical Research

BJRL: Bulletin of John Rylands Library

BL: British Library

Blair J 2007 *Waterways and Canal-Building in Medieval England* Oxford University Press

Bodl: Bodleian Library, Oxford,

Bodl Rawl B352: Rawlinson MSS B352, Account Book of Browne's Hospital 1494-1534.

Bohna M L 2000 Political and criminal violence in fifteenth century England, in R W Kaeuper (ed) 2000 *Violence in Medieval Society* Boydell pp 91-104.

Bolton J L 1980 *Medieval English Economy 1150-1500* Dent

Bridbury A R 1975 edn *Economic Growth: England in the later Middle Ages* New York: Barnes and Noble

Bridbury A R 1981 English Provincial Towns in the Later Middle Ages *Econ Hist Rev* 2nd series 34 pp 1-24

Bridbury A R 1982 *Medieval English Clothmaking: an economic survey* Heinemann

Bridbury A R 1992 *The English Economy from Bede to the Reformation* Boydell

Bridges *Northants:* J Bridges 1791 *History and Antiquities of Northamptonshire* London: Payne

Britnell Elites: R H Britnell 2000 Rural and urban elites in England during the later Middle Ages, http://www.dur.ac.uk/r.britnell/articles/Elites.htm accessed 27-08-2010.

Britnell R H 1997 *Closing of the Middle Ages? England 1471-1529* Blackwell

Britnell R H 1998 The English economy and the government 1450-1550, in Watts 1998 pp 89-116

Britnell R H 2000 The economy of British towns 1300-1540 in Palliser 2000 pp 313-333

Britnell R H 1993 *The Commercialisation of English Society 1000-1500* Cambridge University Press

Britnell R H and Hatcher J (eds) 1996 *Progress and Problems in Medieval England: essays in honour of Edward Miller* Cambridge University Press

Burgess C 1988 'A fine thing vainly invented': an essay on purgatory and pious motive in later medieval England, in Wright 1988 pp 56-84

Burghley MSS: additional lists of Burghley House archives in preparation (advance copies of some of these lists have been seen with gratitude)

Butcher 1717: R Butcher (written in 1626 and published in 1717) *The Survey and Antiquities of the Towns of Stamford in the county of Lincoln and Tottenham High Cross in Middlesex* London

Butcher 1727: revised edition of Butcher 1717 published in Peck's *Antiquarian Annals of Stamford* 1727

Butcher Rent: A F Butcher 1979 Rent and the urban economy, *Southern History* 1 pp 11-43

CAD: *Catalogue of Ancient Deeds*

Cal Papal Reg: *Calendar of Papal Registers*

Cal Wills Husting: R R Sharpe (ed) 1889 *Calendar of wills proved and enrolled in the Court of Husting, London 1258-1688* London: Corporation of City of London 2 vols

Carpenter C 1995 The Stonor circle in the fifteenth century, in Archer and Walker 1995 pp 175-200

Carrel H 2000 Disputing legal privilege: civic relations with the church in late medieval England *JMH* 35. 3 pp 279-296

Carus-Wilson E M 1954/1967 *Medieval Merchant Adventurers* Methuen

Carus-Wilson, Haberget: E Carus Wilson 1969 Haberget *Med Arch* 13 pp 148-166

Carus-Wilson, Wash: E Carus-Wilson, 1962-3 Medieval trade of the ports of the Wash *Med Arch* 6-7 pp 182-201

Carus-Wilson E M and O Coleman 1963 *England's Export Trade 1275-1547* Oxford: Clarendon

C Ch R: *Calendar of Charter Rolls*

CCR: *Calendar of Close Rolls*

CCW: *Calendar of Chancery Warrants*

Cely Letters: H E Malden (ed) 1900 *Cely Letters* Camden Society 3rd series 5 parts

CFR *Calendar of Fine Rolls*

Childs W 1991 'To oure losse and hindraunce': English credit to alien merchants in the mid-fifteenth century, in Kermode *Enterprise* pp 68-98

Chron Petrob: *Chronicon Petroburgense* ed T Stapleton Camden Society vol 47 1849

CIM: *Calendar of Inquisitions Miscellaneous*

CIPM: *Calendar of Inquisitions Post Mortem*

Clark L S (ed) 2003 *The Fifteenth Century III: Authority and subversion* Boydell

Clark *Rule:* L Clark (ed) 2008 *Rule, redemption, and representations in late medieval England and France, Fifteenth Century* vol VIII, Boydell

Clark P and Slack P (eds) 1972 *Crisis and Order in English Towns* Routledge

Clay R M 1966 edn *The Medieval Hospitals of England* Cass

Clayton et al 1994: D J Clayton, R G Davies and P McNiven (eds) 1994 *Trade, Devotion and Governance* Sutton

CLBL: *Calendar of Letter Books of City of London*

Clough C H (ed) 1982 *Profession, Vocation and Culture in Later Medieval England* Liverpool University Press

CMVA: Corpus Vitrearum Medii Aevi, www.cvma.ac.uk

Cobb H S (ed) 1990 *Overseas Trade of London: exchequer customs accounts 1480-1* London Record Society vol 27

Condon M 1990 From caitiff and villain to *pater patriae*: Reynold Bray and the profits of office, in Hicks 1990 pp 137-168

Cornwall J C K 1988 *Wealth and society in early sixteenth century England* Routledge

Coss P 2007 Hilton, lordship and the culture of the gentry, in Dyer et al *Hilton* pp 34-52.

CRO: Records in Coventry Record Office

Coventry, Holy Trinity Guild: M D Harris (ed) 1935 *Register of Guild of Holy Trinity, St Mary, St John the Baptist and St Katherine of Coventry,* Dugdale Society vol 13

Coventry Leet Book: M D Harris (ed) 1907 *Coventry Leet Book 1420-1555* EETS

Cox 1913: J C Cox 1913 Parish churches of Northamptonshire illustrated by will in the reign of Henry VIII, part ii, *Archaeological Journal* 70 pp 217- 430.

CPL: *Calendar of Papal Letters*

CPR: *Calendar of Patent Rolls*

CSP: *Calendar of State Papers Domestic*

CUL: Cambridge University Library

Cullum P H 1994 'For Pore People Harberies': What was the function of the *Maisonsdieu?* in Clayton et al 1994 pp 36-54

Cullum P H 2010 Vowesses and female lay piety in the province of York 1300-1530 *JMH* 36 i pp 21-41

Cuming G J (ed) 1967 *The province of York* Studies in Church History vol 4, Leiden: Brill

CY: Canterbury and York Society publications

CY *Chicheley* : CY 42, 45, 46, 47 *Register of Henry Chicheley archbishop of Canterbury 1414-1443*

CY 73 *Fleming: Register of Richard Fleming bishop of Lincoln 1420-31*

CY 78 *Morton:* Register *of John Morton archbishop of Canterbury 1486-1500*

CY *Visit:* A Hamilton Thompson (ed) 1915 *Visitations of Religious Houses in the diocese of Lincoln, 1420-36,* 3 vols; reprint 1969, Canterbury and York Society vols 17, 24, 33; and Lincoln Record Society vols 7, 14, 21

Davies R R 1968 Baronial accounts, income and arrears in the later Middle Ages, *Econ Hist Rev* 2 series 21 pp 211-229

Davis V 2002 Contribution of university-educated secular clerics to pastoral life of the English church, in C M Barron and J Stratford (eds) 2002 *Church and Learning in later medieval society: essays in honour of R B Dobson* Tyas pp 255-272

DCD: Dean and Chapter of Durham Archives

Dimmock S 2001 English small towns and the emergence of capitalist relations c1450-1550, *Urban History* 28 pp 5-24

Dinn R B 1990 Baptism, spiritual kinship and popular religion in late medieval Bury St Edmunds *BJRL* 72 pp 93-106

Dinn R 1992 Death and rebirth in late medieval Bury St Edmunds, in Bassett 1992 pp 151-169

Dobson R B 1967 The foundation of perpetual chantries by citizens of later medieval York, in Cuming 1967 pp 22-38

Dobson R B 1973 Admissions to the freedom of the city of York in the later Middle Ages *Econ Hist Rev* 2 series 26 pp 1-22

Dobson R B 1977 Urban decline in late medieval England *TRHS* 5th series 27 pp 1-22

Dobson R B 1992 Citizens and chantries in late medieval York, in D Abulafia, M Franklin and M Rubin (eds) 1992 *Church and City 1000-1500: essays in honour of Christopher Brooke* Cambridge University Press pp 311-332

du Boulay F R H 1970 *An Age of Ambition: English society in the late Middle Ages* Nelson.

Duby G (ed) 1988 The growth of individualism in the fourteenth and fifteenth centuries, in G Duby and P Braunstein (eds) 1988 *A History of Private Life II: Revelations of the Medieval World* Cambridge, Massachusetts: Belknap Press pp 85-156

Duffy E 2006 *Marking the Hours: English people and their prayers 1240-1570* Yale

Duffy E 2005 (second edn) *The Stripping of the Altars* Yale

Dyer Alan 1991/1995: Alan Dyer 1991/1995 *Decline and growth in English Towns 1400-1640* Macmillan/Cambridge University Press

Dyer 2000: Alan Dyer 2000 Urban decline in England 1377-1525, in Slater 2000 pp 266-288

Dyer C 1989 Consumer and market in later middle ages *Econ Hist Rev* 2 series 42 pp 305-327

Dyer C 1992 Small-town conflict in the later Middle Ages: events at Shipston-on-Stour, *Urban History* 19 pp 183-210

Dyer C 2000 Small towns 1270-1540, in Palliser 2000 pp 505-37

Dyer, Capitalists: C Dyer 1991 Were there any capitalists in fifteenth-century England? in Kermode, *Enterprise* pp 1-24

Dyer *Standards*: Dyer C 1998 *Standards of Living in the later Middle Age: social change in England c1200-1520* Cambridge University Press

Dyer et al *Hilton*: C Dyer, P Coss and C Wickham (eds) 2007 *Rodney Hilton's Middle Ages: an exploration of historical themes,* Past and Present Supplement 2.

Econ Hist Rev: Economic History Review

EETS: Early English Text Society

EHR: English Historical Review

Emden *Cantab*: Emden A B 1963 *A Biographical Register of the University of Cambridge to 1500* Cambridge

Emden *Oxon*: Emden A B 1974 edn *Biographical Register of the University of Oxford to 1500* Oxford University Press

Emmerson Brasses: R Emmerson 1978 William Browne's taste in brasses, *Transactions of the Monumental Brass Society* 12. 4 pp 322-5

Engl Chron: J S Davies (ed) 1856 *English Chronicle* Camden series 1 vol 64 (reprint 1968)

Esser R 2007 'They obey all magistrates and all good lawes … and we thinke our cittie happie to enjoye them': migrants and urban stability in early modern English towns *Urban History* 34 1 pp 64-75

Exch Jews:: *Calendar of the Plea Rolls of the Exchequer of the Jews preserved in the Public Record Office*, edited by J. M. Rigg, Jewish Historical Society of England., 1905

Exeter-NRA: records of the Exeter family at Burghley House as listed by National Register of Archives, lists in NRO

Fairford: S Brown, L MacDonald (ed) 2007 *Fairford Parish Church: a medieval church and its stained glass* Sutton

Fenwick C C 1998 *The Poll Taxes of 1377, 1379, and 1381* Oxford University Press

Fleming Oligarchy: P W Fleming 2001 Telling tales of oligarchy in the late medieval town, in Hicks 2001 pp 177-193

Fleming Charity: P W Fleming 1984 Charity, faith and the gentry of Kent 1422-1529, in Pollard 1984 pp 36-58

Foedera: T Rymer 1967 edn *Foedera* Gregg

Gairdner J (ed) 1872-4 (1983 edn) *The Paston Letters* Constable (Sutton) 3 vols

GCC 266/670: Gonville and Caius College MSS, Cambridge, St Katherine's Guild Book (see Rogers *Gild Book*)

Gibbons *Wills* A Gibbons 1888 *Early Lincoln Wills* Lincoln

Gilchrist R 1992 Christian bodies and souls: the archaeology of life and death in later medieval hospitals, in Bassett 1992 pp 101-118

Giles K 2000 *The Archaeology of Social Identity: guildhalls in York c1350-1630* London: British Archaeological Reports 315

Goldberg P J P 1988 Women in fifteenth-century town life, in Thomson *Towns* pp 107-128

Goldberg P J P 2004 *Medieval England: a social history 1250-1550* Arnold

Goldberg P J P 1999 Performing the Word of God: Corpus Christi in the northern province; Plays passing from craft gilds to civic control, in D Wood (ed) *Life and Thought in the Northern Church c1100-c1700* pp 145-170

Gothic: R Marks and P Williamson 2003 *Gothic: art for England 1400-1547* London: Victoria and Albert Museum

Grace P 2009 Family and familiars: the concentric household in late medieval penitentiary petitions *JMH* 35 2 pp 189-203

Granshaw L and Porter R (eds) 1989 *The Hospital in History* Routledge

Gray Benevolence: Gray H L 1932 The first benevolence, in A H Cole, A L Dunham and N S B Gras (eds) 1932 (reprint 1969) *Facts and Factors in Economic History* Cambridge Mass: Harvard University Press pp 90-113

Gray 1436: H L Gray 1934 Incomes from land in England in 1436 *EHR* 49 pp 607-639

Greenway *Huntingdon* : D Greenway (ed) 1996 *Henry Archdeacon of Huntingdon: Historia Anglorum* Oxford: Clarendon

Griffiths, Bureaucracies: R A Griffiths 1980 Public and private bureaucracies in England and Wales in the fifteenth century *TRHS* 30 pp 109-130 (reprint in R A Griffiths 1991 *King and Country: England and Wales in the fifteenth century* Hambledon)

Griffiths *Henry VI*: R A Griffiths 1981 *The Reign of King Henry VI* Sutton

Griffiths, Intentions: R A Griffiths 1975 Duke Richard of York's intentions in 1450 and the origins of the Wars of the Roses *JMH* 1 pp 187-209

Griffiths *Patronage*: R A Griffiths (ed) 1981 *Patronage, the Crown and the provinces in later medieval England* Sutton

Haberget, see Carus-Wilson

Hadwin J F 1983 Medieval lay subsidies and economic history, *Econ Hist Rev* 2nd series 36 pp 200-217

Hanham *Cely Letters*: A Hanham (ed) 1975 *The Cely Letters 1472-1488* EETS

Hanham *Celys*: A Hanham 1985 *The Celys and their World* Cambridge University Press

Hanham, Wool: A Hanham 1982 Profits in English wool exports 1472-1544 *BIHR* pp 139-147

Harl. Soc.: publications of Harleian Society

Harl: Harleian Manuscripts (British Library)

Harriss, Aids: G L Harriss 1963 Aids, loans and benevolences *Historical Journal* 6.1 pp 1-19

Harriss, Struggle: G L Harriss 1960 The struggle for Calais: an aspect of the rivalry between Lancaster and York *EHR* 75 pp 30-53

Harrod W 1785 *Antiquities of Stamford and St Martins* Stamford 2 vols

Hartley J S and Rogers A 1974 *Medieval Religious Foundations of Medieval Stamford* University of Nottingham

Harvard: Harvard Law School Library Special Collections, English Deeds Collection, Deed 343 (Hollis AQC4965)

Hatcher *Plague*: J Hatcher 1977 *Plague, Population and the English Economy 1348-1530* Macmillan

Hatcher, Slump: J Hatcher 1996 The great slump of the mid-fifteenth century, in Britnell and Hatcher 1996 pp 237-272

Haward W I 1933 Financial transactions between the Lancastrian government and the merchants of the Staple from 1449 to 1461, in Power and Postan 1933 pp 293-320.

HB: Stamford borough records, Hall Book (in Town Hall, Stamford); fol = folio numbers in original text; page numbers = Rogers 2005, edition of first part of this record (available on www.stamfordhistory.org)

Heale *Priories*: M Heale 2004 *Dependent Priories of Medieval English Monasteries* Boydell

Hicks M A (ed) 1990 *Profit, Piety and Professions in later medieval England* Sutton

Hicks M A (ed) 2001 *Revolution and Consumption in late medieval England* Boydell

Hill J W F 1948 *Medieval Lincoln* Cambridge University Press

Hilton, Urban Property: R H Hilton 1967 Some problems of urban real property in the Middle Ages, in C. H. Feinstein (ed) 1967 *Socialism, Capitalism and Economic Growth: essays presented to Maurice Dobb* Cambridge pp 326-337.

HKW: R A Brown, H M Colvin and A J Taylor 1982 *History of King's Works: Middle Ages* HMSO

HMC: Historical Manuscripts Commission

HMC de l'Isle: HMC vol 77 de l'Isle and Dudley 3 vols 1925

Holland P 1988 The Lincolnshire Rebellion of March 1470 *EHR* 103 pp 849-869

Holmes P 1986 The great council in the reign of Henry VII *EHR* 101 pp 840-862

Horrox R 1983 *The de la Poles of Hull* Hull: East Yorkshire Local History Society

Horrox, Gentry: R Horrox 1988 Urban gentry in the fifteenth century, in Thomson *Towns* pp 22-44

Horrox, Patronage: R Horrox 1981 Urban patronage and patrons in the fifteenth century, in Griffiths *Patronage* pp 145-166

Horrox R and Hammond P W (eds) 1979 *British Library Harl 433* Richard III Society and Sutton

Horrox R and Ormrod W M 2006 *Social History of England 1200-1500* Cambridge University Press

Hughes J 1988 *Pastors and visionaries: religious and secular life in late medieval Yorkshire* Boydell

Huizinga J 1976 *Waning of the Middle Ages* Harmondsworth: Penguin

Innes-Parker C 2002 The 'gender gap' reconsidered: manuscripts and readers in late medieval England *Studia Anglica Posnaniensia: International Review of English Studies* 38

Italian Relation of England edited C A Sneyd 1847 Camden Society, original series vol 37

Ives E W 1983 *The common lawyers of pre-reformation England: Thomas Kebell, a case study* Cambridge University Press

James M 1983 Ritual, drama and social body in the late medieval English town *Past and Present* 98 pp 3-29

JBAA: Journal of the British Archaeological Association

JBS: Journal of British Studies

JMH: Journal of Medieval History

Johnson *York*: P A Johnson 1988 *Richard Duke of York 1411-1460* Oxford

Jones M K and Underwood M 1992 *The King's Mother: Lady Margaret Beaufort, countess of Richmond and Derby* Cambridge

Kennedy Ruth 2003 Spalding's Alliterative Katherine Hymn: a guild connection from the south-east Midlands? EETS 321 pp 455-482

Ker *Libraries*: N R Ker 1964 edn *Medieval Libraries of Great Britain* London: Royal Historical Society, and supplement 1987

Kermode J 1982 The merchants of three northern English towns, in Clough 1982 pp 7-50

Kermode *Enterprise*: J Kermode (ed) 1991 *Enterprise and Individuals in fifteenth century England* Sutton

Kermode *Merchants*: J Kermode 2002 *Medieval Merchants: York, Beverley and Hull in the later middle ages* Cambridge

Kermode, Oligarchies: J Kermode 1988 Obvious observations on the formation of oligarchies in late medieval English towns, in Thomson *Towns* pp 87-106.

Knighton's Chronicle ed J R Lumby (Rolls series) 1895

Kowaleski M 1995 *Local Markets and Regional Trade in Medieval Exeter* Cambridge University Press

Kowaleski M 2000 Port towns: England and Wales, in Palliser 2000 pp 467-494

Kowaleski M and Goldberg Jeremy (eds) 2008 *Medieval Domesticity: home, housing and household in medieval England* Cambridge University Press.

L and P Henry VIII: *Letters and Papers of Henry VIII*

LAO: Lincoln Archives Office

LAO, parish records: notes taken from records of parishes of Stamford before their removal to LAO; the call numbers in LAO are not known (see PG).

Langdon J 2004 *Mills in the Medieval Economy: England 1300-1540* Oxford University Press

Laughton et al 2001: J Laughton, E Jones, C Dyer 2001 Urban hierarchy in the later Middle Ages: a study of the East Midlands *Urban History* 28 3 pp 331-357

Laynesmith J L 2003 Constructing queenship at Coventry: pageantry and politics at Margaret of Anjou's 'secret harbour', in Clark 2003 pp 137-147

Leche accounts: accounts of John Leche churchwarden of St Mary's church Stamford, in NRS 16 Morton pp 4-5

Lee J 2009 Urban policy and urban political culture: Henry VII and his towns *Historical Research* 82 pp 493-510

Leland: L Toulmin Smith (ed) 1964 *The Itinerary of John Leland* Centaur 5 vols

Linc Dioc Docs: A Clark (ed) 1914 *Lincoln Diocesan Documents* EETS vol 149

Loans: K B McFarlane 1947 Loans to the Lancastrian kings: the problem of inducement *Cambridge Historical Journal* 9 pp 51-68

Lloyd *Wool Trade:* T H Lloyd 1977 *The English Wool Trade in the Middle Ages* Cambridge University Press

LRS: Lincoln Record Society

LRS 1 R E G Cole (ed) 1911 *Lincolnshire Church Notes by Gervase Holles 1634-1642*

LRS 5 C W Foster (ed) 1914 *Lincoln Wills*

LRS 7 A Hamilton Thompson (ed) 1914 *Visitations of Religious Houses in the Diocese of Lincoln vol i*

LRS 14 A Hamilton Thompson (ed) 1918 *Visitations of Religious Houses in the Diocese of Lincoln vol ii* (Alnwick Visitation part i)

LRS 18 F M Stenton (ed) 1922 *Gilbertine Charters*

LRS 21 A Hamilton Thompson (ed) 1929 *Visitations of Religious Houses in the Diocese of Lincoln vol iii* (Alnwick Visitation part ii)

LRS 22 *Assize* D M Stenton (ed) 1926 *The Earliest Lincolnshire Assize Rolls 1202-1209*

LRS 36 W S Thomson (ed) 1944 *Lincolnshire Assize Roll 1298*

LRS 52 R M T Hill (ed) 1958 *Sutton's Register vol iv*

LRS 55 W D Simpson (ed) 1960 *Building Accounts of Tattershall Castle 1434-1472*

LRS 57, 58 M Archer (ed)1963 *Repingdon's Register 1405-1419 vols i and ii*

LRS 60 R M T Hill (ed) 1965 *Sutton's Register vol v*

LRS 61 M Bowker (ed) 1967 *Episcopal Court Book 1514-1520*

LRS 64 R M T Hill (ed) 1969 *Sutton's Register vol vi*

LRS 74 M Archer (ed) 1963 *Repingdon's Register 1405-1419 vol iii*

LRS 78 *Inquest:* B W McLane (ed) 1988 *1341 Royal Inquest*

LRS 81 A K McHardy (ed) 1992 *Clerical Poll-Taxes of the Diocese of Lincoln 1377-1381*

LRS 86 A K McHardy (ed) 1997 *Royal Writs to John Buckingham Bishop of Lincoln 1363-1398*

Lutton R 2006 *Lollardy and Orthodox Religion in Pre-Reformation England: reconstructing piety* Boydell

Lutton R and Salter E (eds) 2007 *Pieties in Transition: religious practices and experiences c1400-1640* Ashgate

Mackman J 2008 'To their grete hurte and finall destruction': Lord Welles' attacks on Spalding and Pinchbeck 1449-1450, in Brand P and Cunningham S (eds) 2008 *Foundations of Medieval Scholarship: records in honour of David Crook* Borthwick Publications pp 183-195

Marks R 1982 A late medieval glass-painting workshop in the region of Stamford and Peterborough, in P Moore (ed) 1982 *Crown in Glory: a celebration of craftsmanship: studies in stained glass* Norwich pp 29-39

Mate M E 2006 *Trade and Economic Developments 1450-1550: the experience of Kent, Surrey and Sussex* Boydell

McIntosh M K 1986 Local change and community control in England 1465-1500, *Huntington Library Quarterly* 49 pp 219-242

McIntosh M K 1988 Local responses to the poor in late medieval and Tudor England, *Continuity and Change* 3 pp 209-245

McIntosh M K 1998 *Controlling Misbehaviour in England 1370-1600* Cambridge University Press,

MCO: Magdalen College, Oxford (Stamford deeds)

McRee B 1987 Religious gilds and regulation of behavior in late medieval towns, in Rosenthal and Richmond 1987 pp 108-122

Med Arch: Medieval Archaeology

Medieval Norwich: C Rawcliffe and R Wilson (eds) 2004 *Medieval Norwich* Hambledon

Miller and Hatcher: E Miller and J Hatcher 1995 *Medieval English Towns, Commerce and Crafts 1086-1348* Longman

Mollat M 1978 transl. *The Poor in the Middle Ages: an essay in social history* Yale

Morgan D A L 1973 The King's affinity in the polity of Yorkist England *TRHS* 5th series vol 23 pp 1-25

Munro J H 1972 *Wool, Cloth and Gold: the struggle for bullion in Anglo-Burgundian trade 1340-1478* University of Toronto Press

Nightingale P 1990 Monetary contraction and mercantile credit in later medieval England *Econ Hist Rev* 2nd series 43 pp 560-575

Nightingale P 2010 Gold, credit and mortality: distinguishing deflationary pressures on the late medieval English economy, *Econ Hist Rev* 2nd series 63 pp 1081-1104

Norris, *Brasses:* M Norris 1992 Later medieval monumental brasses: an urban funerary industry and its representation of death, in Bassett 1992 pp 184-209

NRO: Northamptonshire Records Office.

NRS: Northamptonshire Record Society publications

NRS 2 *Pytcheley*: W T Mellows (ed) 1927 *Henry of Pytcheley's Book of Fees*

NRS 5 *Assize*: D M Stenton (ed) 1930 *Earliest Northamptonshire Assize Rolls 1202-1203*

NRS 9, 12, 13, 18 W T Mellows (with D H Gifford, vol 18) (ed) 1939, 1941, 1947, 1956 *Peterborough Local Administration*

NRS 16 *Morton*: P I King (ed) 1954 *Book of William Morton, almoner 1448-1467*

NRS 33 *Obedientiaries*: J Greatrex (ed) 1984 *Account Rolls of Obedientiaries of Peterborough*

NRS 43 *Pilsgate* : M E Briston and T M Halliday (eds) 2009 *Pilsgate Manor of the Sacrist of Peterborough c 1404*

ODNB: *Oxford Dictionary of National Biography*

OHS: Oxford Historical Society

OHS 20 G Little (ed) 1891 *Greyfriars in Oxford*

OHS 32 M Burrows (ed) 1896 *Collectanea III*

OHS 52 *Brazenose Quatercentenary Monographs* vol ii 1909

Oldland J 2010 The allocation of merchant capital in early Tudor London *Econ Hist Rev* 63 pp 1058-1080

Orme N 2006 *Medieval Schools: from Roman Britain to Renaissance England* Yale

Orme N and Webster M 1995 *The English Hospital 1070-1570* New Haven: Yale

Owen D M 1971 *Church and Society in Medieval Lincolnshire* Lincoln: History of Lincolnshire

Palliser D M 1988 Urban decay revisited, in Thomson *Towns* pp 1-21

Palliser D M 1994 Urban Society, in Horrox 1994 pp 132-149

Palliser D M (ed) 2000 *Cambridge Urban History of Britain* 3 vols Cambridge University Press

Paston Letters: N Davis (ed) 1971 *Paston Letters* 3 vols Oxford University Press

Payling S J 1992 Social mobility, demographic change and landed society in late medieval England *Econ Hist Rev* 2nd series, 45 pp 51-73

Payling S J 1995 Politics of family: late medieval marriage contracts, in R H Britnell and A J Pollard (eds) 1995 *The McFarlane Legacy* Sutton pp 21-48

Peberdy R B 1994 The economy, society and government of a small town in late medieval England: a study of Henley-on-Thames from c1300 to c1540, unpublished Ph D thesis, University of Leicester

Peck F 1727 (reprint 1969) *Academia Tertia Anglicana, or Antiquarian Annals of Stanford* London

PG: notes taken from original records of the parish of St George, Stamford (now deposited in LAO)

Phythian-Adams C 1972 Ceremony and the citizen: the communal year at Coventry 1450-1550, in Clark and Slack 1972 pp 57-85

Phythian-Adams C 1977 Rutland reconsidered, in A Dornier (ed) 1977 *Mercian Studies* Leicester University Press pp 63-84

Phythian-Adams *Desolation*: C Phythian-Adams 1979 *Desolation of a City: Coventry and the urban crisis of the late Middle Ages* Cambridge University Press

Piper 1980: Alan Piper 1980 St Leonard's Priory, Stamford, *Stamford Historian* 5 pp 5-25

Pipewell: A R Bell, C Brooks and P Dryburgh 2006 *Leger est aprendre mes fort est arendre: wool, debt and the dispersal of Pipewell Abbey 1280-1320 JMH* 32 pp 187-211

Platts G 1985 *Land and People in Medieval Lincolnshire* Lincoln: History of Lincolnshire

Pollard A J [Tony] (ed) 1984 *Property and Politics: essays in late medieval English his*tory Sutton

POPC: *Proceedings and Ordinances of the Privy Council* 6 vols

Postan M M (ed) 1973 *Medieval Trade and Finance* Cambridge University Press

Postan Credit: M M Postan 1928 Credit in medieval trade, *Econ Hist Rev* 2nd series 1 pp 234-61 (reprinted in Postan 1973 pp 1-27)

N J G Pounds N J 2000 *History of the English Parish* Cambridge University Press

Power E 1926 English wool trade in the reign of Edward IV *Cambridge Historical Journal* 2 pp 17-35

Power E 1933 The wool trade in the fifteenth century, in Power and Postan 1933 pp 39-90

Power E 1937 edn *Medieval People* Penguin

Power E 1941 *Wool Trade in English medieval history* Oxford University Press

Power E and Postan M M (eds) 1933 *Studies in English Trade in the fifteenth century* Routledge

PRO: Public Record Office of The National Archives

Pronay and Cox: N Pronay and J Cox (eds) 1986 *Crowland Chonicle Continuations 1459-86* Sutton for Richard III Society

Pugh T B 2001 Estates, finances and the regal aspirations of Richard Plantagenat (1411-60) duke of York, in Hicks 2001 pp 71-88

Pugh York: T B Pugh 1986 Richard Plantagenet 1411-60 duke of York as king's lieutenant in France and Ireland, in J G Rowe (ed) 1986 *Aspects of Late Medieval Government and Society, essays presented to J R Lander* pp 107-141

Ramsay J H 1892 *Lancaster and York: a century of English history 1399-1485* 2 volumes Clarendon

RCHME: Royal Commission for Historical Monuments England

RCHME 1975 *Northamptonshire* vol 1

RCHME *York*: RCHME 1981 *York* vol. 5

RCHME *Stamford*: RCHME 1977 *The Town of Stamford* HMSO

Rec Comm: publications of the Record Commission

Rich E E 1937 *The Ordinance Book of the Merchants of the Staple* Cambridge University Press

Richmond C 1998 Patronage and Polemic, in Watts 1998 pp 65-88

Richmond *Hopton* : C Richmond 1981 *John Hopton: a fifteenth century Suffolk gentleman* Cambridge University Press

Rigby *Grimsby*: S H Rigby 1993 *Medieval Grimsby: growth and decline* Hull University Press

Rigby S H 2010 Urban population in late medieval England: the evidence of the lay subsidies *Econ. Hist. Rev.* 2s 63 pp 391-417

Rigby *BJRL* S H Rigby 1990 Urban society in the early fourteenth century *BJRL* 72 pp 169-184

Rigby Oligarchy: S H Rigby 1988 Urban 'oligarchy' in late medieval England, in Thomson *Towns* pp 62-86

Roffe D 1994 *Stamford in the thirteenth century: two inquisitions from the reign of Edward I* Stamford: Paul Watkins

Rogers Alan (ed) 1965 *The Making of Stamford* Leicester University Press

Rogers Alan (ed) 2005 *William Browne's Town: the Stamford Hall Book volume 1: 1465-1492* Stamford: Stamford Survey Group

Rogers, Archives: A Rogers 2008 William Browne's title deeds and late medieval Stamford *Archives* 34 pp 1-7

Rogers, Calais: Alan Rogers 1977 Our Man in Calais *Stamford Historian* 1 pp 14-21

Rogers *Deeds*: Alan Rogers 2012, *People and Property in Medieval Stamford: a catalogue of title deeds from the twelfth century to 1547* Bury St Edmunds: abramis

Rogers, Fairfax: Rogers A 2007 A fifteenth century family Bible from Northamptonshire? *Nottingham Medieval Studies* 51 pp 167-179

Rogers, Fermour: Rogers A 2008 Fermour vs Stokes of Warmington: a case before Lady Margaret Beaufort's council, c1490-1500 *Northants Past and Present* 61 pp 30-41

Rogers, *Gild Book*: Rogers A 2011 *The Act Book of St Katherine's Gild, Stamford, 1480-1534* Bury St Edmunds: abramis

Rogers, Parl: Rogers A (forthcoming) The Parliamentary representation of Stamford from Edward IV to Henry VII, *Nottingham Medieval Studies*

Rogers, Stokes: Rogers A 2011 Eton's first 'poor scholar': Sir William Stokes of Warmington, Northamptonshire (c1425-1485) and his family in the fifteenth century *Northants Past and Present* 64 pp 5-21

Rogers, Wills: Rogers A 2008 Some kinship wills of the late fifteenth century from Stamford, Rutland and the surrounding area *Rutland Record* 28 pp 279-299

Rogers A and Hill N forthcoming *New Light on the founding of Browne's Hospital, Stamford 1475-1509*

ROLLR: Record Office of Leicester, Leicestershire and Rutland

Rorig F 1967 Engl transl *The Medieval Town* Batsford

Rosenthal J T 2001 Local girls do it better: women and religion in late medieval East Anglia, in Biggs et al 2001 pp 1-20

Rosenthal J and Richmond C (eds) 1987 *People, Politics and Community in the Later Middle Ages* Sutton

Ross C 1997 edn *Edward IV* Yale

Rosser, Lichfield: A G Rosser 1987 The town and guild of Lichfield in the late Middle Ages *Transactions of South Staffordshire Archaeological and History Society* 27 pp 39-47

Rot Parl: Rotuli Parliamentorum Record Commission [I have used the older version rather than the Given-Wilson edition]

Rubin *Corpus Christi*: Miri Rubin 1991 *Corpus Christi; the eucharist in late medieval culture* Cambridge University Press

Rubin M 1991 Small groups: identity and solidarity in the late middle ages, in Kermode *Enterprise* pp 132-150

Salter 1526: H E Salter (ed) 1909 *Subsidy of 1526* Blackwell

Salter E 2006 *Cultural Creativity in the early English Renaissance: popular culture in town and country* Palgrave Macmillan

Salzman L F 1952/1967 *Building in England down to 1540* Clarendon

Saul, Brass: N Saul 2008 Bold as brass: secular display in English medieval brasses, in P Coss and M Keen (ed) 2008 *Heraldry, Pageantry and Social Display in Medieval England* Boydell pp 169-94

Scofield: C L Scofield 1967 *The Life and Reign of Edward IV* 2 vols Cass

Selden Soc: publications of Selden Society

Selden Soc 46: H Hall (ed) 1930 *Select cases on the Law Merchant 1239-1633 vol* ii

Shaw Wells: D G Shaw 1993 *Creation of a Community: the city of Wells in the middle ages* Oxford University Press

Sheail J 1998 *Regional Distribution of Wealth in England as indicated in the 1524-5 lay subsidy returns* 2 vols List and Index Society, 25, 29

Simcoe: Devon Record Office, Exeter, Simcoe collection (mainly from Elmes family).

SJCC: Archives of St John's College, Cambridge

Slater T R (ed) 2000 *Towns in Decline AD 100-1600* Ashgate

Smith Bill 2000 Financial priorities of Lancastrian Government 1450-1451, in Thornton 2000 pp 168-183

Somerville *Lancaster:* R Somerville 1953 *History of the Duchy of Lancaster* vol i *1265-1603* HMSO

Steel A B 1954 *The Receipt of the Exchequer 1377-1485* Cambridge University Press

St Nicholas Gild: W and V A James (eds) 2004 *Roll of St Nicholas Gild* London Record Society vol 39, 2 vols

Stonor Letters: C L Kingsford (ed) 1919 *Stonor Letters* 2 vols Camden Society third series vol 29 and 30 (facsimile, edited C Carpenter 1996, Cambridge University Press)

Sturman W A 1944 History of the nunnery of St Mary and St Michael outside Stamford, unpublished London University M A thesis

Sutton, Staple: A F Sutton 2008 An unfinished celebration of the Yorkist accession by a clerk of the Merchant Staplers of Calais, in Clark *Rule* pp 135-151

Sutton *Tates:* A F Sutton 1998 *A Merchant Family of Coventry, London and Calais: the Tates c 1450-1515* London: Mercers' Company

Tanner N 1977 *Lollards in diocese of Norwich* Camden Society 4th series 20

Test. Vet.: N H Nicolas 1826 *Testamenta Vetusta* 2 vols London

TH: Town Hall records, Stamford

Thomson *Towns:* J A F Thomson (ed) 1988 *Towns and Towns People in the fifteenth century* Sutton

Thornton T (ed) 2000 *Social Attitudes and Political Structures in the fifteenth century* Sutton

Thrupp S L 1948/1962 *The Merchant Class of Medieval London 1300-1500* Chicago University Press/Ann Arbor

Tooley: J Webb 1962 *The Great Tooley of Ipswich: portrait of an early Tudor merchant* Suffolk Record Society

Toppes: Barringer C and Sigsworth N (eds) 2002 *Robert Toppes of Norwich: the life and times of a late medieval Norwich merchant* Norfolk and Norwich Heritage Trust

Toulmin Smith J and L 1870/1999 *English Gilds* EETS/Ann Arbor

TRHS: *Transactions of Royal Historical Society*

Vale: M L Kekewich, C Richmond, A F Sutton, L Visser-Fuchs and J L Watts (eds) 1995 *The Politics of England: John Vale's Book* Sutton

VCH: Victoria County History

VCH *Lincs*: VCH *Lincolnshire* vol ii

VCH *Northants*

VCH *Oxfordshire*

Virgoe 1450: R Virgoe 1982 The parliamentary subsidy of 1450 *BIHR* 55 pp 125-138

Virgoe 1481: R Virgoe 1989 The benevolence of 1481 *EHR* 104 pp 15-45

Warren *Anchorites*: A K Warren 1985 *Anchorites and their Patrons in Medieval England* Berkeley: University of California Press

Watts J L (ed) 1998 *The End of the Middle Ages? England in the 15th and 16th Centuries* Sutton

Watts J L 1995 Polemics and politics in the 1450s, in Vale pp 3-42

Wedgwood J 1936 *History of Parliament 1436-1509*, vol 2 *Biographies* HMSO

Westlake H F 1919 *The Parish Gilds of Medieval England* SPCK

Wilkins L J 2007 *Women in 13thC Lincolnshire* Boydell and R Hist Soc

Williams D (ed) 1989 *Early Tudor England* Boydell

Withington P 2005 *The Politics of Commonwealth: citizens and freemen in early modern England*, Cambridge University Press

Wolffe B 1981 *Henry VI* New Haven: Yale

Wood D (ed) 2003 *Women and Religion in Medieval England* Oxford

Wood D (ed) 2004 *Medieval Money Matters* Oxford: Oxbow

Workman H B 1926 *John Wycliff* 2 vols Oxford

Wren *Ports*: W J Wren 1976 *Ports of the Eastern Counties* Dalton

Wright H P 1890 *The Story of the Domus Dei of Stamford: the Hospital of William Browne* London: Parker

Wright S J (ed) 1988 *Parish, Church and People: local studies in lay religion 1350-1750* Hutchinson

WRO, Savernake: Wilts and Swindon Record Office, Savernake Estate Records

Yates M 2007 *Town and Countryside in Western Berkshire c1327-c1600: social and economic change* Boydell

INDEX

Adam Thomas, William 141-2, 260

Agnes Stokes/Browne 103, 154-5, 210, 212, 224, 229, 258-9, 273-4, 276-7, 285, 304

agriculture 33-34, 62, 170, 189-90, 273

Alderman of Stamford 9-10, 22, 40, 43, 46-7, 49-59, 60, 66, 71, 74, 78, 181-4, 238; deputy 203, 316

Alice Broune/Botoner/Bradmedewe 49, 102, 135, 239, 258-60, 265, 280, 284-5, 291, 305, 311, 313

alien merchants, Flemings, Florentine, Frescobaldi, Genoese, German, Lombards, Italian 12, 17-19, 44-5, 49, 128-9, 131, 136, 144, 264-5, 305; *see also* Jews

All Saints Place 56

All Saints vicarage 56, 91,122, 158, 210, 241, 259, 264, 292, 313

anchoress 43, 91, 153, 208-9, 219-21, 225-8, 231-2, 234, 278-9, 312

Angel, Angel in the Hoop, Aungel 41, 157, 175-77, 248, 292

Ankes Alice 281

Anneys Marchaunt 284

Anteloppe inn 41, 91

antiquarians in Stamford 21

Apethorpe family 42

appanage (East Midlands) 102, 105

apprentices 42, 56, 61, 65, 128, 136, 190, 197, 281

arbitration 193, 198, 211

Archduke Philip of Austria 268

Ardern Richard 45-6

Arketil John, Margery 218

Armeston William 163

arms, coats of (family and borough) 9, 23, 249, 267, 289, 296-7, 303-4, 314

Ashburne Thomas 13

Ashby St Ledgers, Northants 257

Ashfield John 311

Ashwell, Herts 305

Aunsell John 305

Babthorp Robert 79

Badgemore, Oxon 175-77

bailiff 59, 171, 181, 195, 197, 272; of Stamford 16, 72, 90-1, 184, 186-7, 197, 200, 202, 204; of Coventry 260; of Henley on Thames 265; of nuns of St Michael, Stamford 43, 197, 219; of Peterborough abbey estates 197; of Ralph lord Cromwell 260; of York estates 43, 75, 81-2, 84, 88, 163, 195

Bainton, Northants 175-77

Bakers street 29

Baliol fee 6

Ballard Robert rector of Helpston 52

Balle John 195

Bangor bishop of 13

Baret John 311

Barford John junior 175-77

Barholm, Lincs 166, 169, 170, 175-77

Barlowe John 281

Barn Hill 56, 121-2

Barnack, Northants 16, 50, 152-3, 169, 175-77

Barnard William 175-77

Barnet 99, 100

Barrowden, Rutland 70

Barton John 128, 161, 311; Richard 54

Basing John 216

Basse John 66, 154, 195

Basset, Bassett Alice, Thomas 27, 141, 161-2, 165, 169, 310

Baynards castle 99, 278

Beauchamp Lady Margaret 69, 271, 281

Beaufort Cardinal 147, 260; Lady Margaret 69, 91, 105, 126, 170, 175-7, 196, 203-4, 206-7, 216, 221, 225, 252, 266, 269, 272, 277-8, 316; *see* Somerset